Real World
Color Management

Real World Color Management

Industrial-Strength Production Techniques

Bruce Fraser
Chris Murphy
Fred Bunting

Peachpit Press

Bruce

To Angela, my angel, for every reason in the world.

Chris

To Mom and Dad.

Fred

*To Yolanda, my mother, who epitomized an intense desire to write,
and to Emily, my daughter, who seems to have inherited that desire even
without (or perhaps despite) my help.*

Real World Color Management

Bruce Fraser, Chris Murphy, and Fred Bunting

Peachpit Press

1249 Eighth Street
Berkeley, CA 94710
510/524-2178
Fax: 510/524-2221

Find us on the World Wide Web at: http://www.peachpit.com
Peachpit Press is a division of Pearson Education

Cover Design: Gee + Chung Design
Cover Illustration: Jeff Brice
Cover Production: George Mattingly

ISBN 0-201-77340-6

9 8 7 6 5 4 3 2

Printed and bound in the United States of America

Overview

The Big Picture

Contents

What's Inside

**CHAPTER 12 The Adobe Common Color Architecture:
Color Management in Adobe Photoshop,
InDesign, and Illustrator** 321

Preface

The Color-Management Conundrum

If you've picked up this book because you simply want us to tell you which buttons to push when you run into this or that application's color-management features, put it down again. Although this book starts from the point of view of a beginner in color and color management, and builds up from there, we don't think a cookbook or color-management book for dummies could do the topic justice—this isn't that book.

However, you don't have to be a rocket scientist (or any other kind) to benefit from this book. What we've learned about color management we've learned the hard way—by using it, making a lot of mistakes, correcting those mistakes, and using it some more. This is a book for color-management users, not for color scientists, and we guarantee that it's completely equation-free.

The reasons we won't just tell you which buttons to push are:

▶ The answers depend on which buttons you've already pushed and what you're trying to achieve.

▶ Application vendors have a distressing propensity for moving or renaming the buttons.

▶ Sometimes, a button will do different things in different situations.

▶ The biggest reason of all—even if we told you which button to push, you wouldn't know what it did or *why* you were pushing it.

Instead, we've aimed for something a little more ambitious, but we hope a great deal more useful. In this book, we've attempted to give you the vocabulary, knowledge, and insight to see beyond the buttons and understand what they do, even if you've never seen these particular buttons before. In terms of the old saw about teaching a man to fish instead of giving a man a fish, we're trying to make you marine biologists!

Why Did We Do This?

We wrote this book for a lot of reasons, some better than others. The biggest one is that hardly a day goes by without at least one of us receiving an email asking if there's a good resource for learning about color management. Well of course there are, but they're almost invariably written by color scientists for color scientists—and while they're both fascinating and indispensable, they tend to be long on equations and theory, and short on practical advice on how to actually *use* color-management tools in production scenarios.

Then there's the other type of color-management resource—the happy marketingspeak that promises to make your printer match your monitor. We wish the people who write these would turn their attention to developing an antigravity drive instead—if they can violate the laws of physics so blithely, they may as well use that ability to produce something that *everyone* can use!

For those of us who have to use color management to produce real work, both the aforementioned types of resource are useful in the same way (as Chris would say) that a bicycle is useful when you have to get from San Francisco to Portland. Hence the need for this book. We've tried to pack in everything we've learned in the close to three decades that we've collectively spent laboring in the vineyards of color management, including, especially, all the things the manuals don't tell you.

Understanding the Big Picture

If you don't understand the Big Picture, the basic underpinnings of color management, it may seem like magic when it works, and like black magic when it doesn't. It isn't magic, of course—it's just some rather clever technology based on some very solid, but limited, science. Human vision is a wondrously complex phenomenon, and a great deal remains to be learned before we can fully explain it.

If you understand the way the technology works, and the scope of the mathematical models on which it's based, you'll have a much easier time making color management work for you, and troubleshooting it when it fails to do so.

Sweating the Details

One of the keys to successful color management—one that the manuals largely ignore—is paying close attention to the myriad factors that influence both the behavior of the various hunks of machinery we use to reproduce color, and the way we perceive that color. Our scanners, digital cameras, monitors, printers, and presses are all physical devices, and hence they're subject to physical influences—heat, humidity, and friction to name but a few—that change the color they produce, and our perception of that color is strongly influenced by the environment in which we view it.

So sweating the details—keeping track of the way your various devices behave, correcting that behavior when necessary, and controlling the environment in which we judge that behavior—is an essential but largely undocumented part of the color-management process. Color management succeeds or fails according to the accuracy with which we can describe the way our color-reproduction devices behave, but if that behavior isn't stable and repeatable, attempting to describe it is like measuring a moving target with a rubber ruler—you probably won't get the same answer twice in a row.

Making it Flow

Color management doesn't exist in a vacuum. Useful, real-world color management is simply a part, albeit a useful and important part, of an entire workflow. But the people who publish the software simply document how their particular piece of the puzzle works, not how it fits into the bigger picture.

Everyone's workflow is to some extent unique, so rather than just laying out a color-management workflow, we've tried to show you how to analyze color management so that you can integrate it into your own workflow as seamlessly as possible, and even refine that workflow to make it more efficient.

Why Did We Think We Could Do This?

It seemed simple when we first conceived the idea. All three of us are premature adopters of color management, with the scars to match, but we've all made color management work in mission-critical scenarios. Needless to say, we grievously underestimated the amount of work this book would entail, and the time it would take us to complete that work—for those of you who have watched the publication date slip ever-farther into the future, the wait is over.

Writing this book forced us to learn things we thought we already knew, and turned up masses of material that fell into the category Fred likes to refer to as "more interesting than relevant." We've tried to limit the contents of the book to the material that's both interesting *and* relevant—we'll save the rest for the *Color Geek Trivia—Millennium Edition* board game. We may have been arrogant when we started out, but we all three are now intimately acquainted with the meaning of the word "hubris."

How the Book Is Organized

Color management is an immensely deep subject—Bruce calls it a bottomless pit—with tendrils stretching into many different areas ranging from the physics and chemistry of our devices, to the behavior of our software and computer systems, to the neurophysics and psychophysics of our perceptual systems, to psychology, and even to language. So we've tried to break it down into manageable categories, and present them in a logical order.

Part I: Introduction to Color Management. In the first four chapters, we try to lay the groundwork for the rest of the book. We put this information first because it's hard to manage color if you don't know what it is, or how your various software and hardware tools represent and reproduce it.

▶ What Is Color?

▶ Computers and Color

▶ Color Management

▶ All About Profiles

Part II: Building and Tuning Profiles. Color management succeeds or fails on the accuracy of the profiles we use to describe the way all our color-reproduction devices behave, so the next five chapters look at tried-and-tested real-world techniques for creating, evaluating, tuning and maintaining device profiles.

▶ Measurement, Calibration, and Process Control

▶ Building Display Profiles

▶ Building Input Profiles

▶ Building Output Profiles

▶ Evaluating and Editing Profiles

Part III: Applications and Workflow. Color management is only useful if you can integrate it into a working production system, so the final nine chapters look at color-management workflow, first from an analytical standpoint, then in terms of the actual tools offered by key applications, and finally as a nuts-and-bolts series of decisions you need to make in order to produce a functioning color-management workflow that suits your needs.

▶ Color-Management Workflow

▶ Color Management in the Operating System

▶ The Adobe Common Color Architecture

- ▶ Color Management in Macromedia FreeHand 10

- ▶ Color Management in CorelDRAW 10

- ▶ Color Management in QuarkXPress

- ▶ Color Management and PDF

- ▶ Automation and Scripting

- ▶ Building Color-Managed Workflows

Part IV: Appendices. This section contains supplementary material that we hope you'll find both interesting *and* relevant.

- ▶ Profile Anatomy

- ▶ Workflow Templates

- ▶ Glossary

Thank You!

We couldn't have produced this book without the help of many individuals we'd like to thank here. Rebecca Gulick, our editor, patiently watched deadlines come and go, yet remained unflappable while quietly polishing our prose in ways that were never intrusive and always elegant. When impending motherhood forced her to concentrate on more important matters (we were *way* late), Carolyn Said stepped into the breach and helped us see the process through to fruition. Lisa Brazieal, our ace production coordinator, made sure our digital files were translated to ink on paper—we'd like to thank her and all our other friends at Peachpit. Emily Glossbrenner produced the index in record time, and delivered it exactly when she'd promised. And special thanks to Angela Reitz for catching all those typos and inconsistencies at the 11th hour—any that remain are entirely our fault.

We owe a debt to our peers and colleagues in the industry, but we'd particularly like to thank Michael Kieran and Don Hutcheson for their constant encouragement and generosity of spirit—both slogged their way through early drafts and provided many helpful suggestions.

Several vendors were generous in providing equipment, support, advice, and encouragement. Special thanks go to Brian Levey at ColorVision; Nick Milley and Tom Lianza at Sequel Imaging; Thomas Kunz, Brian Ashe, and Roland Campo at GretagMacbeth; Bonnie Fladung and Marc Levine at Monaco Systems, Inc.; Karl Lang and Carla Ow at Sony; John Zimmerer at Apple Computer, Inc.; Steve Upton at www.chromix.com; Thomas Knoll and Chris Cox at Adobe Systems, Inc.; Mark Duhaime at Imacon USA; Eric Magnusson at Left Dakota, Inc.; John Panozzo at Colorbyte Software; Mark Geeves at BESTColor; Dan Caldwell and Bob Burnett at Integrated Color Solutions; and Parker Plaisted and Eddie Murphy at Epson America.

Bruce. "Thanks to all my fellow color geeks, especially Andrew Rodney (the Digital Dog), Bruce Lindbloom, and Ian Lyons, all of whom share their knowledge and expertise selflessly; Mike Ornellas for always asking the hard questions; Mike 064 Freeman and Wendy Bauer for playing music with me for the last 20 years without undue complaints; to all the good folks on the ColorSync User's List; and most of all to Angela, for her patience, wisdom, strength, and love."

Chris. "For at least cushioning the fall to insanity, if not preventing it entirely, I thank Jay Nelson, Ben Willmore, and Eric Magnusson for their patience and advice. A special thank you to John Zimmerer, Kevin DePalmer, and Michael Kieran who actually got me started on this path; to Mike Rodriguez and Martin Bailey for providing their knowledge of standards, prepress workflow, and PDF; to Nathan Wade for automation and scripting insights; and to Andrew Rodney for being so gracious with his knowledge, on-going encouragement, and attempts to teach me 'Oh come on, just keep it!' And lastly to His Most Imperial Highness, who saw the beginning of this project but not the end, and the Orthutangans— *ik mar beyvoo d'rin!*"

Fred. "My thanks can start nowhere but with Dr. Ed Granger, my color mentor; Larry Baca, Rob Cook, Michael Solomon and everyone at Light Source; the good folks I worked with at X-Rite; Thad McIlroy and The Color Resource; Ty Roberts, Mickey Mantle, and all my friends at Gracenote; and my new friends at Pixar. On a personal level, my gratitude to those who have known and encouraged me throughout this effort, and somehow still like me: Lynn Harrington, my best friend and first color student; Alyson Gill, who makes it so I don't ever have to worry about Emily; Eric Cave, advisor on things academic and co-producer with Alyson of the colorful Meghan; Paul and Alex, my supporting siblings; my Nobody Famous mates; and my students and colleagues at CCSF. But saving best for last, I have to thank my father Frederick Bunting for his great strength and wisdom, but also for exposing me to the incredible beauty that is good engineering."

Contacts and Resources

We welcome email saying nice *or* not-so-nice things about this book. You can reach us at rwcm@colorremedies.com. And as we're made aware of the inevitable errata, we'll post updates, and some useful resources, at www.colorremedies.com/realworldcolor/.

PART I

Introduction to Color Management

What Is Color?

Reflections on Life

"It's not easy being green," sang the velvet voice of Kermit the Frog, perhaps giving us some indication of how the frog felt to be a felt frog. While none of us may ever know the experience of "being green," it's worth reflecting (as we are all reflective objects) on the experience of "seeing green."

You don't have to be a color expert to use color management. But if you're totally unfamiliar with the concepts behind the technology, color management may seem like magic. We don't expect you to become as obsessed with color as we are—indeed, if you want any hope of leading a normal life, we advise against it—but we do recommend that you familiarize yourself with the fundamentals we lay out in this chapter.

▶ They'll help you understand the problem that color management addresses. The whole business of printing or displaying images that look like realistic depictions of the things they portray depends on exploiting specific properties of the way humans see color. Color management is just an extension of that effort.

▶ They'll explain some of the terminology you'll encounter when using color management software—terms like *colorimetric*, *perceptual*, and *saturation*, for example. A little color theory helps explain these terms and why we need them.

▶ The strengths and weaknesses of color management are rooted in our ability (or inability) to quantify human color vision accurately. If you understand this, your expectations will be more realistic.

▶ Color theory explains why a color viewed in a complex scene such as a photograph looks "different" from the same color viewed in isolation. Understanding this helps you evaluate your results.

▶ You need to understand the instruments you may use with color management. This chapter explains just what they measure.

But we have to 'fess up to another reason for writing this chapter: color is just really darned interesting. While this chapter sets the stage and lays the foundation for other chapters in this book, we hope it will also spark your curiosity about something you probably take for granted—your ability to see colors. If you're intimidated by scientific concepts, don't worry—we won't bombard you with obscure equations, or insist that you pass a graduate course in rocket science. It's not absolutely necessary to understand all of the issues we cover in this chapter to use color management. But a passing familiarity with these concepts and terms can often come in handy. And you may well come to realize that, although you've probably done it all your life, in reality "it's not easy seeing green."

Where Is Color?

If you want to manage color, it helps to first understand just what it is, so let's start by examining your current definition of color. Depending on how much you've thought about it—if you're reading this book, you've probably done so more than most—you may have gone through several definitions at various times in your life, but they've probably resembled one of the following statements:

Color is a property of objects. This is the first and most persistent view of color. No matter how much we may have philosophized about color, we all still speak of "green apples," "red lights," and "blue suede shoes."

Color is a property of light. This is the textbook counterclaim to the view of color as a property of objects. Authors of color books and papers love to stress that "light is color" or "no light, no color."

Color happens in the observer. This concept captures our imagination when we encounter optical illusions such as afterimages, successive contrast, and others that don't seem to originate in the objects we see. Color is something that originates in the eye or the brain of the observer.

The correct answer, of course, is a blend of all three. All are partially true, but you don't have to look far to find examples that show that none of the three statements, by itself, is a complete description of the experience we call color.

Color is an *event* that occurs among three participants: a light source, an object, and an observer. The color event is a sensation evoked in the observer by the wavelengths of light produced by the light source and modified by the object. If any of these three things changes, the color event is different (see Figure 1-1)—in plain English, we see a different color.

We find it interesting that the three ingredients of the color event represent three of the hard sciences: physics, chemistry, and biology. Understanding how light affects color takes us into the physics of color;

Figure 1-1
The color event

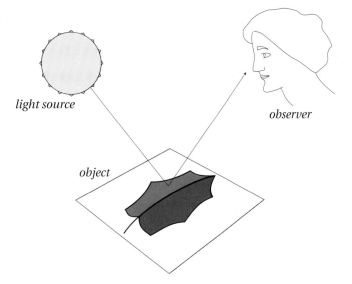

light source

observer

object

A color event always has three participants.

understanding how objects change light involves the chemistry of surfaces and how their molecules and atoms absorb light energy; and understanding the nature of the observer takes us into biology, including the neurophysiology of the eye and brain, and the threshold of the nether regions of psychology. In short, color is a complex phenomenon.

The next sections explore this simple model of the color event in more detail. We begin with light sources, then move on to objects, and then spend a bit more time with the subject most dear to you and us, namely, you and us (the observers).

Light and the Color Event

The first participant in the color event is light. The party just doesn't get started until this guest arrives. But all light isn't created equal: the characteristics of the light have a profound effect on our experience of color. So let's look at the nature of light in more detail.

Photons and Waves

Many a poor physics student has relived the dilemma faced by 18th-Century scientists as to whether light is best modeled as a particle (the view held by Sir Isaac Newton) or as a wave (as argued by Christian Huygens). Depending on the experiment you do, light behaves sometimes like a particle, sometimes like a wave. The two competing views were eventually reconciled by the quantum theorists like Max Planck and Albert Einstein into the 'wavicle' concept called a *photon*.

You can imagine a photon as a pulsating packet of energy traveling through space. Each photon is born and dies with a specific energy level. The photon's energy level does not change the speed at which the photon *travels*—through any given medium, the speed of light is constant for all photons, regardless of energy level. Instead, the energy level of the photon determines how fast it *pulsates*. Higher-energy photons pulsate at higher frequencies. So as these photons all travel together at the same speed, the photons with higher energy travel shorter distances between pulses. In other words, they have shorter *wavelengths*. Another way to put it is that every photon has a specific energy level, and thus a specific wavelength—the higher the energy level, the shorter the wavelength (see Figure 1-2).

The wavelengths of light are at the order of magnitude of *nanometers*, or billionths of a meter (abbreviated *nm*).

The Spectrum

The *spectrum* refers to the full range of energy levels (wavelengths) that photons have as they travel through space and time. The part of this spectrum that tickles our eye is a small sliver from about 380 nm to about 700 nm that we call the *visible spectrum*, or simply, *light* (see Figure 1-3).

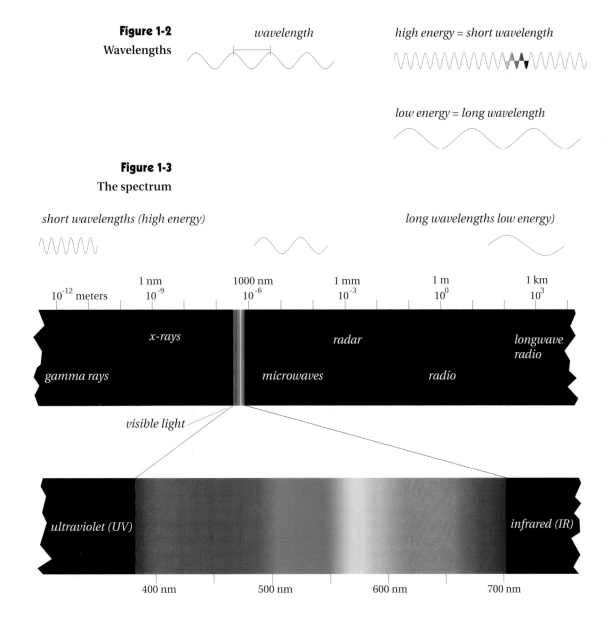

Figure 1-2
Wavelengths

wavelength

high energy = short wavelength

low energy = long wavelength

Figure 1-3
The spectrum

short wavelengths (high energy)

long wavelengths low energy)

1 nm
10^{-9}

1000 nm
10^{-6}

1 mm
10^{-3}

1 m
10^{0}

1 km
10^{3}

10^{-12} meters

x-rays

radar

longwave radio

gamma rays

microwaves

radio

visible light

ultraviolet (UV)

infrared (IR)

400 nm

500 nm

600 nm

700 nm

Our eyes respond only to this tiny sliver of the full electromagnetic spectrum, and they have varying responses to different parts of this sliver—the different wavelengths evoke different sensations of color. So we've come to associate the different wavelengths with the colors they evoke, from the reds at the low-energy end (longer wavelengths at about 700 nm) through the oranges, yellows, and greens to the blues and violets at the high-energy end (shorter wavelengths at about 380 nm). Of course, there's nothing in the electromagnetic spectrum itself that prevents us from naming more or fewer than six bands. Newton, for example, labelled a seventh band, indigo, between the blues and violets. (Many historians believe that Newton was looking for symmetry with the seven notes of the musical octave.)

But no matter how many bands you label in the spectrum, the order—reds, oranges, yellows, greens, blues, and violets—is always the same. (Fred and Bruce spent early years in a British school system, and were taught the mnemonic "Richard of York Gained Battles in Vain," while in the U.S., Chris was introduced to the strange personage of Mr. "ROY G. BiV.") We could reverse the order, and list them from shortest to longest wavelength (and hence from highest to lowest energy and frequency—the lower the energy, the lower the frequency, and the longer the wavelength,) but green would always lie between blue and yellow, and orange would always lie between yellow and red.

In the graphic arts, we're mainly concerned with visible light, but we sometimes have to pay attention to those parts of the spectrum that lie just outside the visible range. The wavelengths that are slightly longer than red light occupy the *infrared* (IR) region (which means, literally, "below red"). IR often creates problems for digital cameras, because the CCD (charge-coupled-device) arrays used in digital cameras to detect light are also highly sensitive to infrared, so most digital cameras include an IR filter either on the chip or on the lens.

At the other end, just above the last visible violets, the range of high-energy (short-wavelength) photons known as the *ultraviolet (UV)* region (literally, "beyond violet") also raises some concerns. For example, paper and ink manufacturers (like laundry detergent manufacturers) often add *UV brighteners* to make an extra-white paper or extra-bright ink. The brighteners absorb non-visible photons with UV wavelengths, and re-emit photons in the visible spectrum—a phenomenon known as *fluorescence.* This practice creates problems for some measuring instruments, because they see the paper or ink differently from the way our eyes do. We address these issues in Chapters 5 and 8.

Spectral Curves

Other than the incredibly saturated greens and reds emitted by lasers, you'll rarely see light composed of photons of all the same wavelength (what the scientists call *monochromatic* light). Instead, almost all the light you see consists of a blend of photons of many wavelengths. The actual color you see is determined by the specific blend of wavelengths— the *spectral energy*—that reaches your eye.

Pure white light contains equal amounts of photons at all the visible wavelengths. Light from a green object contains few short-wavelength (high-energy) photons, and few long-wavelength (low-energy) photons—but is comprised mostly of medium-wavelength photons. Light coming from a patch of magenta ink contains photons in the short and long wavelengths, but few in the middle of the visible spectrum.

All of these spectral energies can be represented by a diagram called the *spectral curve* of the light reflected by the object (see Figure 1-4).

Figure 1-4

Spectral curves

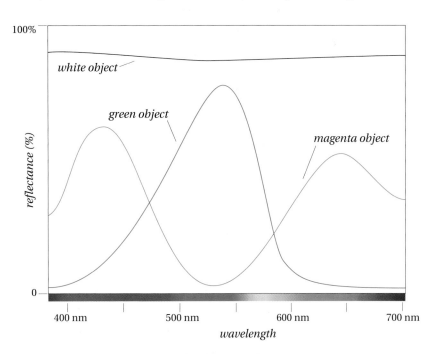

Spectral curves of three objects

Light Sources

A *light source* is just something that emits large quantities of photons in the visible spectrum. Just as with objects, we can draw the spectral curve of the light energy emitted by the light source at each wavelength (see Figure 1-5).

Figure 1-5

Light sources

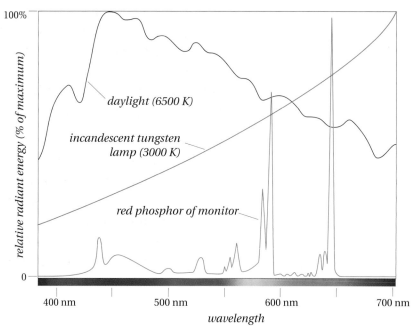

Spectral curves of three light sources

We care about several main kinds of light sources:

▶ **Blackbody radiators** are light sources whose photons are purely the result of thermal energy given off by atoms. Lightbulbs and stars such as our sun are examples of near-perfect blackbodies. The wavelength composition (i.e. 'color') of radiation emitted by a blackbody radiator depends only on its temperature, and not what it's made of. So we use *color temperature* as a way of describing the overall 'color' of a light source. (See the sidebar "*The Color of White*" later in this chapter.)

▶ **Daylight** is the result of our most familiar blackbody radiator, the sun, and an enormous filter we call the atmosphere. It's probably the most important of all light sources since it's the one under which our visual system evolved. The exact wavelength composition of daylight depends on the time of day, the weather, and the latitude (see the black curve in Figure 1-5).

▶ **Electric discharge lamps** consist of an enclosed tube containing a gas (such as mercury vapor or xenon) that's excited by an electric charge. The charge raises the energy level of the gas atoms, which then re-emit the energy as photons at specific wavelengths, resulting in a 'spikey' spectral curve. Manufacturers use various techniques, such as pressurizing the gas or coating the inside of the tube with phosphors, to add other wavelengths to the emitted light. *Fluorescent lamps* are the most common form of these lamps. The phosphors coating the inside of the tube absorb photons emitted by the gas and re-emit them at other wavelengths.

▶ **Computer monitors** are also light sources—they emit photons. CRT (cathode-ray tube) monitors use phosphors on the inside of the front glass to absorb electrons and re-emit photons at specific wavelengths (either red, green, or blue). The red phosphor in particular is characteristically spikey (see the red curve in Figure 1-5). We'll describe monitors in more detail, including other types of monitors such as LCDs, in Chapter 6.

Illuminants

The word *illuminant* refers to a light source that has been measured or specified formally in terms of spectral energy. The *CIE* (*Commission Internationale de l'Eclairage,* or the International Commission on Illumination)—a body of color scientists and technologists from around the world that has accumulated a huge amount of knowledge about color since the 1920s—has specified a number of CIE Standard Illuminants.

▶ **Illuminant A** represents the typical spectral curve of a tungsten lamp (a standard lightbulb). This is the green curve in Figure 1-5.

▶ **Illuminant B** represents sunlight at a correlated color temperature of 4874 K. This is seldom used, if ever.

▶ **Illuminant C** is an early daylight simulator (correlated color temperature 6774 K). It has been replaced by the D illuminants, although you occasionally still find it.

Figure 1-6
Color temperature

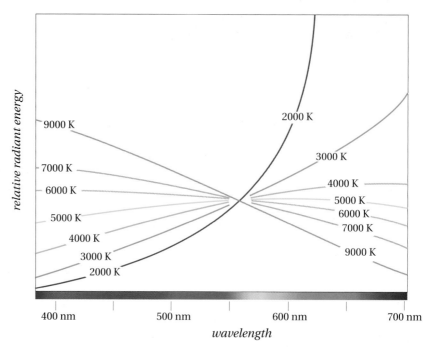

Spectral curves of a blackbody at various temperatures

▶ **Illuminants D** is a series of illuminants that represent various modes of daylight. The most commonly used D illuminants are D50 and D65 with correlated color temperatures of 5000 K and 6504 K respectively. The D65 spectral curve is the black curve in Figure 1-5.

▶ **Illuminant E** is a theoretical 'equal energy' illuminant that doesn't represent a real light source, and is mostly used for calculations.

▶ **Illuminants F** is a series of 'fluorescent' illuminants that represent the wavelength characteristics of various popular fluorescent lamps. These are named F2, F3, and so on, up to F12.

The Object and the Color Event

The second participant in the color event is the object. The way an object interacts with light plays a large role in determining the nature of the color event, so in this section we examine the various ways that objects interact with light, and the ways that this interaction affects our experience of color.

The Color of White

Many of the light sources we use—such as lightbulbs or sunlight—produce light in a characteristic way that gives us a handy terminology to describe the color of light: *color temperature*. Every dense object radiates what's called *thermal energy*. Atoms re-emit energy that they've absorbed from some process such as combustion (burning of fuel), or metabolism (burning off those fries you had for lunch). At low temperatures, this radiation is in the infrared region invisible to humans, and we call it *heat*. But at higher temperatures the radiation is visible and we call it *light*.

To study this phenomenon, physicists imagine objects where they have eliminated all other sources of light and are only looking at the radiation from thermal energy. They call these objects *blackbody radiators*. If you're standing in a pitch-black room, you are a blackbody radiator emitting energy that only an infrared detector, or an owl, can see. Stars (such as our sun) are almost perfect blackbodies as they aren't illuminated by any

other light source, and the light they emit is almost entirely from the heat their atoms have absorbed from the furnaces in the stars' cores. A light bulb in a dark room is an almost-perfect blackbody radiator—all the light is from a heated filament of tungsten. A candle is mostly a blackbody (although if you look closely, you can see a small region of blue light that's due to direct energy released by the chemical reaction of burning wax rather than absorption and re-emission of energy). To see a blackbody in action, turn on your toaster in a darkened kitchen.

Figure 1-6 shows the spectral curves of a blackbody at various temperatures. (Temperatures are in *kelvins (K)*, where a kelvin is a degree in the physicist's temperature scale from absolute zero.) At lower temperatures, the blackbody gives off heat in the in the low-energy/long-wavelength part of the visible spectrum, and so is dominated by red and yellow wavelengths. At 2000 K we see the dull red we commonly call "red hot." As the temperature gets higher, the curve shifts

gradually to the higher-energy/shorter wavelengths. At 3000 to 4000 K, the light changes color from dull red to orange to yellow. The tungsten filament of an incandescent lightbulb operates at about 2850 to 3100 K, giving its characteristic yellowish light. At 5000 to 7000 K, the blackbody's emitted light is relatively flat in the visible spectrum, producing a more neutral white. At higher temperatures of 9000 K or above, short wavelengths predominate, producing a bluer light.

This is the system we use to describe colors of "white light." We refer to their "color temperature" to describe whether the light is orange, yellowish, neutral, or bluish. Purists will remind you that the correct term is actually *correlated color temperature* as most emissive light sources—including daylight (which is filtered by the earth's atmosphere), fluorescent lamps, and computer monitors—aren't true blackbody radiators, and so we're picking the closest blackbody temperature to the apparent color of the light source.

Reflection and Transmission

An object's surface must interact with light to affect the light's color. Light strikes the object, travels some way into the atoms at the surface, then re-emerges. During the light's interaction with these surface atoms the object absorbs some wavelengths and reflects others (see Figure 1-7), so the spectral makeup of the reflected light isn't the same as that of the

Figure 1-7   Reflection

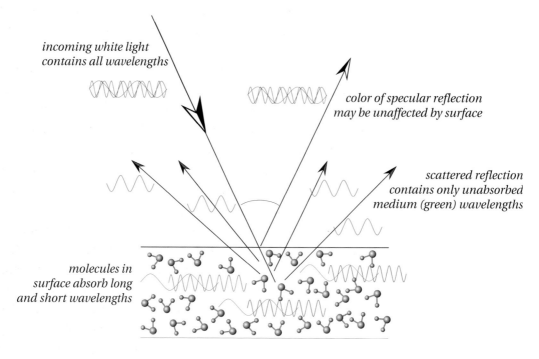

incoming white light
contains all wavelengths

color of specular reflection
may be unaffected by surface

scattered reflection
contains only unabsorbed
medium (green) wavelengths

molecules in
surface absorb long
and short wavelengths

Surface of a reflective object

incoming light. The degree to which an object reflects some wavelengths and absorbs others is called its *spectral reflectance*. Note that if you change the light source, the reflectance of the object doesn't change, even though the spectral energy that emerges is different. Reflectance, then, *is* an invariant property of the object.

A *transmissive* object affects wavelengths in the same way as the reflective object just described, except that the transmissive object must be at least partially translucent so that the light can pass all the way through it. However, it too alters the wavelength makeup of the light by absorbing some wavelengths and allowing others to pass through.

The surface of a reflective object or the substance in a transmissive object can affect the wavelengths that strike it in many specific ways. But it's worth pausing to examine one phenomenon in particular that sometimes bedevils color management—the phenomenon known as *fluorescence*.

Fluorescence

Some atoms and molecules have the peculiar ability to absorb photons of a certain energy (wavelength), and emit photons of a lower energy (longer wavelength). *Fluorescence*, as this phenomenon is called, can sometimes change one type of visible wavelength into another visible wavelength. For example, the fluorescent coating inside a sodium lamp absorbs some of the yellow wavelengths emitted by the electrically excited sodium vapor, and re-emits photons of other wavelengths in order to produce a more spectrally balanced light.

But fluorescence is most noticeable when the incoming photons have wavelengths in the non-visible ultraviolet range of the spectrum, and the emitted photons are in the visible range (usually in the violets or blues). The result is an object that seems to emit more visible photons than it receives from the light source—it appears "brighter than white."

Many fabric makers and paper manufacturers add fluorescent brighteners to whiten the slightly yellow color of most natural fibers. To compensate for the slow yellowing of fabrics, many laundry detergents and bleaches have fluorescent brighteners, often called 'bluing agents' (because they convert non-visible UV light to visible blue). We all have fond memories of groovy 'black lights'—lamps designed to give off light energy in the violet and ultraviolet wavelengths—and their effects on posters printed with fluorescent inks, on white T-shirts, and yes, even on teeth, depending on the brighteners in the toothpaste we had used!

Fluorescence crops up in unexpected places in color management—we'll alert you when they are something to look out for. For now, it's enough to know that fluorescence can be an issue in three cases:

▶ Whenever a measurement instrument (a spectrophotometer, colorimeter, scanner, digital camera, or film) is more responsive to UV light than our eye is (which has no response at all).

▶ Whenever artificial light sources (such as lamps, flashbulbs, or scanner lamps) emit more or (more likely) less UV than daylight, which includes a sizeable amount of UV.

▶ Whenever a colorant (ink, wax, toner, etc.) or paper used for printing has fluorescent properties that make it behave unpredictably depending on the light source used to view it (as unpredictability is the nemesis of color management).

The Observer and the Color Event

Of the three participants in our simple model of the color event, you, the observer, are by far the most complex. Your visual system is way more complex than a blackbody radiator or a hemoglobin molecule, so much so that we still have a great deal to learn about it. It starts with the structures of the eye, but continues through the optic nerve and goes deep into the brain. In this section, we look at various models of human vision that form the basis of color management.

Trichromacy: Red, Green, Blue

If there's one lesson you should take from this chapter, it's that **the fundamental basis for *all* color reproduction is the three-channel design of the human retina**. Other features of human vision—such as opponency, color constancy, and non-linearity, all of which we cover in this section—are important, but the fact that the human eye has three types of color sensors (corresponding roughly to reds, greens, and blues) is what lets us reproduce colors at all using just three pigments on paper, or just three phosphors in a monitor.

The eye. Your eye is one of the most beautiful structures in nature. (We hope you don't think we're being too forward.) Contrary to popular belief, the main task of focusing light into an image at the back of the eye is handled not by the lens, but by the *cornea*, the curved front layer of the eye. The lens makes minor focus adjustments as the tiny muscles that hold it in place adjust its shape, but it does two important things for color vision. First, the lens acts as a UV filter, protecting the retina from damaging high-energy ultraviolet light—so even if the retina could see into the UV range (and some experiments show that it can), the lens is partly responsible for our inability to see UV light, unlike other visual systems, such as honeybees, birds, scanners, and digital cameras. Second, the lens yellows as we age, reducing our ability to see subtle changes in blues and greens, while our ability to see reds and magentas is hardly affected. Our discrimination in the yellows is always fairly weak, regardless of age.

The retina: rods and cones. The *retina* is a complex layer of nerve cells lining the back of your eye (see Figure 1-8). The nerve cells in the retina that respond to light are called *photoreceptors*, or often just *receptors*.

Figure 1-8   The human eye

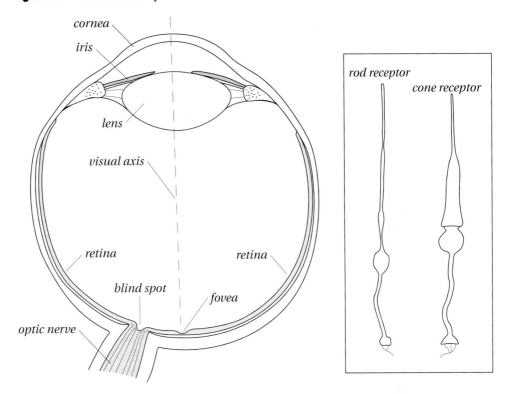

Cross-section of the right eye from above. Most color vision happens in the fovea, where the three types of cones far outnumber the rods. Inset shows the shape of the rod and cone cells, which is where they get their names.

Receptors come in two types, called *rods* and *cones* because of their shapes. Rods provide vision in low-light conditions, such as night-vision. They're sensitive in low levels of light and are largely blinded by daylight conditions. Cones are a more recent development in the evolution of the mammal retina and function in bright light conditions. We have far more rods than cones throughout most of the retina (about 120 million rods to about 6 million cones), except in a little indentation in the very center of the retina, called the *fovea*, where cones outnumber rods (about 150,000 cones, with a small number of rods, falling off to a completely rod-free region in the center of the fovea called the *foveola*). This center region, where you have the highest density of photoreceptors, also provides the best acuity (for example, to read these letters, you're focusing the image of the letters on your fovea). It's also where your primary color vision happens.

Three types of cones. While all the rods in your retina are essentially the same, the cones fall into three types. One responds primarily to the long wavelengths of light and has little response in the middle or short wavelengths. One responds primarily to the middle wavelengths, and the third responds to the short wavelengths (see Figure 1-9). Many people call these the red cones, green cones, and blue cones respectively because of the colors we normally associate with these three regions of the spectrum, but it's less misleading to refer to them as the long-, medium-, and short-wavelength cones (or L, M, and S) respectively.

Trichromacy and tristimulus. Two related and often confused terms are *trichromacy* and *tristimulus*. The term *trichromacy* (also known as the *three-component theory* or the *Young-Helmoltz theory* of color vision) refers to the theory, now well verified, that we have three receptors for color (the three types of cones).

Figure 1-9

Peak sensitivities

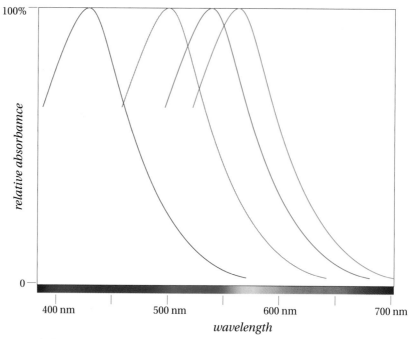

The peak wavelengths of the photoreceptor pigments. The three cone photoreceptors have peak absorptions at 420 nm, 530 nm and 565 nm respectively. The rod photoreceptor (gray line) has a peak absorption at 499 nm.

The term *tristimulus* refers to experiments and measurements of human color vision involving three color stimuli, which the test subject uses to match a target stimulus (see Figure 1-10). In other words, trichromacy refers to our three color receptors, and tristimulus refers to the experiments that use three stimuli to verify and measure trichromacy. The most comprehensive tristimulus model has been defined by the CIE and forms the basis for color management.

The importance of trichromacy for the graphic arts is that **we can simulate almost any color by using just three well-chosen primary colors** of light. Two colors are not enough—no matter how carefully you choose them, you cannot duplicate all colors with two primaries. And four colors is unnecessary—any color you can produce with four colors of light you can reproduce with just a well-chosen three.

Additive primaries. It's the trichromatic structure of the human retina that makes possible what we know as the *additive primary colors* (see

Figure 1-10
Tristimulus experiment

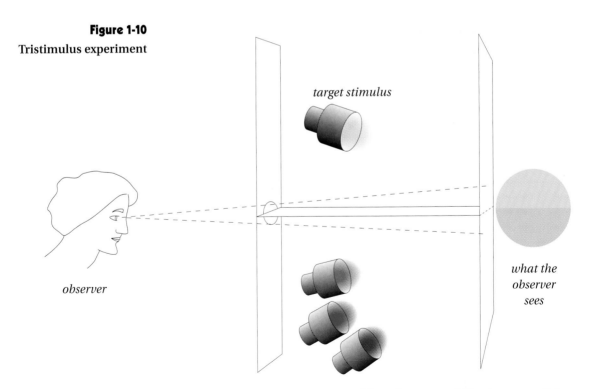

target stimulus

observer

what the
observer
sees

The observer adjusts the intensities of the red, green, and blue lamps until they match the target stimulus on the split screen.

Figure 1-11). If you choose three light sources with overlapping spectra that divide up the visible spectrum roughly into thirds, each one adds wavelengths that tickle one or more of your eye's three receptors. Divide the spectrum roughly into thirds and you get three light sources that we would call red, green, and blue. Starting from black (no wavelengths), the three colors *add* wavelengths—hence "additive color"—until you get white (all wavelengths in even proportions).

Subtractive primaries. Trichromacy is also the source of our *subtractive primaries*—cyan, magenta, and yellow (see Figure 1-11). Rather than adding wavelengths to black, they act to subtract wavelengths from an otherwise white source of light. In other words, the term "cyan ink" is just a name for "long-wavelength-subtractor," or simply "red-subtractor"— it subtracts long (red) wavelengths from white light (such as that reflected from otherwise blank paper). Similarly, magenta ink is a "medium-wavelength-subtractor," or a "green-subtractor." And yellow is a "short-wavelength-subtractor," or a "blue-subtractor."

Figure 1-11
Primary colors

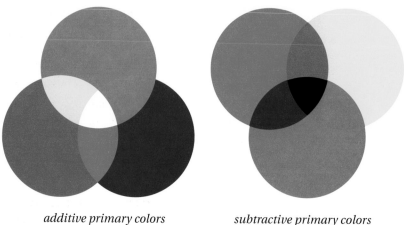

additive primary colors   *subtractive primary colors*

But the bottom line is that both additive and subtractive primaries work by manipulating the wavelengths that enter our eyes and stimulate our three cone receptors. This manipulation, when done cleverly, stimulates our three receptors in just the right proportions to make us feel like we are receiving light of a certain color.

There are still a few more points to make about trichromacy.

Color spaces. The three primary colors not only allow us to define any color in terms of the amount of each primary, they also allow us to plot the relationships between colors by using the values of the three primaries as Cartesian coordinates in a three-dimensional space, where each primary forms one of the three axes. This notion of *color spaces* is one you'll encounter again and again in your color management travails.

Relationship with the spectrum: why not GRB or YMCK? Have you have ever wondered why we have the convention that RGB is always written in that order (never GRB or BRG)? Similarly, CMYK is never written YMCK (except to specify the order in which inks are laid down, or when adding a twist to a certain Village People song). Well, now you know why:

▶ The colors of the spectrum are usually listed in order of decreasing wavelength: red, orange, yellow, green, blue, and violet—ROYGBV.

▶ The additive primaries divide this spectrum roughly into thirds, corresponding to the reds, greens, and blues. So ROYGBV leads to RGB.

▶ We write the subtractive primaries in the order that matches them to their additive counterparts (their opposites). Thus RGB leads to CMY.

You may find this last convention handy for remembering complementary colors. For example, if you're working on a CMYK image with a blue cast, and can't remember which channel to adjust, just write RGB, and then under it CMY. The additive primaries match their subtractive complements (Y is under B because yellow subtracts blue). So to reduce a blue cast, you increase Y, or reduce both C and M.

Artificial trichromats (scanners, cameras, etc.). We also use trichromacy to make devices that simulate color vision. The most accurate of these are *colorimeters*, which we'll describe later in this chapter. A colorimeter tries to duplicate the exact tristimulus response of human vision. More common examples of artificial trichromats are cameras, which use film sensitive to red, green, and blue regions of the spectrum, and scanners and digital cameras, which use sensors (CCDs) with red, green, and blue filters that break the incoming light into the three primary colors. When the 'receptors' in these devices differ from *our* receptors, the situation arises where they see matches that we don't and vice versa. We discuss this phenomenon, called *metamerism*, later in this chapter.

Opponency: Red-Green, Blue-Yellow

Some fundamental features of human color vision not only are unexplained by trichromatic theory, but seem to contradict it.

The strange case of yellow. Many of us grew up with the myth that the primary colors are red, yellow, and blue—not red, green, and blue. Studies have shown that more cultures have a name for 'yellow' than have a name even for 'blue'—and our own color naming reveals a sense that 'yellow' is in a different, more fundamental category than, say, 'cyan' and 'magenta'. Even though Thomas Young first demonstrated that you can make yellow light by combining red and green light, it seems counterintuitive. In fact, it's difficult to imagine any color that is both red and green at the same time.

Other effects unexplained by trichromacy. The fact that we can't imagine a reddish green or a greenish red is evidence that something more is going on than just three independent sensors (trichromacy). The same holds for blue and yellow—we can't imagine a yellowish blue. The effects of simultaneous contrast and afterimages shown in Figures 1-12 and 1-13 are other examples—the absence of a color produces the perception of its opposite. Finally, anomalous color vision (color blindness) usually involves the loss of color differentiation in pairs: a person with anomalous red response also loses discrimination in the greens, and a person who has no blue response also has no yellow response.

Figure 1-12
Simultaneous contrast

The two Xs look dramatically different in brightness and color, but as shown by where they touch, they are identical. (Based on a painting by Josef Albers)

Figure 1-13

Successive contrast

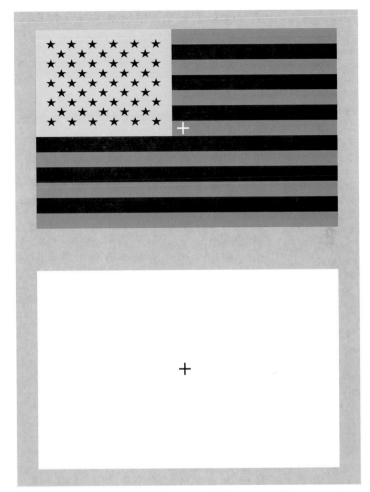

Instructions: stare at the white cross in the center of the upper image for a full minute. Then quickly look down at the lower area, and stare at the black cross.

After a few seconds and some blinking, the afterimage should appear. Note that the colors are chosen to demonstrate green-red, yellow-blue, and black-white opponency.

Opponency. Experiments and observations by Ewald Hering in the late 1800's focused on these *opponent* pairs. Why is it that we can have reddish-yellows (orange), blue-greens, and blue-reds (purples), but no reddish-greens and no yellowish-blues? To say that something is both red and green at the same time is as counterintuitive as saying that something is both light and dark at the same time. The *opponent-color theory* (also known as the *Hering theory*) held that the retina has fundamental components that generate opposite signals depending on wavelength.

The key point is that the color components in the retina aren't independent receptors that have no effect on their neighbors, but rather work as antagonistic or *opponent* pairs. These *opponent pairs* are light-dark, red-green, and yellow-blue.

Reconciling opponency and trichromacy. While the advocates of the opponency and trichromacy theories debated for many years which theory best described the fundamental nature of the retina, the two theories were eventually reconciled into the *zone theory of color.* This holds that one layer (or zone) of the retina contains the three trichromatic cones, and a second layer of the retina translated these cone signals into opponent signals: light-dark, red-green, yellow-blue. The zone theory has held up well as we continue to learn more about the layer structure of the retina, and use simple neural-net models that explain how opponent signals can emerge from additive signals (see Figure 1-14).

Figure 1-14

Trichromacy and opponency in the retina

First zone (or stage): layer of retina with three independent types of cones

Second zone (or stage): signals from cones either excite or inhibit second layer of neurons, producing opponent signals

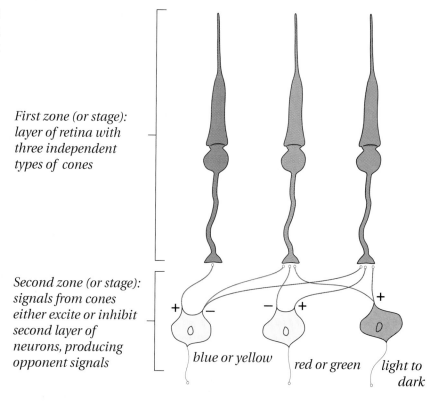

blue or yellow   red or green   light to dark

Opponency and trichromacy in the CIE models. If all this opponency and trichromacy stuff is about to make your head explode, let us assure you that it's very relevant to color management. In Chapter 2 we'll look at the CIE models of color vision, which are used as the basis for color management computations, but the important point here is that many of the CIE models—such as CIE LAB used in Photoshop and in most color management systems (CMSs)—incorporate aspects of both trichromacy and opponency. CIE LAB is based on the results of tristimulus experiments such as the one described in Figure 1-10, but it represents colors in terms of three values that represent three opponent systems: L* (lightness-darkness), a* (red-green opposition), and b* (blue-yellow opposition).

So using LAB, we can convert trichromatic measurements (measurements made with instruments that duplicate the responses of our cone receptors) to values in an opponent-color system. Achieving this wasn't simple, and it's far from perfect (as we will discuss in Chapter 2), but it's very clever, and surprisingly successful as a model, particularly when you consider that it was designed simply as a test of the reigning theories of color vision, not as a workhorse for computer calculations for the graphic arts industry.

Metamerism

If you've encountered the term "metamerism" you've probably heard it referred to as a problem or as an "error" of human vision. But—as programmers love to say—it's not a bug, it's a feature. Not only is metamerism inherent in trichromatic vision, it's the feature that makes color reproduction possible.

In simple terms, *metamerism* is the phenomenon whereby two different color samples produce the same color sensation. By "different color samples" we mean two objects that have different spectral characteristics. So, remembering our light-object-observer definition of color, if the objects are different but they produce the same 'color' (the same color sensation), this match may be dependent on (1) the light illuminating both color samples, or (2) the observer viewing the two color samples. Under different lighting, or to a different observer, the two samples may not match.

Two spectrally different color samples that produce the same color sensations are called *metamers*. Or we say that the two colors are *metameric* under certain lighting or to a certain type of observer.

You may run into different, seemingly contradictory definitions of metamerism. For example, many books give one of the following two definitions:

▶ Metamerism is when two color samples produce the same color sensation under certain lighting.

▶ Metamerism is when two color samples produce different color sensations under certain lighting.

Actually, metamerism is when *both* of these events happen to the same pair of color samples. The two color samples match under some, but not all, lighting. The first statement focuses on the match that can be made using radically different spectra. The second statement focuses on the fact that the match is tenuous. The reason you need to understand metamerism is that virtually all our color-matching activities rely on making a metameric match between two colors or sets of colors—comparing a chrome on a light table with a scanned image on a monitor, or comparing a proof with a press sheet. It's highly unlikely that the two samples will have identical spectral curves, but thanks to metamerism, we can make them match—at least in some lighting conditions.

Relationship between two color samples. Metamerism is always a relationship between *two* color samples—a single color sample can't be metameric any more than it can be identical. You may hear some people refer to "a metameric color," or talk about a printer having "metameric inks," but we think that this usage is both confusing and wrong. A printer with inks that were *truly* metamers of each other would be pointless— the inks would all appear to be the same color under some lighting condition. What they *really* mean is that the inks have spectral properties that make their appearance change more radically under different lighting conditions than most other inks.

Why metamerism happens. Metamerism happens because the eye divides all incoming spectra into the three cone responses. Two stimuli may have radically different spectral energies, but if they both get divided up between the three cone types, stimulating them in the same way, they appear to be the same color.

In the terms of our light-object-observer model (remember Figure 1-1), the color 'event' is a product of three things: the wavelengths present in the light source; the wavelengths reflected from the object or surface; and the way the wavelengths are divided among the three receptors (the cones in the eye).

What matters isn't the individual components, but the product of the three. If the light reaching your eye from object A and object B produces the same cone response, then you get the same answer—the same color sensation (see Figure 1-15).

Figure 1-15

Metamerism

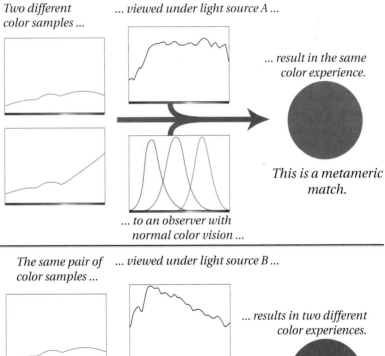

Two different color samples ...

... viewed under light source A ...

... result in the same color experience.

... to an observer with normal color vision ...

This is a metameric match.

The same pair of color samples ...

... viewed under light source B ...

... results in two different color experiences.

... to same observer ...

This is a metameric mismatch.

Objects can only reflect those wavelengths that are present in the light source. Source B contains fewer red wavelengths than source A, so the samples that appear to match under source A produce a mismatch under source B.

Metamerism in everyday life. If you've ever bought two "matching" items in a store—a tie and a handkerchief, or a handbag and shoes—only to find that they look different when viewed in daylight or home lighting, you've experienced metamerism. Fred has pairs of white jogging socks that match when he puts them on indoors, but when outdoors one looks noticeably bluer than the other, probably (he theorizes) because they were washed separately using laundry detergents with different UV brighteners. Catalog-makers cite as a common problem the fact that a clothing item shown in a catalog doesn't match the color of the item received by the customer—perhaps a result of a metameric match that was achieved in the pressroom that failed in the customer's home.

These examples illustrate the fragile nature of all color-matching exercises—when we match colors, we're almost always creating a metameric match under a specific lighting condition. That's why we use standard lighting conditions when we evaluate proof-to-press matches.

In theory, if the catalog publisher knew the conditions under which the catalog would be viewed, she could tailor the color reproduction to that environment, but in practice, it's just about impossible to know whether prospective customers will look at the catalog in daylight on their lunch hour, under office fluorescent lighting, at home under incandescent lighting, or curled up by a cozy fire under candlelight.

Ultimately, metamerism problems are something we simply have to accept as part of the territory, but if you're working in an extreme case—like designing a menu for a fancy restaurant that will be viewed mostly under candlelight—you may want to test important matches under a variety of viewing conditions.

Metamerism is your friend. You need to make peace with metamerism. Many people first encounter metamerism as a problem—a color match achieved at great effort under certain lighting fails under different lighting because of odd properties of certain inks or paper. But it's not, as some people describe, an error of our visual system. It's just an inevitable side-product of the clever solution evolution produced for deriving wavelength, and hence color information, using only three types of sensors.

More importantly for color management, metamerism is what makes color reproduction possible at all. Metamerism lets us display yellows or skin tones on a computer monitor without dedicated yellow or skin-color phosphors. Metamerism lets us reproduce the green characteristic of chlorophyll (the pigment found in plants) without chlorophyll-colored ink—or even an ink we would call green (see Figure 1-16)!

Figure 1-16
Metamerism in action

Thanks to metamerism, we can reproduce the color of this leaf in print without using a single drop of green ink.

Without metamerism, we'd have to reproduce colors by duplicating the exact spectral content of the original color stimulus. (Incidentally, this is what we have to do with sound reproduction—duplicate the stimulus of the original sound wavelength by wavelength.) If you think your ink costs are high today, imagine if you had to have thousands of colors of ink instead of just four!

Camera and scanner metamerism. We mentioned that a metameric relationship between two color samples is dependent not only on the light source, but also on the specific observer viewing the two samples. A pair of color samples can produce one color sensation to one observer, but a different color sensation to a second observer. This "observer metamerism" is sometimes an issue with color management when the observer is one of our artificial trichromats.

If a scanner's red, green, and blue detectors respond differently than our cone sensors, the scanner can see a metameric match where you and I see separate colors, or conversely, a pair of samples may appear identical to us but different to the scanner (see Figure 1-17). This is sometimes called *scanner metamerism,* and we shall see in Chapter 8 that this is the reason it's difficult to use a scanner as a measurement device for making profiles. Similarly, if a film or digital camera has different sets of metameric matches than we do, we would call this *camera metamerism,* and while there's little that color management can do about it, you need to be aware of it as an issue.

Figure 1-17

How scanner metamerism happens

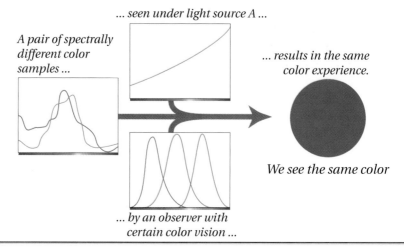

A pair of spectrally different color samples ...

... seen under light source A ...

... results in the same color experience.

We see the same color

... by an observer with certain color vision ...

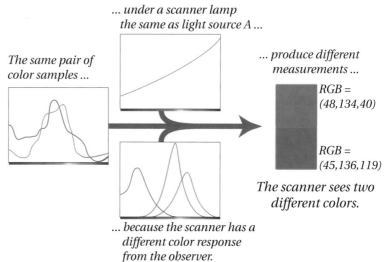

The same pair of color samples ...

... under a scanner lamp the same as light source A ...

... produce different measurements ...

RGB = (48,134,40)

RGB = (45,136,119)

The scanner sees two different colors.

... because the scanner has a different color response from the observer.

Non-Linearity: Intensity and Brightness

Another important property of the human visual system is that it's *non-linear.* All this means is that our eyes don't respond in a one-to-one fashion to the *intensity* (the number of photons reaching your eye as you might count them with a light meter) by reporting *brightness* (the sensation you feel) to the brain. When you double the intensity, you don't see the light as twice as bright. If things were that simple, if you drew a graph of intensity versus brightness, this would be a straight line as in Figure 1-18a, and we would call this *linear* response. Instead the relationship between intensity and perceived brightness looks like the graph in Figure 1-18b. To perceive something about twice as bright, we have to multiply the intensity by about nine!

Figure 1-18

Linear and non-linear response

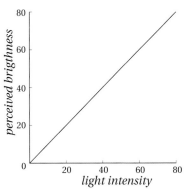

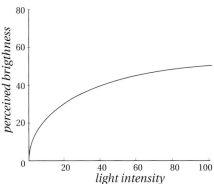

a. *Linear response—light intensity translates directly to brightness.*

b. *Non-linear response—increased light intensity produces progressively smaller increases in brightness.*

This non-linearity is common in human perception. If you double the intensity of a sound, you don't hear it as twice as loud. If you put two sugar cubes in your coffee instead of your normal one, you don't taste it as twice as sweet. The degree of non-linearity varies for different senses, but they often shape as Figure 1-18b.

Our non-linear responses are what allow our sensory systems to function across a huge range of stimuli. The difference in intensity between a piece of paper illuminated by daylight and the same piece of paper illuminated by moonlight is about 1,000,000:1. But nerve cells can respond (in the number of nerve firings per second) only at a range of about 100:1, so a huge number of inputs have to map to a small number of outputs. Non-linearity lets our sensory systems operate over a wide range of environments without getting overloaded.

The good news is that just because our response is non-linear doesn't mean it's complicated. We could have evolved a totally wacky response curve instead of the nice simple one in Figure 1-18b. Instead, this simple curve resembles what mathematicians call a power curve. In fact, using the trick of graphing the logarithms of intensity and brightness simplifies the curve even more, turning it into a straight line that can be characterized by its slope. (If you aren't familiar with logarithms, see the sidebar "*What's a Logarithm, and Why Should I Care?*") Many of the scales we use to measure perception are logarithmic scales, including decibels, which measure perceived loudness, and Optical Density (OD), which measures how dark or light an object appears.

The non-linear nature of our response to light impinges on color management in several ways, but the most important is that the various devices we use to measure light have linear responses. To relate these measurements to human perception, we have to translate them from the linear realm of light to the non-linear realm of perception (see "*We Cannot Truly Measure Color, Only Light,*" later in this chapter.

So next time someone accuses you of being non-linear, you can respond, "yes I am, and glad to be that way!"

Achromatic Component: Brightness

The term *brightness* refers to our perception of intensity (the number of photons reaching our eye). Of the three color attributes—brightness, hue, and saturation—we tend to think of brightness as different from the other two, in part because we can detect variations in brightness even when there isn't enough light (or enough different wavelengths in the light) to see color.

On a dark night, our vision is produced by our rods, which have no color response, but we can still see differences in brightness, and if we view objects under monochromatic light, everything takes on the color of the light, but again we still see differences in brightness.

Brightness describes the *quantity* of light ("how much"), while hue and saturation describe the *quality* of light ("what kind"). Detecting variations in brightness is the fundamental task of vision itself, while color, as established by hue and saturation, is just icing (albeit some tasty icing). Vision is fundamentally about "counting photons," while color deals with "categorizing" these photons into differing types.

So color scientists often speak of the *achromatic* and *chromatic* attributes of a source of light or color. The *achromatic* attribute is brightness as we perceive it independently from color, and the *chromatic* attributes are those that we commonly associate with color, independent of brightness. Most mathematical models of human color vision, including the ones that lie at the heart of color management, treat brightness separately

What's a Logarithm, and Why Should I Care?

A logarithm is a handy way to express numbers that vary over huge ranges. For example, if a set of values ranges from 0 to 1,000,000, you'll probably want much more precision when you compare values between 1 and 10 than you will when comparing values in the 100,000 to 1,000,000 range. For example, you might notice when the price of a movie ticket goes up from $7 to $8, but when buying a house you probably don't care as much about the difference between $247,637 and $247,638. The numbers at the upper end are not only unwieldy, they have an unnecessary amount of precision.

Logarithms are a nice way to deal with this problem. Instead of imagining all the numbers from 0 to 1,000,000 lined up on a huge ruler so that the distance between any two numbers is always the same, a logarithmic scale compresses the distance between any two numbers as the numbers get higher. In this way, the distance between 0 and 10 is the same as the distance between 10 and 100. So between 0 and 10 you have tick marks for 1, 2, 3, etc. but between 10 and 100 you have tick marks for 10, 20, 30, etc. You end up with a ruler that looks like Figure 1-19.

The nifty thing about such a scale is that when you take a non-linear response function like that shown in Figure 1-18b, and graph the logarithms of the values (what's called a *log-log* graph), the result is a straight line again (see Figure 1-20)!

This is why, when we measure some physical value with the purpose of predicting how our nervous system perceives that stimulus, we use some sort of logarithmic quantity. For example, what we call *density* is a logarithmic function derived from a measurement of light intensity and gives us a measurement of perceived darkness. Another example is the unit we call a *decibel*, which is also a logarithmic function derived from sound intensity, and which gives us a measurement of perceived loudness.

Figure 1-19

A logarithmic scale

Figure 1-20

A log-log graph of Figure 1-18b

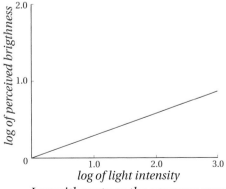

Logarithms turn the response curve into a straight line.

from the chromatic attributes. We discuss these models in Chapter 2, *Computers and Color.*

Brightness vs. lightness. In color science, we draw a distinction between *brightness* and *lightness*. For most purposes, the two words mean the same thing—they both refer to the eye's (non-linear) perception of intensity. But the strict definition is that *lightness* is relative brightness. In other words, lightness is the brightness of an object relative to an absolute white reference. So lightness ranges from "dark" to "light" with specific definitions of black and white as the limits, while brightness ranges from "dim" to "bright" with no real limits. The distinction matters because we can measure lightness and assign specific numerical values to it, while brightness is a subjective sensation in our heads.

Chromatic Components: Hue and Saturation

Brightness is a property of all vision, but hue and saturation pertain only to color vision. Together, they're known as the chromatic components of color vision, as distinct from the achromatic component of brightness.

Hue. Defining the word *hue* as an independent component of color is like trying to describe the word "lap" while standing up. There are multiple definitions for hue—some more vague than others. We've even seen hue defined as "a color's color."

The most precise definition is that hue is the attribute of a color by which we perceive its dominant wavelength. All colors contain many wavelengths, but some more than others. The wavelength that *appears* most prevalent in a color sample determines its hue. We stress the word "appears" because it may not be the actual dominant wavelength—the color sample simply has to produce the same response in the three cone types in our eyes as the perceived dominant wavelength would. In other words, it produces a metameric match to a monochromatic light source with that dominant wavelength.

A more useful and equally valid definition of hue is that it's the attribute of a color that gives it its basic name, such as red, yellow, purple, orange, and so on. We give these names to a region of the spectrum, then we refine individual color names by adding qualifiers like bright, saturated, pale, pure, etc. Thus, red is a hue, but pink is not—it can be described as a pale or desaturated red. The set of basic names that people use is quite subjective, and varies from language to language and culture to culture. As you'll see later in this chapter when we talk about psychological aspects of color, this connection between hue and color names can be fairly important to color reproduction.

Saturation. Saturation refers to the purity of a color, or how far it is from neutral gray. If hue is the perceived dominant wavelength, saturation is the extent to which that dominant wavelength seems contaminated by other wavelengths. Color samples with a wide spread of wavelengths produce unsaturated colors, while those whose spectra consist of a narrow hump appear more saturated. For example, a laser with a sharp spike at 520nm would be a totally saturated green (see Figure 1-21).

Figure 1-21
Spectra and saturation

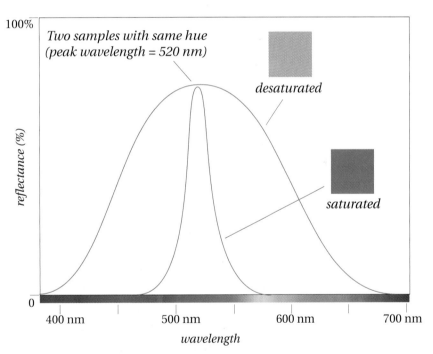

Both samples have the same peak wavelength, so they appear to be the same hue, but the narrow spectrum contains fewer contaminating wavelengths and hence appears more saturated.

Representations of hue, saturation, and brightness. Most hue diagrams and color pickers represent hue as an angle around some color shape, and saturation as the distance from the center. For example, the Apple color picker accessed from most Macintosh graphics applications shows a disk with neutral grays in the center and saturated pure hues at the edge. The disk represents all the colors at a single brightness level, so each disk is a cross-section of the full space of possible colors. Brightness is represented as a third axis ranging from black to white along which all these cross-sections are piled, resulting in a color cylinder, sphere, or double-cone (see Figure 1-22). You choose colors by first picking a brightness value, which takes you to a certain cross-section, then choosing a point on the disk representing the hue (the angle on the disk) and the saturation (the distance from the center of the disk).

Figure 1-22

Hue, saturation, and brightness

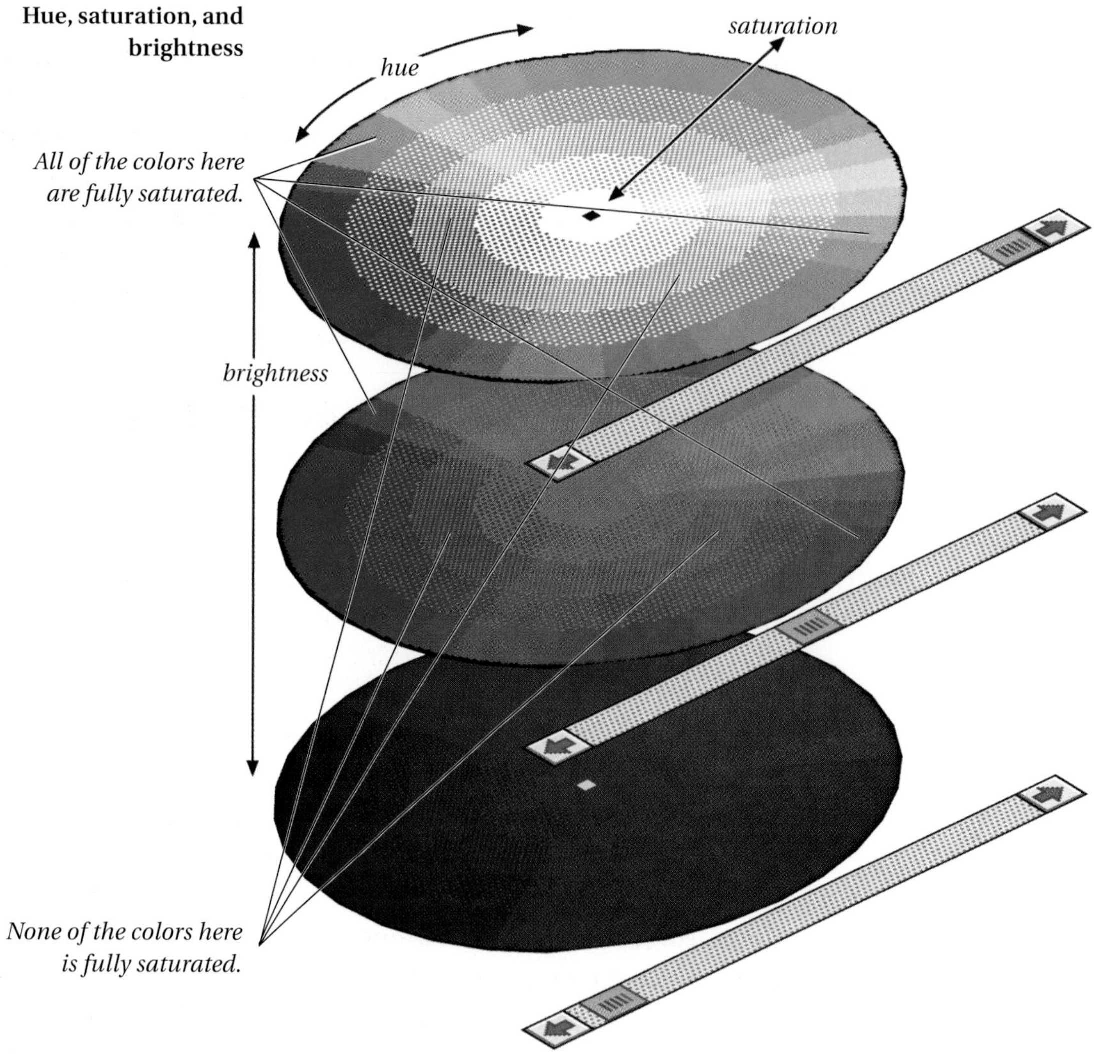

saturation

hue

All of the colors here are fully saturated.

brightness

None of the colors here is fully saturated.

Measuring Color

All the preceding knowledge about color would fall into the category that Fred likes to call "more interesting than relevant" if we couldn't draw correlations between what we expect people to see and things we can physically measure. The whole purpose of color management is ultimately to let us produce a stimulus (photons, whether reflected from a photograph or magazine page) that will evoke a known response (the sensation of a particular color) on the part of those who will view it.

Fortunately, we *are* able to draw correlations between perceived color and things we can measure in the real world, thanks to the people who have not only figured out the complexities of human vision but have modelled these complexities numerically. We need numerical models to manipulate and predict color using computers, because computers are just glorified adding machines that juggle ones and zeroes on demand. We'll look at the numerical models in more detail in Chapter 2, *Computers and Color*, but first we need to look at the various ways we can count photons and relate those measurements to human perception, because they form the foundation for the models.

We Cannot Truly Measure Color, Only Light

"Measuring color" is really an oxymoron. We've pointed out that color is an event with three participants—a light source, an object, and an observer—but the color only happens in the mind of the observer. One day we may have both the technology and a sufficient understanding of the human nervous system to able to identify which of the zillions of electrochemical processes taking place in our heads corresponds to the sensation of fire-engine red, but for now, the best we can do is measure the stimulus—the light that enters the observer's eye and produces the sensation of color. We can only infer the response that that stimulus will produce. Fortunately, thanks to the work of several generations of color scientists, we're able to draw those inferences with a reasonable degree of certainty.

We use three main types of instruments to measure the stimuli that observers—our clients, our customers, our audience, and ourselves—will eventually interpret as color. They all work by shining light with a known spectral makeup onto or through a surface, then using detectors to measure the light that surface reflects or transmits. The detector is just a photon counter—it can't determine the wavelength of the photons it is counting—so the instrument must filter the light going to the detector. The differences between the three types of instruments—densitometers, colorimeters, and spectrophotometers—are the number and type of filters they use, and the sensitivity of their detectors.

▶ **Densitometers** measure *density*, the degree to which reflective surfaces absorb light, or transparent surfaces allow it to pass.

▶ **Colorimeters** measure *colorimetric* values, numbers that model the response of the cones in our eyes.

▶ **Spectrophotometers** measure the spectral properties of a surface; in other words, how much light at each wavelength a surface reflects or transmits.

Densitometry

Densitometry plays an indirect but key role in color management. Density is the degree to which materials such as ink, paper, and film absorb light. The more light one of these materials absorbs, the higher its density. We use densitometry as a tool for *process control*, which is (to grossly oversimplify) the art and science of ensuring that our various devices are behaving the way we want them to. In prepress, we use densitometers to assure that prepress film is processed correctly. In the pressroom, we use densitometers to make sure that the press is laying down the correct amount of ink—if it's too little, the print will appear washed out, and if it's too much, the press isn't controllable and ink gets wasted.

We also use densitometers to *calibrate* devices—changing their behavior to make them perform optimally, like doing a tune-up on your car. We use densitometers to linearize imagesetters, platesetters, and proofers, ensuring that they produce the requested dot percentages accurately. Some monitor calibrators are densitometers, though colorimeters and spectrophotometers are more often used. We discuss calibration and process control in more detail in Chapter 5, *Measurement, Calibration, and Process Control.*

You may never use a densitometer—they're quite specialized, and most of their functions can be carried out equally well by a colorimeter or spectrophotometer—but it's helpful to understand what they do.

Reflectance (R) and transmittance (T). Densitometers don't measure density directly. Instead, they measure the *ratio* between the intensity of light shone on or through a surface, and the light that reaches the detector in the instrument. This ratio is called the *reflectance* (R) or the *transmittance* (T), depending on whether the instrument measures reflective materials such as ink and paper, or transmissive materials such as film.

Densitometers use filters that are matched to the color of the material you are measuring, so that the detector sees a flat gray. Pressroom densitometers, for example, have filters matched to the specific wavelengths reflected by cyan, magenta, yellow, and black inks, so that they always measure the dominant wavelength. This means first that you have to know and tell the densitometer exactly what it is measuring, and second, that you can only use a densitometer to measure materials for which it has the appropriate filter.

Density is a logarithmic function. Density is computed from the measurement data using a logarithmic function, for several reasons. First, as we've seen, the human eye has a non-linear, logarithmic response to intensity, so a logarithmic density function correlates better to how we see brightness. Second, it correlates better with the thickness of materials like printing inks or film emulsions, which is one of the main functions of densitometers. Third, a logarithmic scale avoids long numbers when measuring very dark materials (such as prepress films).

To see what this means, imagine a surface that reflects 100% of all the light that strikes it—a so-called *perfect diffuser*. Its reflectance, R, is 1.0, and its density is 0. If we consider other surfaces that reflect half the light, one-tenth the light, and so on, we derive the following values:

Reflectance (R)	Density (D)
1.0	0.0
0.5	0.3
0.1	1.0
0.01	2.0
0.001	3.0
0.0001	4.0
0.00001	5.0

Notice how a number like 5.0 is far more convenient than 0.00001?

One of the characteristic requirements for a densitometer is that it has a very wide *dynamic range*. In fact, the dynamic range of other devices (e.g. scanners and printers), media (prints vs. film), or even images (low-key, high-key) is expressed in terms of density units, typically abbreviated as D (density) or O.D. (optical density). For example, the dynamic range of a scanner is expressed in terms of the D_{min} (minimum density) and D_{max} (maximum density) at which the scanner can reliably measure brightness values.

Colorimetry

Colorimetry is the science of predicting color matches as typical humans would perceived them. In other words, its goal is to build a numeric model that can predict when metamerism does or does not occur. To be considered a success, a colorimetric model must do both of the following:

▶ Where a typical human observer sees a match (in other words, metamerism) between two color samples, the colorimetric model has to represent both samples by the same numeric values.

▶ Where a typical human observer sees a difference between two color samples, not only should they have different numeric representations in the model, but the model should also be able to compute a *color difference* number that predicts *how different* they appear to the observer.

The current models available aren't perfect, but thanks to the pioneering work of the CIE, they're robust enough to form the basis of all current color management systems. If CIE colorimetry is all just so much alphabet soup to you, the one key fact you need to know is that the various CIE models allow us to represent numerically the color that people with normal color vision actually see. Compared to that one insight, the rest is detail, but if you want to really understand how color management works and why it sometimes fails to work as expected, it helps to have a basic understanding of these details. So let's look at the body of work that forms the core of color management, the CIE system of colorimetry.

The CIE colorimetric system. Most modern colorimetry and all current color management systems are based on the colorimetric system of the

CIE, which we introduced at the beginning of this chapter. This system contains several key features.

▶ **Standard Illuminants** are spectral definitions of a set of light sources under which we do most of our color matching. We introduced you to the Standard Illuminants A through F, but in the graphic arts world, the two most important are D50 and D65.

▶ **The Standard Observer** represents the full tristimulus response of the typical human observer, or in plain English, all the colors we can see. Most colorimeters use the *2˚* (1931) Standard Observer, but there's also a *10˚* (1964) Standard Observer. The latter arose as a result of later experiments that used larger color samples that illuminated a wider angle of the fovea and found a slightly different tristimulus response. It's rare that you'll encounter the 10° observer, but we'd be remiss if we didn't mention it.

▶ **The CIE XYZ Primary System** is a clever definition of three imaginary primaries derived from the Standard Observer tristimulus response. (The primaries are imaginary in that they don't correspond to any real light source—it's impossible to create a real light source that stimulates only our M or S cones—but the response they model is very real.) Not only does every metameric pair result in the same XYZ values, but the primary Y doubles as the average luminance function of the cones—so a color's Y value is also its luminance.

▶ **The CIE xyY diagram** is a mathematical transformation of XYZ that makes a useful map of our color universe. It shows additive relationships—a straight line between two points represents the colors that can be created by adding the two colors in various proportions (see Figure 1-23). But it's important to note that XYZ and xyY don't factor in the non-linearity of the eye, and so the *distances* are distorted.

▶ **The uniform color spaces** (**LAB, LUV**) are two color spaces that were defined by the CIE in an attempt to reduce the distortion in color distances. Both compute the lightness value L^* in exactly the same way—it's approximately the cube root of the luminance value Y (which is a rough approximation of our logarithmic response to luminance). Both attempt to create a space that is *perceptually uniform*—in other words, distances between points in the space predict how different the two colors will appear to a human observer. As a result, the spaces also have features that resemble hue, saturation, and brightness, and (in the case of L*a*b*) our three opponent systems. LAB has largely replaced LUV in most practical applications, and while it isn't perfect (it exaggerates differences in yellows and underestimates them in blues, for example), it's pretty darn useful. The quest for a perfectly uniform color space continues, but thus far LAB has stood the test of time.

▶ **Color difference (ΔE) calculations** offer an easy way to compute the color difference between two samples. If you measure the two colors, plot them as points in the uniform space, and then compute the distance between them, that distance will by definition, correlate well to the difference a human observer will see. This value is called ΔE (pronounced "delta-E"—delta is the Greek letter 'D' we commonly use to represent a difference).

Figure 1-23

The xy chromaticity chart

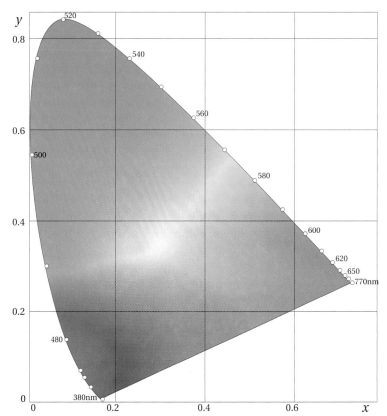

Colorimeters. Colorimeters measure light through filters that mimic approximately the human cone response, and produce numerical results in one of the CIE color models. Most colorimeters have user-selectable reporting functions that let you obtain the color's values in CIE XYZ, CIE LAB, CIE LUV, or other colorimetric spaces, as well as measuring the E value between two color samples.

While colorimeters are very flexible in their reporting functions, they have important limitations in the colorimetric assumptions they must make. Specifically, they're limited to a specific Standard Illuminant and Standard Observer, though some colorimeters let you switch between different illuminants (such as a D50 and a D65 option).

Colorimeters can't detect metamerism. They can tell whether or not two samples match under the specific illuminant they use, but they have no way of telling if that match is metameric—dependent on the illuminant—or if the samples really do have identical spectral properties that would make them match under all illuminants. Fortunately, for most color-management purposes, computing a color match under a single illuminant is enough.

Colorimetry and color management. Colorimetry is the core of color management, because it allows us to define color unambiguously as it will be seen by humans. As you'll learn in Chapter 2, *Computers and Color*, the systems we use to represent color numerically in our everyday image, illustration, and page-layout files are fundamentally ambiguous as to the actual color they represent. Colorimetry allows color management systems to remove that ambiguity. And in Chapter 3, *Color Management—How It Works*, you'll see how colorimetry lets color management systems compute the numbers that we send to our various color-reproduction devices—monitors, desktop printers, proofing systems, and printing presses—to ensure that they reproduce the desired colors. For now, just accept the fact that color management systems feed on colorimetry.

Spectrophotometry

Spectrophotometry is the science of measuring spectral reflectance, the ratio between the intensity of each wavelength of light shone onto a surface and the light of that same wavelength reflected back to the detector in the instrument. Spectral reflectance is similar to the reflectance (R) measured by a densitometer and then converted to density, with one important difference. Density is a single value that represents the total number of photons reflected or transmitted. Spectral reflectance is a set of values that represent the number of photons being reflected or transmitted at different wavelengths (see Figure 1-24). The spectrophotometers we use in the graphic arts typically divide the visible spectrum into 10 nm or 20 nm bands, and produce a value for each band. Research-grade spectrophotometers divide the spectrum into a larger number of narrower bands, sometimes as narrow as 2 nm, but they're prohibitively expensive for the types of use we discuss in this book.

Figure 1-24

A metameric pair

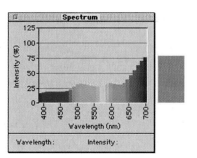
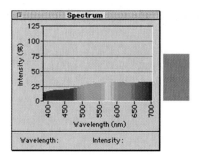

Measured spectra of the GATF/RHEM Light Indicator, which contains patches that match only under D50 lighting.

*Appearance under
D50 lighting*

*Appearance under
D65 lighting*

Spectrophotometry and color management. Spectral data has direct uses in graphic arts—such as when some press shops check incoming ink lots for differences in spectral properties—but spectrophotometers are more often used in color management as either densitometers or colorimeters.

The spectral data spectrophotometers capture is a richer set of measurements than those captured by either densitometers or colorimeters. We can compute density or colorimetric values from spectral data, but not the other way around. With spectral data, we can also determine whether or not a color match is metameric, though color management doesn't use this capability directly.

In color management, a spectrophotometer's real value is that it can double as a densitometer or colorimeter or both, and it is usually more configurable than the densitometer or colorimeter at either task. Sometimes a dedicated densitometer or colorimeter may be better suited to a specific task such as measuring the very high densities we need to achieve on prepress film, or characterizing the very spiky response of the red phosphor in a monitor. But in most cases, a spectrophotometer is a versatile Swiss-Army knife of color measurement.

Where the Models Fail

The CIE colorimetric models are pretty amazing, but it's important to bear in mind that they were designed only to predict the degree to which two solid color swatches, viewed at a specific distance, against a specific background, under a specific illuminant, would appear to match. Color management takes these models well beyond their design parameters, using them to match complex color events like photographic images. In general, color management works astonishingly well, but it's important to realize that our visual system has complex responses to complex color events that the CIE models we currently use don't even attempt to address. A slew of phenomena have been well-documented by—and often named for—the various color scientists who first documented them, but they typically point to one significant fact: unlike colorimeters and spectrophotometers, humans see color in context.

So there's one caveat we'll make repeatedly in this book: while color management uses colorimetry for purposes of gathering data about device behavior, the ultimate goal of color management is *not* to get a colorimetric match, but rather to achieve a pleasing image. Sometimes a colorimetric match is great, but sometimes that match comes at the expense of other colors in an image. And sometimes two colors can differ colorimetrically and yet produce a visual match when we view them in context.

Features like simultaneous and successive contrast (see Figures 1-12 and 1-13) and color constancy (see below) aren't modeled by colorimetry and can't be measured using a colorimeter. Sometimes it's an advantage to have an instrument that isn't distracted by these issues—such as when you are collecting raw data on device behavior to feed to a color management system or profile maker. But when it comes time to evaluate results, don't reach for your colorimeter as a way to judge success. A well-trained eye beats a colorimeter every time when it comes to evaluating final results.

Here are just a few visual phenomena that color management ignores.

Color Constancy

Color constancy is one of the most important features of the visual system, and it's so ingrained a mechanism that you're rarely aware of it. Color constancy, sometimes referred to as "discounting the illuminant," is the tendency to perceive objects as having a constant color, even if the lighting conditions change. In other words, even if the wavelength composition (the spectral energy) of the light coming from the object changes, our visual system picks up cues from surrounding objects and attributes that change to the lighting, not to the object.

What may surprise you is how basic a feature color constancy is to the nervous system. It doesn't involve memory, much less higher-level thought at all, but seems to be rooted in low-level structures in our visual system. In fact, color constancy has been verified in animals with as simple a nervous system as goldfish (see Figure 1-25). In humans, color constancy seems to be the result of center-surround fields similar to those responsible for opponency, but instead of occurring in the second layer of the retina, as opponency is, the center-surround fields responsible for color constancy seem to be located in the visual cortex of the brain, and they're far more complex than those responsible for opponency.

Figure 1-25
Color constancy

Color constancy has been demonstrated in goldfish.

Devices don't have color constancy. Cameras don't have color constancy. Film doesn't change its response depending on the illumination in the scene. This is why a photographer has to match the film response to the lighting. Digital cameras with automatic white balance *do* change their response depending on the illumination in the scene, but they don't do so in the same way humans do. If a digital camera captures an image of a white horse standing in the shade of a leafy tree, it will faithfully record the greenish light that's filtered through the leaves and then reflected from the horse, producing a picture of a green horse. But humans know there's no such animal as a green horse, so they "discount the illuminant" and see the horse as white.

Similarly, colorimeters can't measure color constancy. They duplicate the tristimulus response of the eye to isolated colors while ignoring the surrounding colors. But even when a device like a scanner *does* measure the colors surrounding an isolated sample, the exact nature of color constancy is so complex that we don't yet have a usable mathematical model that would let color management compensate for it.

Color constancy and color management. While color management does not have a model of color constancy to work with, it can do many things without it. The important thing for color management to do is to preserve the *relationships* between colors in an image. This is the difference between what we call *perceptual* and *colorimetric* renderings (see Chapter 3, *Color Management—How It Works*). When it's possible to render some but not all of the colors with complete colorimetric accuracy, it's often perceptually more pleasing to render them all with the same inaccuracy than to render some faithfully and some not.

Color constancy is one reason why neutrals are important: neutrals—especially the highlights in a printed picture that take their color from the paper—form the reference point for colors. If the neutrals are off, the entire image appears off, but it's hard to pinpoint why. It takes training to 'ignore' color constancy and say, "the neutrals are blue" when your visual system is trying to say, "the neutrals are neutral."

A final point about color constancy and color management: color constancy presents an argument that the color temperature of lighting isn't as important as some people think. It still *is* important, but not at the expense of everything else. For example, when calibrating your monitor, you usually have the choice between setting your monitor to a

D50 or D65 white point. (Monitor calibration, and the differences between D50 and D65 white points, are described in Chapter 6, but you don't need to understand these details to understand this point.) Many people choose D50 in order to match the exact white point color of the viewing environment, which is usually a D50 lighting booth. But we, along with many other practitioners, recommend D65 because we think you'll be happier looking at a bright white D65 monitor than a dingy yellow D50 one, even if the D50 monitor is colorimetrically closer to the D50 lighting booth. Matching brightness levels between two viewing environments may be as important as, or even more important than, matching the color temperature—color constancy will do a lot to adapt to slight differences in color temperature.

Psychological Factors: Color Names and Memory Colors

Now we turn to the psychological attributes of color. These involve aspects of judgment that are not well understood. Some of these psychological attributes may be learned. Some may even be cultural. But these attributes relate to the way we talk about color in our *language*.

Names and color reproduction. Earlier in this chapter, we defined hue as the attribute of a color by which it gets its basic name. This connection between hue and basic names isn't just a philosophical nuance, but may be one of the most important things to remember about color reproduction. If nothing else, it sets a minimum bar for reproduction quality. We're generally fussier about discrepancies in hue than we are about discrepancies in brightness or saturation between a target color and its reproduction, or between a displayed color and its print. If the hue is different enough to cross some intangible boundary between color *names*—such as when your reds cross slightly into the oranges, or your sky crosses a tad into the purples—then people notice the hue shift more, perhaps because they now have a way to articulate it. The good news is that this is often the first step in solving the problem—by being able to put a name to the hue shift, you can begin to look for the source of the problem (too much yellow ink in the reds or too much magenta in the blues).

Memory colors. One effect that all graphic artists are aware of is that of *memory colors.* These are the colors such as skin tones, green grass, or sky blue that we are very familiar with. These colors matter more than others because we have such a strong memory of them. As our friend (and color-management critic) Dan Margulis likes to say, the color on the left of Figure 1-26 is a color, but the one on the right is a COLOR. The evaluation of the quality of a color reproduction is weighted by the fact that some colors are more important to get "right" than others. We put "right" in quotes because our ingrained memory of these colors is often quite inaccurate. Even if everything is colorimetrically perfect, if the skin tones aren't what the viewer expects, the image looks "wrong"; if the skin tones fit the expectation, but a sweater went a little too red, few people will notice, unless the picture is in a sweater catalog.

Figure 1-26
A color and a COLOR!

In summary, there are psychological aspects of human color perception that we can't (yet) model mathematically, so color management simply can't address them. Even the best color management must leave room for human intervention at strategic points. And you have to be aware of where color management needs your help, as we'll be pointing out throughout the book.

Lessons for Color Management

We conclude this long chapter on color science with a summary of some of the main lessons we should keep in mind for color management.

▶ Lighting is important … our eye is best designed to work under certain conditions …

▶ … but it's not absolute. The visual system has a tremendous ability to adapt. (See the section, *Color Constancy.*)

▶ Watch out for fluorescence with certain papers or inks, or when making scanner profiles. (See the section, *Fluorescence.*)

▶ Metamerism is the basis for color matching and hence the basis for color management. (See the section, *Metamerism.*)

▶ Train yourself to see your red, green, blue response. With practice, you can recognize all colors as mixtures of red, green, and blue. (See the section, *Trichromacy: Red, Green, Blue.*)

▶ Train yourself also to think in blue-yellow, red-green opponencies. If you want to reduce the yellow in an RGB image, which has no yellow channel, you can increase its opponent color, the blue channel. (See the section, *Opponency: Red-Green, Blue-Yellow.*)

▶ Watch for hue shifts that move a color into a different color name category. These will be obvious to viewers and signal a significant problem. (See the section *Psychological Factors: Color Names and Memory Colors.*)

▶ There are colors, and there are COLORS (COLORS have different values to us emotionally). (Again, see the section, *Psychological Factors: Color Names and Memory Colors.*)

▶ Colorimetry is the basis for the quantification of colors. Color management is based on mathematical models of color closeness provided by colorimetry. (See the section, *Colorimetry.*)

▶ Colorimetry isn't perception. Relationships *between* colors are more important than the colors themselves. This is an important point to understand when we look at the difference between colorimetric and perceptual renderings. (See the section, *Color Constancy.*)

Computers
and Color

Color by the Numbers

Computers know nothing about color except what we humans tell them. They're just glorified adding machines that juggle ones and zeros to order. One of the many ways we use numbers on the computer is to represent color. To do that, we need some kind of mathematical model of color. Applying mathematical models to reality is always tricky, but it's particularly so when dealing with something as slippery and subjective as color. The great mathematician, Sir Isaac Newton, made many important discoveries about color, but as far as we know he never tried to model it mathematically. Instead he went onto simpler subjects like inventing calculus and discovering the mechanical laws of the universe.

In Chapter 1, we explained that color is really something that only happens in our heads—it's the *sensation* we experience in response to different wavelengths of light. When we talk about measuring color, what we're measuring isn't really color itself, but rather the stimulus that evokes the sensation of color—the makeup of the light hitting our retinas. We can correlate light measurements with the color people experience, but the correlation isn't perfect.

In this chapter, we'll examine the various number systems we use to represent color, explain what these numbers mean, and show how, without color management, the same set of numbers will produce very different colors in different situations.

Color by the Numbers

In the previous chapter, we explained how it's possible to produce all the colors people can see using only red, green, and blue light—the "additive" primary colors. When we reproduce color on a physical device, whether it's a monitor, a piece of transparency film, or a printed page, we do so by manipulating red, green, and blue light.

In the case of true RGB devices such as monitors, scanners, and digital cameras, we work with red, green, and blue light directly. With film and printing, we still manipulate red, green, and blue light, but we do so indirectly, using CMY pigments to subtract these wavelengths from a white background—cyan absorbs red light, magenta absorbs green light, and yellow absorbs blue light—hence the term "subtractive" primary colors. Most digital color is encoded to represent varying amounts of either R, G, and B or C, M, and Y, or, in commercial printing and some (but not all) desktop printers, C, M, Y, and K (for BlacK). (See the sidebar "Why CMYK?")

Unfortunately, these mathematical models of color are quite ambiguous. You can think of an RGB or CMYK file as containing, not color, but rather a *recipe* for color that each device interprets according to its own capabilities. If you give 20 cooks the same recipe, you'll almost certainly get 20 slightly different dishes as a result. Likewise, if you send the same RGB file to 20 different monitors, or the same CMYK file to 20 different presses, you'll get 20 slightly (or in some cases, more than slightly) different images. You can readily see this in any store that sells television sets. You'll see twenty televisions all lined up, of various makes and models, all tuned to the same station, and all producing somewhat different colors. They're receiving the same *recipe* but their different characteristics generate different visible results. This even happens within the same make and model of television.

The RGB and CMYK models originated in the analog rather than the digital world. Neither was designed as an accurate mathematical description of color: they're really *control signals* that we send to our various color devices to make them produce something that we eventually experience as color. So you should always think of RGB or CMYK numbers as tuned for a specific device.

Why CMYK?

Why CMYK rather than CMY? In theory, pure cyan absorbs 100% of red light just as pure magenta and yellow fully absorb green and blue light respectively. A combination of perfectly pure cyan, magenta, and yellow colorants would absorb all light, which people would see as black (if they could see it all—the only perfectly black objects we're aware of in this universe are black holes, which we can't see directly). When one or more colorants aren't 100% pure, some light is reflected instead of being absorbed. This is why many toner-based devices have a greenish three-color black, and why three-color black on a printing press is usually a muddy brown. The colorants are simply not perfect. Photographic dyes come close, but inks and toners, for example, have to satisfy many different physical requirements besides color, such as adhering to the paper and each other, drying in a reasonable length of time, being fade-resistant, and being affordable. This almost invariably involves compromising the color purity. So to get a better black that will absorb as much light as possible, as neutrally as possible, we use black ink. Another good reason for printing with black ink is that black-only objects such as text are a lot easier to print when you don't have to perfectly align the cyan, magenta, and yellow versions.

You may also wonder why it's CMYK rather than CMYB. There's general agreement that referring to black as "B" would lead to confusion with Blue. Press operators often refer to cyan and magenta as blue and red, which is, of course, incorrect and not something we personally encourage. But it's an ingrained, time-honored practice, and trying to change it is, as our friend and colleague Herb Paynter would say, "a hill that ain't worth dyin' on." There are various theories as to why "K" was chosen, but the likeliest, in our view, is that it refers to "key"—the master plate to which the other three colors are registered. Since black is the darkest color, it's usually used as the key because it's the easiest to see. Whatever the reason, we print with CMYK, not with CMYB.

Analog Origins

The numbers in RGB and CMYK files don't really represent color. Instead, they represent the amounts of *colorants*—the things our devices use to make a color. Both RGB and CMYK were used in the analog world long before they were translated to the digital world.

CMYK printing has been around as a mass-market commercial process since the early 1920s, and until pre-press went digital in the 1970s, CMYK separations were made optically by photographing the original art through C, M, Y, and neutral-density (for the black plate) filters. The earliest scanners used analog RGB signals. The scanners' RGB signals were typically converted directly to analog CMYK which was used to expose film from which printing plates were made. When we started making color digitally, we simply used digital RGB and digital CMYK to mimic their analog predecessors. In short, it was the easiest way to make the transition to digital color, but not necessarily the best way.

Monitor RGB. When we display color on a monitor, we do so by spraying streams of electrons that strike *phosphors*. Phosphors are chemical and mineral compounds that emit light when they're struck (the technical term is *excited*) by a beam of electrons. Color monitors use three different phosphors painted on the inside of the faceplate that emit red, green, and blue light, respectively. By varying the strength of the electron beam, we can make the phosphors emit more or less red, green, and blue light, and hence produce different colors (see Figure 2-1).

Figure 2-1

Monitor phosphors

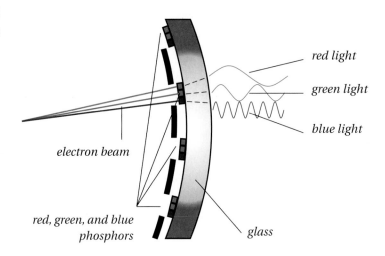

But the precise color that the monitor produces depends on the type of phosphors used, their age, the specific circuitry and other characteristics of the monitor, and even the strength of the magnetic field in which the monitor is located. All monitors' phosphors produce something we recognize as red, green, and blue, but there are at least five quite different phosphor sets in common use, and the phosphors can vary substantially even in a single manufacturing batch. Factor in individual preferences for brightness and contrast settings, and it's highly unlikely that any two monitors will produce the same color from the same signal, even if they're two apparently identical monitors bought on the same day.

Scanner RGB. When we capture color with a scanner or digital camera, we do so using monochromatic light-sensitive sensors and red, green, and blue filters. Each sensor puts out a voltage proportional to the amount of light that reaches it through the filters, and we encode those analog voltages as digital values of R, G, and B. The precise digital values a scanner or camera creates from a given color sample depend on the makeup of the light source and the transmission characteristics of the filters. As with monitor phosphors, scanner and camera filters vary from vendor to vendor, and they also change with age. Scanner lamps also vary both from vendor to vendor and with age, and the light source in a digital camera capture can range from carefully controlled studio lighting to daylight that varies from exposure to exposure, or even, with scanning-back cameras, over the course of a single exposure. So it's very unlikely that two capture devices will produce the same RGB values from the same color sample.

Printer CMYK. When we print images on paper, we usually do so by laying down dots of cyan, magenta, yellow, and black ink. In traditional halftone screens, the spacing is constant from the center of one dot to the next, but the dots vary in size to produce the various shades or tints. Many desktop printers and some commercial press jobs use different types of screening, variously known as *error diffusion* or *stochastic screens*, where each dot is the same size, and the color is varied by printing a greater or smaller number of dots in a given area (see Figure 2-2, and the sidebar, "Pixels, Dots, and Dithers," later in this chapter).

Figure 2-2
CMYK halftone

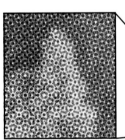

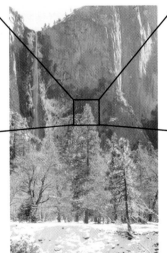

In a conventional CMYK halftone, dot placement is regular, and the illusion of different tonal values is produced by varying the size of the dots.

In a CMYK diffusion dither, the size of the dots is regular, and the illusion of different tonal values is produced by varying the dot placement.

Pixels, Dots, and Dithers

Wherever possible we try to avoid nitpicking about terminology, but the practice of using the terms "dpi" (dots per inch) and "ppi" (pixels per inch) interchangeably inevitably leads to confusion, because dots and pixels are distinct entities with different properties. Some digital mavens insist on using the term "spi" (samples per inch) rather than dpi when discussing scanner resolution—*that's* nitpicky.

Pixels represent varying levels of density. A single pixel can not only be red, green, and blue at the same time, but have different intensities of red, green, and blue, rather than just on or off. This is where we get the term *continuous tone*. A monitor is an example of a continuous-tone device.

But most digital hard-copy output devices aren't continuous-tone. Instead of pixels, they print dots of ink or toner, which are either on or off, present or absent. Digital printers' resolution is expressed in dots per inch, which describes the number of locations per inch in which the printer can either print a dot, or not print a dot. We can't vary the density of ink, nor can we vary the size of the dot. Rather, we can only tell the output device whether or not to print a dot at each location. A 600-dpi laser printer, can print, or not print, 600 dots per linear inch, while a 2400-dpi imagesetter has to make that same decision 2400 times per linear inch. Each dot has the same density—the only thing we can control is the location of the dots.

We make digital printers produce the *illusion* of continuous tone by arranging these equally sized, constant-density dots using some kind of *dithering*—a way of arranging the dots in a pattern that isn't obvious to the eye. Back in the analog days, prepress folks converted continuous-tone originals to *halftones*—a kind of dither where the dots are constant-density and equally spaced, varying in size to produce the illusion of darker or lighter shades—by projecting the original onto plate material through color filters and a screen like the ones you find on a screen door. The holes in the screen acted as pinhole lenses, producing large dots in the dark areas and smaller ones in the light areas.

Most presses still use this kind of dithering, but to make a digital halftone on an imagesetter or platesetter, we arrange its printable dots into larger groups called *halftone cells* or *halftone spots*. We simulate the traditional analog halftone by turning dots on and off in a cell. This type of dither is also known as "AM (Amplitude Modulation) screening," or "conventional halftone."

But the precise color that the printer produces depends on the color of the inks, pigments, or dyes, the color of the paper stock, and the way the colorants interact with the paper, both chemically and physically. Inkjet printers commonly show color shifts over time (most obvious in neutrals) when ink and paper aren't appropriately matched. Color laser printers and color copiers are very susceptible to humidity change. On a commercial press, the color can vary with temperature, humidity, prevailing wind, and the state of the press operator's diet and marriage, but that's another story! So it's very unlikely that two different printing devices will produce the same color from the same set of CMYK values.

Halftoning converts continuous tone images, such as digital files or scans, from pixels into dots so the image can be reproduced on an inkjet printer or a printing press, for example. The best-known type of halftoning is sometimes called *ordered dither* or "conventional halftone dot" in addition to the aforementioned "AM screening". A different kind of halftoning, *error diffusion*, also goes by names such as "FM screening" and "stochastic screening".

AM screening varies the size of the dots, but not their location. Darker areas have larger dots and lighter areas have smaller dots (or no dots). This type of halftoning is common for printing presses as a carry over from making plates through a "screen."

Because of the pattern generated with AM screening, undesirable artifacts can occur with multiple inks when their "screens" conflict with each other. Combating this necessitates rotating each inks' screen to avoid these conflicts, hence the term "screen angles."

The other kind of dithering, error diffusion or FM screening, is used on most inkjet printers, and occasionally on presses too. FM screening varies the location of the dots, but not their size. Darker areas have more dots closer together while the lighter areas have fewer dots dispersed farther apart. The more random nature of FM screening gives high resolution inkjet output the appearance of continuous tone. FM screening is sometimes used on press, but since small variations in press behavior are exaggerated much more by FM screening than by AM screening, it's usually limited to premium jobs in shops that have gained considerable experience using FM screens.

Dye sublimation, and photographic output methods are considered continuous tone because the colorants' density can be controlled, so dots, and therefore halftoning. aren't needed.

The importance of this to color management is that ICC-based color management only works on pixels, not dots, but the final output is more often than not created with dots. The effect of screening algorithms can affect what we see compared to what was measured and predicted by the color management system (CMS).

So we need to take the screening algorithm into account when we color-manage a device, because different screening algorithms will produce different tonal renderings. (See "Tone Reproduction Characteristics," later in this chapter.)

Digital Evolutions

The point of the previous section is that RGB and CMYK are fundamentally analog concepts—they represent some amount of *colorants*: the dyes, inks, phosphors, or filters we use to control the wavelengths of light. RGB devices such as televisions, monitors, scanners, and digital cameras to this day, and for the forseeable future, all have analog components—things that work in terms of continuous voltages: magnets, lenses, mirrors, and phosphors and filters baked in chemical labs. CMYK printers still deal with the idiosyncracies of chemical inks, dyes, and pigments on sheets of mashed wood pulp that we call "paper."

However, RGB and CMYK numbers are nevertheless … numbers. This has made them ripe for adoption into the digital age where numbers themselves take the form of bits and bytes (see "How the Numbers Work," later in this chapter).

Over the years we've seen more and more analog components replaced by digital. The Darwinian force that drives this evolution is, very simply, money. Digital components are faster, cheaper, and (most importantly from the point of view of color management) repeatable and predictable. All of these benefits translate directly into monetary savings.

But keep in mind two things about this evolution. First, it's incremental. Companies usually produce products that are small improvements over previous technologies—despite what their marketing brochures say. New products and subcomponents of products must coexist with old, and new technologies must be usable by people who have worked with old components for years. Second, because of this incremental evolution, digital RGB and CMYK are often designed to mimic their analog predecessors. The result has been that digital color-reproduction equipment often has odd little idiosyncracies that might not be there if the things had been designed from the ground up to be digital, or mostly digital, devices.

An example is the evolution of the imagesetter, the output device that generates the film used to image plates for offset lithography. Imagesetters evolved from the analog methods of imaging film using photographic techniques—for example, projecting a photographic negative through a fine screen to produce a halftone image (hence the terms "screening" and "screen frequency"). This analog photographic process was replaced by computers controlling lasers that precisely exposed the film microdot by microdot, but these imagesetters still needed traditional analog darkroom equipment, chemistry, and photographically skilled technicians to develop the film. However, bit by bit, even the darkroom processing was replaced by digitally controlled processor units that control all aspects of film development.

But why did we need film at all? Because extremely expensive (and therefore not expendable) printing presses had almost as expensive platemakers that required film for platemaking, and because creating an analog proof from the film was the only affordable method in place for creating a contract between the print client and printer (premium jobs sometimes use actual press proofs—in effect, separate press runs for proofing only—but they're brutally expensive). Nowadays, however, as platemaking and digital proofing technologies become more reliable, film itself is being skipped (with obvious cost benefits), and the digital process is being extended from the computer right up to the platesetter itself, even including digital platemakers that image the plates right on the press rollers.

What does all this mean for digital RGB and CMYK numbers and color management? It means that all the digital computation and control of the numbers exercised by color management are only as good as their ability to model the behavior of analog components. Digital color management *alters the numbers* to compensate for the behavior of the various analog components. As such, the strengths and weaknesses of color management lie entirely in how well our digital manipulations model the behavior of the analog parts, including that most important analog 'device' of all, the viewer's eye.

In a moment we'll examine the key parameters that describe the analog behavior of color-reproduction devices. But first, we should examine the *digital* part of digital color—the numbers—a bit more closely.

How the Numbers Work

Let's pause for a moment and examine the systems we use for representing—or, more accurately, *encoding*—colors as numbers in a computer. We'll take this the opportunity to clarify a few points that often confuse people about the basics of digital color, which propagates into confusion about color management. Even if you're extremely familiar with the basics of bits, bytes, tones, and colors, this section is worth reviewing as we make a few key points about the difference between colors-as-numbers and colors as "Real World" experiences.

The system computers use for encoding colors as numbers is actually quite simple: colors are comprised of *channels*, and each channel is sub-divided into *tone levels*. That's it! We start with a simple model of color perception—the fact that colors are mixtures of red, green, and blue in various intensities—and then we adapt this model for efficient storage, computation, and transportation on computers. The number of channels in our encoding system is usually three, to correspond to our basic three-primary way of seeing colors. The number of tone levels in our encoding system is usually 256, to correspond to the minimum number of tone levels we need to create the illusion of *continuous tone*—to avoid the artifacts known as *banding* or *posterization*, where a viewer can see noticeable jumps between one tone level and the next (see Figure 2-3).

Figure 2-3

Levels and posterization

256 shades of gray provides the illusion of continuous tone.

With only 128 shades of gray, some tonal detail is lost, and we start to see hints of posterization.

With only 64 shades of gray, we see banding in the gradients and in the sky.

Why 256 Levels?

This number, 256, seems arbitrary and mysterious to some people, but it crops up so many times in computers and color that it's worth making your peace with it. It's not that mysterious. We want to be able to represent enough tone levels so that the step from one tone level to the next is not visible to the viewer. It turns out the that number of tone levels needed to produce the effect of a smooth gradient is about 200 for most people. So why not encode only 200 levels? Why 256? For two reasons.

Headroom. It's useful—in fact, essential for color management—to have some extra tone levels in our data so that the inevitable losses of tone levels at each stage of production (scanning, display, editing, conversion, computation, printing) don't reintroduce banding.

Bits. The second reason is just that we use bits to represent these tone level numbers. Seven bits would let us encode only 128 tone levels (2^7), which would be a surefire way to get banding in our skies and blotches on the cheeks of our fashion models. Eight bits lets us encode 256 tone levels (2^8), which gives us just enough, plus a little headroom. The third reason we go with eight bits is that computer storage is already organized in terms of bytes, where a byte is a unit of exactly eight bits. This quantity of eight bits is already so useful—for example, it's perfect for storing a character of type, which can be any of 256 letters and punctuation marks in a western alphabet—that it seems a cosmic coincidence that a byte is also the perfect amount of memory to encode tone levels for the human visual system. Engineers love those cosmic coincidences!

Millions of Colors

So *8-bit encoding*, with its 256 tone levels per channel is the minimum number of bits we want to store per channel. With RGB images, storing eight bits for each of the three channels gives us 24 bits total (which is why many people use the terms "8-bit color" and "24-bit color" interchangeably to mean the same thing). The number of colors encodable with 256 tone levels in each of three channels is $256 \times 256 \times 256$, or (if you pull out your calculator) about 16.8 million colors! Quite a lot of encodable colors for our 24 bits (or three little bytes) of storage!

Although this basic 3-channel, 8-bit encoding is the most common because it's based on human capabilities, we can easily expand it as needed to encode more colors for devices other than the human eye, either by adding channels or by increasing the number of bits we store for each channel. For example, when we're preparing an image for a CMYK printer, we increase the number of channels from 3-channel to *4-channel encoding*, not because we need more encodable colors (in fact, we need fewer) but because it's natural to dedicate a channel to each of the four inks.

Similarly, we often go from 8-bit to *16-bit encoding* when saving images captured with a scanner capable of discerning more than 256 levels of RGB (the so-called "10-bit," "12-bit," and "14-bit" scanners—although, because we store files in whole bytes, there are no 10-bit, 12-bit, or 14-bit files, only 8-bit or 16-bit files).

A key point to remember is that this is all talking about the number of *encodings*, the set of numeric color definitions we have available. But just as in the San Francisco Bay Area there are far more telephone numbers than there are actual telephones, with computer color the number of *encodable* colors far exceeds the number of *reproducible* colors. In fact, it far exceeds the number of *perceivable* colors. And even if we make devices such as high-end scanners that can "perceive" more tone levels than the human eye, we can always expand our encoding model to handle it. All that matters is that each perceivable color has a unique encoding, so there are always more encodable colors than we need—just as the phone company must ensure that every telephone has a unique telephone number, so it had better have more telephone numbers than it really needs.

We make this point because it's a key step to understanding the difference between colors as abstract numbers and how those numbers are actually rendered as colors by "Real World" devices—printers, monitors, scanners, etc. When you look at how those numbers are actually interpreted by a device, the number of actual "Real World" colors, drops dramatically! (See the sidebar "Color Definitions and Colors.")

So while it's useful to understand how the numbers work—why we see numbers like 256 or 16.8 million crop up everywhere—don't forget that they're just numbers … until they're interpreted by a color device as colors.

In the next section we'll look at what gives the numbers a precise interpretation as colors. These are the analog parts of our color devices, the things that color management systems need to measure to know how to turn number management into color management.

Color Definitions and Colors

Lots of people confuse the number of color definitions with the number of colors. For example, we mentioned that colors intended for a CMYK printer are naturally encoded in four channels. Does 8-bit CMYK really represent $256 \times 256 \times 256 \times 256$ or 4.3 billion encodable colors?! Theoretically, yes. Four arbitrary channels produce 4.3 billion encodings, but when we assign the interpretations C, M, Y, and K to those four channels, we realize that the fourth channel (K) doesn't seem to add many colors. In fact, many of the CMYK encodings represent the same color. For example, 50C, 50M, 50Y, 0K theoretically encodes the same shade of gray as 0C, 0M, 0Y, 50K, so there's a lot of redundancy. Now one could argue that the extra K values contribute additional tonal levels to the CMY channels, but this starts to get way more complicated than we need to get here. Let's just say that the total number of encodable colors in 8-bit CMYK is far less than 4.3 billion.

As another example, we mentioned that there are scanners that claim to be able to see far more than the 256 tone levels encodable in eight bits. These tout 10-bit, 12-bit, or even 14-bit capability. Many people confuse this with the scanner's *dynamic range*, the range from brightest white to darkest dark in which the scanner can distinguish tonal variation reliably. Some scanner vendors may actually claim that these "high-bit" scanners give a larger dynamic range than 8-bit ones. This is nonsense—the dynamic range is an analog limitation of the capture device and has nothing whatsoever to do with bit depth. Higher bit depths simply allow us more editing flexibility by slicing the device's dynamic range into more discrete steps. You can think of dynamic range as the height of a staircase, and bit depth as the number of steps that staircase contains. Obviously, if we want to keep the steps as small as possible (which we do, to avoid posterization or banding), a higher dynamic range needs more steps than a smaller one, but there's no direct relationship between the two.

Why the Numbers Vary

In the coming chapters we'll look at the specifics of measuring the behavior of display devices (monitors), input devices (scanners and digital cameras), and output devices (printers and proofing systems), but here we'll look briefly at the basic parameters that vary from device to device.

All devices vary in certain basic parameters. These are the things you'll measure if you are making your own profiles, and which must remain stable for your color management system to work effectively.

The three main variables are:

▶ The color and brightness of the colorants (**primaries**).

▶ The color and brightness of the **white point** and **black point**.

▶ The **tone reproduction characteristics** of the colorants.

These concepts aren't new to color management or unique to digital devices. They're all variables introduced by analog components like inks on paper, phosphors and analog voltages in monitors, and filtered sensors in scanners. While digital components rarely vary much, analog components vary a great deal in design, manufacturing, and condition.

Colorants (Primaries)

The first, most obvious factor that affects the color a device can reproduce are the colorants it uses to do so. On a monitor, the primaries are the phosphors. In a scanner or digital camera, the primaries are the filters through which the sensors see the image. In a printer, the primaries are the process inks, toners, or dyes laid down on the paper, but, because the subtractive color in CMYK printers is a bit more complicated than the additive color in RGB monitors, we usually supplement measurements of the primaries with measurements of the secondaries (the overprints—Magenta+Yellow, Cyan+Yellow, and Cyan+Magenta) as well (see Figure 2-4).

The exact color of the colorants determines the range of colors the device can reproduce. This is called the color *gamut* of the device. We care not only about the precise color of the primaries, but also how bright they are. In technical terms we often refer to the *density* of the primaries, which is simply their ability to absorb light.

Figure 2-4

Subtractive primary and
secondary colors

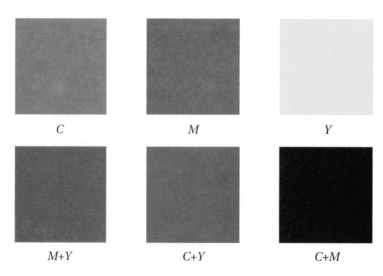

White Point and Black Point

Besides the primaries, the other two points that define the gamut and hence need to be measured and monitored in a device are the *white point* and *black point*. Books (and people) often talk about the white point and black point in very different terms: with the white point, they're usually concerned with the *color* of white, while with the black point they're more concerned with the *density* (the darkness) of black. In fact, we can talk about both color and density of either the white point or the black point—the difference is only a matter of emphasis. With the white point, the color is more important than its density, and with the black point, the density is more important than its color.

The color of the white point is more important than its density because the eye uses the color of this white as a reference for all other colors. When you view images, the color of white on the monitor or the color of the white paper on a printed page affects your perception for all the other colors in the scene. This *white point adaptation* is an instantaneous and involuntary task performed by your eye, so the color of white is vital. This is why, as we'll see in Chapter 6, we often sacrifice brightness during monitor calibration to get the color of the white point correct. Similarly, when looking at a printed page, it's important to remember that the color of the white point is determined as much by the light that illuminates the page as by the paper color itself.

With black point the emphasis shifts towards density as a more important variable than color. This is because the density of black determines the limit of the *dynamic range*, the range of brightness levels that the device can reproduce. Getting as much dynamic range as possible is always important, as this determines the capacity of the device to render *detail*, the subtle changes in brightness levels that make the difference between a rich, satisfying image and a flat, uninteresting 'mistake.'

On a monitor, we try to calibrate so that we get just enough brightness differences near the bottom end to squeeze some extra detail out of our displayed shadows.

On a printer, we can improve both the color and the density of the black point by adding our friend K to the CMY colorants. Adding K lets us produce a more neutral black point than we could with our somewhat impure C, M, and Y inks, and using four inks rather than three gets us much denser (darker) blacks than we could using only C, M, and Y.

On a scanner, the software lets you change the density of the white and black points from scan to scan either manually or automatically, but for color management we need to use a fixed dynamic range, so we generally set the black and white points to the widest dynamic range the scanner can capture.

Measuring the color and density of the white and black points is usually one of the steps in preparing to use any device in a color management system. You also need to watch out for changes in these values over time, so that you know when to adjust either the device itself or your color management system accordingly.

Tone Reproduction Characteristics

Measuring the precise color and density of the primaries, white point, and black point is essential, but these points only represent the extremes of the device: the most saturated colors, the brightest whites, and the darkest darks. To complete the description of a device, the color management system also needs to know what happens to the "colors between the colors" (to paraphrase a well-known desktop printer commercial).

There are several ways to measure and model devices' tone-reproduction characteristics. The simplest, called a *tone reproduction curve* (TRC), defines the relationship between input values and resulting brightness values in a device. Most analog devices have similar curves that show gain (increase) in the darkness levels that affect the midtones most and taper off in the hightlights and shadows. In monitors, scanners, and digital cameras this is called a *gamma curve*. Printers exhibit a slightly different *dot gain* curve, but the two are similar (see Figure 2-5).

Some printers have much more complicated tonal responses that can't be represented adequately by a simple curve. In these cases, we use a lookup table (LUT), which records representative tonal values from light to dark.

When you take measurements in the process of calibrating or profiling a device for color management, you're measuring the tone-reproduction characteristics of the device as well as the primaries and black/white points. You should try to get a feel for the things that can alter these tonal characteristics—such as changing to a different paper stock, or adjusting the contrast knob on your monitor—because when a device's tone-reproduction characteristics change, you'll have to adjust your color management system to reflect the changes.

Figure 2-5

Tone reproduction curves

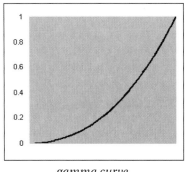
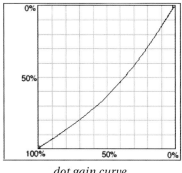

gamma curve   *dot gain curve*

Device-Specific Color Models

We call RGB and CMYK *device-specific* or *device-dependent* color models, because the actual color we get from a given set of RGB or CMYK numbers is specific to (it depends on) the device that's producing the color. Put simply, this means two things:

▶ The same set of RGB or CMYK numbers will produce different colors on different devices (or on the same device with different paper, if it's a printer or a press—see Figure 2-6).

▶ To produce the same color on different devices, we need to change the RGB or CMYK numbers we send to each device—see Figure 2-7.

The problems we face as a consequence are:

▶ How do we know what color the numbers in an RGB or CMYK file are supposed to represent? In other words, what does "255, 0, 0" mean? Yes, it means 'red,' but precisely what red? The red of your monitor, or Chris's or Fred's? The red sensor in your scanner or Bruce's digital camera?

▶ How do we know what RGB or CMYK numbers to send to a device to make it produce a desired color? In other words, even if we know precisely what 'red' we're talking about, what RGB numbers do we send to Chris's monitor, or what CMYK percentages do we send to Fred's color laser printer to reproduce that precise red … if it's possible to reproduce it at all?

Figure 2-6

Same numbers,
different color

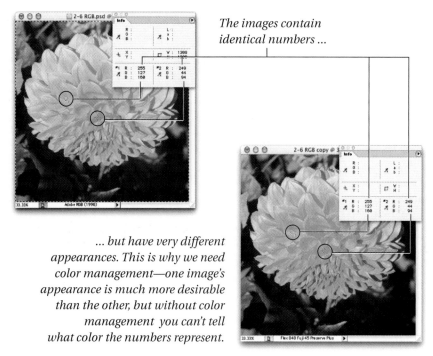

*The images contain
identical numbers ...*

*... but have very different
appearances. This is why we need
color management—one image's
appearance is much more desirable
than the other, but without color
management you can't tell
what color the numbers represent.*

Figure 2-7

Same color,
different numbers

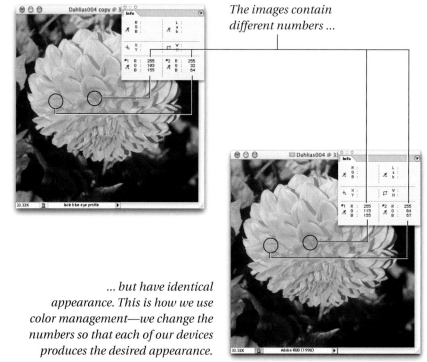

*The images contain
different numbers ...*

*... but have identical
appearance. This is how we use
color management—we change the
numbers so that each of our devices
produces the desired appearance.*

Color management systems allow us to solve both problems by attaching absolute color meanings to our RGB and CMYK numbers. By doing so, the numbers cease to be ambiguous. Color management allows us to determine the actual color meaning of a set of RGB or CMYK numbers, and also lets us reproduce that actual color on another device by changing the numbers we send to it. But to do so, color management has to rely on a different kind of numerical model of color, one that's based on human perception rather than device colorants.

Device-Independent Color Models

Fortunately, we have several numerical models of color that are *device-independent.* Instead of using the numbers required to drive a particular device to produce color, device-independent color models attempt to use numbers to model human color perception directly.

The device-independent color models in current use are based on the groundbreaking work we mentioned in Chapter 1 by a body of color scientists and technicians known as the *Commission Internationale de l'Eclairage,* or CIE—in English, the name means "International Commission on Illumination"—and the CIE is the international standards body engaged in producing standards for all aspects of light, including color.

In 1931, the CIE produced a mathematical model of color with the formidable-sounding name CIE XYZ (1931). This model was unique in that it tried to represent mathematically the sensation of color that people with normal color vision would experience when they were fed a precisely defined stimulus under precisely defined viewing conditions. Since that original work was done, the CIE has produced a wild alphabet soup of color models with equally opaque names—CIE LCh, CIELUV, CIE xyY, CIELAB, and so on, all of which are mathematical variants of CIE XYZ.

You don't need to know the differences between the various models in order to use color management effectively. In fact, outside of measuring the colors a device produces as part of the profiling process, you needn't deal with any of the CIE models directly. But it *is* important to understand the distinction between device-dependent models like RGB and CMYK, and device-independent models like CIE XYZ and CIELAB.

RGB and CMYK just tell machines how much colorant to use: they tell us nothing about the actual color the machines will produce in response. The CIE models describe the specific color that someone with normal color vision would see under very precisely described viewing conditions, but tell us nothing about what we need to do to make a particular monitor, scanner, or printer produce that color. To manage color in the real world, we need to use both device-independent and device-specific color models.

CIELAB

The CIE color model you're most likely to interact with is CIELAB (LAB). You can actually save images in the LAB model, and edit them in Adobe Photoshop, Heidelberg's LinoColor, and several other applications. LAB also plays a central role in color management, as you'll learn in the next chapter.

If you've ever tried editing a LAB file in Photoshop, you've probably concluded that LAB is not the most intuitive color space around. It is, however, based on the way our minds seem to judge color. It uses three primaries, called L* (pronounced "L-star"), a* and b*. L* represents lightness, a* represents how red or green a color is, and b* represents how blue or yellow it is. (Remember, red-green and blue-yellow are *opponent* colors—they're mutually exclusive. There's no such thing as a greenish-red or a bluish-yellow.)

LAB, by definition, represents all the colors we can see. It's designed to be perceptually uniform, meaning that changing any of the primaries by the same increment will produce the same degree of visual change. In practice, it's not perfect, but it *is* pretty darn good, and more to the point, nobody has as yet presented an alternative that is both a clear improvement and can be implemented using the computing power available on today's desktop. Many of the problems we have with LAB stem from the fact that we use it to do things for which it was never intended (see the sidebar, "LAB Limitations").

Despite its flaws, CIE LAB allows us to control our color as it passes from one device to another by correlating the device-specific RGB or CMYK values with the perceptually based LAB values that they produce on a given device. LAB acts as a form of universal translation language between devices, or, as Bruce is wont to say, "a Rosetta Stone for color." It allows us to express unambiguously the *meaning* of the colors we're after.

LAB Limitations

At some point in your color management travails, you'll almost certainly run into a situation where CIE colorimetry says that two colors should match, but you see them as being clearly different. LAB does have some inherent flaws. It's not as perceptually uniform as it's supposed to be. It also assumes that colors along a straight hue-angle line will produce constant hues, changing only in saturation. This assumption has proved false, particularly in the blue region, where a constant hue angle actually shifts the hue towards purple as blue becomes less saturated. But it's also helpful to bear in mind the purpose for which LAB was designed.

The design goal for LAB was to predict the degree to which two solid color samples of a specific size, on a specific background color, under very specific lighting, at a specific viewing distance and angle, would appear to match to someone with normal color vision. It was never designed to take into account many of the perceptual phenomena we covered in Chapter 1, such as the influence of surround colors. Nor was it designed to make cross-media comparisons such as comparing color displayed on a monitor with color on reflective hard copy.

Yet color management systems try to make LAB do all these things and more. When we color-manage images, we do so pixel by pixel, without any reference to the surrounding pixels (the context) or the medium in which the pixels are finally expressed (dots of ink on paper or glowing pixels on a monitor). So it's not entirely surprising that the model occasionally breaks down. If anything, it's surprising that it works as well as it does, considering the limited purpose for which it was designed.

The good news is that the theory and practice of color management are not dependent on LAB, even though most color management systems today use LAB as the computation space. The basic theory stays the same and the practice—the "Real World" part of this book—does not depend too much on the computation model. As developers come up with fixes and workarounds to LAB's flaws, as well as alternative color models, they can just swap out LAB like an old trusty car engine that has served us well. In the meantime, LAB continues to be the worthy workhorse of the color-management industry.

Figure 2-8

LAB imperfections

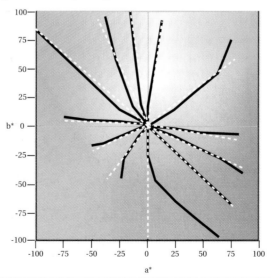

This figure shows the a,b plane of LAB, where hue is shown by the angle, and saturation by the distance from the center, which represents neutral gray (a and b both equal 0). In theory, the dashed lines should represent constant hues, but actual constant perceived hues produce the solid lines shown in the figure. The hue shift is most pronounced in the red and blue regions.

Alphabet Soup

According to the citations we've been able to turn up, the official names are CIE XYZ (1931), abbreviated as CIE XYZ, CIE L*a*b* (1976), abbreviated as CIELAB, and CIE L*u*v* (1976), abbreviated as CIELUV. We haven't found a canonical abbreviation for CIE LCh (the primaries are referred to as $L^* C^*_{uv} h_{uv}$) or CIE xyY, so we abbreviate them as CIE LCh and CIE xyY.

If you want to be pedantic, CIE L*a*b* and CIE L*u*v* are incorrect. No one seems to have any serious objection to using CIE Lab and CIE Luv, which are more consistent with CIE XYZ, CIE LCh, and CIE xyY, but using the * superscript or the $_{uv}$ subscript is excessively fiddly (and is also technically incorrect) unless you're using the long name of the space, or referring to the individual primaries. While we're at it, how many angels can dance on the head of a pin?

But there's another aspect to the device-dependence problem that color management addresses.

Mismatching—the Limits of the Possible

We use color management to reproduce faithfully the colors in our source file on one or another target device—a monitor, a printer, a film recorder, or a commercial press. But it's often physically impossible to do so, because each of our devices is limited by the laws of physics as to the range of tone and color it can reproduce.

Device Limitations—Gamut and Dynamic Range

All our output devices (both printers and monitors) have a fixed range of color and tone that they can reproduce, which we call the devices' *color gamut*. The gamut is naturally limited by the most saturated colors the device has to work with, its primaries. You can't get a more saturated red on a monitor than the red of the monitor's phosphor. You can't get a more saturated green on a printer than you can get by combining solid cyan and yellow ink.

Output devices (printers and monitors) also have a finite *dynamic range*—the range of brightness differences they can reproduce. On a monitor the darkest black you can display is the black that results if you send RGB value 0,0,0 to the monitor (which, if you have turned the brightness control too high, may be quite a bit brighter than all the phosphors completely off). The brightest white on a monitor is the white you get when all three phosphors (R, G, and B) are glowing at maximum—

although you usually have to calibrate your monitor to a less-bright white point in order to get a more color-accurate white. On a printer, the brightest white you can render is the whiteness of the paper, and the darkest black is the highest percentages of the four inks you can print on top of each other without resulting in a soggy mess (usually considerably less than all four inks at 100%).

Input devices (scanners and digital cameras) don't have a color gamut because there is no sharp boundary between colors that they can "see" and colors that they can't—no matter what you put in front of them, they're going to see *something*. Instead, we say they have a *color mixing function*, the unique mixture of red, green, and blue values that they will produce for each color sample. This leads to a problem known as *scanner metamerism*, which we described in Chapter 1, but is not the same as the gamut issue we are describing here.

However, although scanners don't have a specific gamut, we can often think of the effective "gamut" of the materials—usually photographic prints or transparencies—that you scan with the scanner, and this effective gamut is usually much wider than any output device you will be using to reproduce these scans. Digital cameras don't have a fixed gamut since they capture color directly from the real world and have to cope with it in all it's multi-hued glory. This makes them tricky to profile.

Although input devices don't have a fixed gamut, they *do* have a fixed dynamic range, the range of brightness levels in which the scanner or digital camera can operate and still tell brightness differences. Below a certain level of darkness—or density—a scanner or digital camera can no longer distinguish between brightness levels, and just returns the value 0, meaning "man, that's dark!" Similarly, above a certain level of brightness, the device can't capture differences in brightness—rarely a problem with scanners, but all too common with digital cameras. Input devices typically have a wider dynamic range than we can reproduce in our output.

This difference between device gamuts and dynamic ranges leads to a problem. If our original image has a wider dynamic range or a wider color gamut than our output device, we obviously can't reproduce the original exactly on that output device.

There's no single "correct" solution to this problem of variable gamuts and dynamic ranges. You "can't get theah from heah," as they say in New England, so you have to go somewhere else instead.

Tone and Gamut Mapping

The dynamic range of our printers, be they desktop color printers, film recorders, or printing presses, is limited by the brightness of the paper at the highlight end, and by the darkest black the inks, dyes, or pigments can produce on that paper at the shadow end. A film recorder has a wider dynamic range than an inkjet printer, which in turn has a wider dynamic range than a printing press. But none of these output processes comes close to the dynamic range of a high-end digital camera. Even a film recorder can't quite match the dynamic range of film exposed in a camera. So some kind of *tonal compression* is almost always necessary.

Similarly, a film recorder has a larger gamut than an inkjet printer, which again has a larger gamut than a printing press, and the gamuts of all three are smaller than the gamut of film, so we need some strategy for handling the out-of-gamut colors.

Gamut size isn't the only problem. We typically think of a monitor as having a larger gamut than CMYK print, and this is true, but monitor gamuts don't wholly contain the gamut of CMYK print. Even though the monitor has a larger gamut, there are some colors we can produce with CMYK ink on paper that monitors simply can't display, particularly in the saturated cyans and the blues and greens that lie adjacent to cyan. So the mismatches between various device gamuts can be as much due to the shapes of those gamuts as to their size—see Figure 2-9.

Color management systems use various gamut-mapping strategies that let us reconcile the differing gamuts of our capture, display, and output devices, but it's important to recognize that not only is there no "correct" way to handle out-of-gamut colors, it's also pretty unlikely that any gamut-mapping strategy, or any automatic method of compressing tone and color, will do equal justice to all images. So color management doesn't remove the need for color correction, or the need for skilled humans to make the necessary decisions about color reproduction. As we've said before, perception of color is uniquely human, and its judgement is decidedly human as well. What color management *does* do is to let us view color accurately and communicate it unambiguously, so that we have a sound basis on which to make these judgements.

Figure 2-9   Gamut plots, gamut sizes, and gamut mismatches

There are various ways to illustrate and compare gamuts, some of which are more complete than others. Two-dimensional gamut representations are invariably incomplete or misleading—they either show a slice of the gamut at a single lightness level or they show a projection of maximum saturation at all levels.

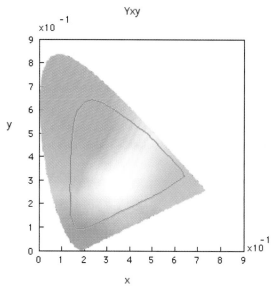

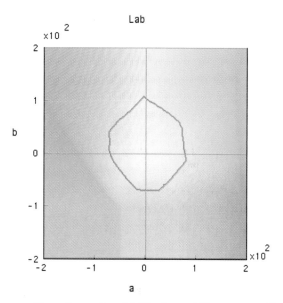

Two-dimensional xyY plots exaggerate some color regions and downplay others, because xyY isn't perceptually uniform.

Two-dimensional LAB plots, while perceptually uniform, are incomplete because they can only show a single lightness level.

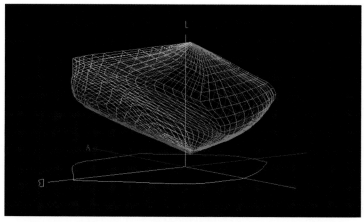

In reality, gamuts are complex three-dimensional shapes. You can tell a great deal more from a three-dimensional gamut plot, such as the one shown at left, than you can from any of the two-dimensional gamut-plotting techniques.

In this three-dimensional LAB gamut plot, the Lightness axis is vertical, the horizontal a axis runs from red to green, and the horizontal b axis runs from yellow to blue.

Figure 2-9 Gamut plots, gamut sizes, and gamut mismatches, *continued.*

When we use plots to compare two devices' gamuts, the differences in plotting techniques become more critical. All three plot types illustrated below show us that the typical monitor has a larger gamut than a sheetfed press, containing many unprintable colors, particularly in the reds, but that the press can also reproduce some colors that the monitor cannot.

The xyY plot at right shows us that the press gamut contains a cyan-green region and a smaller yellow-orange region that the monitor can't display, but it exaggerates the size of both while minimizing the monitor's unprintable reds.

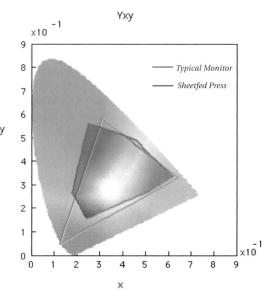

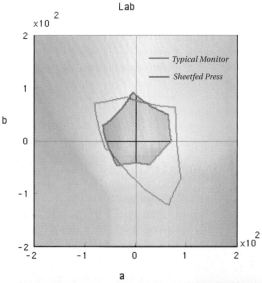

The LAB plot at left provides a more accurate depiction of the relative sizes of both the gamuts themselves and of the regions where they mismatch, but still doesn't tell the whole story.

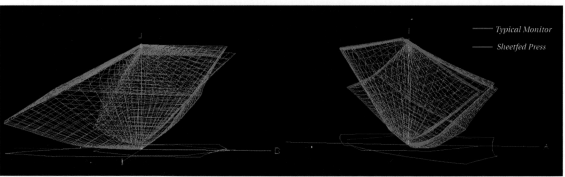

The three-dimensional LAB plots reveal the exact nature of the gamut mismatch, showing the monitor's unprintable blues and the press's undisplayable light yellows, left, and the monitor's unprintable reds and light greens, and the press's undisplayable dark greens and cyans, right.

Figure 2-9 Gamut plots, gamut sizes, and gamut mismatches, *continued.*

In some cases, such as the one shown below, two-dimensional plots may simply give the wrong answer, as in this comparison between a sheetfed press and an Epson Stylus Photo 2200 printer (you might want to make this kind of comparison if you were considering using the Epson inkjet as a proofing device, for example).

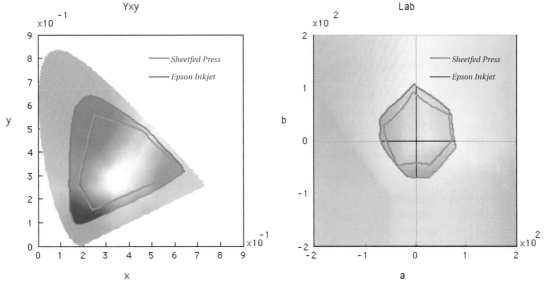

Both 2-D plots indicate that the Epson inkjet's gamut completely encompasses that of the press.

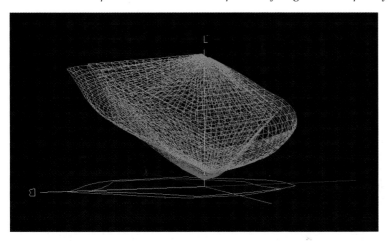

A 3-D comparison tells a rather different story. While the inkjet has a good overall match to the sheetfed press, it can't reproduce some of the dark, saturated colors of which the press is capable—which would be important if you were printing a shoe catalog, for example. When you really know your way around gamut plots, you'd also conclude that a whiter paper stock in the inkjet would provide a closer highlight match to the press,

One final point about gamuts: a device's color gamut isn't the same thing as a device's color space. The gamut simply represents the limits—the whitest white, the blackest black, and the most saturated colors of which the device is capable. A device's color space includes not only the gamut boundary, but also the tonal information that tells you what goes on inside that boundary. For example, a newspaper press will likely have a fairly large discontinuity between paper white and the lightest actual color it can lay down, because newsprint can't hold small dots of ink. That fact isn't conveyed by the gamut, but is a property of the device space. So the gamut is one of the important properties of a device's color space, but not the only important property.

Color is Complex

If all this sounds dauntingly complicated, that's because we're laying out the complexity of the issues color management must address. Actually *using* a color management system isn't that complicated, despite what sometimes seems like a conspiracy on the part of applications vendors to make it appear that way. But if you don't understand the underpinnings of color management, it may seem like magic. It isn't magic, it's just some pretty cool technology, and in the next chapter we'll look in detail at how color management actually performs the complex tasks of changing the numbers in our files to make the color consistent.

Color Management

How It Works

For 1400 years, reading Egyptian hieroglyphics was a lost art. In 1799, a chance discovery by a soldier in Napoleon's conquering army changed all that. The Rosetta stone, as his find was named, allowed the brilliant French linguist Jean François Champollion to unlock the secret of hieroglyphics because it contained the same text in three different scripts, hieroglyphics, demotic script, and Greek, the last two of which were already known.

Depending on your background and training, RGB or CMYK numbers may seem about as comprehensible as Egyptian hieroglyphics: fortunately, thanks to the work of the CIE that we introduced in Chapter 1, color management is able to use the perceptually based CIE LAB and CIE XYZ color spaces as a Rosetta stone for color, letting us translate our color from one set of device-specific RGB or CMYK numbers to another.

In Chapter 2 we broke the sad news that the numerical systems we most often use for representing color on our computers—RGB and CMYK—are fundamentally ambiguous. They aren't descriptions of color. Instead, they're control signals, or instructions, that make devices like monitors and printers produce something that we can experience as color. In this chapter we'll discuss how a color management system (CMS) works to reconcile the RGB and CMYK control signals with the perceptually based CIE numbers.

Color management systems have to perform two critical tasks:

▶ They have to figure out what perceived colors our RGB and CMYK numbers represent.

▶ They have to keep those colors consistent as we go from device to device.

Most discussions of color management focus on the second task, but it's important to realize that until you do the first, the second is impossible—you can't match a color until you know what it is! It's also useful to set realistic expectations—see the sidebar, "The WYSIWYG Myth," later in this chapter.

The details of implementing color management and using it in our applications can be insanely complex, since each application vendor seems to insist on developing its own unique interface and terminology, but the fundamental workings of color management systems are relatively simple. Color management systems really do only two things:

▶ They attach a specific color meaning to our RGB or CMYK numbers, making them unambiguous. With color management, we always know what color a given set of numbers represents.

▶ They change the RGB or CMYK numbers that we send to our various devices—a monitor display, an inkjet printer, an offset press—so that each produces the same colors.

Some CMS implementations may appear to do more complicated things, but on closer examination, anything a CMS does *always* boils down to a combination of these two tasks. In Part III of this book we'll discuss the many ways you can use a CMS, but in this chapter we'll look at what a CMS actually does.

Once you understand what a CMS really does, you'll find that it's a lot easier to wade through all the various menus and dialog boxes that applications use to control color management. First, though, let's look briefly at why we need color management in the first place.

The Genesis of Color Management

In the old days, life was a lot simpler. We didn't need color management in what we might call the *one-input-one-output workflow*. All images were scanned by a professional operator using a single scanner producing CMYK tuned to a single output device. Spot colors were handled either by mixing spot inks or by using standard CMYK formulas in swatch books. Accurate monitor display was unheard of. The system worked because the CMYK values the scanner produced were tuned for the output device, forming a closed loop that dealt with one set of numbers.

Fast-forward to the third millennium. For input, we now have not only high-end drum scanners, but also high-end flatbed scanners, desktop flatbeds, desktop slide scanners, and digital cameras. On the output end, we not only have more diverse web and sheetfed presses with waterless inks, soy inks, direct-to-plate printing, and HiFi color, but also digital proofers, flexography, film recorders, silk screeners, color copiers, laser printers, inkjets, and even monitors as final output devices. This diversity breaks the old closed loop workflow into a zillion pieces.

The result is a huge number of possible conversions from input to output devices (see Figure 3-1). Instead of one input and one output device, today we have to deal with a very large number (which we'll arbitrarily label m) of input devices and an equally large number (which we'll arbitrarily label n) of output devices. With an m-input/n-output workflow, you need $n \times m$ different conversions from input to output. We'll let you do the math, but if you have more than a handful of inputs or outputs, which most of us do, things quickly become unmanageable.

Figure 3-1
n×m input to
output conversions

m input devices

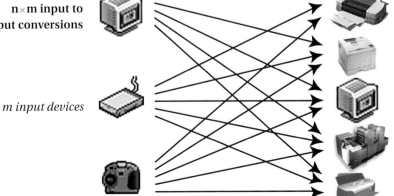

n output devices

The ingenious solution provided by color management is to introduce an intermediate representation of the desired colors called the *profile connection space*, or PCS. The role of the PCS is to serve as the hub for all our device-to-device transformations. It's like the hub city for an airline. Rather than have separate flights from 10 western cities (San Francisco, Seattle, Los Angeles, etc.) to 10 eastern cities (Boston, Atlanta, Miami, etc.) for a total of a hundred flights, the airline can route all flights through a major city in the middle, say Dallas, for a total of only 20 flights.

The beauty of the PCS is that it reduces the m×n link problem to *m+n* links. We have *m* links from input devices to the PCS, and *n* links from the PCS to the various output devices (see Figure 3-2). We need just one link for each device.

Figure 3-2
n+m input to
output conversions

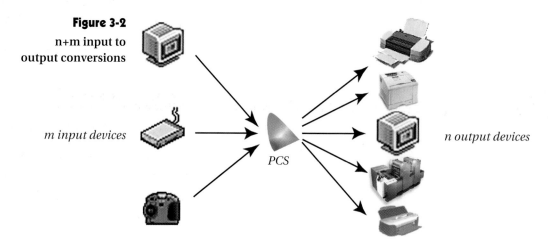

m input devices   *n output devices*

PCS

Each link effectively describes the color reproduction behavior of a device. This link is called a *device profile*. Device profiles and the PCS are two of the four key components in all color management systems.

The WYSIWYG Myth

While the desire for WYSIWYG (What You See Is What You Get) was a driving force behind the development of color management, color management isn't just about achieving WYSIWYG, which in its extreme sense is an impossible goal. While color management goes a long way towards making a monitor simulate the limitations of a printer, monitors and printers have fundamentally different viewing environment issues, so there will always be differences between what you see on your monitor and what you get on your printer. We point this out to counter both the overzealous hype of color-management advocates who may claim that color management gives you true WYSIWYG, and the detractors who claim that color management is a failure because it hasn't delivered on its promise of WYSIWYG.

In fact, we question whether any system has ever achieved the extreme interpretation of WYSIWYG. A traditional film-based proof certainly produces a close visual match to the press sheet, but we've never seen one that was identical to the press sheet. Our belief is that *any* proofing system requires some interpretation on the part of the user. Color management won't make your monitor and your printer produce identical color, but it *will* produce a close and consistent visual match that, with very little learning, you can use as a pretty accurate predictor of the final output.

The Components of Color Management

All ICC-based color management systems use four basic components:

▶ **PCS.** The profile connection space allows us to give a color an unambiguous numerical value in CIE XYZ or CIE LAB that doesn't depend on the quirks of the various devices we use to reproduce that color, but instead defines the color as we actually see it.

▶ **Profiles.** A profile describes the relationship between a device's RGB or CMYK control signals and the actual color that those signals produce. Specifically, it defines the CIE XYZ or CIE LAB values that correspond to a given set of RGB or CMYK numbers.

▶ **CMM.** The CMM (Color Management Module), often called the *engine*, is the piece of software that performs all the calculations needed to convert the RGB or CMYK values. The CMM works with the color data contained in the profiles.

▶ **Rendering intents.** The ICC specification includes four different rendering intents, which are simply different ways of dealing with "out-of-gamut" colors—colors that are present in the source space that the output device is physically incapable of reproducing.

The PCS

The PCS is the yardstick we use to measure and define color. As we hinted earlier in this chapter, the ICC specification actually uses two different spaces, CIE XYZ and CIE LAB, as the PCS for different profile types. But unless you're planning on writing your own CMS, or your own profile-generation software (in which case you'll need to learn a great deal more than the contents of this book) you needn't concern yourself greatly with the differences between the two. The key feature of both CIE XYZ and CIE LAB is that they represent *perceived* color.

It's this property that makes it possible for color management systems to use CIE XYZ and CIE LAB as the "hub" through which all color conversions travel. When a color is defined by XYZ or LAB values, we know how humans with normal color vision will see it.

Profiles

Profiles are conceptually quite simple, though their anatomy can be complex. We'll look at different kinds of profiles in much more detail in Chapter 4, *All About Profiles,* (or for a truly geek-level look at the contents of profiles, see Appendix A, *Anatomy of a Profile*). For now, though, we'll concentrate on their function.

A profile can describe a single device, such as an individual scanner, monitor, or printer; a class of devices, such as Apple Cinema Displays, Epson Stylus Photo 1280 printers, or SWOP presses; or an abstract color space, such as Adobe RGB (1998) or CIE LAB. But no matter what it describes, a profile is essentially a lookup table, with one set of entries that contains device control signal values—RGB or CMYK numbers—and another set that contains the actual colors, expressed in the PCS, that those control signals produce (see Figure 3-3).

A profile gives RGB or CMYK values meaning. Raw RGB or CMYK values are ambiguous—they produce different colors when we send them to different devices. A profile, by itself, doesn't change the RGB or CMYK numbers—it simply gives them a specific meaning, saying, in effect, that this set of RGB or CMYK numbers represent *this* specific color (as defined in XYZ or LAB).

By the same token, a profile doesn't alter a device's behavior—it just describes that behavior. We'll stress this point in Chapter 5 when we discuss the difference between calibration (which alters the behavior of a device) and profiling (which only describes the behavior of a device), but it's a sufficiently important point that it bears repeating.

The ICC—Some Historical Perspective

In the late 1980s and early 1990s, many companies—most notably, Adobe, Agfa, Electronics for Imaging, Hewlett-Packard, Kodak, Linotype-Hell, Pantone, Tektronix, and Xerox—developed color management systems that used profiles to solve the device-to-device color-matching problem. However, the profiles from one company's solution weren't usable by others, and consumers were limited to the profiles created for a specific color management system.

Apple Computer recognized that this problem of incompatibility of profiles had to be addressed at the operating system level, and in 1993 it introduced ColorSync, a color-management architecture built into the Macintosh operating system. Apple also started the ColorSync Consortium, which consisted of companies using the ColorSync profile format as well as shaping its development.

This consortium of companies later became known as the

International Color Consortium, or *ICC*. One of the consortium's goals was extending this profile architecture from the Macintosh to Windows and Unix computers. The central document of the ICC is the *ICC Profile Format Specification*, which describes an open profile format that all vendors can use. By defining a format that allowed consumers to mix and match profiles created by different vendors, the ICC standardized the concepts of profile-based color management.

Converting colors always takes two profiles, a source and a destination. The source profile tells the CMS what actual colors the document contains, and the destination profile tells the CMS what new set of control signals is required to reproduce those actual colors on the destination device. You can think of the source profile as telling the CMS where the color came from, and the destination profile as where the color is going to.

Figure 3-3
Profiles

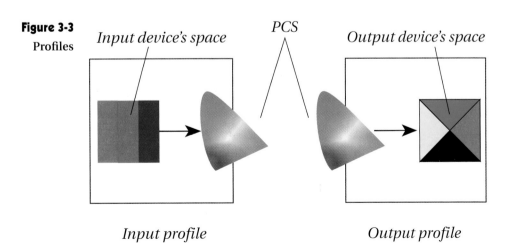

A profile contains two sets of values, RGB or CMYK device control values, and the corresponding CIE XYZ or CIE LAB values that they produce.

The CMM

The Color Management Module, or CMM, is the software "engine" that does the job of converting the RGB or CMYK values using the color data in the profiles (see the sidebar, "What Does CMM Stand For?"). A profile can't contain the PCS definition for every possible combination of RGB or CMYK numbers—if it did, it would be over a gigabyte in size—so the CMM has to calculate the intermediate values. (See the sidebar, "Why do we need CMMs at all?")

The CMM provides the method that the color management system uses to convert values from source color spaces to the PCS and from the PCS to any destination spaces. It uses the profiles to define the colors that need to be matched in the source, and the RGB or CMYK values needed to match those colors in the destination, but the CMM is the workhorse that actually performs the conversions.

When do you care about the CMM? You rarely have to interact with the CMM—it just lurks in the background and does its thing. But if you have multiple CMMs—Bruce's Mac has CMMs loaded from Adobe, Agfa, Apple, Heidelberg, Kodak, and X-Rite, for example—it's often useful to know which one is being used for any given operation.

Why should you care? Well, ICC-compliant CMMs are designed to be interoperable and interchangeable, but they differ in their precision and their calculations of white point adaptation and interpolation (using the profile points as guides), and some profiles contain a "secret sauce" tailored for a particular CMM.

The differences in precision tend to be subtle and often profile-specific. If you have multiple CMMs installed, and you get strange results from one, it's always worth trying another.

What Does CMM Stand For?

The acronym CMM has been known to stand for several different things—*Color Management Module, Color Matching Method, Color Manipulation Model*—but all the names mean the same thing. Our preference is *Color Management Module*, as this captures the essence of what the engine is—a drop-in component in a modular color management system. But it doesn't really matter what it's called as long as there is agreement on what it is.

Why Do We Need CMMs At All?

A profile for an input device can't contain the PCS definition for every possible combination of RGB values, nor can an output profile list the CMYK values for every possible PCS color. For example, as each of the three channels of an RGB device contains 256 discrete values (0-255), an RGB space contains about 16.7 million possible RGB values. If an RGB device profile contained the PCS definition of each of the 16.7 million RGB values, and if you dedicated only three bytes for each of those PCS definitions, the single RGB profile would occupy more than 48 megabytes! Profiles of this size would quickly become prohibitively large when you started embedding profiles in images and in page-layout documents that contain color from multiple sources.

So rather than storing a point for every possible RGB value (in an input profile) or every possible PCS color (in an output profile), the CMM describes a way of computing points from existing points—the process called *interpolation*. This reduces dramatically the number of points that need to be stored in the profiles.

The simplest CMM assumes that we do this interpolation in CIE LAB. In fact, if we use LAB as the PCS itself, then the CMM would seem to have little to do at all. Just take the LAB values produced by the input profiles, find the nearest PCS value found in the output profile, and look up the output value. However, in practice this has not produced stellar results. LAB is simply not as perceptually uniform as we need for this type of computa-

tion. So different vendors have different mechanisms for doing this interpolation.

Some supplement LAB with some clever math to compensate for its known inaccuracies. Others avoid LAB altogether and convert to some other space for purposes of interpolation. Still others create profiles that support additional, private conversion spaces in addition to supporting one of the two required conversion spaces (XYZ or LAB).

The continuing battle over which one of these strategies produces the best color management results is one of the reasons why so many vendors hawk their own CMM, claiming that theirs produces results superior to those produced by competing ones.

The different math for white point adaptation can be more obvious. As we explained in Chapter 2, *Computers and Color*, white comes in many different flavors, and our eye adapts automatically to the flavor of white with which it's currently confronted, judging all other colors in reference to that white. So we usually convert the white of the source space to the white of the destination space when we do color conversions. Some CMMs have difficulty doing this with some profiles, translating white to a "scum dot" with one percent of ink in one or more channels, instead of paper white. Switching to a different CMM will often cure this problem.

The differences in math for interpolation can range from subtle to dramatic. Many CMMs have fixed notorious problems with LAB, such as skies that seemed to turn noticeably purple, by implementing clever tricks in the interpolation mathematics.

The practice of building "secret sauce" into profiles directly contravenes the goal of an open, interchangeable profile format. Kodak is the main offender in this case. If you use a profiling tool that builds in customizations for a particular CMM, you may get slightly better results using the preferred CMM, but in our experience, the differences have been so slight that we question the value of the practice.

How the CMM is chosen. Profiles contain a tag that lets them request a preferred CMM when it's available, though they *must* be able to use any ICC-compliant CMM if the preferred one is unavailable. This becomes an issue on Mac OS if you set the choice of CMM to Automatic in the ColorSync control panel. Doing so allows each profile to select its preferred CMM. It also means that unless you do a lot of detective work, you'll have no idea which CMM is in use at any given moment.

The Macintosh and Windows operating systems, and almost all color-managed applications, let you override the profiles' preferred CMM and choose a specific CMM for all color-management tasks. We recommend that you choose one CMM and stick to it, experimenting with others only if you run into a specific problem or if you're trying to get a specific advantage touted by a CMM vendor.

Rendering Intents

There's one more piece to the color-management puzzle. As we explained in Chapter 2, each device has a fixed range of color that it can reproduce, dictated by the laws of physics. Your monitor can't reproduce a more saturated red than the red produced by the monitor's red phosphor. Your printer can't reproduce a cyan more saturated than the printer's cyan ink. The range of color a device can reproduce is called the *color gamut.*

Colors present in the source space that aren't reproducible in the destination space are called *out-of-gamut* colors. Since we can't reproduce those colors in the destination space, we have to replace them with some other colors, or since, as our friends from New England are wont to remark, "you can't get theah from heah," you have to go somewhere else. Rendering intents let you specify that somewhere else.

The ICC profile specification includes four different methods for handling out-of-gamut colors, called *rendering intents* (see Figure 3-4). *Perceptual* and *saturation* renderings use gamut compression, desaturating all the colors in the source space so that they fit into the destination gamut. *Relative* and *absolute colorimetric* renderings use gamut clipping, where all out-of-gamut colors simply get clipped to the closest reproducible hue.

▶ **Perceptual** tries to preserve the overall color appearance by changing all the colors in the source space so that they fit inside the destination space while preserving the overall color relationships, because our eyes are much more sensitive to the relationships between colors than they are to absolute color values. It's a good choice for images that contain significant out-of-gamut colors.

▶ **Saturation** just tries to produce vivid colors, without concerning itself with accuracy, by converting saturated colors in the source to saturated colors in the destination. It's good for pie charts and other business graphics, or for elevation maps where saturation differences in greens, browns, or blues show different altitudes or depths, but it's typically less useful when the goal is accurate color reproduction.

▶ **Relative colorimetric** takes account of the fact that our eyes always adapt to the white of the medium we're viewing. It maps white in the source to white in the destination, so that white on output is the white of the paper rather than the white of the source space. It then reproduces all the in-gamut colors exactly, and clips out-of-gamut colors to the closest reproducible hue. It's often a better choice for images than perceptual since it preserves more of the original colors.

▶ **Absolute colorimetric** differs from relative colorimetric in that it doesn't map source white to destination white. Absolute colorimetric rendering from a source with a bluish white to a destination with yellowish-white paper puts cyan ink in the white areas to simulate the white of the original. Absolute colorimetric is designed mainly for proofing, where the goal is to simulate the output of one printer (including its white point) on a second device.

When you use a CMS to convert data from one color space to another, you need to supply the source profile and the destination profile so it knows where the color comes from and where the color is going. In most cases, you also specify a rendering intent, which is how you want the color to get there. When you aren't given a choice, the application chooses the profile's default rendering intent, which is set by the profile-building application and is usually the perceptual rendering intent.

Figure 3-4 Rendering intents

This figure shows the MacBeth Color Checker target rendered to the CMYK profile we used to make this book, using each of the four rendering intents. Each rendering is accompanied by a plot in the a,b plane of LAB space showing the original colors in green, and their rendered equivalents in red. (We didn't plot the grays, because they tend to shift only in luminance, which is the third axis of LAB and is not shown on a,b plots.)

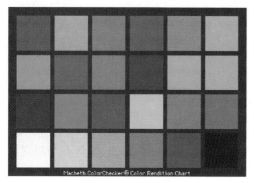

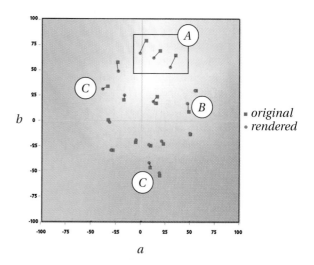

Perceptual rendering

Perceptual rendering tries to compress the source gamut into the destination gamut in such a way that overall color relationships are preserved.

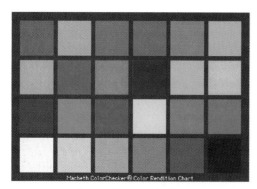

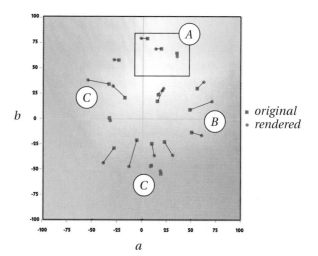

Saturation rendering

Saturation rendering maps fully saturated colors in the source to fully saturated colors in the destination without concern for accuracy.

Figure 3-4   Rendering intents, *continued*

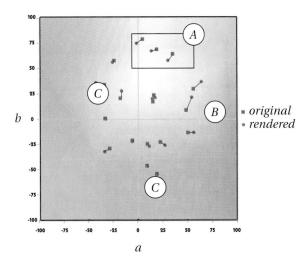

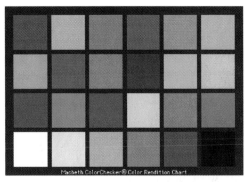

Absolute colorimetric rendering

Absolute colorimetric rendering attempts to reproduce all source colors, including white, as exactly as possible.

(A)   *Out-of-gamut colors*

(B)   *These colors are largely within gamut but get different treatment from each rendering intent.*

(C)   *These colors are desaturated by perceptual rendering, but not by the colorimetric rendering intents.*

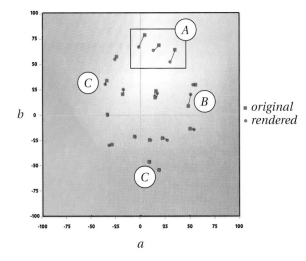

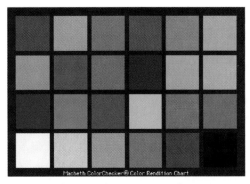

Relative colorimetric rendering

Relative colorimetric rendering scales the source white to the destination white and adjusts all other colors proportionally.

Figure 3-4   Rendering intents, *continued*

In most cases, the differences between perceptual, relative colorimetric, and saturation rendering are quite subtle. Absolute colorimetric rendering produces very different results from the other three since it doesn't perform white point scaling, and hence is usually used only for proofing. Notice the difference in the saturated reds between the perceptual and relative colorimetric treatments of the image below, and the hue shift of the reds in the saturation rendering.

Perceptual rendering

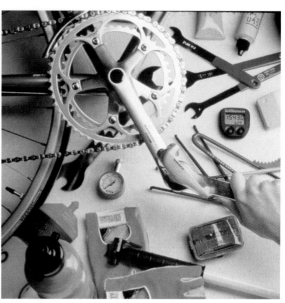

Relative colorimetric rendering

Saturation rendering

Absolute colorimetric rendering

Color Management in Action

Let's look at how the different color-management components interact. We've told you that a CMS does only two things:

▶ Assign a specific color meaning to RGB or CMYK numbers.

▶ Change the RGB or CMYK numbers as our color goes from device to device, so that the actual color remains consistent.

We accomplish the first by assigning or embedding a profile in our document. We accomplish the second by asking the CMS to convert from the assigned or embedded source profile to a chosen output profile.

Assigning and Embedding Profiles

Most color-managed applications let you assign a profile to images and other colored objects. For example, Photoshop allows you to assign a profile to an image. When you do so, you're defining the meaning of the RGB or CMYK values in the image by assigning the image a profile that describes where it came from, such as a scanner or digital camera. A page-layout document may have multiple images or illustrations in a single document and will allow you to assign a profile to each one. For example, you may have some scanned images and some digital camera captures. You'd want to assign the scanner profile to the scans, and the digital camera profile to the camera captures, so that the CMS knows what actual colors the scanner RGB and digital camera RGB numbers represent.

Most color-management-enabled applications also let you embed profiles inside documents such as images or page-layout files when you save them. Doing so lets you transfer documents between applications or computer systems without losing the meaning of the RGB or CMYK values used in those documents (see Figure 3-5).

Note that assigning or embedding a profile in a document doesn't change the RGB or CMYK numbers; it simply applies a specific interpretation to them. For example, if we embed the profile for Bruce's Imacon scanner in an RGB document, what we're doing is telling the CMS that the RGB numbers in the document represent the color that the Imacon scanner saw when it recorded these RGB numbers.

Figure 3-5
Profile embedding

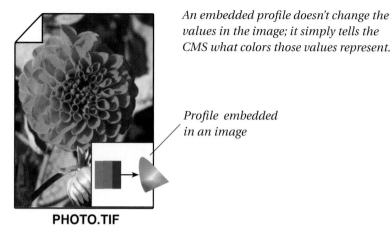

An embedded profile doesn't change the values in the image; it simply tells the CMS what colors those values represent.

Profile embedded in an image

PHOTO.TIF

Some people find it counter-intuitive that if we assign a different profile—for example, the Adobe RGB (1998) working space—the RGB numbers in the image don't change, but the image's appearance does. It does so because we've changed the meaning of the RGB numbers—the actual colors those numbers represent.

Assigning or embedding a profile is a necessary first step before you can convert the color for output on another device. This may be done automatically by scanner or camera software, it may be done explicitly by the user, or it may be done implicitly by a color-managed application— most color-managed applications let you specify default RGB and CMYK profiles, which they automatically assign to color elements that don't already have a profile embedded. This assigned or embedded profile is used as the source profile when you ask the CMS to perform a conversion.

Converting with Profiles

To convert an image from one profile's space to another's—actually changing the RGB or CMYK numbers—we have to specify two profiles, a source profile and a target or destination profile. The source profile tells the CMS where the numbers in the document come from so that it can figure out what actual colors they represent. The destination profile tells the CMS where the document is going to so that it can figure out the new set of RGB or CMYK numbers needed to represent those same actual colors on the destination device (see Figure 3-6).

Figure 3-6
Converting with profiles

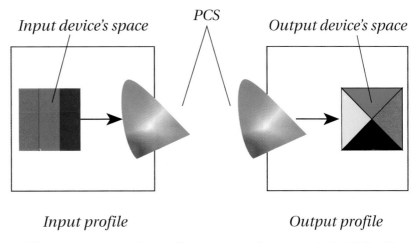

Input device's space   *PCS*   *Output device's space*

Input profile   *Output profile*

*When you convert using profiles, you must always supply the CMS with a
source (input) profile and a destination (output) profile.*

For instance, if Chris shoots an image with a digital camera, he ends
up with an RGB image—but not just any RGB image, rather a "Chris's
Nikon D1 RGB" image. So he needs a profile for the digital camera in
order to tell the CMS how Chris's Nikon D1 sees color. That is the source
profile—it describes where the color numbers came from and what
perceived colors they represent. Chris wants to convert the image to
CMYK so it can go into a magazine article—but not just any CMYK
image, rather a "*Color Geek Monthly* CMYK" image. So he needs a
profile for *Color Geek Monthly*'s press to tell the CMS how the press
reproduces colors. Now the CMS has the necessary information to figure
out which perceived colors the original image RGB numbers represent
and which CMYK values it needs to send to the press to reproduce those
colors.

It may seem counter-intuitive, but converting colors from one profile's
space to another's doesn't change the color appearance—preserving the
color appearance is the whole point of making the conversion.

The usefulness of converting colors becomes clearer when you
consider why you use conventional color-correction techniques. When
you print out an image on an inkjet printer and it comes out too green
overall, with an excessively-yellow gray balance in quarter-tones and too
much cyan and yellow in shadows, what do you do? You color-correct it
using curves, hue/saturation, replace color, and any other tools you feel
comfortable with, until it prints out the way you want. You're changing

the numbers in the image to produce the color appearance you want. Conversions made with profiles find the proper device values for you, automatically.

Color management doesn't take a bad image and make it look good on output. Instead, it makes the output faithfully reflect all the shortcomings of the original. So color management doesn't eliminate the need for color correction. Instead, it simply ensures that once you've corrected the image so that it looks good, your corrections are translated faithfully to the output device.

How Conversions Work

First, the conversion requires you to select four ingredients:

The source profile. This may be already embedded in the document, applied by the user, or supplied by a default setting in the operating system or application.

The destination profile. This may be selected by a default setting in the operating system or application, or selected by the user at the time of conversion (for example, choosing a printer profile at the time you print).

The CMM. This may be chosen automatically as the destination profile's "preferred" CMM, or selected by the user either at the time of conversion, or as a default setting in the operating system or application.

A rendering intent. This may be selected by the user at the time of conversion, or as a default setting in the operating system or application. Failing that, the "default" rendering intent in the destination profile is used.

The color management system then performs the series of steps shown in Figure 3-7.

That's really all that a CMS ever does. Some CMS implementations let you do multiple conversions as a single operation—Photoshop, for example, lets you print an inkjet proof that simulates a press from an image that's in an RGB editing space. But when you break it down, all that's happening is conversions from one profile's space to another's, in sequence, with different rendering intents at each step.

Figure 3-7 A color space conversion

1. *The CMS looks at the source profile and builds a table that correlates source RGB (or CMYK), with PCS values, using relative colorimetric rendering.*

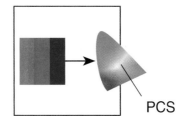

PCS

2. *The CMS looks at the destination profile and builds a table that correlates PCS values with destination CMYK (or RGB) values, using the selected rendering intent, or, if none is selected, the profile's default rendering intent.*

PCS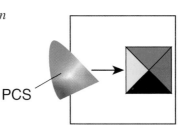

3. *Using the interpolation algorithm defined in the CMM, the CMS connects the two tables together through the common PCS values and builds a table that goes directly from source to destination.*

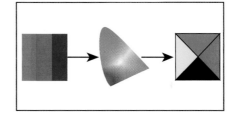

4. *The CMS passes each pixel in the source image, or color in the source art- work, through the table, converting the values from source to destination.*

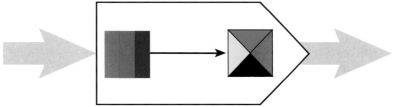

Conversions and Data Loss

It may seem from the foregoing that you can simply convert your color from device space to device space as needed. Unfortunately, that's not the case: if you're dealing with typical 8-bit per channel files, where each channel contains 256 possible levels, each conversion you put the file through will lose some of these levels due to *rounding error*.

Rounding errors happen when you convert integers between different scales—for example, 55 degrees Fahrenheit and 56 degrees Fahrenheit both convert to a brisk 13 degrees Centigrade as a product of rounding to the nearest integer value. The same kinds of errors occur when you convert 8-bit RGB or CMYK channels to PCS values.

To put this in context, we should hasten to point out that almost any kind of useful editing you perform on files made up of 8-bit channels will result in some levels getting lost. So it's not something to obsess about. But it *is* something to bear in mind.

The High-Bit Advantage

If you start with 16 bits of data per channel, your color suffers much less from rounding error, because instead of having only 256 possible input values per channel, you have 65,536! You'll still get rounding errors, but you have so much more data to start with that they become insignificant. There's no such thing as a free lunch, but high-bit conversions come pretty close. However, just converting an existing 8-bit per channel file to 16 bits won't buy you anything—you have to start out with real high-bit data.

Rounding error is simply something you need to keep in mind when constructing color-managed workflows—you generally want to put your color through as few conversions as possible.

Color Management Is Simple

We've deliberately kept things conceptual in this chapter, and we've left out a lot of details. But until you understand the basic things that a CMS does, the details won't make any sense. Keep in mind the fundamental concepts behind color management—an assigned or embedded profile describes the actual colors represented by RGB or CMYK numbers, and a conversion from one profile to another keeps those actual colors consistent by changing the numbers that get sent to the output—and the details, which we'll continue to feed you throughout this book, will make a great deal more sense.

All About Profiles

Describing Devices

If color management is as simple as we say it is in Chapter 3, *Color Management—How It Works*, you may be wondering why you even need this book. The answer is that, while color management is simple, color *reproduction* is not. The various machines we use to reproduce color are prey to a host of factors that affect their behavior, and color management is blissfully unaware of them—unless they are captured in a profile.

Color management systems know nothing about the various devices they drive *except* for the information that's recorded in the profiles for those devices. All the intelligence in color management systems— rendering intents, previewing capabilities, simulations—is built into the device profiles. So it's essential that you obtain or create accurate profiles for your various devices. We tell you how to create device profiles later in the book, but to make good ones, you need to know a little about what comprises them and how they work.

What Are Device Profiles?

Contrary to prepress legend, profiles aren't magic, nor are they made by elves during the full moon in Orthutanga.

A profile is just a file that correlates device color values with corresponding device-independent color values that represent the actual color people see. The device values are expressed as the control signals—usually RGB or CMYK—that we send to our devices to make them reproduce color. The corresponding device-independent values that represent the color they reproduce are expressed in the profile connection space (PCS)—either CIEXYZ or CIELAB. (Refer to Chapter 3 for more on the PCS.)

The device profile contains information about the three main variables that describe how a device is behaving:

▶ Gamut—the color and brightness of the colorants (primaries)

▶ Dynamic range—the color and brightness of the white point and black point

▶ Tone-reproduction characteristics of the colorants.

(We tell you more about these variables in Chapter 2 in the section, "Why the Numbers Vary.")

Some kinds of profiles may contain additional information, such as instructions for handling out-of-gamut colors, more detailed tone-reproduction information, or special "secret sauce" information that's only used with a particular CMM.

Profile Classes

Profiles come in a few varieties, or *classes*: *input profiles* describe scanners and digital cameras; *display profiles* describe monitors and LCD displays; and *output profiles* describe printers and presses.

Some people confuse the term *input profile* with *source profile*, and *output profile* with *destination profile*. Input and output profiles refer to distinct types of devices that these profiles represent, whereas source and destination profiles refer to temporary roles two profiles take at the moment a color conversion happens. We describe source and destination profiles in "Using Profiles—Source and Destination," later in this chapter.

One factor that differentiates the three types of profiles is whether they are one-way or two-way—that is, whether they allow the CMS to convert from device space to PCS and from PCS to device space. Input profiles only have to define the conversion from the input device's color space to the PCS. You can't view or output color on a scanner or digital camera, so there's really no need to convert color to scanner or digital camera space. Input profiles simply tell the CMS how people would see the color the scanner or camera captures (see Figure 4-1).

Figure 4-1

One-way and two-way profiles

Communication between the CMS and display profiles is two-way, so the CMS can send the right RGB values to the monitor to reproduce a requested color, and can interpret monitor RGB values to reproduce them on output devices.

Profiles let the CMS translate between different devices' RGB and CMYK values using the PCS as a common language.

Communication between the CMS and input profiles is one-way, because the CMS simply needs to know what colors the input RGB numbers represent.

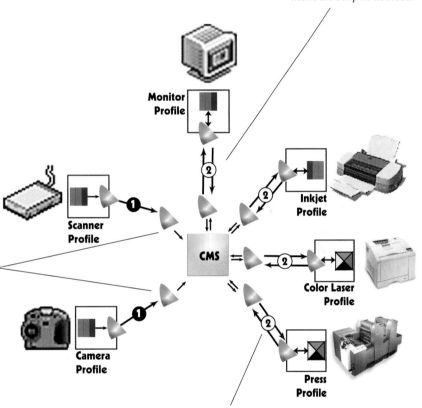

Communication between the CMS and output devices must also be two-way so the CMS can translate output CMYK or RGB to monitor RGB for soft-proofing, and can translate between different output RGB or CMYK so that it can, for example, reproduce press CMYK on an RGB inkjet.

On the other hand, display profiles must be two-way because your display acts as both an input and an output device. If you create or edit a color based on its appearance on your monitor, you're using the monitor as an input device: the CMS needs to know what color you're seeing on the monitor so that it can reproduce it on a printer, press, or another display. The CMS looks at the monitor RGB values being displayed and uses the profile to calculate what actual color those RGB values represent. Conversely, when you display an image on your screen, the monitor is the output device: the CMS evaluates the image's embedded profile to determine what actual colors are represented by the numbers in the file, and then uses the monitor profile to calculate the monitor RGB values needed to display those colors accurately.

Output profiles are always two-way profiles, too. We use them not only to convert from the PCS to the output color space for printing, but also to display files already converted to output space on the monitor, or to convert a press CMYK image to some other output device's space for proofing. When you display a CMYK image on your RGB monitor, the CMS relies on the CMYK output profile to tell it how to convert the numbers back to the PCS and, ultimately, to monitor RGB.

The device-to-PCS transform is known as the *backwards transform*, and the tables that specify it are known as the *AtoB tables*, while the PCS-to-device transform is known as the *forward transform*, and the tables that specify it are known as the *BtoA* tables (see Figure 4-2).

Figure 4-2

Matrix and table-based profiles

Matrix profiles contain tags that describe the CIE XYZ values of the primaries, which form the matrix, plus tags that describe the tone reproduction characteristics of each colorant.

Table-based profiles use lookup tables to define the conversion between device color and LAB for each rendering intent (AtoB), and between LAB and device color for each rendering intent (BtoA).

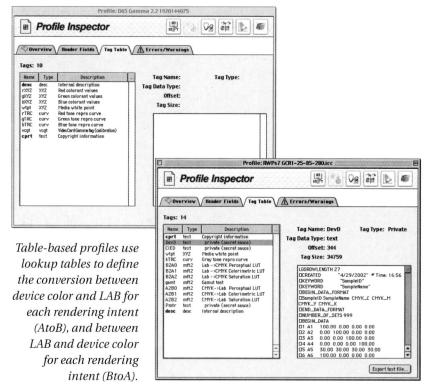

Matrix-Based Vs. Table-Based ICC Profiles

Profiles can be either matrix-based or table-based. Both types include the device's white point, but they differ in the way they represent the device's tone-reproduction attributes. This is why some profiles are tiny while others can weigh in at over a megabyte, and why some profiles seem to produce identical results no matter which rendering intent you choose while others produce very different results with each rendering intent.

The simplest way to store a conversion from one three-channel space to another—such as from RGB to XYZ—is to use a mathematical model known as a 3x3 *matrix*. A 3x3 matrix is an array of nine numbers that can convert any triplet of numbers, such as (20, 30, 40), to another triplet, such as (1.83, 2.0, 3.67). In ICC profiles, the 3x3 matrix consists of the XYZ values for each of the three colorants (primaries) of the device. The profile also contains one or more numbers defining the tone curve of each colorant. The device numbers are passed through the tone curves before conversion using the 3x3 matrix. Matrix profiles always use CIE XYZ as the profile connection space.

The other way to store the conversion is in a *lookup table*, or LUT, which is a table of numbers that lets you look up any input value and find its corresponding output value. The profiling package decides the number of points in the LUT, and vendors often compete on the tradeoff between the quality afforded by more sample points and the increased size and decreased speed of the profile. LUT-based profiles always use CIE LAB as the profile connection space.

Matrices are much smaller than lookup tables because you always store only nine numbers for the matrix, whereas the size of a LUT depends on the number of sample points it contains, which can number into the hundreds or thousands. Matrices are reversible—the same matrix lets you convert numbers in either direction. But matrices are only good for devices with fairly simple tone curves, like scanners and basic CRT-based monitors. For more complex devices, like printers, matrices just don't contain enough information.

Matrix-based profiles only contain information for a single rendering intent, which is assumed to be relative colorimetric, even if the user interface of the application calling the conversion lets you choose perceptual or saturation.

Matrix profiles *do* support absolute colorimetric rendering in addition to relative colorimetric; absolute colorimetric doesn't require additional tables because it's computed from the relative colorimetric intent using the white point value.

Lookup tables can represent extremely complex devices just by adding more points in the table. They also have an advantage in that they aren't limited to three-channel devices, so they can describe four-channel devices such as CMYK printers, or even printers with higher numbers of inks. But lookup tables get very large when you add more data points, and since the tables are unidirectional, you need a separate table for each direction.

Input and display profiles can be matrix-based *or* table-based, which is why you may find that profiles made by one vendor are much larger than those from another. Display profiles are always bidirectional. Some input profiles are also bidirectional, though it seems a little pointless to convert color to a scanner or digital camera space.

Output profiles are the largest profiles by far; they must be table-based and must store two tables (one for each conversion direction) for each of the three rendering intents, perceptual, relative colorimetric, and saturation. So a typical output profile has six lookup tables!

Stimulus and Response

One easy way to visualize the process of making profiles is to think in terms of stimulus and response. Empirical science often boils down to poking things and seeing what happens. Profilers work by sending a stimulus to the device, obtaining a response, and then comparing and correlating the two. In other words, they poke the device with known RGB or CMYK values, and then measure what the device produces.

For a display device, the profile maker sends a stimulus in the form of known RGB values and then measures the colors those RGB values cause the monitor to display. The measurements are made with an instrument that captures PCS (XYZ or LAB) values. Then it constructs a profile that correlates the RGB values and their PCS equivalents. Hence the profile can tell the CMS what actual color will results from a given set of RGB values. The profile can also tell the CMM what RGB values are needed to display a specific color (see Figure 4-3).

Figure 4-3
Monitor calibrators

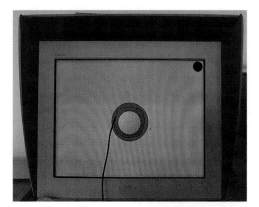

Monitor profiling and calibration packages send known RGB values to the monitor and measure the color that results with an instrument like the ones shown here. They use the first set of measurements to calibrate the monitor, adjusting its behavior, and a second set to create the monitor profile.

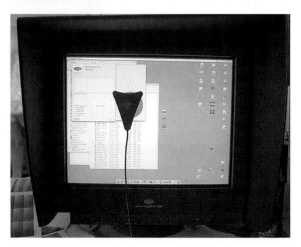

For an output device such as a printer, the profile maker sends known RGB or CMYK values to the printer and then measures the printed output. Again, it builds a profile that correlates the stimulus and the response, so that the CMS can tell from the profile what actual color will result from specific RGB or CMYK values, and what RGB or CMYK values are needed to print a specific color (see Figure 4-4).

Figure 4-4   The IT8.7/3 target

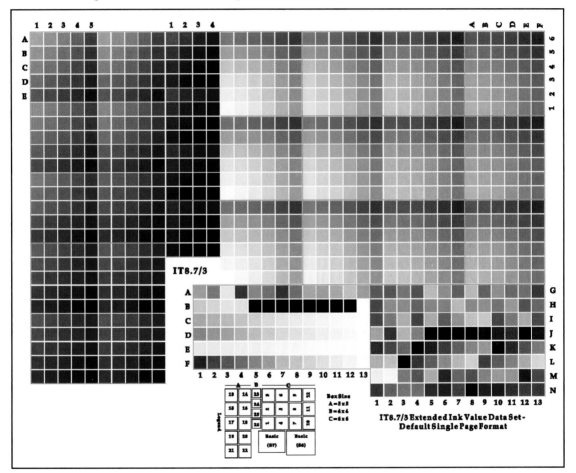

The IT8.7/3 target is a standard target for profiling CMYK output devices. It contains patches with 0%, 10%, 20%, 40%, 70% and 100% of each ink in all possible combinations, plus 13-step ramps of each ink. In addition, rows K and L contain near-neutral patches using finer increments. Profiling packages use this target to model all the colors CMYK devices can produce.

For an input device such as a scanner, the process differs only in that the measurements are usually already done for you. The stimulus in this case is a scanning target that's either supplied with the profiling package or obtained from a third-party vendor. Scanner targets are always accompanied by a data file that records the LAB or XYZ values of the color patches. You scan the target, and then feed the scanner profiler the scan and the target data file. The profiler compares the RGB values in the scan and the LAB or XYZ values in the target data file and builds a profile that tells the CMS how the scanner sees color (see Figure 4-5).

Figure 4-5

The HCT scanner target and reference data file

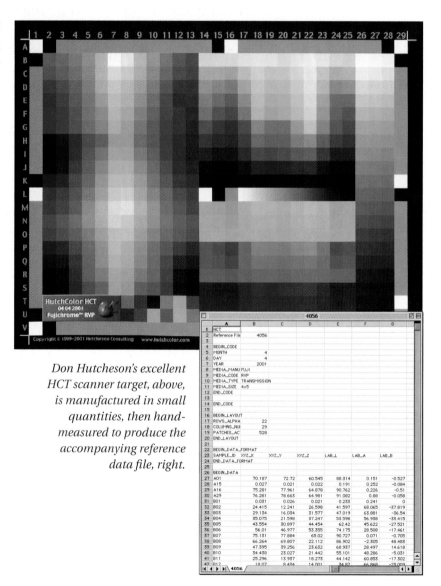

Don Hutcheson's excellent HCT scanner target, above, is manufactured in small quantities, then hand-measured to produce the accompanying reference data file, right.

Profile Limitations

There are three limitations in this process of creating profiles that you need to keep in mind.

First, the profile maker can't cover the entire set of possible device signals. For example, a printer profiler can't send every possible combination of CMYK values to the printer to see what results—at one percent increments, doing so would require a target with 100,000,000 patches! Even if you had the equipment (and the patience) to measure all these patches, storing that many sample points in a lookup table would produce output profiles in the gigabytes.

So interpolation is unavoidable, both at the time the profile is created and when it is used by the color management system. We mention this because it helps explain what the CMM does, and why some color conversions are slower than others. Many people assume that with a big enough lookup table there would be no need for a CMM because there would be no interpolation, or at the least all CMMs should produce the same results with the same profiles. While in theory this is true, in practice, interpolation is unavoidable, which is why some vendors try to find better interpolation systems with different CMMs.

The second limitation is that profiles can't make devices do things they cannot do. If a printer can't produce a certain shade of red, a profile won't somehow make it magically produce that color. The profile describes the gamut of the device, but it can't enlarge the gamut.

The third limitation is that the profile is only as accurate as the measurements on which it's based. A profile is a snapshot of the way the device was behaving when the measurements were captured. The majority of color devices drift over time, so you need to take steps to ensure that the device is behaving the way you want it to before you profile, and you need to take steps to keep it behaving that way after you profile; otherwise the profile will no longer provide an accurate description of the device's behavior, and you won't get the color you want. We discuss this topic in more detail in Chapter 5, *Measurement, Calibration, and Process Control*, and in the following three chapters that deal with the specifics of building display, input, and output profiles, respectively.

Using Profiles—Source and Destination

By itself, a profile does nothing at all—even when a profile is *embedded* in a file. It's only when you're converting colors from one device to another that a profile becomes active. At that time, the color management system doing the conversion needs to know where the colors came from and where they are going—and thus requires *two* profiles to do the color conversion.

In a color conversion, the profile you're converting *from* is the *source profile*, and the profile you're converting *to* is the *destination profile*.

Source and destination profiles aren't types or classes of profile—they're just temporary *roles* that two profiles play when a color management system uses them to convert colors from one device to another. Input profiles are almost invariably used only as source profiles—it makes much more sense to convert color *from* a scanner or camera space than to convert it *to* a scanner or camera space—but output and display profiles are equally at home as source and destination profiles. For example, if you have an image from an RGB scanner that you want to print on a press, you'd convert it using the scanner RGB profile as the source and the press CMYK profile as the destination. But if you then wanted to proof the converted CMYK image on an RGB inkjet printer, you'd perform another conversion using the CMYK press profile as the source and the RGB inkjet profile as the destination.

Generic Profiles

Just about every color device sold nowadays comes with one or more generic ICC profiles made by the device manufacturer and describing the typical behavior of the device model rather than the specific behavior of the individual unit. Some of the more rabid color-management enthusiasts will tell you that all such profiles are useless. While it's probably true that the inappropriate or over-optimistic use of generic profiles—profiles that were made from something other than the measured behavior of your particular unit—have caused far more than their fair share of color-management headaches, some generic profiles are a great deal more useful than others.

Generic profiles are useful when they're for very stable devices that display little or no variation from unit to unit in manufacturing, or little or no variation from batch to batch in consumables. The profiles that accompany many inkjet printers, for example, fall into this class: you may get slightly better results from a custom profile, but the generic ones are nevertheless quite useful. Generic profiles are also useful in representing standard conditions, such as SWOP (Specifications for Web Offset Publications), that define how a press should behave, or for common mainstream proofing systems.

Generic profiles are useless (Bruce would say worse than useless; Chris would say somewhere between lethal and catastrophic) for unstable devices, or for ones that display significant unit-to-unit variation, such as CRT displays. CRTs not only have a lot of unit-to-unit variation fresh from the factory, they drift over time *and* they offer controls that let you change their behavior radically, making generic monitor profiles a cruel joke at best.

Color Space Profiles

Thus far in this chapter, we've confined our discussion of profiles to *device* profiles—profiles that describe the behavior of an actual physical device or a class of physical devices. But there are also profiles that describe device-independent color spaces such as CIE LAB or CIE XYZ—these are known, logically enough, as color space profiles.

In recent years, another type of profile has become commonplace—device-independent RGB profiles. Technically, these aren't color space profiles as defined in the ICC spec—they're built like display profiles and appear to the CMS as display profiles—but in practice they behave a lot more like color space profiles than device profiles. They don't represent devices, so they aren't subject to variability, and they're always accurate. We'll discuss these profiles more fully in Chapter 10, *Color-Management Workflow*.

Good Profiles

One entirely reasonable way to decide whether your profiles are accurate enough is simply to look at the results you're getting and decide whether or not you're happy with them. But if you bought this book, chances are that you're less than satisfied with what color management is currently doing for you. In the next four chapters, we look at building profiles, and reveal our techniques for making sure that your profiles give you the best results from your devices and that your devices keep behaving the way your profiles think they do.

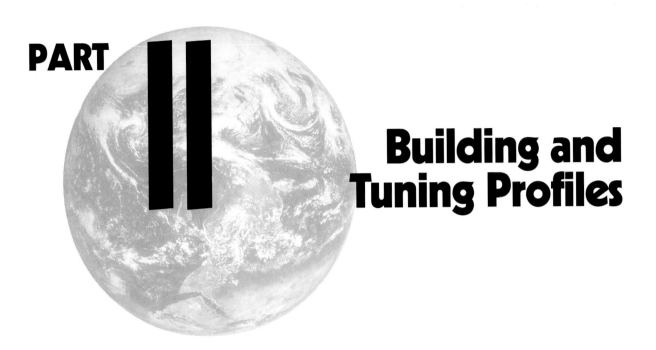

PART II

Building and Tuning Profiles

5

Measurement, Calibration, and Process Control

"The Map Is Not the Territory"

Whether you attribute the above quotation to British artist Ralph Rumney and the Situationist International movement, or to Alfred Korzybski, the father of general semantics, you probably didn't picture either of them slaving over a hot spectrophotometer or wrestling with rendering intents. As far as we know, both were blissfully unaware of color management. But the quotation contains an important lesson for would-be color managers: just as the map is not the territory, in color management, the profile is not the device. If your map doesn't reflect the territory accurately, you'll get lost, and if your profiles don't provide an accurate description of your device's behavior, your color output will be unpredictable.

In Chapter 4, we explained that color management lives or dies by the accuracy of the profiles used. Profiles are essentially snapshots of a device's behavior, so if the profiled device's behavior changes, the profiles are no longer accurate and you won't get the color you expected. In this chapter, we'll talk about keeping our devices' behavior in sync with the profiles that describe them. It's the part of color management that most often gets overlooked because it's something you need to do outside of the color management system.

Keeping Track of Device Drift

Process control is the art and science of tracking and compensating for variability. In the realm of color management, it means keeping track of the way our devices are behaving and either *calibrating* them (adjusting their behavior to keep it in sync with our profiles), or *characterizing* them (building new profiles that reflect their current behavior).

► *Calibration* is the act of changing a device's behavior to achieve some desired state. We calibrate for many reasons, but for color management, the most important reason is to make the device behave consistently so that the profile that describes it remains accurate.

► *Profiling*, which is often called *characterization,* is the process by which we record a device's behavior into a *profile.* It doesn't change the device's behavior; it just records how this device makes color and what colors it can (and cannot) reproduce.

Calibration is like performing a tune-up on your car. You're actually changing the behavior of the device (in this case, your car's engine) by adjusting something. Profiling, on the other hand, is like getting a printout of the mechanic's report—the car's current levels of hydrocarbons and carbon monoxide emissions, RPM measurements of idle speed, and so forth—that describe the car's current behavior. Just as you can get an emissions report with or without a tune-up first, with color management you can profile (characterize) a device with or without calibrating it first. Calibration actually changes the way a device behaves, whereas profiling simply describes how the device was behaving at the time the profile was created.

If a device isn't stable—if its behavior changes over time—then simply profiling it, as Bruce likes to point out, is like trying to measure a moving target with a rubber ruler. The point is not that it's impossible; it's just much harder than measuring a stationary target with a rigid ruler. Ideally, process control is accomplished through calibration alone. It's easier to calibrate an unstable device to make sure that it's behaving the way the profile says it is. In some cases, though, we simply have to accept a certain amount of instability. In those cases, process control will require either more frequent profiling or basing the profile on a device's average behavior.

Stimulus and Response

Calibration and profiling are often confused because the steps involved seem very similar on the surface. Both processes involve sending a *target* of known color signals—the *stimulus*—to a device, measuring the color that results—the *response*—and then feeding the results into some software. With some kinds of devices, such as monitors, calibration and profiling are performed at the same time by the same pieces of software or hardware.

But calibration and profiling are separate processes with different goals. When you profile, you simply record the response and encode it in a profile. When you calibrate, you use the stimulus and response to actually change the device's response. For example, when you set a monitor's white point, the calibration software sends a stimulus—RGB 255, 255, 255—to the monitor, examines the response that's detected by the measuring instrument, and keeps adjusting either the monitor guns or the lookup table in the video card until the response matches the white point that you requested.

Some devices simply can't be calibrated because they don't have anything you can adjust. Desktop scanners, for example, generally have no user-accessible calibration features. The same holds true for non-PostScript inkjet printers. In these cases, you just have to keep track of the device's behavior and reprofile if it drifts too far (which is relatively rare).

In all cases, though, you need to control all the variables that can make the device produce a different response to stimuli than the one the profile predicts. We'll look in detail at the kinds of things that introduce variability for different device types in the following chapters that deal with building profiles, but here's a quick rundown.

Controlling Variables

Some sources of variability are inherent in the devices themselves, and we have to account for those either with calibration or by reprofiling, but others are controllable with nothing more than a little common sense. Here are a few sources of variability that may or may not be obvious but that nonetheless need to be kept under control.

Software settings. Input, display, and output devices are all subject to having their behavior controlled by software. For example, scanners often have autoexposure routines, and some printers have automatic color-correction routines that do different things depending on image content. These features defeat color management before it starts because they make the device respond inconsistently—they'll typically try to increase the contrast on a flat image, for example. The color management breaks because it expects the device to always produce the same response to a given stimulus, so you need to turn these features off. Figure 5-1 shows the kinds of things that happen when you fail to do so.

Slightly less obviously, different resolution settings may change the color rendition—more so on display and output devices than on scanners and digital cameras. So you need to keep your resolution settings consistent or build profiles for each setting.

Often, something as seemingly innocuous as a software update may change the device's behavior. So you need to be vigilant, make sure that you keep all your software settings consistent and update only when necessary.

Media and consumables. Probably the biggest variables that affect output devices are the inks, toners, dyes, or waxes that form the color, and the paper or other substrate on which they're laid down.

The same inks can produce radically different colors when you change paper stocks, for example. So, if you switch to a different brand of ink (or toner, etc.) or paper, you'll almost certainly need to reprofile the device. We could write a 2,000-word article on this topic alone, but it wouldn't change the reality: even if you buy paper or inks consistently from the same supplier, watch out for manufacturing variations, or unannounced manufacturing changes. If your device behavior suddenly seems to change immediately after you've loaded new consumables, the new consumables are probably the culprit.

A related issue is that many inkjet printers use media settings to control ink limits and black generation. We always make a point of double-checking these settings before pressing the Print button, because if they're wrong they have a dramatic impact on the appearance of the print, and more often than we'd like, media settings in the printer driver that appear to be sticky, aren't. Figure 5-2 shows how the wrong media settings can ruin a print.

Figure 5-1   The effect of autoexposure routines

The image at right shows the results of applying a profile, created with autoexposure turned off while scanning the profiling target, to a scan also made with autoexposure turned off. It produces an image with clean neutrals and good saturation.

The image at left results from neglecting to turn off autoexposure while scanning the profiling target, producing a rather useless profile that imposes poor gray balance and noticeably reduced saturation.

Autoexposure off while profiling and scanning

Autoexposure on while profiling, off while scanning

The image at right is the result of failing to defeat autoexposure while scanning both the profiling target and the image. In this case it produced a heavy blue-purple color cast. On another image, the results would be different, but almost certainly just as bad because autoexposure randomizes the scanner's response.

Autoexposure on while profiling and scanning

Figure 5-2   The importance of correct media settings

Matte media settings on matte paper

Glossy media settings on matte paper

Matte media settings on glossy paper

Hardware settings. If the device in question has knobs, sliders, or switches, they need to be set correctly. In particular, the brightness and contrast controls on CRT monitors have a radical effect on the tone and color the monitor produces. Once they're set correctly, make sure that they stay set that way by taping them down or using the monitor's setup features.

Controlling Variability

Even if you control all the aforementioned variables, at least some of your devices will still exhibit some kind of variability. CRT monitors drift over time, color laser printers react to changes in temperature and humidity, inkjet printers almost invariably need some drying time for the ink to reach its final color, and printing presses are subject to so many mechanical, chemical, and physical variables that a slew of books have been written on controlling them. For color management to work, you need to account for the inherent variability in your devices. There are three ways to do this:

▶ Calibrate the device, changing its behavior back to the state in which it was profiled.

▶ Make a new profile that describes its new state.

▶ Collect data that describes the range of variability you deem acceptable, average that data, and build a profile from the average.

Typically, you need to use a combination of all three methods. But to control variability, you need to know that it's happening. You could just wait until you see that something's wrong, but a much more reliable method is to use measurements to track the variation.

The Multiple Roles of Measurement

Measurement plays a key role in both calibration and profiling. If you're serious about building your own profiles, you need some kind of measuring instrument. We'll discuss the different types of instruments in Chapter 6, *Building Display Profiles*, and Chapter 8, *Building Output Profiles*, but for now, we'll point out the many useful things measuring capability brings outside of the profiling process.

You need to make measurements to build display and output profiles. (The only reason you don't need to make measurements to build input profiles is that the target you use to do so has already been measured for you.) But measurement plays other, equally important roles.

We use measuring instruments to calibrate our various devices, or at least those that *can* be calibrated, but how do we know how often we need to calibrate a particular device? Measurement provides the answer. How about those devices that can't be calibrated? Keeping a log of measurements lets you decide when the device has changed sufficiently to require reprofiling.

We don't mean to suggest that you go hog-wild and measure everything in sight every 10 minutes, but investing a modest amount of time making some carefully planned measurements both before and after profiling will save you time, frustration, and premature hair loss.

Evaluating Devices

The first role of measurement is to *evaluate* the device—to find out just what kind of a beast we're dealing with. If it's a monitor, can it still reach a high enough brightness level while maintaining a decent black? If it's an output device, does it produce clean neutrals and reasonably even tonal gradations while achieving the best color gamut of which it's capable?

Measurement can help you answer all these questions. When the answers aren't to your liking, measurement can play other roles:

▶ You can use measurements to calibrate the device to a better-behaved state.

▶ You can use measurements to arrive at better driver settings.

▶ You can use measurements to decide that the device in question simply isn't a candidate for color management.

We'll go into much more detail on the kinds of issues that affect different types of devices in the next three chapters. For now, we just want to give you the Big Picture.

Calibrating Devices

As we said earlier, calibration means adjusting a device's behavior so that it produces a specific, known response to stimuli—in plain English, it always produces the same color in response to a given set of numbers. But we don't just calibrate our devices to any old state. In fact, there are three possible goals for calibration, which we list here in order of importance for color management.

▶ **Stability**. Profiling is much more likely to be successful when the device we're profiling is stable, so that the same stimulus will always provoke the same response—the same set of RGB or CMYK numbers will always make the device produce the same color.

When the device's response drifts over time, the profile becomes progressively less accurate and the colors get further and further away from the desired ones. To keep the color right, you must calibrate the device often enough to bring its response back to the desired aim point. If the device has no user-accessible calibration features, you need to track the changes so that you know when it's time to reprofile (see "Monitoring Devices," later in this chapter).

▶ **Optimization (linearization)**. Once we've made the device stable, a second objective is to make the device perform optimally, so that we're using as much of the device's dynamic range and color gamut as possible, while still delivering smooth and predictable tonal gradations (see Figure 5-3).

Figure 5-3
Before and after
linearization

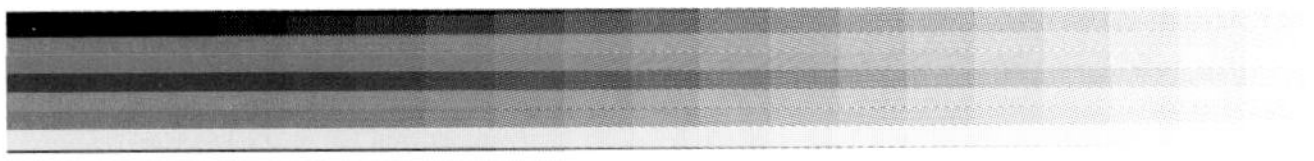

21-step ramps before linearization

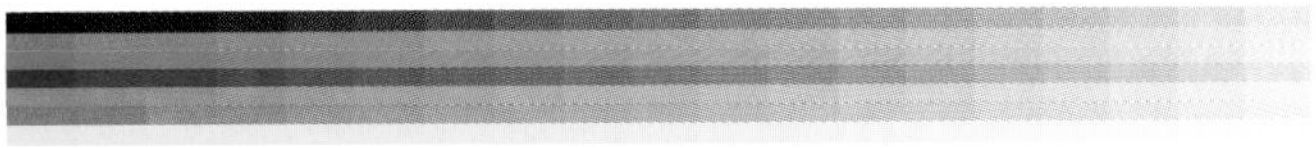

21-step ramps after linearization

▶ **Simulation**. If we've managed to make the device both stable and optimal, we may want to take the extra step of simulating another device. For example, we may adjust the white luminance of a monitor to match the brightness of white paper in a light box, or adjust the ink curves of a proofer to simulate a certain press. As long as we can do this without compromising the device's behavior, it can make less work for the color management system.

These three goals sometimes compete. We might be able to tweak a press to produce denser blacks by increasing ink densities, but doing so may make it less stable. In this case we'd almost certainly choose stability over dynamic range.

Once you've got the device behaving the way you want it to, it's time to profile it, which again uses measurement. But the role of measurement doesn't end when you build the profile. Most devices are subject to some kind of variation over time, and if you don't account for that variation your profile will become progressively less accurate. So the last role of measurement is to track your device's behavior over time and make sure that it's still behaving the way the profile says it does.

Monitoring Devices

The simplest way to check for device drift is to wait until you notice that the color is wrong. Unfortunately, it's also the most expensive way, particularly if you notice that the color is wrong on a press run costing tens or hundreds of thousands of dollars. It's also inefficient: most color outcomes involve at least two, and sometimes more than two profiles. If you wait until something has gone wrong, all that you know is that something has gone wrong—you don't know which of the possible suspects is really the culprit.

A few well-planned measurements, on the other hand, can tell you when a device is drifting too far and when it's time to recalibrate or reprofile. Measurement can help you determine the drying time your inks need on your inkjet paper, or how often you need to recalibrate your color laser printer, and can alert you to unannounced manufacturing changes in consumables, saving you a ton of time and frustration. This is what good process control is all about.

Working Outside the System

The big lesson you need to take away from this chapter is that color management is the map, not the territory, and all too often the territory is shifting sand. No matter how good your profiles are, they only reflect what your devices were doing when you captured the input target, printed the output target, or measured the color swatches on your display. Unless you take positive steps to make sure that your various devices keep behaving the way the profiles say they do, your best efforts will be doomed to failure and frustration.

If, on the other hand, you spend a modest amount of time before profiling to make sure that the device is behaving properly, and after profiling to make sure that it keeps behaving that way, you'll create the necessary conditions for the color management system to do its job—namely, helping you produce great color with no surprises. In the next three chapters, we'll look in detail at all the things you need to do before, during, and after building profiles for your display, input, and output devices.

Building Display Profiles

Your Window to Color

Who said "the eyes are the windows to the soul"? Well, Guillaume de Salluste Du Bartas, the 16th century French poet and diplomat, did pen the line, "These lovely lamps, these windows of the soul," and Shakespeare's Richard III did say, "Ere I let fall the windows of mine eyes." But the line everyone remembers seems to stem from the 1955 movie, "The Ladykillers," where Alec Guiness' Professor Marcus asks, "And didn't someone say, 'The eyes are the windows of the soul'?" and Katie Johnson's Mrs. Wilberforce replies, "I don't really know. But, oh, it's such a charming thought, I do hope someone expressed it." Of course, since then many people have.

Whether or not you happen to be one of them, one thing is certain: your monitor is the window to the world of digital color. Monitor profiles—or more accurately, *display profiles*—are key to the big payoff of color management: the instantaneous preview of all your color-managed materials. We can't stress enough the importance of good monitor calibration and profiling to a well-oiled color management system. You *may* be able to get by with vendor-supplied profiles for input and output devices, but effective color management really demands a custom profile for each display.

As with any other type of profiling, building display profiles is a process of comparing known values with measured ones—in this case, the profiling software displays a series of color patches with known RGB values, and compares them with measurements from a colorimeter or spectrophotometer. And as with any other type of profiling, you want to get the device behaving properly before you profile it. The difference between monitor profiling and other types is that monitor profiling packages actually help you get the device behaving well before you profile it, because they combine the functions of calibration and profiling.

This occasionally gives rise to some confusion—see the sidebar, "Muddying the Waters," later in this chapter—but generally speaking, it's easier to calibrate and profile displays than it is to calibrate and profile just about any other type of device.

Note that we say calibrating and profiling *displays*, not monitors. You're really calibrating and profiling the combination of the video driver, the video card, and the actual monitor—in short, the whole display system. So it's very helpful to understand just how monitor calibration is achieved. Profiling the calibrated result is really the trivial part of the exercise.

Display Calibration

When you calibrate a display, you (or your calibration software) adjust three, or sometimes four, things:

▶ The luminance of monitor white, expressed either in foot-lamberts or in candelas per meter squared (cd/m^2).

▶ The color of monitor white, usually expressed in Kelvins.

▶ The tone response curve of the display system, expressed as a gamma value.

▶ Optionally, the luminance of monitor black, expressed either in foot-lamberts or in candelas per meter squared (cd/m^2).

Where you make these adjustments depends on the capabilities of your monitor.

What to Adjust

There are two ways to change the behavior of a display. You can adjust the controls on the monitor itself, or you can adjust the signals that get sent to the monitor by tweaking the values in the video card's lookup table, or videoLUT. It's always preferable to make the adjustments to the monitor itself, because when you tweak the videoLUT, it's essentially the same as editing an 8-bit channel—you start out with 256 levels, but you end up with a smaller number.

However, the only way to adjust the display gamma is in the videoLUT, so you'll always be doing some tweaking there—the goal is to keep the videoLUT tweaks to a minimum. The degree to which you can do so is dictated by the controls your monitor offers, and, to some extent, the controls offered depend on the type of monitor you're using.

▶ The workhorse of computer displays is still the CRT (cathode ray tube). A cathode ray is a stream of electrons that are fired from one end of an enclosed glass tube to the other. The electrons originate from *electron guns* that spray a beam of electrons onto the inside face of the tube, which is coated with *phosphors*—chemical compounds that kick off photons (light) of specific wavelengths when they're struck by electrons. Color monitors use three phosphors in the mixture coating the inside of the CRT—the red phosphor, the green phosphor and (you guessed it) the blue phosphor. The voltages sent from the video card control the bursts of electrons from the electron gun, and hence the amount of light emitted by the phosphors.

▶ The new kid on the block, and gaining fast in the world of computer displays, is the LCD (liquid crystal display). The liquid crystals that give this type of monitor its name have the peculiar property of changing shape in response to electrical currents. When sandwiched between layers of polarized glass or plexiglass, they act as filters that modulate the *backlight,* a fluorescent light behind a diffuser that produces all the light the display emits.

CRT monitor controls. Every CRT we've ever seen has controls for contrast and brightness (which really control white luminance and black luminance, respectively). Most offer some degree of control over the color of white, either as a series of presets, as a continuously variable control, or as separate gain controls for the red, green, and blue channels. A few high-end monitors also offer red, green, and blue bias controls, which set the black level for each channel.

LCD monitor controls. Because of the way they work, the only real control possible on LCD monitors is the brightness control, which controls the brightness of the backlight. Some LCDs, particularly those with analog rather than digital interfaces, supply software controls that mimic those found in CRTs, but they're just tweaking the videoLUT, not adjusting the behavior of the monitor itself.

The upshot of all this is that with a CRT monitor, you may be able to adjust the white luminance, black luminance, and color temperature in the monitor itself, while with an LCD monitor, the only thing you can really adjust in the monitor is the white luminance. This has some implications for your choice of calibration aim points. See "Choosing Calibration Settings," later in this chapter.

Calibration and Profiling Tools

There are essentially four different types of calibration/profiling packages.

▶ Packages that are bundled with a monitor

▶ Standalone instrument-and-software bundles

▶ Standalone software packages that support different instruments

▶ Visual calibrators

Let's deal with the last first. If you're at all serious about color management, we don't recommend visual monitor calibration. The very same adaptability that makes our eyes incredibly useful organs for living on Planet Earth makes them pretty useless as calibration devices—the goal of calibration is to return the device to a known, predictable state, and while our eyeballs are very good at making comparisons, they're lousy at determining absolutes. If your viewing environment is completely stable—essentially, a windowless cave—you *may* be able to get by with a

Muddying the Waters

We've mentioned several times in this book the rule that profiles merely describe—a single profile doesn't change anything. But for every rule, there's an exception, and the exception to this particular rule is most display profiles. Display profiling blurs the distinction between calibration and profiling in two ways:

▶ The instrument and software packages we use to calibrate and profile monitors usually perform both tasks as a single operation.

▶ Many monitor profiles contain calibration information that actually changes the behavior of the display.

Fred remembers his jaw dropping in shocked dismay the first time he selected a new monitor profile in a beta version of what was then called the Monitors & Sound Control Panel and saw his monitor flash to a new white point.

This shredded the simple rule that a profile merely *described* device behavior but didn't *change* device behavior. The culprit, if you wish to call it that, is the "vcgt" tag found in many monitor profiles, which stores the calibration data that gets downloaded to the videoLUT—the gamma and, possibly, white point corrections.

When you load a display profile that has a vcgt tag, it downloads the contents of this tag to the videoLUT, and hence changes the behavior of the display. We confess that we have mixed feelings about this, and we could hash out all the arguments, pro and con, but the bottom line is that it's a done deal—monitor profiles can, and often do, change the behavior of the display system.

There are still a few monitor profiling packages that don't write a vcgt tag into the profile. Instead, they use a startup application, which downloads the calibration data to the videoLUT. The major downside to this approach is that if you choose a display profile written by one of these packages *after* startup, the matching calibration data probably won't get downloaded to the videoLUT, with the unhappy result that the display won't behave the way the profile thinks it does.

We suspect that this approach's days are numbered for that very reason. But if you do use such a package, be careful.

visual calibrator, but in our opinion, you'd be penny-wise and pound-foolish to do so. But if you must, see the sidebar, "Visual Calibration," later in this chapter.

Monitor/Calibrator bundles. Monitors that come with a bundled calibrator are, thus far, invariably CRTs. These are "smart" packages in the sense that the communication between monitor and host is two-way, allowing the calibration software to adjust the monitor's internal controls in response to feedback from the measuring instrument. Early models used a serial cable to communicate with the host CPU, but the current ones all use USB. (This means that they occupy two USB ports, one for communication between monitor and host, the other for the measuring instrument.)

Figure 6-2

Monitor calibrators

 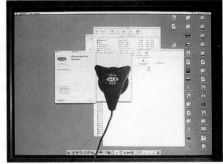

Warning: If you're calibrating an LCD monitor, make sure that you use an instrument expressly designed for LCDs. The suction cups used to attach calibration instruments to CRTs will rip the coating right off the front of an LCD monitor, rendering it useless. (Dead LCD monitors aren't heavy enough to make good doorstops.)

Some instruments are more influenced by ambient light than others. A monitor hood can help shield the face of the monitor from ambient light, so that less of it is reflected into the instrument. With CRT monitors, we generally recommend working in a fairly low ambient light anyway, so if you find that ambient light is making your instrument produce inconsistent results, you may want to consider paying some attention to your viewing environment. See "Viewing Environment" in Chapter 9, *Evaluating and Editing Profiles*.

Choosing Calibration Settings

To a great extent, the whole notion of monitor calibration standards stems from the days before the display was taken out of the color management chain, and represented an attempt to make all monitors behave identically by calibrating them to the same white point and gamma. Of course, this never worked, and has been supplanted by the current approach of color-managing the data that gets sent to the video card, using the profile that represents the behavior of the specific display in question.

So from the narrow color-management point of view, it doesn't really matter what calibration settings you choose—all that matters is that your display profile represents the behavior of your display as accurately as possible.

However, other considerations come into play. For example, if some of your work lies outside the color-management realm, you may want to calibrate your monitor to a recognized standard. And even if all your work *is* color-managed, your display will behave better at some settings than others. The one thing you always want to avoid is making major corrections in the videoLUT, because doing so reduces the number of discrete levels your display can reproduce—the bigger the correction, the fewer levels.

Adjustments that you can make to the monitor itself, on the other hand, are "free"—there's no loss—so a major consideration in choosing calibration settings is the means available to you to achieve them. All calibrators ask you for two target values:

▶ white point

▶ gamma.

The three of us, by separate paths, have come to the same recommended calibration settings: calibrate your monitor to a white point of 6500 K and a gamma of 2.2. You can just take our word for it, and skip the rest of this section. But we think it's useful to understand *why* we like white point-6500 K, and gamma-2.2.

Target White Point

The white point of the monitor plays an important role for your eye. As described in Chapter 1, your eye judges all colors relative to some neutral baseline that it considers white. The three of us unanimously recommend that you calibrate your monitor to 6500 K even though many people think of 5000 K as the standard viewing white point in graphic arts. Here's why.

The eye has a tremendous ability to adapt to different white-point environments. However, the eye works best when it's operating in a white point closest to that environment most familiar to it through millions of years of evolution—namely daylight. So the discussion quickly reduces to which of the two most commonly used daylight standards, D50 (5000 K correlated color temperature) or D65 (6500 K correlated color temperature), is best. (See Chapter 1 if you are unfamiliar with these white point terms.) If you have a D50 viewing booth, this might seem to tip the scales toward setting your monitor to 5000 K so that your monitor and print-viewing environment have identical white points. But long experience has told us that this doesn't work the way the theory would seem to predict—see "Monitor-to-print comparisons," in Chapter 9, *Evaluating and Editing Profiles.*

A second factor is that many uncalibrated CRTs, especially older models, are pretty darned blue, with a color temperature closer to 9300 K, though the better current CRTs have a native white point closer to 6500 K. In either case, to move the white point to 5000 K, we have to limit the output of the display's blue channel, lowering the overall brightness and dynamic range. This is why many people (including us) often find a 5000 K monitor to be a bit too dim, dingy, and … well … too darned yellow.

So instead, it's worth remembering the sentence that started off this explanation. The eye has a tremendous ability to adapt to different white-point environments. The eye takes a little bit of time to adjust to a change in brightness, but it has little trouble looking at a color image in a 6500 K monitor and then moving to view the same image printed out and mounted in a viewing booth. It's the relationships *within* the image or page that you're evaluating. As long as you give the eye a good adaptation environment, and both environments are of approximately equivalent brightness, then you should have no problems.

If your software has more than just two choices for white point, you have another option—you can perform iterative calibrations to find the white point setting that best approximates a sheet of paper in your viewing booth. Some people in extremely color critical environments, with control over all of their equipment, including the paper being used, have found this to be useful. We, however, prefer to deal with the color of paper white in the printer profile, and concentrate on matching the brightness of the monitor and the viewing booth.

Target Gamma

The recommended setting for gamma depends somewhat on how much work you do outside the color-managed environment. Without color management, the general practice has been to choose a gamma that best simulated the mid-tone characteristics of the target medium—in

English, if you're going to print, you want your monitor to have similar tone reproduction characteristics to your printer.

This, supposedly, is why Macintosh displays have traditionally been assumed to have a gamma of 1.8—the default table in Macintosh video cards is set to produce an approximate display gamma of 1.8, and calibration instructions have long touted 1.8 as the "standard Macintosh gamma" when calibrating your monitor. Why 1.8? A monitor gamma of 1.8 roughly approximated the dot-gain curve of the Apple LaserWriter. This served as a poor-man's color management (actually a grayscale management, as this was well before the days of color management, since the displays being used at the time were monochrome). If an image looked good on a monitor calibrated to gamma 1.8, then it would look reasonable when printed without much adjustment.

But with color management, simulation is now the job of the color management system, and specifically, of the printer profile. So instead, we recommend that you calibrate your monitor to a gamma of 2.2, for the simple reason that, in all our testing, we've found that calibrating to around gamma 2.2 produces the smoothest display of gradients, with little or no visible banding or posterization.

If you're picky, like us, you may want to go further, and use the techniques described in "Checking the Display," in Chapter 9, *Evaluating and Editing Profiles*, to find the ideal gamma for your particular display. On the other hand, if you've been happily calibrating your monitor to D50, to gamma 1.8, or to both, don't feel you have to change it just because we say so—as long as you have an accurate monitor profile, the differences between the various calibration aim points are pretty darned subtle.

How Often Should I Calibrate?

With CRT monitors, we recommend calibrating weekly. At minimum, you should calibrate monthly—some of the high-end systems like the Barco Calibrator V and the Sony Artisan are pretty insistent that you recalibrate after 30 days. We know people who calibrate their monitors every day, which seems excessive, but harmless.

With LCD monitors, the jury is still out. The dyes in LCD cells wear at a much slower rate than the phosphors in CRTs—it's unlikely to be an issue in a human lifespan. The backlight, however, will decay slowly over time. We calibrate our LCDs weekly to be on the safe side, but you can probably get by with less-frequent calibration than with CRTs.

Before Calibration

The first thing to do before calibrating your monitor is to make sure that it's worth calibrating. On a CRT, turn the contrast control all the way up, on an LCD, turn the brightness control all the way up. If the result is something other than a display that's *at least* a hair brighter than you'd like, the monitor is probably a candidate for replacement rather than calibration—calibrators work by turning things *down*, so if the display, running wide open, isn't as bright as you'd like, it'll be even worse after calibration.

Warm-Up Time

Before calibrating a CRT, make sure it's been on and in use for at least 30 minutes, and preferably for an hour so that it's reached its stable operating temperature. If you have any energy-saving software that turns the monitor off when not being used, make sure this doesn't kick in during the warm-up period. (If you use this as your excuse for a little Web surfing every morning, we won't tell anyone.) Regular screensavers (those floatie fishies or flying toasters) are fine, as are the simpler ones that just display a black screen, as long as they don't actually turn the monitor off.

LCD monitors need little, if any, warmup time—the backlight reaches its operating temperature in about the time it takes to boot your computer.

Resolution, Refresh, and Other Monitor Settings

Make sure that all the other monitor settings are finalized before you calibrate. Just changing the resolution from say 1280×1024 to 1152×864, or changing the refresh rate from 85 to 75 Hz, can affect the overall brightness output of the monitor. So can changing the geometry settings on the display—reducing the size of the displayed image on the monitor targets the electron guns on a smaller area of phosphors, which slightly increases the brightness of the image.

Tip: Extend the Life of Old Monitors. If you followed the instructions on evaluating your monitor and didn't achieve satisfactory brightness, it may be time for a new monitor. However, to try and squeeze some extra brightness back into the monitor, you can:

▶ use the geometry controls on the front panel of the monitor to reduce the horizontal and vertical size of the displayed image

▶ reduce the refresh frequency from, say, 85 Hz to 75 Hz

▶ reduce the resolution from, say, 1280×1024 to 1152×864 or even 800×600.

The refresh frequency and resolution settings can be found in the Display Settings or Control Panel on your system, but be careful that you select a combination that supports true 24-bit color (millions of colors).

It's OK to change these settings, but you must do so *before* you calibrate, and if you commonly change any of these parameters, you need to recalibrate for each change. Also, it should go without saying—but we'll say it anyway—that you should have your monitor set to display true 24-bit color (millions of colors).

Cleaning the Screen

It's important to make sure your screen is free of dust and fingerprints before calibration, because they can introduce inaccuracies into the readings. In the case of CRT monitors, they can also cause the sensor to fall off halfway through the calibration process, which can be a major frustration and a hazard for your keyboard and measuring instrument.

Use a weak solution of mild detergent or a cleaning product specifically formulated for monitors. *Don't* use regular glass cleaners that contain ammonia or other harsh solvents—most high-end CRTs have antiglare coatings that can easily be wrecked by household glass cleaners, and the coatings on LCDs are even more fragile.

Precalibration—Setting the Analog Controls

In addition to specifying the color temperature and gamma of the display, calibrators ask you to set the dynamic range by choosing white and black luminance. In some packages, this step—setting the analog controls on the monitor—is handled as part of the calibration process. Others, such as Colorvision's OptiCAL and PhotoCAL, use a separate application, PreCAL, to step you through optimizing the monitor's contrast, brightness, and color temperature settings. Smart monitors with bundled calibrators, such as the Barco Calibrator V, the LaCie Electron/BlueEye, and the Sony Artisan Color Reference System, handle this task automatically, and usually more accurately.

Setting White Luminance

Some packages allow you to specify a value for white luminance—how bright you want the monitor to be. Others simply adjust the monitor to an internal (and sometimes undocumented) preset value. With CRT monitors, when given a choice, we opt for a value somewhere between 85 and 95 cd/m², or 24 and 28 foot-lamberts.

Most of today's CRTs can reach a higher luminance—sometimes much higher—for a while. It's always tempting to crank up the white luminance to get the maximum possible contrast ratio, but when you do so, you're shortening the useful life of the monitor. If you follow our recommendations, a decent CRT should be able to achieve the specified luminance for at least three years, often for longer.

With LCD monitors, we simply go for the maximum luminance the calibrator will allow: we usually look for an automatic setting.

Unless we're using a calibrator that adjusts the monitor automatically, we start out by turning the contrast all the way up and the brightness all the way down—most calibrators tell you explicitly to do so, anyway. The non-automatic varieties generally provide some kind of display that indicates the target luminance and the current measured luminance. You then adjust the contrast control (on CRTs) or the brightness control (on LCDs) to make the two match. Figure 6-3 shows some typical examples.

Setting Black Level

Setting the black level is quite a bit trickier than setting the white. If you set it too low, you'll clip some shadow levels, and if you set it too high, your blacks will be washed out. To further complicate matters, most of the instruments we use to calibrate monitors have diminishing accuracy as the sample gets darker, and the light output of CRT monitors gets progressively less stable the closer it gets to black.

This is where systems that adjust the monitor's controls automatically have a huge advantage. They take hundreds of measurements and average them. Calibrators that step you through these same adjustments manually also take many measurements of black, but the problem then becomes how to present these measurements to the user in a useful form.

Figure 6-3

Setting white luminance

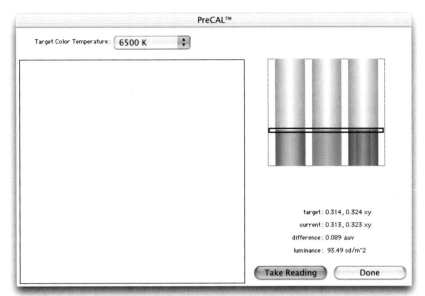

ColorVision's PreCAL lets you take a measurement and reports the measured luminance. You adjust the contrast control and repeat the process until you achieve the desired luminance.

GretagMacbeth's EyeOne Match, above, measures continuously. You adjust the contrast control until the white indicator lines up with the black one.

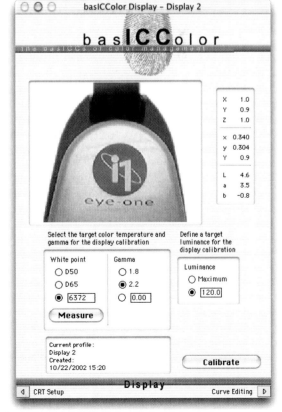

Integrated Color Solutions' basICColor Display, when used with LCD monitors, simply lets you define a target luminance.

On CRTs (and on a very few LCDs), you adjust the black level using the brightness control (which is really what the techies call an *offset*). Most LCDs don't offer a black-level control, so you simply have to accept what the calibrator gives you. We've seen many cases where the indicator of the current measured black level jumps around, making it quite hard to determine when you've arrived at an optimal setting. In this situation, the key is patience. Don't expect the indicator to magically stop moving around—it won't. Instead, just keep making *small* adjustments to the black level. Gradually, the results will converge on the target point.

Some calibrators let you set the black level visually, instead—they usually show a dark gray patch against a black one. With this approach, it's very easy to set the black level too low, which results in clipping potentially useful shadow values. The goal is to set the black level a hair (since you're working visually, more technical definitions don't apply) higher than no signal at all. Figure 6-4 shows some different approaches to setting the black level.

Setting the black level is by far the most difficult part of monitor calibration. It's worth learning the quirks of your chosen calibration system and working with them to get the most consistent results possible. See "Black-point check" in Chapter 9, *Evaluating and Editing Profiles*, for some techniques that can help you refine the black-point setting.

Setting the Color Temperature

In CRT monitors, the color temperature is adjusted by changing the individual gains on the red, green, and blue guns. With LCDs, it can only be accomplished by filtering the backlight, so we generally leave LCDs at their native white point, which is usually close to 6500 K anyway.

But the level of control that CRTs offer varies from model to model. Typically, CRTs offer one (or more) of the following:

▶ Several preset color temperature settings (typically 5,000 K, 6500 K, and 9300 K, though some offer additional presets)

▶ Continuously-variable color temperature

▶ Gain controls for two of the three guns

▶ Gain controls for all three guns.

Figure 6-4

Setting black level

ColorVision's OptiCAL, above, uses a visual target to help you set the black level.

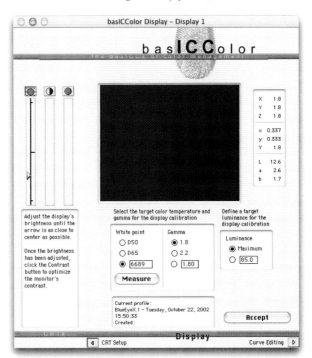

GretagMacbeth's EyeOne Match, above, and Integrated Color Solutions' BasICColor Display, right, both measure black continuously and provide feedback via a slider. When it lines up with the target, you've set the black level correctly.

So how you get to the desired color temperature depends on the monitor controls. Again, with automatic systems, the software takes care of the necessary adjustments automatically. Many of the manual calibrators tell you to skip this adjustment if your monitor doesn't have individual R, G, and B gains, but we find it useful on all CRTs (see Figure 6-5).

CRTs with presets. We always start out with the preset closest to our desired color temperature, but the presets are often off by a considerable amount, almost invariably giving a lower color temperature than the preset value. In that case, we may try going to the next-higher preset. For example, if the 6500 K preset measures as 6100 K, and the monitor offers a 7500 K preset, we'll use that instead. Once we've determined the best preset to use, we'll skip this step in future calibrations.

CRTs with continuously-variable color temperature. Again, the color-temperature labels on the color-temperature control are often significantly off from the real, measured color temperature. We adjust the color temperature to get as close as possible to the desired result.

CRTs with gain controls. We find that it doesn't make a whole lot of difference whether the monitor offers control over two or three of the channels—we rarely adjust more than two, anyway. Most calibrators show you where the guns are now, and where they need to be. Make the adjustments until you get as close as possible. (How close this is varies considerably with different monitors, different instruments, and different software—after you've gone through the process a few times you'll develop a sense of how far you can go before you reach the point of diminishing returns.)

Calibration and Profiling

At this point, you've done all the difficult stuff—setting the analog controls is really the only part of calibrating and profiling the monitor that requires user intervention. The software displays patches on the screen, looks at the measurements from the instruments, and makes the necessary tweaks to the videoLUT. Then it displays some more patches,

Figure 6-5

Setting white point

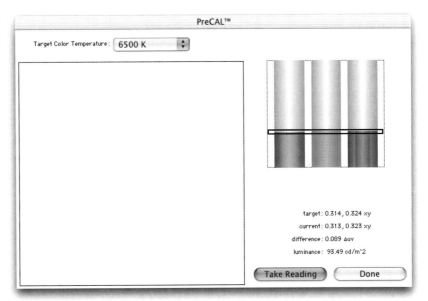

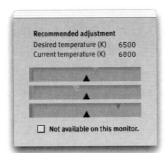

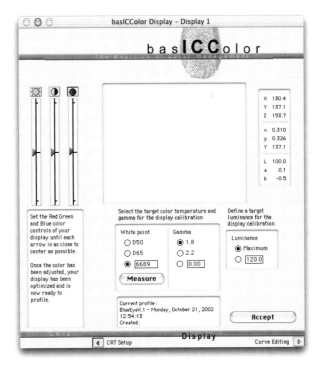

Clockwise from top: ColorVision's PreCAL, Integrated Color Solutions' basICColor Display and GretagMacbeth's EyeOne match all provide a graphic display of the current RGB levels and how they need to be adjusted to achieve the requested white point.

looks at the measurements, and builds a profile. There are, however, a few things that can go wrong.

Make sure that some screensaver software doesn't kick in during calibration. Any good calibration software should detect when this happens, and, in fact, most have code that prevents it. Nevertheless, if your floatie fishies appear during calibration, you may have to adjust the screensaver's settings, or disable it altogether. And of course, you'll have to restart the calibration process.

It's possible to throw off a calibration by allowing your mouse pointer to move across the measurement area during a measurement. Most calibrator programs nowadays are able to hide the pointer if it enters the measurement area, or at the least can detect when this happens and beep angrily at you, but there are still exceptions. It's just good advice to keep the pointer safely off to the side and don't touch anything during calibration.

If you use the calibration process as an opportunity to take whatever kind of break you need, check that the calibrator is still attached to the monitor when you come back. The industrial design of instruments intended to attach to the monitor has greatly improved since the early days, but it's still by no means unheard-of for the instrument to fall off before the calibration is done. In that case, you need to start over.

Saving the Monitor Profile

Regardless of what type of calibrator you are using, the last thing it does seems like such a tiny afterthought, but is the key to getting this laboriously calibrated monitor into your color management system—saving and naming the monitor profile.

Some people create a new profile each time by including the date in the filename. We think this is silly—the condition that the old monitor profile described no longer exists since you've recalibrated the monitor. We recommend that you just overwrite the previous profile—the old ones are useless and just clutter your system.

Most profilers automatically save the profile in the correct location and load it as the profile that describes the monitor, even in dual-monitor systems. Unless you *really* know what you're doing, let the software save the profile in its preferred location, which varies on

Visual Calibration

We're tempted to say that visual calibration is an oxymoron—calibration means bringing a device back to a known state, and the adaptive nature of our eyes makes it just about certain that you won't be able to hit the same aim point twice by visual methods alone. We don't recommend visual calibration, but if you must, here are some pointers that you may find helpful.

▶ All the directions about warmup time and resolution settings apply to visual calibration just as they do to instrumented calibration.

▶ The viewing environment is much more critical for visual calibration than for instrumented calibration. The ideal is a darkened room, but if that's impractical, at least try to make sure that you always calibrate under the same lighting conditions—if the ambient light is dramatically different from one calibration to the next, the results almost certainly will be, too.

▶ All visual calibrators start out with an existing profile. Try to choose one that bears some general resemblance to the monitor you're calibrating. Ideally, you should start out with a profile that describes a monitor that uses the same phosphors as yours. Failing that, if your monitor is an aperture-grille type (a Trinitron or Diamondtron), choose a profile that describes that type of monitor, and if it's a shadow-mask monitor, use a shadow-mask profile. Sony and Mitsubishi are the leading providers of the former type; Hitachi is the leading provider of the latter.

▶ If the calibration tool offers a choice between a single gamma and individual gammas for red, green, and blue, choose the latter.

▶ Gamma adjustments are almost always carried out by having you move a slider until a solid color matches a dither pattern. It's easy to do this with red and green, but it's just about impossible to do with blue. So when you adjust the blue gamma, don't look at the target—look at your neutral gray desktop instead (of course, your desktop pattern *is* a neutral gray rather than pink marble or your favorite picture of your cat). It's very easy to see what's happening to the neutrals—aim for the blue setting that gives you a neutral gray.

▶ Visual calibrators are designed with CRTs in mind. If you attempt to use them with LCD monitors, all bets are off!

different operating systems. On Mac OS 9, save the profile in the ColorSync Profiles folder in the System Folder (some calibrators save the profile in the Displays folder inside the ColorSync folder—either way is fine).

On Mac OS X, the situation is a little trickier. Some calibrators save the profile in the /Library/ColorSync/Profiles/Displays folder if you're logged in as an Admin user, thereby making the profile available to all users. Others save it in the ~/Library/ColorSync/Profiles/Displays folder—that's your "Home" Library, which is unavailable to other users. Eventually, we hope Apple will make up its mind whether monitor profiles should go with the user or with the monitor, but meanwhile we advise leaving the profile wherever the calibrator saves it.

On Windows 98, save the monitor profile in Windows/System/Color. On Windows XP, Windows 2000, and Windows ME, save the monitor profile in WinNT/System/Spool/Drivers/Color. On Windows NT, save the profile in WinNT/System32/Color.

Piece of Cake

Monitor calibration and profiling is really very straightforward, which is just as well, because it's the lynchpin of a color managed workflow. Most people say they want to trust their monitor, and calibration and profiling is the first step in attaining that goal. Often, though, it's an iterative process. See "Checking the Display," in Chapter 9, *Evaluating and Editing Profiles*, for techniques to help you evaluate and improve your display calibration and profiling.

Building Input Profiles

Starting Out Right

To get the color you want, you first have to know what that color is. Telling the CMS what that color is, is the fundamental role that input profiles play. We must stress upfront that input profiles don't automatically give you great color or remove the need for color correction—they just tell the CMS what colors your capture device sees. So a good input profile will faithfully render the dark and murky appearance of an underexposed image or the washed-out appearance of an overexposed one.

Moreover, some types of input are difficult-to-impossible to profile. Digital cameras shot in the field rather than the studio are difficult to profile because the light source is all over the place. Color negative scans are basically impossible to profile for a raft of reasons, the main ones being:

▶ Nobody makes a color-negative scanning target.

▶ Unless you like orange, inverted images, you don't want to reproduce what's on the film.

▶ The orange mask on negatives varies so much with exposure that, even if someone did make negative targets, they'd only work if your negatives were exposed the same way the target was.

However, if you're scanning prints or reversal (positive) film, or you're shooting digital captures under controlled lighting, good input profiles can be significant time-savers. Scanner profiles are so easy to build that there's relatively little reason not to do so. Digital camera profiles, however, are quite a bit harder, for reasons that we'll examine a little later. First, let's look at the similarities between profiling scanners and profiling digital cameras.

Input Profile Basics

The process of building input profiles is the same as building other types of profiles in that we compare device values—almost always RGB in the case of input devices—with measurements in a device-independent color space such as CIE XYZ or CIE LAB. The difference is that with input profiles, the measurements have, in the vast majority of cases, already been done for you.

Input Profiling Targets

Input profiling targets always have two components:

▶ The physical target that you scan or shoot

▶ A target description file (TDF) that contains measurements of the color patches on the target.

The main difference between inexpensive and expensive input profiling targets is the accuracy of the measurements in the target description file. Inexpensive targets are manufactured in fairly large batches, and the measurements are carried out on a small sample of the total batch. As a result, some targets' TDFs in the batch are more accurate than others. Expensive targets are manufactured in smaller batches, and measured individually, so the TDFs are generally a lot more accurate.

Of course, if you have an instrument capable of doing so, you can always measure the profiling target yourself and plug the measurements into the target description file that accompanied the target. This is easy to do with reflective targets, quite difficult with large-format transparency targets (you need a transmissive spectrophotometer, and the affordable ones force you to position each patch manually), and extremely difficult with 35mm transparencies (you need a very specialized transmissive spectrophotometer with a very small aperture, and they're both rare and expensive).

Scanner Targets. By far the most common scanner targets in use are the IT8.7/1 (transmissive) and IT8.7/2 (reflective) targets, which are available from several different vendors on several different film stocks. Kodak's version, the Q-60, follows the IT8 standard (see Figure 7-1).

Figure 7-1

The IT8.7/1 and
IT8.7/2 targets

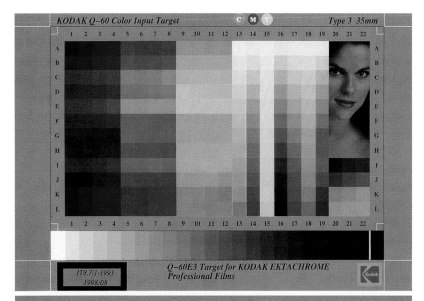

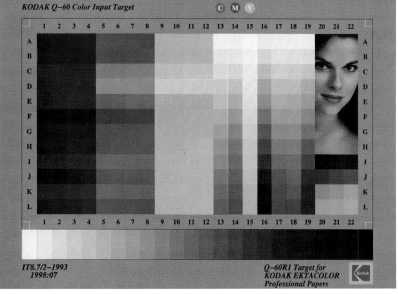

One frequently asked question is, do I need to make different profiles for different film stocks? We hesitate to give a definitive verdict, but based on our experience, we don't think so. The image-forming dyes used in film stocks as different as Kodak Ektachrome and Fuji Velvia are almost identical—the differences come from the image-capture dyes, and a profile simply records how the capture device sees color. The colors may be quite different on a Kodak and a Fuji IT8 target, but as long as the TDF is accurate, we've found that they produce extremely similar profiles.

We've built profiles using Don Hutcheson's excellent hand-measured HCT targets (you can find out all about them at www.hutchcolor.com), using both the Kodak and Fuji versions, and we've found that they produce almost identical profiles that are capable of characterizing scans from either film stock very well. Of this much we're certain. You're definitely better off buying one individually-measured target than buying batch-measured targets on different stocks.

We prefer the HCT target to the IT8 not only for the accuracy of the TDF, but also because it contains a better sampling of colors, particularly dark, saturated colors, and we find that it simply produces a better profile than the IT8 (see Figure 7-2).

Figure 7-2
The HCT target

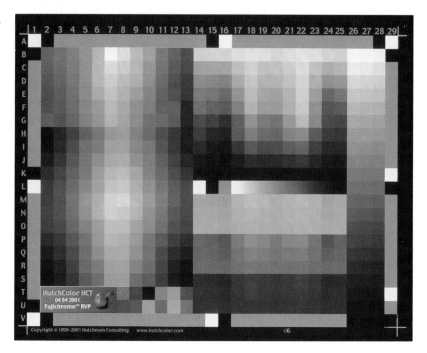

Digital camera targets. There are only two digital camera targets that have gained any significant degree of support in profiling packages, the 24-patch Macbeth ColorChecker, and the newer 237-patch GretagMacbeth ColorChecker DC. The latter was specifically designed for profiling digital cameras (hence the DC in the name), and includes a series of white, gray and black patches around the perimeter designed to let the profiling software compensate for uneven lighting (see Figure 7-3).

Figure 7-3

Macbeth ColorChecker and GretagMacbeth ColorChecker DC

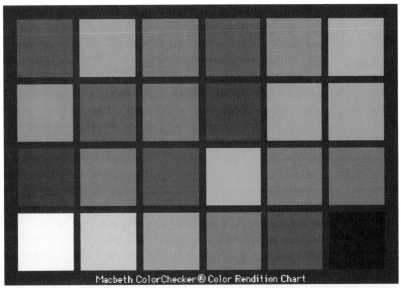

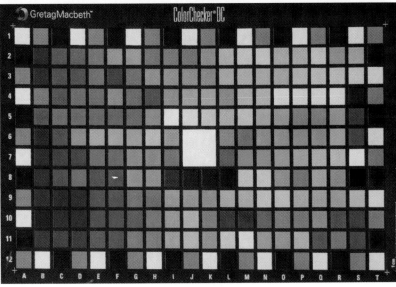

All of which sounds like a great idea. But the available evidence seems to suggest that the ColorChecker DC is a great example of good intentions gone awry. Our own experience, and just about all the anecdotal evidence we've been able to collect, suggests that the original 24-patch ColorChecker almost always results in better camera profiles. Certainly the DC target is harder to light—it's larger, and some of the patches react very strangely to polarized light.

The one situation where we prefer the ColorChecker DC is for profiling cameras in the field under available (that is, uncontrollable) light, for the simple reason that the black, white, and gray patches around the perimeter of the target help the profiling tool compensate for uneven lighting. If you can control the lighting, you're better off doing so and using the smaller target.

We do suggest that you measure the 24-patch ColorChecker yourself. The formulation has changed at least three times over the years, and while the patches from each formulation appear similar to the human eye, they appear rather differently to digital cameras.

Input Device Variables

As with any other type of device, it's vital that you control all the variables that can affect your input device's performance before you profile it. There are really only three factors that affect capture devices such as scanners and digital cameras:

▶ The light source

▶ The color filters

▶ The software settings.

In scanners, the light source is stable in all but the least expensive models, and is almost always compensated for by an internal calibration before each scan. In digital cameras, however, the light source is a huge variable—this is why scanners are easier to profile than digital cameras. How you account for differences in the light source depends on the capabilities of the camera.

The color filters on scanners and cameras change over the life of the device, but so slowly that it'll probably take five years or more before you need to reprofile.

With scanners, the biggest variable by far is the software settings. Software settings are also important with digital cameras, but in rather different ways, so from here on it makes more sense to deal with scanners and cameras separately. We'll start with the easier option, scanners, first.

Building Scanner Profiles

Building scanner profiles is relatively easy—the key to doing so successfully lies in setting up the scanner software correctly, then keeping it set that way. The first goal is to get the scanner behaving consistently. Once you've achieved that, the second goal is to get the scanner behaving optimally.

Stabilizing the Scanner's Response

To make a good scanner profile, the first thing you need to do is to make sure that the scanner responds the same way to every image you scan. If the scanner uses features that tailor its response to the image at hand, you're back to chasing the proverbial moving target with the rubber ruler!

So you need to turn off any features that set black or white points, remove color casts, or do anything else automatically in response to the image content. Less obviously, you need to turn off any sharpening in the scanner—sharpening is also a feature that produces different results depending on image content.

There are, however, two automatic features that we've found are benign with regards to color management (and are extremely useful in their own right). Applied Science Fiction's Digital ICE surface-defect removal and GEM (Grain Enhancement Module) noise-reduction technologies don't, in our experience, interfere with color management, so if your scanner is equipped with them, and you like what they do, by all means leave them active. (A third ASF technology, Digital ROC, is inimical to color management, but since it's designed to work on faded or color-casted originals—where you *don't* want to reproduce what's on the film—it's unlikely that you'd want to use color management and Digital ROC at the same time.)

A very few scanner drivers make it impossible to defeat the auto settings—the ones we run into over and over again are those for the

Polaroid Sprintscan series. Not all models are effected, but some members of the family have auto-exposure hardwired into the scanner firmware. You can't really profile these scanners. If you're using a scanner whose auto features are undefeatable, or if you're scanning color negatives, use the techniques described in "Bringing Color into a Color-Managed Environment" in Chapter 10, *Color-Management Workflow*, instead.

Optimizing the Scanner's Response

Once the scanner is stable—you've turned off auto-everything—the next task is to make sure that it's behaving optimally. The default tone curves on most scanners, whether a lowly desktop flatbed or a Heidelberg drum scanner, produce images that are pleasantly contrasty and saturated, but tend to compress shadow detail and distort darker colors.

If your scanner software allows you to set the output gamma, we recommend setting it somewhere in the range of 2.6 – 3.0. See "Objective Test for Input Profiles" in Chapter 9, *Evaluating and Editing Profiles*, for a technique that allows you to determine the scanner's optimum gamma. For further reading, we recommend Don Hutcheson's excellent paper entitled *"Scanning Guide,"* which is available for download in PDF format from www.hutchcolor.com.

Our usual approach to color-managed scanning is to run the scanner "wide open" with no black-point or white-point correction, and capture the maximum bit depth the scanner allows. We then do any necessary corrections, including optimizations for different output processes, in an image editor such as Adobe Photoshop.

However, if your scanner allows it, you can achieve significant productivity gains by performing color correction and conversion to output space in the scanner software. The downside is that your corrections will be based on whatever size prescan the scanner software provides. But whether you bring raw scans onto an image editor or do conversions and corrections on the scanner, the procedure for building the profile is the same.

Scanning the Target

The target scan doesn't have to be particularly high-resolution—we usually aim for a file in the 5–12 MB range for 24-bit scans, 10–24 MB for

48-bit scans. Make sure that you've set all the scanner parameters correctly, and try to mount the target as straight as possible. If you're profiling a flatbed scanner, it's a good idea to mask the rest of the bed—the area that isn't covered by the target—to minimize distortions from unwanted reflections.

We usually scan the target as a high-bit TIFF file. If your profiling software doesn't accept high-bit TIFFs, you can downsample the target scan to eight bits per channel in Photoshop, or just scan in 24-bit RGB. We always open the target scan in Photoshop before feeding to the profiler, and perform any necessary rotation and cropping (you set the final crop in the profiling package—cropping in Photoshop just minimizes the amount of data you're slinging around). We also check each patch for dust and scratches, and spot out any defects with Photoshop's clone tool (see Figure 7-4).

Figure 7-4

Massaging the target scan

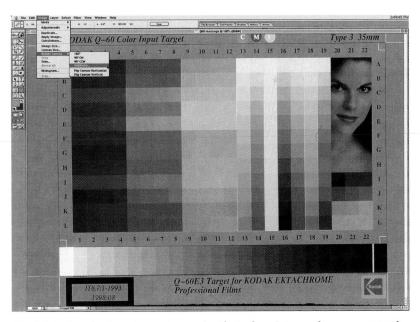

Straightening the target scan is easy in Photoshop. We use the measure tool to measure the angle of one of the lines that should be horizontal, then choose Arbitrary Rotate. The opposite angle is automatically entered, so clicking OK results in a straightened scan. Make sure that the interpolation method is set to Nearest Neighbor to preserve the integrity of the color patches.

Tip: Check Your Policies Before Opening the Target Scan. When you're building input profiles, it's vitally important that you don't change the RGB values in the target scan, so make sure that you don't have any automated conversions specified in your image editor. We also recommend that you make a point of never, ever, embedding a profile in any color-management target, including scans or captures of input profile targets.

Building the Scanner Profile

Once you've got the target scan in the best shape possible, all that remains is to build the profile. The user interface may vary from profiler to profiler, but they all work in fundamentally the same way.

First, you're asked to open the target reference file, which contains the measured color data for the target. Then you're asked to open the target scan (see Figure 7-5).

Figure 7-5

Cropping the target scan

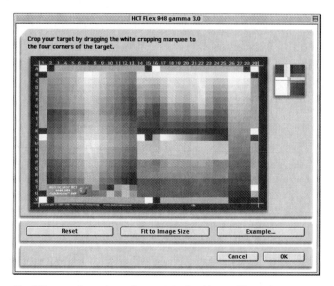

Profiling tools such as GretagMacbeth's Profilemaker Pro, above, let you crop the target exactly to the index marks so that the software can identify the color patches correctly.

The profiler now has all the information it needs to build the profile. Some packages offer choices of profile size, gamut mapping, or gray tracking. We haven't found any consistency as to which options work best—it varies from device to device and from profiler to profiler. Since the actual profile-building process is so quick, we suggest you simply try each option and then use the techniques described in "Input Profiles" in Chapter 9, *Evaluating and Editing Profiles*, to determine which options work best for the device at hand.

Most profilers ask you to name and save the profile before calculating it, and all reasonably recent ones default to the correct location for saving. Once you've entered the name and clicked the Save (or Build, or Calculate) button, the profiler does the calculations and builds the profile. On a reasonably current computer, this process usually takes well under a minute.

Building Digital Camera Profiles

The actual profile-building process for digital cameras is pretty much identical to that for scanners—you provide the profiling package with a target reference file and a capture of the target, and then it crunches the numbers and builds a profile. What makes digital cameras much harder to profile than scanners is the inherent differences in the ways they're used.

Where scanners have a fixed and reasonably stable light source, digital cameras do not. Moreover, scanners, for the most part, capture originals that have already been reduced to three or four colors of dye or ink, while digital cameras have to capture real-world objects in all their diversity. So metamerism—where the capture device sees colors differently from the way we do—is much more commonly a problem with digital cameras than it is with scanners.

Controlling the Camera's Response

With digital cameras, the strategy that works for scanners—locking the device's response—is totally useless. You *need* the camera to react differently to different scenes so that it can accommodate lighting conditions that vary in both dynamic range and color temperature.

Controlling the camera's response to dynamic range is basic photography—lighting and exposure. There are plenty of good books on the subject, so we'll say no more except to stress, once more, that when you're profiling a camera, lighting the target evenly and capturing both the highlights and shadows, is critical.

Control over color temperature, on the other hand, depends largely on the capabilities of the camera. Most digital cameras offer some kind of automatic white-balancing feature, but we haven't found any of these particularly reliable. Instead, we tend to rely on gray-balancing using a gray card. How you gray-balance depends on the camera.

In-camera gray-balancing. This is the best-case scenario: you expose a gray card, and the camera software adjusts the response of each channel to produce a neutral gray. Most scanning-back cameras offer this feature, but most other types of cameras do not.

Click-balancing during image acquisition. Many camera drivers allow you to apply gray balance by clicking on an area that you know should be neutral. The driver then applies that gray balance to all selected images. This method is popular with one-shot color cameras. It works better than simply editing the image once it's been acquired, because the gray balance is applied to the processing of the raw (grayscale) camera data that produces the color image (see Figure 7-6).

Figure 7-6

Click-balancing
multiple images

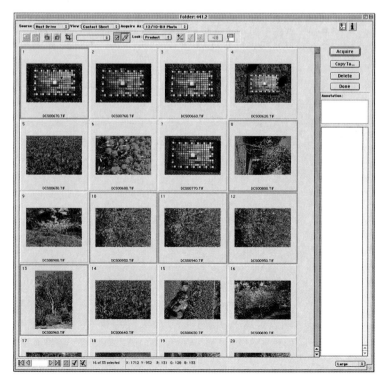

Tip: Shoot a Gray Card. While you can often find something in an image that you know should be neutral gray, if you take a quick shot of a gray card at the beginning of each shoot and whenever the lighting changes significantly in color temperature, then you *know* that you have an unambiguous reference on which to click-balance all the frames for that lighting setup.

If your camera lacks either of these features, it probably isn't a candidate for profiling. Instead, simply open the images in a well-chosen editing space, and use your calibrated monitor as your guide for any necessary edits.

Capturing the Target

Make sure that the target is lit as evenly as possible, and try to capture it as squarely as possible. Most profiling tools will ignore small perspective distortions, but if they're more extreme you may get a bad profile, or the software may simply reject the capture.

Some cameras, notably the Kodak DCS series, offer a "linear" (gamma 1.0) capture mode which supposedly is the best choice for profiling. We confess that we've had a notable lack of success with this (and it also produces very dark thumbnails that make image identification in the acquire module nearly impossible). If your camera offers high-bit captures, however, by all means use them.

Building the Camera Profile

The process for building camera profiles is basically identical to that for building scanner profiles. You provide the profiling tool with a target description file and a captured TIFF image of the target, crop the target, and press a button. The profiling tool then calculates the profile, and you're done.

Well, not quite. More than any other profile type, we find that camera profiles usually require careful evaluating and editing. In Chapter 9, *Evaluating and Editing Profiles*, we look in depth at the techniques for doing so.

Starting Out Right

A good input profile can be a valuable time-saver. Good scanner profiles produce scans that reproduce exactly what's on the film, which is usually the best starting point for an image. Camera profiles are a bit more slippery. We've found that even with the best camera profiles, we'll still have to make significant edits to tone, and when camera metamerism rears its head, to color, too. But even in the worst-case scenarios, a good camera profile will at least nudge the image in the right direction, saving you time and effort. Which is really, after all, what color management is about.

Building Output Profiles

Final Destinations

Output profiles do more than just deliver your known, calibrated color to your output device. They're also the map you use when you're deciding where you want to drive that color. Output profiles not only help the color management system (CMS) produce the right numbers to represent your color on the output device, but they also help the CMS show you, on your display or on another printer, how the output device will render the color *before* you print it. Most of our captured images contain colors that our output devices can't reproduce, so we have to decide how we want to handle these out-of-gamut colors: the output profile is the map that shows you the possible destinations. If that map doesn't describe the territory accurately, you're liable to get lost, and if an output profile doesn't describe the behavior of your output device accurately, your color won't end up where you expected it to.

This capability to preview the results before they happen is one of the most valuable things color management brings to the table—it lets you use relatively inexpensive devices like monitors and inkjet printers to predict what will happen when you send your color to much more expensive devices like printing presses or digital film recorders, so you can take any necessary corrective action beforehand.

But to do so, the color management system needs accurate profiles. The process of building a profile is quite simple—you feed the profiling software some measurements, and it munches them and spits out a profile—but just as profile accuracy makes or breaks color management, the accuracy of the data you collect makes or breaks the profile.

If you skipped straight to this chapter without reading Chapter 5, *Measurement, Calibration, and Process Control*, because you figured it didn't apply to you, Stop, Do Not Pass Go, Do Not Collect $200. If you just print the profiling target, measure it, and let the profiling software do its thing, you *may* get a decent profile. But the chances will be a lot higher if you spend some time making sure that the device you're profiling is working properly before you print the profiling target—that's why we spent a whole chapter harping about calibration and linearization.

In this chapter, we talk in detail about the things you have to do before profiling to make sure that the data you collect represents the behavior of the device you're profiling as accurately as possible, and after profiling to make sure that your device keeps behaving the way the profile expects it to. Even if you don't plan to build your own profiles, relying instead on any of the many reputable profile-building services available online or through consultants, you need to make sure that the profiling target gets printed properly, and you need to be aware of the things that can affect your device's behavior, and hence the accuracy of its profile, after the profile is built.

The Moving Target and The Rubber Ruler

As we pointed out in Chapter 5, *Measurement, Calibration, and Process Control*, profiles are snapshots in time. In the case of output profiles, all that they can do is to describe how the output device was behaving when it printed the profiling target.

But most output devices change over time, though different kinds do so in different ways. So unless you like trying to measure moving targets with rubber rulers, you need to develop strategies for making sure that you collect good data to build the profile and for keeping the device's behavior in sync with the profile. In this chapter, we'll point out the kinds of variability that plague different types of output devices, and suggest strategies both for collecting good data and for tracking the device's behavior so that you know the data remains good. The primary tool for doing all these things is the measuring instrument.

Measuring Instruments

If you're serious about building output profiles, a dedicated measuring instrument is essential.

In theory, you can use either a reflective colorimeter or a reflective spectrophotometer to build output profiles. In practice, we recommend reflective spectrophotometers because they offer the most bang for the buck. They don't cost a whole lot more than colorimeters, but they're more accurate and versatile.

Do yourself a favor and choose an instrument that's directly supported by your profiling software. If you're a tinkerer by nature, you can probably figure out the data format your profiling software expects—the patch order, the measurement type, and the actual formatting of the file—and then export the measurements to a text file that your profiling software can read, but it's a lot of work! (Bruce remembers using Red Ryder 10.1, a venerable Macintosh terminal emulator, to take readings with a Gretag SPM50, and blames it for a considerable amount of hair loss.) It's just so much simpler to use a device that your profiling software can talk to directly.

There *are* profiling packages that use a flatbed scanner to measure the printed targets, but in the final analysis, scanner-based profilers are like the talking horse: what's amazing isn't how well they do it, but that they do it at all. We don't recommend them.

Measurement Geometry

Spectrophotometers have two different flavors of *measurement geometry*—the direction from which the light strikes the sample, and the direction from which that light is collected. Instruments with d/0° or 0°/d geometries are often known as "integrating sphere" or simply "sphere" instruments. They measure the color of the sample without regard to surface texture and are most often used in the formulation of paints, inks, plastics, and other colored materials. In the graphic arts world, we favor instruments with a 0°/45° or 45°/0° geometry (the two are functionally equivalent), because they make measurements that correspond more closely to the way the sample appears to the human eye, taking into account surface texture and its effect on the apparent color (see Figure 8-1).

Most sphere instruments offer an option to "exclude the specular component" when measuring, which produces a measurement more like the 45°/0° geometry; so if you do use a sphere instrument, use this option if it's available.

Figure 8-1

Measurement geometries

In a 0°/45° instrument, the sample is illuminated by a light beam that's perpendicular to the surface. The detector reads the light that's reflected at a 45-degree angle.

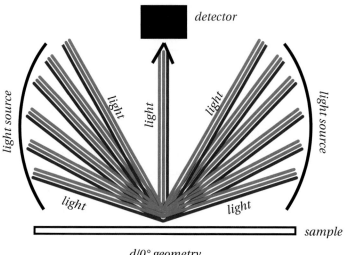

light source

light

light

detector

sample

0°/45° geometry

detector

light source

light

light

light

light source

light

light

sample

d/0° geometry

In a d/0° instrument, the sample is illuminated by a diffuse light source that lights the sample evenly from all angles. The detector reads the light that's reflected perpendicular to the surface.

Aperture Size

All spectrophotometers measure light through an opening, or *aperture*. Most of the spectrophotometers used in color management have a measurement aperture of around 4–8 mm in diameter. Smaller aperture sizes are pretty rare, but some instruments have larger apertures in the 12–15 mm range. The disadvantage of larger apertures is that you have to print targets so that the patches are large enough to be read individually by the instrument, which uses more paper—a concern if you're profiling expensive art papers or specialty photo-inkjet papers.

However, there are two situations where a larger aperture can help. One is when you're profiling output with very low line screens, such as billboard printers, where a small aperture may not capture a large enough area to correctly determine the ratio of coverage between the halftone dots and the paper on which they're printed. The other is when you're profiling a "noisy" print process, such as uncoated watercolor paper or canvas on an inkjet printer, where each patch contains substantial variation. The larger aperture effectively averages out the "noise."

Filters

Some papers contain fluorescent brighteners that convert ultraviolet light into visible blueish light, fooling our eyes into thinking the paper is whiter and brighter. (Many laundry detergents use a similar technique, which is why they're often blueish in color.)

Unlike our eyes, spectrophotometers don't have white point adaptation and aren't fooled by paper brighteners, so they see the paper as being blueish. Profiling tools compensate by adding the complementary color, yellow, so the resulting output may have a yellow cast from highlights to midtones, or sometimes even green quartertones, as the yellow ink and bluish paper combine.

One way to deal with this problem is to use a spectrophotometer with a UV filter. Bruce sees this as the colorimetric equivalent of sticking your fingers in your ears and yelling lalalalala—it deals with the problem by pretending that it isn't there—but he admits that it can produce better results than no UV filtering. The only spectrophotometer we know of that has user-switchable UV filters is the Spectrolino. Other instruments, such as the X-Rite DTP-41, come in two versions, one with a (permanent) UV filter and one without.

We'd prefer to see profiling tools handle UV brighteners intelligently, rather than pretending that they weren't there—GretagMacbeth's ProfileMaker 4.1, for example, has an option to detect and compensate for optical brighteners—but thus far it's the exception rather than the rule.

Polarizing filters are sometimes useful for measuring very glossy papers, particularly when the gloss has a directional component. We've found them more useful with dye-sublimation printers than with glossy inkjet papers. They're also used in instruments designed to measure wet ink on press. (For process control when you're profiling, you must let the ink dry before you measure it!)

Backing

The ISO standard recommendation is to measure targets on a black backing. While we hesitate to disagree with such an august body, we feel bound to point out that measuring over black can create problems when the stock you're measuring is thin or translucent, because the black backing results in artificially low luminance readings. (Unless, that is, your final output will be viewed on a black backing, which is typically not the case with thin papers.)

Our recommendation for translucent papers is to measure over a stack of blank stock where possible, or, if you're using a strip reader (which makes stacking paper impractical), to measure over white instead—strip readers such as the DTP-41 generally give you the choice. A white backing will still skew the measurements slightly, but much less so than a black one will.

Handheld Instruments

Handheld instruments are great for making spot color measurements—you position the measurement aperture on the sample and press the measure button. They're handy for process control, where you need to take relatively few measurements, but most profiling tools require you to measure hundreds or even thousands of color patches.

With a handheld instrument, you position the measurement aperture on the first patch, press the measure button, move the aperture to the second patch, press the measure button, and so on, several hundred times. Handheld instruments are usually less expensive than the automated varieties and can produce very good results. They're great if you're on a tight budget, have plenty of time and strong wrists, and only need to make profiles occasionally—we've used them more often than we care to remember—but if you're like us, you'll find about halfway through measuring your first target that you'd really like an instrument that offers more automatic data collection.

Handheld reflective spectrophotometers include the Color Savvy ColorMouseToo! CM2S and the X-Rite Digital Swatchbook (DTP-22). Handheld reflective/emissive spectrophotometers, which can measure monitors as well as hard copy, include the various incarnations of the venerable Colortron series, which still receives some degree of support from X-Rite, Spectrostar's Spectrocam, and GretagMacbeth's Spectrolino and EyeOne Pro.

Figure 8-2

Handheld
Spectrophotometers

Part of Bruce's collection of handheld spectrophotometers, old and new. Clockwise from left: ColorMouseToo! CM2S, Colortron II, X-Rite DTP-22 Digital Swatchbook, and GretagMacbeth EyeOne Pro.

The Spectrocam and EyeOne Pro offer a unique measuring capability that other handheld spectrophotometers lack. In addition to taking spot readings like other handhelds, you can also use them in a "scanning" mode by dragging them over a row of patches on an appropriately designed target (the instruments need targets where each patch is significantly different from its neighbors to figure out where one patch ends and another starts). These instruments offer a very quick way of collecting data at relatively low cost. The only real downside is that it's relatively difficult to design your own targets, which is a fairly esoteric concern.

XY Plotters

XY plotters are the most automated reflective spectrophotometers. They use a mechanism that moves the reading head in both dimensions across the face of the target, so you can program them to read an entire target automatically. XY plotters demand the least human interaction for reading patches, but many of them don't make it easy to measure a single color or a custom set of colors. The two most commonly used XY instruments are GretagMacbeth's Spectroscan (see Figure 8-3) and X-Rite's Spectrofiler. But the two are very different and are suited to different tasks.

The Spectroscan is actually made up of two parts—the handheld Spectrolino previously mentioned and a mechanized table with a robot arm that moves the Spectrolino from patch to patch. The Spectroscan measures targets up to 31×24 cm (12.2×9.4 inches) on material up to 1.5 mm in thickness. It lets you specify measurement positions to within 0.25 mm and to average multiple measurements per patch, which makes it very useful for measuring "noisy" print processes such as inkjet on rag paper, where there may be substantial variation within each color patch. Measurement is automatic, but quite slow. On the plus side, once you've started the measurement process, you can simply walk away and come back when it's done.

Figure 8-3
GretagMacbeth's
Spectroscan

Bruce's Spectroscan at work

X-Rite's Spectrofiler is more specialized—it's designed to make fast measurements of targets printed in the trim area of a press sheet, either control bars for process control or specially formatted targets for profiling. The patches can be as small as 3.8×1.6 mm, with target widths up to 80 inches (less-expensive versions of the instrument handle 20-inch and 40-inch sheets, respectively). It measures an appropriately formatted extended IT8 target in under four minutes.

Printing the target in the trim area lets you piggyback target printing onto a money-making press run, so the Spectrofiler is great for profiling presses, but it's less suited to dealing with smaller-format output devices.

Strip Readers

Strip readers are generally the fastest measurement instruments available, although a handheld scanning spectrophotometer like the EyeOne Pro or Spectrocam can come close. They need more human involvement than XY plotters—you need to load the strips into the instrument and keep them properly aligned—and they're ill suited to making spot measurements for comparison or process control. But they're quick and efficient for reading profiling targets.

There's really only one strip reader that's widely supported by profiling tools—the X-Rite Autoscan Spectrophotometer DTP-41. It's a fast, efficient workhorse for making ICC profiles and is also directly supported by some Electronics for Imaging Fiery RIPs and the BestColor proofing RIP as a calibration instrument.

Profiling Packages

All profiling packages work by comparing known reference data with measurement data. In the case of output profiles, they compare known RGB or CMYK values (the ones in the profiling target) with the LAB values we obtain by measuring the printed target. Profiling packages run the gamut (pun intended) from relatively inexpensive (<$100) scanner-based packages to industrial-strength solutions with price tags to match ($2500–$5000). Generally speaking, we find that you get what you pay for, though depending on your needs, you may find that you don't always use everything you pay for! For example, if your profiling activities are focused on RGB inkjet printers, you don't need sophisticated control over black generation and other CMYK separation parameters. Likewise, if you're working with a handheld measuring instrument, the ability to define custom targets with thousands of patches probably isn't of great interest.

All output profilers work in basically the same way—they provide a profiling target that you print on the device you're profiling, you measure the target, feed the measurements to the profiler, and then it chews on the measurement data and spits out a profile. (For details on the chewing, see the sidebar, "Profile Creation.") But within those broad confines, you'll find plenty of differences. We can't possibly review every profiling package in this book—it would get out of date very quickly if we did—so instead, we'll give you a quick rundown of the kinds of features on which different packages compete.

Instrument Support

We don't think there's been any collusion between the vendors, but they all seem to have made a conscious decision to support as many of the instruments in common use as they possibly can—this is true even of vendors like GretagMacbeth, who make instruments in addition to profiling software.

Most profiling packages can support any instrument by importing measurements as text files, but it's a lot more convenient if the package actually drives the instrument directly. With handheld instruments, direct support usually means that the target is displayed on the monitor with a cursor showing you which patch to measure—very helpful when you stop to answer the phone halfway through a target. With automated instruments, it's perhaps less important but still a real convenience.

With instruments that require specially formatted targets, such as X-Rite's DTP-41 strip reader or the handheld scanning EyeOne from GretagMacbeth and Spectrocam from Spectrostar, the profiler may limit you to a subset of all the available targets. We can't say we've ever found this to be a real problem, but in some situations—for example, if you want to measure the industry-standard IT8.7/3 target to compare your press's behavior with published standards—you may have to do some searching to find an IT8.7/3 formatted for the EyeOne or Spectrocam. (You can always measure it one patch at a time, but that's quite tedious. See the following two tips.)

Profile Creation

Just what do output profilers do when they, as we rather simplistically put it, "chew on the measurements?" In practice, they have to do quite a lot. As we pointed out in Chapter 4, *All About Profiles*, every output profile contains six tables, one in each direction between device RGB or CMYK and PCS values for each rendering intent. Building all these tables takes quite a bit of work.

Profiles generally don't use the raw measurement data to build the profile. For example, the profiles we used to print this book were made from a profiling target containing 875 patches, producing 875 measurements. But each AtoB table contains only 17 grid points, each one of which has four values for C, M, Y, and K and three values for L*, a* and b*. (A profile that contained grid points for each measurement would get very large, very quickly, because it would contain 875 points, each of which had four values for C, M, Y, and K, and three values for L*, a*, and b*!) So the first thing the profiling package does is to interpolate the measurement data down to a manageable size, and build the AtoB1 table, which contains the relative colorimetric rendering intent. Then it calculates the AtoB0 (perceptual) and AtoB2 (saturation) rendering intents.

To go in the opposite direction, the profiling package uses double the number of grid points—33 in this case—to improve accuracy. (The profiling tool knows what LAB colors result from the CMYK values in the target, but it doesn't have any actual data going in the other direction.) So it has to interpolate the AtoB tables to twice the number of grid points, then reverse the tables so that they go from LAB to device values to produce the BtoA tables.

That's the simplified view. In addition, the profiling tool may apply some smoothing to the data, it may build in some "secret sauce" to work around some of the limitations of LAB, or it may do other things that we've yet to figure out. But whatever the story, when you see a progress bar during the profile creation process, rest assured that the profiling tool is doing some pretty hefty calculations.

Tip: Download Targets from Different Vendors. Your profiling tool may not offer a target formatted for your instrument, but chances are that some other vendor does. Most profiling tools are available as downloads in demo mode—you need to buy a dongle or license key to actually save profiles, but you can download the package and use the targets and target reference files contained in the package without buying anything. The only tricky part is formatting the target reference file for your particular profiling tool (see the next tip).

Tip: Use a Spreadsheet to Format Target and Measurement Files. The one speed bump in using both measurement files and target reference files that weren't created by, or designed for, your profiling tool is getting them into the format your profiling tool expects. We find that the best approach is to use a spreadsheet program like Microsoft Excel to reformat measurement and target reference files. They're almost always tab-delimited text, so you can easily switch things around by simply moving the columns in the spreadsheet.

Profilers almost always include sample measurement files. Use one of these as a template to figure out the data format the profiling tool wants (see Figure 8-4). Likewise, profiling tools almost always include target reference files that record the RGB or CMYK values for each patch in the target. You need to take the target reference file for the "foreign" target and reformat it for your profiling tool.

Figure 8-4
Target data reference files

IT8.7 CMYK Ref.txt

	A	B	C	D	E
1	Date:	9/4/97	Time:	13:47	
2	BEGIN_DATA_FORMAT				
3	Sample_Name	CMYK_C	CMYK_M	CMYK_Y	CMYK_K
4	END_DATA_FORMAT				
5	BEGIN_DATA				
6	A1	100	0	0	0
7	A2	0	100	0	0
8	A3	0	0	100	0
9	A4	100	100	0	0
10	A5	100	0	100	0
11	A6	0	100	100	0
12	A7	100	100	100	0
13	A8	70	70	0	0
14	A9	70	0	70	0
15	A10	0	70	70	0
16	A11	40	40	0	0
17	A12	0	40	40	0
18	A13	40	40	40	0
19	A14	40	0	40	0
20	A15	20	20	0	0
21	A16	20	0	20	0
22	A17	0	20	20	0
23	A18	100	0	0	100
24	A19	0	100	0	100
25	A20	0	0	100	100
26	A21	100	100	0	100
27	A22	100	0	100	100
28	A23	0	100	100	100
29	A24	100	100	100	100
30	A25	0	0	0	100
31	A26	0	0	0	0

IT8.7 CMYK Ref.txt

GretagMacbeth's target reference file for the IT8.7/3 target

BC 2200 Proto PL.TAR

	A	B	C	D	E	F
1	basICColor	print	3c	Definition	File	
2	RGB	Profile	Target	Definition		
3						
4	KEYWORD	CONTROL				
5	KEYWORD	SAMPLE_LOC				
6						
7	LINEARIZATION:					
8		CYAN:				
9		0	47.25	75.82	90.11	100
10		0	60	67.84	76.08	100
11		MAGENTA:				
12		0	47.25	75.82	90.11	100
13		0	60	67.84	76.08	100
14		YELLOW:				
15		0	47.25	75.82	90.11	100
16		0	60	67.84	76.08	100
17	BEGIN_DATA_FORMAT					
18	SAMPLE_ID	SAMPLE_LOC	CONTROL	CMY_C	CMY_M	CMY_Y
19	END_DATA_FORMAT					
20						
21	BEGIN_DATA					
22	1	1A1	N	49	49	49
23	2	1A2	N	100	100	100
24	3	1A3	N	0	0	0
25	4	1A4	N	100	100	100
26	5	1A5	N	0	0	0
27	6	1A6	N	60	5	13
28	7	1A7	N	40	76	0
29	8	1A8	N	25	60	0
30	9	1A9	N	0	100	60
31	10	1A10	N	40	25	25

BC 2200 Proto PL.TAR

Intergrated Color Solutions' target reference file for the BasICColor Print 3c RGB target

Targets

One of the biggest areas of difference between profiling packages is in the profiling targets they use. Most packages support the IT8.7/3 target for CMYK profiling, but the IT8.7/3 has some shortcomings—its main usefulness is as a standard for publishing reference data for print standards—so most packages also offer one or more proprietary CMYK targets. There are no standard targets for RGB output profiling—each profiling package uses its own proprietary RGB target(s).

Besides any special requirements imposed by your instrument, the big difference between different packages' targets is the number of patches they require you to measure. Most packages need at minimum two to three hundred measurements, some require closer to a thousand, and some give you the option of measuring several thousand patches. Don't assume that more measurements always means a better profile in the end—in our experience, it depends very much on the profiling software and the device being profiled. A very general guideline is: the closer your device is to being linear and gray balanced, the fewer patches you need; and the more non-linear and/or color casted the device, the more patches you need. In some cases you can end up introducing noise when profiling very linear devices if you measure too many patches. But no matter what, your mileage will vary.

If you're working with a handheld instrument, you probably want to measure the smallest number of patches possible—the difference between three hundred and eight hundred patches translates to a lot of time and a lot of stress on your wrists! When you have to measure a large number of patches with a handheld instrument, you also run a greater risk of mismeasurement, which will produce a bad profile. With an automated instrument, the number of patches is obviously less of an issue, and it's common for packages to provide feedback in the form of an error message if mismeasurement occurs.

Some profiling tools also let you generate your own custom targets. This is strictly for the hardcore color geek, and the only situation where we've found it's worthwhile to do so is to improve the grayscale behavior of RGB output devices. It's a *lot* of work, and the improvements, while real, are modest. Figure 8-5 shows targets used by a variety of profiling packages.

Figure 8-5

Profiling targets

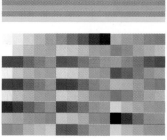

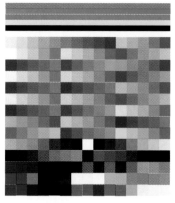

Profiling targets come in all shapes and sizes, but they all attempt to do the same thing— provide the profiling tool with a sufficiently representative sample of the device's behavior to build an accurate profile.

Heidelberg PrintOpen RGB target

Heidelberg PrintOpen CMYK target

Both pages of Integrated Color Solutions' Print 3c RGB target

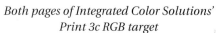

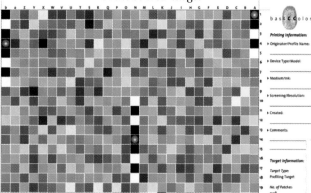

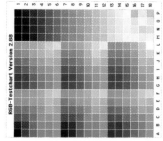

GretagMacbeth's TC2.88 RGB test chart

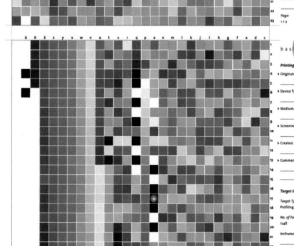

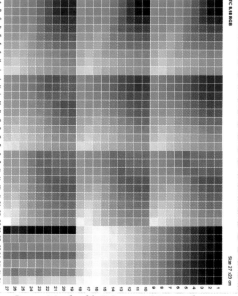

GretagMacbeth's TC9.18 RGB test chart (designed by Bill Atkinson)

Figure 8-5

Profiling targets, *continued*

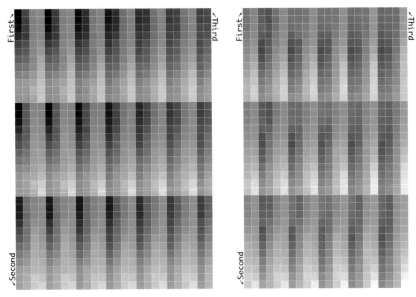

Both pages of MonacoPROFILER's 1728-patch RGB target

The IT8.7/3 CMYK target

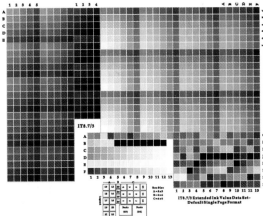

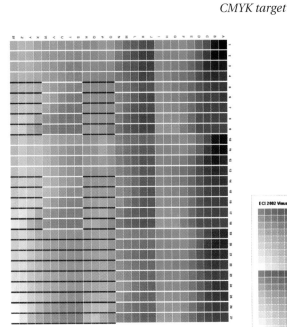

ColorVision's Profiler Pro 729-patch RGB test chart

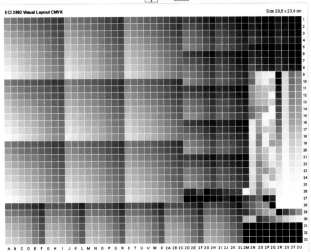

The ECI 2002 CMYK target, designed by the European Color Initiative. It combines the IT8.7/3 with the proposed IT8.7/4.

Data Averaging

If you're planning on profiling an inherently variable printing process such as a press or color copier, you'll almost certainly need to measure multiple targets and average the results. Some profiling tools will do this for you. You can always open the measurement files in a spreadsheet program such as Microsoft Excel and average them there, but having the profiling tool do it for you is much more convenient.

Tip: Download GretagMacbeth's MeasureTool. ProfilerPro is available as a demo download from GretagMacbeth's Web site. You need to buy a license to unlock the ProfileMaker and ProfileEditor applications, but the MeasureTool application offers two very useful capabilities even when the package is running as a demo—it lets you compare measurement files, and it lets you average measurement files. So if your profiling package doesn't offer data averaging, you can always use MeasureTool to average your measurements before feeding them to your profiler.

Linearization

Some profiling packages make profiling a two-step process, whereby you first print and measure a linearization target, like the one shown in Figure 8-6, to determine the linearity of the printer—the degree to which changes in the control signals produce proportional changes in the printed color. The profiler then uses the measurements to generate a profiling target that's optimized for the specific device.

Some of these packages take this feature further, allowing you to reprint and measure the linearization target (which has many fewer patches than the full-blown profiling target), and use these measurements to update an existing profile. In most cases, you need to build the original profile using the linearization step to be able to re-linearize and update the profile.

Figure 8-6
Linearization target

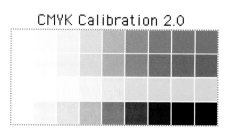

CMYK Calibration 2.0

Do these packages work any better than those that don't offer linearization? In extreme cases—for example, when a device starts to plug up, producing the same color at any value higher than 70%—they can. They work by changing the values in the profiling target (and its accompanying target reference file) to eliminate redundancy by lightening the patches so that they lie inside the usable range of the printer.

If you're working with a CMYK RIP that supports linearization, it's usually easier to linearize the device through the RIP prior to profiling—that way, you eliminate the need for linearizing the profiling target. However, some RIPs do a better job, or are easier to use, than others, so when in doubt, experiment. Bear in mind that if you linearize part-way in the RIP and the rest of the way in the profiling tool, you're mutiplying the number of variables you need to keep under control. You may get the best possible results that way, but at the cost of introducing more opportunities to screw up.

Parameter Controls

Most profiling tools offer explicit control over CMYK separation parameters such as total ink limit, black ink limit, and black generation, although a few entry-level packages simply offer presets for different CMYK processes. More advanced packages offer control over black start (the point, typically some considerable distance from the highlights, where black ink is first introduced), black shape (the rate at which black ink is introduced as the color gets darker), and black width (the strength of the Gray Component Replacement, or GCR, which dictates how far from the neutral axis black ink is introduced into color combinations). Figure 8-7 shows the separation parameters offered by some of the leading profiling packages.

A few packages let you control the trade-offs that are made in rendering out-of-gamut colors using the perceptual rendering intent, letting you choose the compromises between maintaining hue, saturation, and lightness. Figure 8-8 shows the rendering controls offered by Heidelberg PrintOpen 4.5 and MonacoPROFILER 4.5.

Figure 8-7

Separation parameters

The controls provided by the three packages shown here are roughly equivalent, even though the terminology differs from package to package.

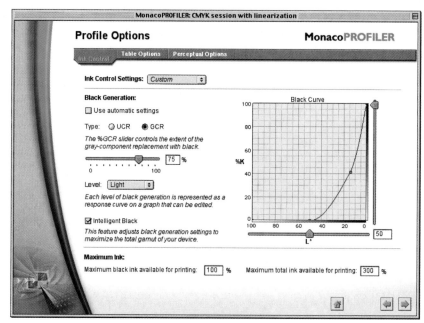

MonacoPROFILER offers control over black and total ink limits, black start, black shape, and GCR strength, in addition to automatic settings.

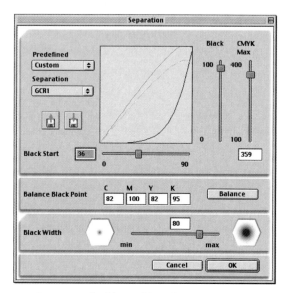

Heidelberg PrintOpen lets you control black and total ink limits, black length, black width, and GCR strength.

GretagMacbeth's ProfileMaker Pro provides control over black and total ink limits, black start, black width, and several presets for black shape.

Figure 8-8

Rendering controls

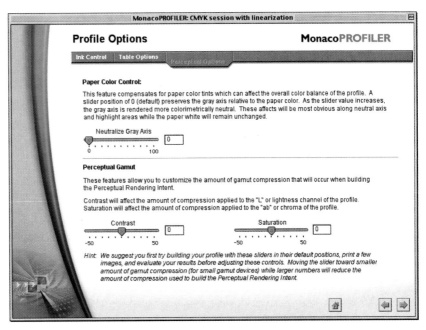

MonacoPROFILER lets you choose how much lightness or saturation to sacrifice for perceptual rendering.

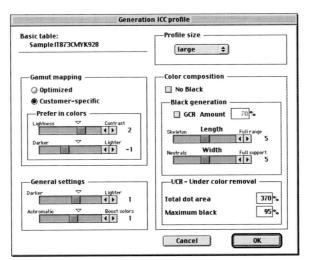

Heidelberg PrintOpen lets you build custom perceptual renderings by controlling lightness and contrast.

Some profilers let you decide whether to aim for a neutral gray axis that's dead-on neutral or one that's neutral relative to the paper stock. In our experience, very blue-white papers can cause profiling packages to overcompensate and make true neutrals appear yellow, while the paper-relative neutrals appear much more neutral even if they don't measure that way.

Profile Editing

Some packages not only generate profiles, but also let you edit them. Profile editing can be extremely valuable, with the important caveat that before you start editing a profile to address a problem, you need to be very sure that the problem does in fact lie in the profile, rather than in the measurement data or the device behavior. See Chapter 9, *Evaluating and Editing Profiles*, for an in-depth discussion of profile editing.

Getting Good Data

If you just print a profiling target, measure it, and feed the measurements to your profiling software, you may be lucky enough to get a good profile—but unless you take special care when printing the target and taking the measurements, it's a lot more likely that you'll get a bad one.

You want to make sure that the output device is working properly when you print the profiling target. Then you want to capture measurements that represent the good working state accurately. Lastly, after you've built the profile, you want to make sure that the device keeps working the way it did when you printed the target, and hence that the profile stays valid. Different device types present different challenges, each of which requires a different remedy, so we'll break the discussion down by types of device, point out the issues you're likely to run into with each type, and suggest remedies. So feel free to skip from here to the device types that interest you.

Opening and Printing the Target

Profiling targets are possibly the only case where we don't care at all about color appearance—all that matters is the numbers in the target files. Therefore, it's absolutely vital that you do nothing to change the numbers in the target files. We make a practice of never, ever, assigning or embedding a profile in a profiling target, both because they're simply unapplicable, and because it's all too easy to trigger an automatic conversion when a source profile is present. (It's possible to trigger one even when there's no source profile, but no workflow is absolutely bulletproof!)

We almost always print our profiling targets from Photoshop, because Photoshop has very explicit color management controls throughout the process. But whatever application you use, you must make sure that the target doesn't get converted when you open it.

You can make life simpler by also making sure that nothing happens to the values in the target when you print it, and that the numbers in the target file simply get sent directly to the printing device. See Chapter 11, *Color Management in the Operating System,* for more information on printer driver color management.

Sometimes you may want to deviate from this strict rule—for example, when profiling an RGB inkjet printer, you may want to use one of the auto-correction features in the printer driver, or when profiling a proofer, you may want to profile on top of linearization curves, or curves set to make the proofer simulate another printing process.

If you do anything like this, be aware that the profile is only valid for that printing condition. When we make profiles in situations like this, we always document exactly what settings we used, and we put some clear indication in both the internal and external name of the profile that it's a non-standard profile that applies to a particular set of printer settings.

Opening the Target

When we open the profiling target, we always make sure that Photoshop's missing profile warning is turned on, and we always choose the Leave as is (don't color manage) option, as shown in Figure 8-9.

Figure 8-9

Opening the target

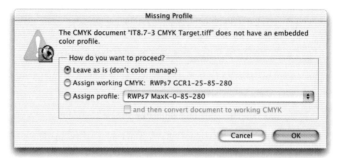

Choose Leave as is (don't color manage) to leave the numbers in the target unchanged.

That way, we don't run the risk of inadvertently embedding a profile—it's all too easy to close the file, get the prompt asking if you want to save, then click the save button. If you assigned a profile, it gets embedded when you save.

Printing the Target

When we print, we always set the Source Space to Document (which, if we opened the target correctly, is always Untagged RGB or Untagged CMYK) and set the Print Space to Same as Source, as shown in Figure 8-10. That way, the numbers in the target are always passed along unchanged to the printer driver.

Figure 8-10

Printing the target

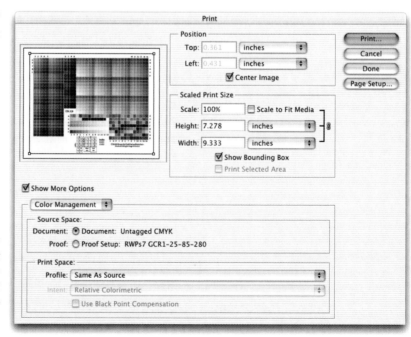

Set the Source Space to Document and the Print Space to Same as Source to pass the unchanged numbers to the printer driver.

Profiling RGB Inkjet Printers

As we've previously pointed out, there's really no such thing as an RGB inkjet printer—they all use cyan, magenta, and yellow inks, most also use black, and some also add "light" versions of the primaries to help improve highlight detail. We call them "RGB inkjets" because the vast majority require RGB signals as their input, forcing us to profile them as RGB devices.

The reason all non-PostScript inkjets function as RGB devices doesn't have anything to do with the devices themselves; it's simply that the data pipeline from the application to the printer driver offered by QuickDraw on the Macintosh or GDI (Graphics Device Interface) on Windows can only pass RGB (or grayscale) data, not CMYK. So even though some applications will let you send a CMYK file to the printer, they perform a hidden conversion back to RGB before handing off the data to the printer driver. (The Mac OS X display architecture doesn't have this limitation—it can pass CMYK as well as RGB or grayscale—but we've yet to see an OS X driver that exploits this capability.)

In theory, inkjets driven by PostScript RIPs should function as CMYK devices, but in practice we've found that a good many PostScript RIPs also perform a hidden CMYK-to-RGB conversion. Sometimes the only way to find out which will give you the better results is to make both RGB and CMYK profiles for such devices, and use the one that performs better.

Before Profiling RGB Inkjets

Inkjet printers are typically very repeatable and stable. RGB inkjets don't offer any calibration features, though they do usually have a plethora of software settings. To get a good RGB inkjet profile, there are three variables you need to worry about.

▶ Software settings in the driver have a huge impact on the printer's behavior—see Figure 5-2 on page 114 for some dramatic examples.

▶ Inkjet prints take time to reach their final, stable color. Even "fast-drying" inks, which appear to be dry when the page comes out of the printer, continue to change color until they reach stability.

▶ Unannounced manufacturing changes in inks or paper can change the color that the printer produces.

Comparing Colors

The ability to compare measured colors is invaluable in color management, whether you're tracking press variation from sheet-to-sheet, comparing different batches of consumables, or determining drying time. Visual comparisons can identify gross problems, but subtle differences can be exaggerated by the profiling process. So some means of comparing measurements and determining how different they are is extremely useful.

Delta-e. By far the most common way of expressing color differences is in CIE LAB delta-e units. Other color-differencing schemes exist, and some are a bit more accurate than LAB, but LAB is still the most widely used. If someone reports delta-e values without any further qualification, it's safe to assume that she means LAB delta-e.

In theory, LAB is perceptually uniform, and in theory one delta-e unit is the smallest difference perceivable by humans with normal color vision, but in practice it falls a little short of that goal. In the saturated yellow region, for example, even viewers with very discriminating color

vision may be hard-pressed to see a 3 delta-e difference, while in midtone neutrals a difference of 0.5 delta-e may be visible.

In production work, a delta-e in the range of 3–6 is usually considered a good commercial match, and a delta-e of less than 2 is considered unattainable due to the many variables in print production. But when you're evaluating device drift or comparing profiling targets, you need to be a little stricter, because small differences in the profiling target can often be amplified in the profile.

Bruce's usual method of tracking device drift on non-calibratable devices such as RGB inkjets is to print and measure the profiling target and then compare the measurements with the ones from which the profile was built. If he finds an average delta-e of more than 2, or a peak delta-e of more than 6, he builds a new profile.

Tools. Most spectrophotometers come with software that lets you compare two LAB values and determine the delta-e difference between them. It's less common to find tools that let you compare

an entire set of measurements and calculate the average and peak delta-e differences.

One well-kept secret is GretagMacbeth's MeasureTool, which is one of the modules in their ProfileMaker Pro software. You can download a demo version of ProfileMaker from GretagMacbeth's Web site (www.gretagmacbeth.com), which doesn't let you save profiles unless you purchase a license. But the MeasureTool application is fully functional, and, for this situation, it allows you to compare two sets of measurements of the same target and shows you the average and peak delta-e values (it even shows you which patches have the highest delta-e values—see Figure 8-13.)

MeasureTool reads the measurement files saved by most profilers directly. A few profilers save the measurements in a format that MeasureTool can't read, but you can open them in a spreadsheet application, and then, using one of the sample files that GretagMacbeth supplies as a template, copy the measurements into one of the sample files so that MeasureTool can read it.

The first two are things you need to take into consideration before you profile. The last one is simply something you need to watch out for when you change consumables.

Media settings. Most inkjets offer settings for different media types, generally those sold by the printer vendor. These settings control the amount of ink laid down, the black generation, and in some cases, the screening algorithm, so they have a huge effect on the print. If you're using vendor-supplied paper, simply choose that paper type. If you're using third-party papers, you'll need to experiment to find out which settings produce the best gamut and the most linear tone scale (often, you'll need to compromise one for the sake of the other). See Figure 8-11.

Figure 8-11

Media settings

The paper settings in most inkjet printer drivers control the ink limits and black generation. Finding the correct settings for your paper is key to getting good profiles.

A target like the one shown in Figure 8-12 is useful for all sorts of tasks, including this one: the ramps let you judge the tonal behavior, while the solid colors let you evaluate the gamut.

Figure 8-12

RGB process control target

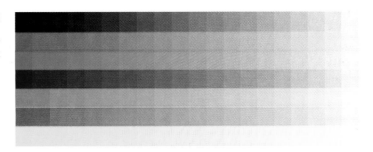

This target contains 21 steps of red, green, blue, cyan, magenta, yellow, and RGB gray (R=G=B).

Don't expect perfection. Our experience has been that if you achieve the maximum gamut, you'll have a fairly non-linear tone scale with some blocking of the shadows. It's often preferable to sacrifice some linearity in favor of a larger gamut—a profile can compensate for non-linearity to some extent, but it can't do anything about the gamut size. Watch out for puddling, bronzing, or ink bleeding, all of which are signs that the printer is laying down too much ink for the paper to handle. If you encounter any of these problems, switch to a media setting that lays down less ink.

Color settings. Most inkjet drivers offer a variety of color-handling options. Epson inkjets, for example, offer options with names like Vivid and Photorealistic, along with some slider controls and a gamma setting. Fortunately, they also offer an option labeled, "No Color Adjustment."

Wherever possible, look for a "raw" setting that just sends the numbers unchanged to the printer driver, like the aforementioned No Color Adjustment. It's the simplest way to profile. In some cases, though, you may find that you get better linearity using some other setting.

Once you determine the settings that yield the best compromise, you can profile this condition, with the important caveat that when you use the profile, you'll always have to have the software settings set the same way you did when you made the profile. This also means that you can't use the profile inside the printer driver, because the place you choose the driver-level color settings is the same place you'd choose the profile—you can only have one or the other, but not both. This isn't a problem when you're dealing with color-managed applications, but it may be if you need to print from a non-color-managed application such as PowerPoint.

Resolution settings. Most of the inkjets we've tried seem to be fairly consistent between different resolution settings, but there's no guarantee that *your* inkjet will work that way.

We find that a single profile works for all supported resolutions on a given paper stock, but if that doesn't seem to be working for you, you can do a quick reality check by printing the RGB process control target shown in Figure 8-9 at the different resolutions, and then measuring each one and comparing the results. See the sidebar, "Comparing Colors," earlier in this chapter. If the average delta-e in LAB between different resolutions is greater than 1, or if the peak delta-e is greater than 6, you'll almost certainly want to build separate profiles for the different resolutions.

Curing time. One of the biggest gotchas that people overlook when profiling is that inkjet prints need time to cure. The ink may appear dry when the paper leaves the printer—it won't smear or rub off—but it almost certainly hasn't reached its final color appearance because the solvents take time to evaporate and the ink takes time to react with the paper coating. Every inkjet we've ever used takes some time for the color to stabilize. (The actual curing time depends on the specific inkset and paper.) If you start measuring the profiling target as soon it leaves the printer, you'll go crazy trying to figure out what's wrong with the resulting profile because you really are measuring a moving target.

The easiest way to determine the length of time your prints need to attain final color is to keep measuring the profiling target with an automated measuring instrument until you see little or no difference between measurement passes. It's time-consuming, but you only need to do it once for each paper and ink combination. It's the combination of paper and ink that is the issue. The same paper will have different curing times with different brands (and sometimes models) of printer that use different inksets, and the same inkset may have radically different curing times on different papers (see Figure 8-13).

Figure 8-13

Comparing measurements

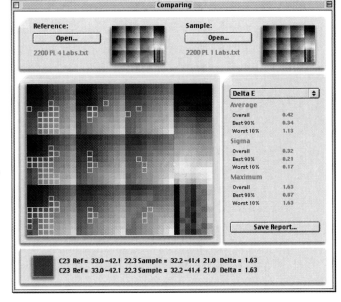

GretagMacbeth's MeasureTool is invaluable for comparing sets of measurements. Note that in this case, measuring the entire target reveals drift in the greens that would remain undetected if you simply measured the primaries.

If you're working with a handheld instrument, though, you probably don't want to torture yourself measuring hundreds or thousands of patches over and over again. Instead, you can use the RGB Process Control target shown in Figure 8-12. Print the target, note the time it was printed—preferably on the target itself—and set it aside for a couple of hours. Then print the target again, noting the time the new one was printed, and make a visual comparison of the two prints.

If you can see visual differences, you know the print takes at least two hours to cure. Re-examine them periodically until they appear identical, and note how long it takes for the second print to look identical to the first one. This gives you a rough estimate of the drying time.

You need to refine this rough estimate with a few well-chosen measurements. Subtle differences between targets that aren't obvious to the naked eye can be amplified during the profile calculation process, so measure *at least* the solid and midtone patches for R, G, B, C, M, Y, and RGB. When the prints have cured, you shouldn't see any differences greater than 0.5 delta-e LAB between targets. See the sidebar, "Comparing Colors," earlier in this chapter.

Creating RGB Inkjet Profiles

Profiling tools usually offer few or, sometimes, no parameters to set for RGB output profiles. A good rule of thumb is to start by building a profile at the default settings offered by the profiling tool and depart from them only when you've found a reason to do so.

Some profiling packages offer a two-step process in which you first print and measure a linearization chart. The profiler then uses the linearization measurements to generate a custom profiling target tailored to the specific printer at hand. Read the accompanying documentation carefully: some packages, such as Integrated Color Solutions' BasICColor Print3/c, recommend using the linearization step for inkjet printers, while others, such as Monaco Systems' MonacoPROOF and MonacoPROFILER, recommend against doing so.

Some packages, including MonacoPROOF, MonacoPROFILER and GretagMacbeth's ProfileMaker, offer a choice of gray rendering as either absolute or relative to the paper. We've noticed that with some very blue-white paper stocks, neutrals that measure dead-on neutral appear yellow to the eye because our eyes always adapt to the paper white. In those situations, rendering gray relative to the paper seems to work better. In the case of ProfileMaker, Preserve Gray Axis will produce neutrals that measure neutral yet look yellow, whereas the Paper Gray Axis will produce neutrals that visually appear neutral. These options apply only to the perceptual rendering intent. Other intents are always built using Paper Gray Axis.

A few packages offer some control over gamut mapping for the perceptual rendering intent. There's no right way to do perceptual rendering: if you're of a mind to experiment, by all means do so, but we suggest starting out with the default.

When you build the profile, it's always a good idea to give it a name that's as informative as possible—one that contains the printer model and the paper stock.

Profiling True RGB Printers

We use the term *true* RGB printers to refer to devices such as the Fuji Pictrography, Cymbolics LightJet, Durst Lambda series, and anything else that images directly onto photosensitive paper or film. These types of devices usually have robust built-in calibration features that make them highly repeatable. The photographic media they use tends to be very stable with no curing time.

The only real source of variability we find in these devices is that the profiling target may print slightly differently depending on its orientation. Color geeks refer to this problem as *anisotropy*—an obfuscatory way of saying that the printer produces slightly different color when printing the same image in portrait and landscape orientations.

In our experience, the effect of anisotropy is usually quite subtle, and unless you're picky, you may not even notice the effect it has on your images printed through the profile.

Before Profiling True RGB Printers

If you do notice anisotropy in the printing of the profiling target, we offer two ways to work around the problem—scrambling the patches on the target, or printing the target four times, rotated 90 degrees each time, and averaging the results. If your profiling package either offers to scramble the patches for you (MonacoPROFILER will do this), or uses a target with a randomized set of patches (such as the ones offered by Integrated Color Solutions' BasICColor Print3c), use the randomized target.

Tip: Use the GretagMacbeth EyeOne Target. Many profiling packages that don't offer random patch arrangements have targets formatted for the EyeOne. Since the EyeOne's scanning mode requires big differences between each patch, the EyeOne targets are, in effect, randomized, which makes them ideal for dealing with anisotropy, even if you're using some other instrument to measure them.

Randomizing the patches yourself might seem like less work than printing and measuring four targets. Trust us—it's not! You not only have to move the patches in the target file itself; you also have to rearrange the numbers in the target description file that the profiler uses to relate the measured values to the control signals that produced them, and the chances are extremely high that you'll screw something up in the process. Just bite the bullet and print the target four times at different rotations!

Creating True RGB Printer Profiles

The options offered by profiling packages for true RGB printers are the same as for RGB inkjets, but they may not always produce the same results.

Of those packages that offer linearization, the ones that don't recommend it for RGB inkjets *do* recommend it for true RGB printers, and vice versa. Rendering gray relative to the paper tends to have a more pronounced effect on these types of printers than on inkjets—if it's available, we recommend trying it as your first choice.

Profiling Three-Color Dye-Sub Printers

Non-PostScript dye-sublimation printers function as RGB devices even though they use CMY dyes. The main variables that plague dye-sublimation printers are anisotropy (though for quite different reasons than true RGB printers) and manufacturing variation in consumables.

Dye-sublimation printers vary in their color performance due to thermal latency: they make color by heating the dyes in the donor ribbon until they sublimate—turn into a gas—and get absorbed by the coating on the paper. The laws of physics limit the speed with which the print head can heat up and cool down, so the color can vary depending on what color was printed immediately before the current one.

As with true RGB printers, the remedies are either scrambling the patches or printing the target at multiple orientations and then averaging the results. We've generally had better results from printing multiple targets than we've had from patch-scrambling, but it means more measurement—so if you're working with a handheld instrument, you may want to use scrambled patches on a single target to avoid excessive wear and tear on your wrists.

Some dye-sub printers also exhibit *directional metamerism*, where the color appearance (and the measurement) changes when you rotate the sample 90 degrees. If you average four targets at different orientations, the difference gets averaged out. If, however, you're measuring a single target, a polarization filter can help (if your spectrophotometer has one).

Some dye-sub printers offer software settings that perform some kind of auto-enhancement on incoming images. Make sure that any such options are turned off before you print the profiling target.

If your profiling package offers a linearization step, it's likely that your dye-sub printer will benefit from it. Other than that, the default settings for your profiler should work well.

Profiling Composite CMYK Printers

CMYK printers differ enormously in dynamic range, gamut, available paper stocks, and inksets. In this section, we'll talk about color laser printers, color copiers, solid ink/wax printers, inkjets, and digital presses. (Printing presses have their own section later in this chapter.) In addition, we'll assume the device is driven by a PostScript RIP.

As with RGB output devices, you first need to make sure that the printer is stable, linearized, and gray-balanced. The different printing technologies are prone to different sources of variability, so we'll deal with each class's typical problems and the strategies for dealing with them, separately.

Once you've stabilized the printing process (we provide guidelines for doing so below under each printer type), printed the target or targets, and collected the measurements, you're ready to build the profile. Most profiling packages offer default settings for the different types of devices, and these are usually the best place to start. The most common options are total ink limit and UCR/GCR settings. More sophisticated packages allow finer control over black generation, including black start, the shape of the black curve, and the amount of GCR. See the sidebars, "Ink Limiting" and "Black Generation," for a discussion of these terms.

In case your package doesn't provide presets for categories of CMYK printers, we've provided starting points for common printer types. These are guidelines, not rules. If you have ink bleeding all over the page and you're using 400% ink, lower the total ink limit! Likewise, if we suggest a medium black generation, but a lighter or heavier amount gives you better results, go with the settings that give you better results.

Before Profiling CMYK Color Laser Printers

Color laser printers, color copiers, and some digital presses form a class of devices generically called *electrophotostatic* devices. In these devices, a laser writes the image onto a light-sensitive drum that converts light into a static charge. The drum then rotates, transferring this invisible image made of patterns of positive and negative charge onto the paper. The paper passes by a toner cartridge containing the first colorant in the form of very small and charged particles, which attach themselves to the oppositely charged areas of the paper. Finally, the paper passes through a heated fusion roller that melts and fuses the toner onto the paper. In older color lasers the process is done separately for each colorant, and in the latest generation all four colorants are applied in a single pass.

We explain this technology because it helps you understand its inherently variable nature. The variability comes from two sources:

▶ Paper needs some humidity to hold a static charge—it can't be completely dry. Variations in humidity translate directly to color variation.

▶ When a toner cartridge is new, there are lots of eager toner particles that are itching to jump on charged paper. Over time, the eager toner particles are gone, leaving behind the less eager toner particles, so there's a steady decrease in the density you can achieve with each colorant.

If you used up the exact same amount of each colorant (extremely unlikely), you'd notice a steady decrease in saturation. More likely, you consume the colorants at different rates, so the relationship in density among the four colorants is constantly changing.

Electrophotostatic printers are a prime example of the moving target. The only solution is frequent calibration—twice a day is typical, and once an hour is not unheard of. The newer generations of machines tend to be more stable than the older ones. So first determine how often you need to calibrate to keep the device reasonably stable—periodically printing and measuring a CMYK process control target like the one in Figure 8-14 is the easiest way to do so.

Figure 8-14
CMYK process control
target

This target contains 21-step ramps of C+M+Y, M+Y, C+Y, C+M, C, M, Y, and K.

We offer two strategies for printing the profiling target:

▶ Calibrate the printer and immediately print the profiling target.

▶ Calibrate the printer, print a series of targets (decide how many you're prepared to measure) throughout the previously determined calibration interval, and average the results.

The first approach will produce a profile that's accurate for the device's optimal behavior. The second will give you a profile that's accurate for the device's average behavior. If you can enforce regular calibration, use the first approach. If you can't guarantee that the device will always be calibrated when necessary, use the second.

Ink Limiting

We don't know of any CMYK printing processes that can use 100% coverage of each of the four colorants. If you apply 400% ink to paper, the paper is likely to disintegrate, whether the ink is being applied by an inkjet printer or a printing press.

But even when the colorants aren't wet, as in the case of color laser, dye-sublimation, or solid-ink printers, maximum density is achieved long before you reach 400% coverage, and in some cases density may even decrease as you add more colorants. So some kind of ink limiting is always needed in CMYK printing.

With composite CMYK printers, you often have the choice of limiting the inks in the profile or in the RIP. If the printer is a type that can take different paper stocks with different ink requirements, such as an inkjet, it's usually easier to set the limits for each paper type in the RIP, and then set the profile ink limits to 400%.

If the printer is either limited to a single paper (dye-sub), or the paper has almost no effect on the point at which the colorants reach maximum density (color laser, solid ink), it doesn't matter where you set the ink limits.

In either case, though, it's critical that you set them in one place or the other, but *not* both. For presses, it makes a great deal more sense to set the ink limits in the profile.

There's never a reason to lay down more colorant than is required to achieve maximum density. There is, however, often a good reason to lay down less.

You may wish to sacrifice some density in favor of stability, but an even more compelling reason is simply to save money by using less ink.

Creating CMYK Color Laser Profiles

Color laser printers and copiers almost always have fixed built-in ink limiting, so you don't want to limit it any further. These devices are usually designed to print business graphics, so the colorants aren't particularly well gray balanced. You'll usually get the best gray balance by forcing as much gray component as possible to print with black ink by selecting a maximum GCR separation. Here are our suggested separation parameters for color laser printers.

▶ Total Ink Limit: 400%

▶ Black Ink Limit: 100%

▶ Black Generation or GCR: Maximum setting

▶ Black Start/Onset: 5-10%.

If prints made through the resulting profile seem oversaturated or plugged in the shadows, it's possible that the printer doesn't have built-in ink limiting (the Xerox DocuColor series is one example). In that case, we suggest the following as a starting point:

Black Generation

Composite CMYK printers usually need a fairly specific black generation scheme, but on presses, the way you introduce black ink to the cyan, magenta, and yellow primaries involves a series of trade-offs that represent one of the most critical aspects of printing. The main reason we use black ink is to produce a denser black than we could obtain with CMY primaries on their own, but important secondary reasons include saving money—black ink is generally cheaper than the colored inks—and avoiding problems on press caused by misregistration or fluctuations in density.

The two basic black generation strategies are Under Color Removal (UCR), and Gray Component Replacement (GCR). UCR separations use black only in the neutral and near-neutral areas, while GCR is a more aggressive strategy that replaces the amount of CMY that would produce a neutral with K, even in colors that are quite a long way from neutral.

Each has its own strengths and weaknesses.

UCR separations are often used on newsprint presses because they're generally less vulnerable to changes in black density—newsprint press operators tend to run up the black until the type looks nice and dense, and a little more black than you'd bargained for can turn a GCR separation to mud. But UCR separations are also used on high-end sheet-fed presses to print content that has important dark, saturated colors such as shoe and leather catalogs.

GCR separations save money by using more black ink relative to the colors, and they can mask slight variations in registration between the colors that would wreck UCR separations. GCR separations also make it easier to maintain gray balance, since most of the neutrals are carried by the black plate and are often used for images whose important details are neutral or close to neutral.

So one key point to make is that the choice of UCR or GCR is dependent not only on the printing process, but also on the image content. When we profile presses, we generally create a family of profiles that differ only in black generation so that we can tailor the separations to the content. Computer screen grabs, for example, generally benefit from a much heavier GCR than we would consider using on scanned photographic images. There's no right answer when it comes to black generation on press, so don't be afraid to experiment.

Most of the work in profiling a press is in collecting the data. Once you've done that, it's trivial to generate profiles with different black generation schemes. You can tell a lot about a profile's behavior without ever committing ink to paper, so don't think that experimenting necessarily involves huge print bills. See "Output Profiles" in Chapter 9, *Evaluating and Editing Profiles*.

- ▶ Total Ink Limit: 260%

- ▶ Black Ink Limit: 100%

- ▶ Black Generation or GCR: Maximum setting

- ▶ Black Start/Onset: 5-10%.

Before Profiling CMYK Inkjets

Most of the things that apply to profiling RGB inkjet printers apply to profiling CMYK inkjet printers as well. The main variable, apart from the software settings in the RIP, is the time the ink needs to stabilize on the paper (see "Curing time," earlier in this chapter).

If your RIP allows it, it's usually easier and more convenient to set ink limits and linearization in the RIP before profiling than it is to apply ink limits and linearization in the profile. You won't get the best possible results by applying ink limits and linearization in both; all you're doing is multiplying the number of variables you have to contend with. Pick one or the other.

Some RIPs apply ink limiting but don't let you control it other than by selecting different paper types. If you want to use a paper that isn't supported directly by the RIP, you'll need to experiment, but you should begin by building a profile that assumes the ink limits have been set in the RIP.

We rarely find a reason to print multiple targets, though if the inkjet printer is very low resolution (such as a billboard printer) or is very noisy (such as when using uncoated watercolor paper), you may benefit from taking multiple measurements and averaging them—which, with a strip reader, may mean printing and reading two targets.

Creating CMYK Inkjet Profiles

Due to the wide array of inkjet printers, paper stocks, and RIP capabilities, the recommendations we give here are guidelines for a reasonable starting point, not hard and fast rules. Coated papers can generally handle more ink than uncoated ones. If your RIP applies ink limiting (whether you can control it or not), we suggest the following as a starting point:

► Total Ink Limit: 400%

► Black Ink Limit: 100%

► Black Generation: Medium to Heavy (not quite Maximum)

► Black Start/Onset: 30%.

If your RIP doesn't apply ink limits, we suggest as a starting point:

▶ Total Ink Limit: 260%

▶ Black Ink Limit: 100%

▶ Black Generation: Heavy (not quite Maximum)

▶ Black Start/Onset: 30%.

Before Profiling Solid Ink Printers

Solid ink printers (aka *crayola-jet* or *crayon-spitters*) aren't popular (perhaps because people don't realize how inconsistent color laser printers can be and aren't aware of solid ink as a viable option). Their main drawback is that the prints are quite delicate—an eraser removes the ink from the paper, heat melts the ink, and sunlight can drastically alter its color.

Solid ink printers work by maintaining a heated reservoir of melted ink. The liquid ink is squirted onto a rotating drum and is then cold-fused with pressure onto the paper. They're very versatile when it comes to paper types—we've even seen one print on a tortilla—and the color is very consistent between different substrates as long as they're white.

Older models of these printers had to be shut down each day, because the liquified ink cooked over time and changed color. Newer printers don't have this problem.

Even though these printers have four inks, we usually profile them either as CMY, or as CMYK with no black generation. We've never found a reason to average multiple targets.

Creating CMYK Solid Ink Printer Profiles

You may need to experiment for the best results. But in the case of the Xerox Phaser 8200, here are the recommended settings. This effectively builds a CMYK profile that generates separations with no black channel— apparently the black channel is best computed by the printer itself:

▶ Total Ink Limit: 300%

▶ Black Ink Limit: 0%

▶ Black Generation: None

▶ Black Start/Onset: Not applicable.

If you end up with disgusting results, fall back to the suggested settings for the color laser or copier.

Before Profiling CMYK Dye-Sublimation Printers

CMYK dye-sub printers operate identically to CMY dye-sub printers except that they have PostScript RIPs. Whether they have three or four colorants, they're still considered CMYK devices. But since they operate identically to non-PostScript dye-sub printers, the same considerations before profiling apply, including printing and averaging of multiple targets in multiple orientations.

Most dye-sub RIPs have fixed, built-in ink limiting. If you should encounter the very rare one that doesn't, don't make the mistake of thinking that dye-sub can handle 400% coverage—you'll typically get less density at 400% than at 320% or so, because the extra heat required to lay down 400% coverage sublimates some of the dye out of the paper and back into the donor ribbon!

Creating CMYK Dye-Sublimation Printer Profiles

If your dye-sub has built-in ink limiting, use the following settings:

▶ Total Ink Limit: 400%

▶ Black Ink Limit: 100%

▶ Black Generation: UCR

▶ Black Start/Onset: 60%.

In the rare case that the dye-sub doesn't have built-in limiting, try:

▶ Total Ink Limit: 320%

▶ Black Ink Limit: 100%

▶ Black Generation: UCR

▶ Black Start/Onset: 60%.

Profiling Printing Presses

Be it lithography, flexography, or gravure, the printing press is The Beast when it comes to printers. On a desktop CMYK printer, you worry about one sheet at a time. On a press, you worry about five thousand sheets at a time. Because mistakes are extremely costly in terms of time and money, you need to take into account some special considerations prior to going down the road of profiling a press.

With other devices, you typically calibrate them to optimal behavior and then profile them. With presses, that's just one option. You may decide on standardized press behavior rather than optimized press behavior. Or you may decide not to profile the press at all (see the sidebar, "Don't Profile the Press?!").

The key factor in deciding how you want your press to behave, and whether or not to profile it, should be your proofing methodology. *The press must be able to match the proof.* If it doesn't, you're in the situation we color geeks technically term *hosed*, and you must either do whatever's necessary to force the press to match your proofs or change your proofing system so that it does a better job of predicting actual press behavior (see "Printing and Proofing" in Chapter 10, *Color-Management Workflow*).

There are essentially two approaches to running presses.

▶ Do whatever's necessary in prepress to massage the data so that it produces the desired result on press.

▶ Treat the press as a $4000/hr. color correction station by adjusting the press to produce a sellable result from questionable separations.

In the latter case, you may as well forget about profiling the press unless you're willing to spend a good deal of time finding a stable and reasonably optimal set of press conditions, and a somewhat larger amount of time retraining the press operators to hit that condition consistently instead of making artistic decisions based on the current job. You may, however, find it worthwhile to profile your proofing system (see the sidebar, "Don't Profile the Press?!," later in this chapter).

Don't Profile the Press?!

Given the variation inherent in printing on a press, as well as the cost, you may want to consider *not* profiling the press. That's right, you read correctly. Consider profiling your contract proofer instead. If you can successfully match your proof on press, and with reasonable ease, it makes sense to make the proofer, rather than the press, your aimpoint. It's a lot easier to get a perfect proof than it is to get a perfect press run that hits your in-house process control target aimpoints dead center.

Traditional contract proofers, such as those that produce film-based laminate proofs, use colorants that are similar to press inks on substrates that make the colorants produce similar dot gains to the press. The great workflow benefit is that you can send exactly the same separations to the proofer and to the press. A few digital proofers, such the Kodak Approval and the Iris inkjet series, offer similar capabilities.

You can create a profile for a contract proofing device by measuring a single target, so it's relatively quick and easy. When you create the profile, simply use the ink limits and black generation you want on press. That way the separations resulting from this profile are press-ready.

In the former situation, profiling the press is eminently practical, but even then you may decide that building a profile, or a family of profiles, for every paper stock is simply too big a headache. If your current proofing system takes the same CMYK data as your press—that is, it doesn't rely on a color conversion between press space and proofer space—and you're confident that you can match your proofs on press, it's easier and cheaper to profile the proofer instead.

If you aren't happy with your proofing system, or it's one that uses profiles to convert from press to proofer space, you'll need to profile the press, but you may only need to make one press profile (see the sidebar, "Profile the Press Once," later in this chapter).

Before Profiling Presses

The first consideration is to get the press behaving in as stable a manner as possible—which means very different things for a brand-new sheet-fed press and a 50-year-old web. This isn't a book about press process control—there are many good ones—so we won't tell you how to do that; we simply point out the necessity of doing so.

A second consideration is whether you want to optimize your press to take full advantage of its capabilities, or whether you want to make your press conform to some kind of standard or reference behavior such as SWOP/TR001 for magazine publication, the nascent sheetfed TR004

Profile the Press Once

What if you aren't happy with your current proofing situation? If you print to more than a handful of paper stocks, it's probably impractical to create and manage press profiles for each paper. One viable strategy is to take a paper stock with middle-of-the-road behavior on press and profile that press/ink/paper combination as an aimpoint for proofing.

Once you've profiled the press and established your aimpoint, you can profile your proofing device, use a color server to make the necessary conversions from your press profile to your proofer profile, and account for varying dot gains on different paper stocks by applying transfer curves in the platesetter or imagesetter. The single press profile then becomes the aimpoint for RGB-to-CMYK conversions and also serves as the source profile for proofing client-supplied CMYK.

standard from GRACoL, ISO 12647-3 for newsprint, or a contract proofing device. See the sidebars "Optimized or Standardized Press Behavior," and "Intentionally Non-Linear," later in this chapter.

Printing a profiling target on press demands a significant commitment of time and money. Moreover, the measurement data you collect from the target run will likely be reused, because building the best possible press profile is almost always an iterative process. So no matter whether you opt for an optimized or standardized press condition, you should treat the target run as a critical job.

Choosing profiling targets. Most profiling packages offer proprietary targets as well as IT8.7/3, largely due to the latter's shortcomings. However, a couple of new standard targets are worth considering:

▶ The proposed IT8.7/4, which is aimed mainly at the packaging market (for characterization of flexographic presses, for example), is expected to perform better than the IT8.7/3 for other CMYK profiling purposes. It contains 950 patches.

▶ The ECI 2002 target from the European Color Initiative, comprising 1,485 patches, is effectively a combination of the IT8.7/3 and the proposed IT8.7/4.

Both targets come in randomized versions. GretagMacbeth already offers the ECI 2002 as their preferred target for profiling presses. We recommend using a randomized target if at all possible (such as the version GretagMacbeth offers for the EyeOne Pro). Otherwise, gang copies of the target in four different orientations and expect to do extra measuring.

Optimized or Standardized Press Behavior

It's possible to have a press condition that's both optimized and standardized, but it's easier to understand if you consider them as separate goals. A fully optimized press is all about maximizing its capability—the lowest possible dot gain, highest ink densities, and best contrast the individual press can achieve, without regard to any external specifications or standards. If your press can do better than a specification, you let it do so.

The problem is that this creates a unique press condition for which there's no standard means of creating separations or proofs. But if you profile the press, your applications can do the necessary conversions to create separations tailored to your unique and optimized press behavior.

Another approach is to make the press conform to some kind of reference. This may involve something relatively easy such as changing ink densities on press, or creating custom transfer curves in your RIP, imagesetter or platesetter (see the sidebar "Intentionally Non-Linear"). Or it may be more involved, such as changing water/ink ratio, temperature, blanket pressure, ink viscosity, ink tack, and dozens of other variables, to essentially force the press into the desired behavior. The desired behavior could be a house-standard proofing system that you want all your presses to match. It could be SWOP/TR 001 to take advantage of file portability, as it is one of the most common targets for color separations in the U.S., or FOGRA in Europe.

With a fully optimized press, you'll need to make a profile for your press because the press behavior is unique, and there's no other way to make separations or proofs. In the second case, you can use good process control to make the press conform to the desired behavior, and you can use either standardized characterization data, such as that provided by SWOP TR 001, FOGRA, or ISO 12647-3, or profile your in-house contract proofing device instead of profiling the press.

When you print a run of targets, you'll have hundreds if not thousands of press sheets from which to choose. We recommend selecting between 10 and 20 sheets to measure and average. There are two equally valid schools of thought on which sheets you want to measure:

▶ Measure targets representing the full range of the press output. Don't measure 10 press sheets in the middle of the stack—get a sample of sheets representing the natural oscillation of press behavior, with some really good press sheets, some average press sheets, and some below-average press sheets that nevertheless wouldn't be rejected.

▶ Measure targets representing the sweet spot of press output. Sample only those press sheets that represent the ideal press behavior you wish it always had from the beginning to the end of a press run.

Intentionally Non-Linear

Linearizing the imagesetter or platesetter should be a regular event in a print shop, because these devices drift so that a 50% dot in an image file ends up creating something other than a 50% dot on film or on plate. Commonly, we linearize imagesetters and platesetters and then compensate for dot gain produced on press in our separations. That's one purpose for profiling a press or contract proofing system.

But there's a legitimate case to be made for intentionally non-linearizing your imagesetter or platesetter in order to force one or more presses to conform to a specific behavior. In fact, it's common in the flexography and print-packaging industries to compensate for large amounts of dot gain in the image- and platesetters, though it seems to be a relatively recent idea in lithography. Using transfer curves, you can compensate for the more subtle variations in the

behavior among presses without having to make custom profiles for each one of them.

In an organization with 10 presses, it's not realistic to make 10 profiles: quite apart from anything else, you can't delay the pre-press department until they know which press will run a job. Instead, use transfer curves to compensate for differences in dot gain, giving all presses the same tone response curve. Then use a single profile for all presses.

This is especially important in CTP (Computer-To-Plate) workflows, where a linear platesetter produces a sharper dot on press than a plate made from film. For these environments to take advantage of file portability and standard separation methods (see the sidebar "Optimized or Standardized Press Behavior)", they need to use the transfer curve function to effectively "add-in" dot gain. That way, these workflows have the

benefits of CTP, while still being able to produce plates with the same dot size as plates made with film for those jobs that need it.

You can even use this method to compensate for the difference in dot gain from different line screen settings. If all other things are equal, the higher the line screen, the higher the dot gain. If you regularly print at 150 and 175 lpi with a particular inkset and substrate, you can use transfer curves to compensate, and use just one profile for both.

But be warned: transfer functions are an expert feature that can cause a great deal of trouble, especially if they're saved into image files. It's a great deal safer to download a transfer curve to the imagesetter or platesetter RIP than it is to build one into an image. Unless you know exactly what you're doing, and have communicated it clearly to your prepress and printing providers, don't mess with transfer curves.

In the first case, the intent is to ensure the profile represents the overall average sellable product from the press. Use this technique when press process control and consistency are acceptable, but not outstanding—you don't have a whole lot of near-perfect sheets or below-average sheets, and most of them are average.

In the second case, the intent is to ensure that average or below-average press sheets don't add noise to the profile. Use this technique when press process control and consistency are excellent. Most press sheets will hit the intended aimpoints; therefore, you want the profile to expect those aimpoints.

Creating Profiles for Presses

While most packages supply default ink limit and black generation settings for different press types, consider them starting points—each combination of press, ink, and paper has its own requirements.

The ink limits for a particular press are usually known (and if they aren't, they should be determined as part of the exercise of stabilizing the press), but black generation is more of an open question. Entry-level packages may simply offer preset UCR and three or four strengths of GCR black curves. More sophisticated packages offer complete control over the black curve shape, start, and end points, and also let you decide how far to extend black away from the neutrals and into saturated colors—see Figure 8-15.

Figure 8-15

Black generation controls

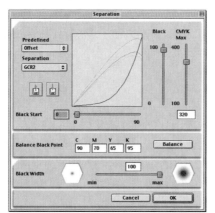

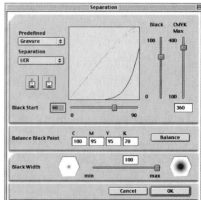

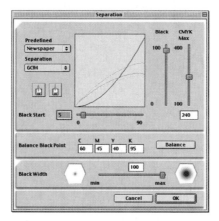

GretagMacbeth's ProfileMaker Pro offers presets for a variety of different press types, but also allows you to control the total and black ink limits, the black start, and the black width, the last of which fine-tunes the extent to which black extends from the neutrals into colors.

When making press profiles, we rarely make a single profile. Instead, we build a family of profiles that differ only in their black generation to accommodate different image types (see the sidebar, "Black Generation," earlier in this chapter). Often, after we've used the profiles, we'll go back to the measurement data and generate new profiles with slightly refined black curves. Until you've used the profiles on live jobs, it's pretty much impossible to tell if your profile would be improved by setting the black start value to 38% rather than 40%, for example. See Chapter 9, *Evaluating and Editing Profiles*, for profile evaluation techniques.

Profiling Multichannel Printers

You might think any printer that uses more than four inks qualifies as a multichannel (sometimes referred to as deviceN Color) printer. Nothing could be further from the truth. In an overwhelming majority of cases, printers that have six, seven, eight, 10, sometimes 18 inks are treated and profiled as either RGB or CMYK. The challenge is in knowing which one.

In most cases, you'll need to make both an RGB and a CMYK profile to see which is better. The RIP or printer driver separates the RGB or CMYK data you send it into the control signals for the specific inks in the printer.

A few inkjet RIPs actually let you control each ink individually and offer support for six-, seven- and/or eight-color ICC profiles. In this case, making such a multichannel profile may be worthwhile. In the case of printing presses, it's really the only way to go because you need multi-channel separations to generate the film and plates for use on press. Be warned, however, that few profiling packages provide support for multichannel profiling, and those that do often do so only at extra cost.

Building multichannel profiles is the trivial part of the task. Printing the target optimally and collecting the measurement data are the tricky parts. No one has massive amounts of experience building multichannel profiles—you're on the bleeding edge—so the best advice we can offer is to remember the guiding principles of profiling:

▶ Do what's necessary to make the device behave the way you want it to.

▶ Print the profiling target while the device is behaving that way.

▶ Make sure that the measurements you collect truly represent the device's behavior.

Checking the Map

If you're careful about following the principles we've laid out in this chapter, you may get perfect profiles on the first try—maps that show exactly where your color will go. Our experience tells us that although a newly-built profile may be very good indeed, it can almost always be improved. In the next chapter, we look at techniques for evaluating and editing profiles.

Evaluating and Editing Profiles

Color Orienteering

In Bruce's native land, Scotland, many otherwise-normal people happily spend rainy Saturday afternoons tramping across heath and bog, peering through wet glasses at the map in hand, pondering how to relate its contents to the ankle-deep water in which they're standing. They're indulging in the grand British pastime of orienteering—negotiating terrain using a map as their guide.

Evaluating and, optionally, editing profiles is a lot like orienteering. The profile is the map, and the device is the territory, but now you're looking at the map from the middle of the territory, possibly in ankle-deep water, and figuring out just how closely the two correspond.

One view of evaluating profiles is that it's an exercise in determining how lost you are. Another is that it's fundamentally futile to try and put a metric on people's subjective preferences. We think it makes sense to find out how inaccurate your maps are. Once you know, you can decide to make them more accurate by editing them to better match the territory, or you can decide to allow for the inaccuracies and learn to head in the right general direction while keeping an eye on the nuances of the terrain.

We have one more reason for putting profiles through some kind of systematic evaluation. Almost all color matches are the product of at least two profiles. If you don't take the necessary steps to evaluate the accuracy of individual profiles in isolation, it's hard to pinpoint the culprit when things go awry.

Judging the Map

Compasses, sextants, and other such devices are indispensable tools for navigation, but at some point, you have to simply look at where you are. By the same token, measurements play an essential role in color management, but when it comes to evaluating profiles, your eye has to be the final arbiter—if it doesn't look right, it's wrong.

But beware of mirages: back in Chapter 1, we pointed out some of the many tricks your eyes can play on you. So when you evaluate a profile, you need to set up your viewing environment so that you can say with certainty that any problems you see do, in fact, lie with the profile.

Your eye must be the final judge, but it doesn't have to be the only judge. We'll show you some objective tests that can help determine a profile's colorimetric accuracy. But these only apply to colorimetric renderings—perceptual renderings always involve subjective judgements, because there's no single correct way to reconcile two different gamuts. So objective tests, while they're useful, don't tell the whole story. At some point, you have to make subjective judgements, and to do that, a stable viewing environment is critical.

You may be tempted to edit profiles to fix problems that really lie in the device calibration or the data collection. We can tell you from bitter experience that doing so is akin to buying a one-way express ticket to the funny farm. It's often quicker and easier to recalibrate and/or reprofile to fix the problem at its source. We tend to use profile editing as a last resort (though it's also an integral part of our workflows), so throughout this chapter we'll point out which problems can be fixed more easily through other means, and which ones are amenable to profile edits.

Viewing Environment

Back in Chapter 3, we pointed out that virtually all the color matches we create are metameric in nature—that is, they're dependent on the light source under which we view them. So when you come to evaluate profiles, it's vital that you view hard-copy samples under a controlled light source such as a D50 light box. But simply plonking an expensive light box into an otherwise-imperfect viewing situation is like sticking a Ferrari engine into an AMC Pacer—it'll cost you plenty, but it may not get you where you wanted to go.

Some color-management purists insist that you must work in a windowless cave with neutral gray walls, floor, and ceiling, and a low ambient level of D50 light, while wearing black or neutral gray clothing. We agree that this represents an ideal situation for evaluating color matches, but it's a distinctly less-than-ideal situation for most other human activities. (We know shops where rooms just like this improved color matching but dramatically increased employee sick days.)

So rather than insisting on ideal conditions, we offer a series of recommendations for reasonable ones. We'll let you decide just how far you want to go towards the ideal.

Surfaces

Surfaces within your field of view—walls, floor, ceiling, desktop—should be as neutral as humanly possible. You most certainly don't want strong colors intruding into the field of view because they'll throw off your color judgement. But pastels can be just as insidious: Bruce moved into a workspace with very pale pink walls, and he found that until he painted them white, he introduced cyan casts into all his images!

If you decide that neutral gray is the way to go, Chris has compiled some paint recommendations from a variety of sources:

▶ California photographer Jack Kelly Clark recommends mixing one gallon of Pittsburgh Paint's pastel-tint white base #80-110 with Lamp Black (B-12/48 PPG), Raw Umber (L-36/48 PPG), and Permanent Red (O-3/48 PPG). Write those numbers down and take them with you to the paint store if you want to try the mix yourself.

▶ A similar Kelly-Moore Paint Co. formula from photographer John Palmer uses a pastel-tint white as a base with three colors to create an interior, flat latex similar to Munsell 8 gray: Lamp Black (4/48 PPG), Raw Umber (27/48 PPG), and Violet (2/48 PPG).

▶ Sherwin-Williams paint code: 2129 ZIRCOM. You'll want flat paint rather than glossy. (Matt Louis, Louis Companies, Arlington, Texas)

If all this seems a bit extreme, the main consideration is to ensure that the field of view you use to evaluate hard copy is neutral, and that color in the room doesn't affect the light you use to view the hard copy. Bear in mind that white walls tend to reflect the color of the ambient light—it's manageable as long as you're aware of it and take steps to control it. Glossy black isn't ideal either, as it can cause distracting reflections.

Lighting

The ISO (International Standards Organization) has set standards for illumination in the graphic arts. For example, ISO 3664 specifies D50 as the standard illuminant for the graphic arts. It also specifies luminosity of 500 lux for "Practical Appraisal" and 2,000 lux for "Critical Comparison." See the sidebar, "Counting Photons," for a definition of lux, lumens, and candelas. The standard takes into account the fact that both apparent saturation and apparent contrast increase under stronger light (these effects are named for the scientists who first demonstrated them—the Hunt effect and the Stevens effect, respectively).

But the standard wasn't created with monitor-to-print matching in mind—it mandates that the ambient illumination for color monitors should be less than or equal to 32 lux and *must* be less than or equal to 64 lux. For monitor-to-print matching, all these values are way too high—the ISO has acknowledged this, and is still working on standards for this kind of match. So until these standards are published and ratified (which may take several years), we offer some practical advice that we've gleaned empirically (that is, by trial and error) over the years.

While it might be mostly a concern for the upcoming board game *Color Geek Trivia–Millennium Edition*, we should be clear that D50 is an illuminant with a very specific spectral power distribution that no artificial light source on the planet can replicate. The term used for most light sources is correlated color temperature for which there are invariably multiple spectra. 5000 K is an example of correlated color temperature, not an illuminant. Different 5000 K light sources have different spectra and produce slightly different appearances.

Ambient light. If you're working with a CRT monitor, you need low ambient light levels because CRTs just aren't very bright. The color temperature of the ambient light isn't terribly important: what *is* important is that you shield both the face of the monitor and the viewing area for hard copy from the ambient light. Filtered daylight is OK. Full sun from a west-facing window is not, both because it's too bright and because it imparts a lot of color to your surroundings.

With some of the latest LCD displays, such as the two Apple Cinema Displays, you can use much higher ambient light levels simply because these displays are so much brighter than CRTs, but the same rules about excessive coloration are as applicable to LCDs as to CRTs.

Counting Photons

Photometry—the science of counting photons—is a basic building block for measuring color. But there's more than one way to count photons, and different methods use different units.

The *luminous flux* (or *luminous power*) is the amount of visible light energy a light source emits over time in all directions. It's computed by measuring the power in watts the light source emits, weighted by the spectral sensitivity of the eye. The unit for luminous flux is the *lumen* (lm), which is the luminous flux a reference light source emits. We use lumens to describe the overall light output of lamps without regard to the lamp's reflectors or the distance from the lamp to what it's illuminating. A typical 100-watt light bulb has a luminous flux of about 1700 lumens.

The *luminous intensity* is the amount of visible light energy over time from a point light source in a given direction. The unit for luminous intensity is the *candela* (cd), which is equivalent to *lumens per steradian* (lm/sr). (A *steradian* is a standard unit of solid angle. Just as an angle cuts out a subsection of a circle, a solid angle forms a cone that cuts out a subsection of a sphere and represents the cone of light travelling out from the point source in the given direction.) The

candela also has an equivalent definition based on the luminous intensity of a reference light source. The candela is one of the fundamental units of measurement (along with such things as grams and meters) defined by the SI (Systém Internationale d'Unités).

The *luminance* refers to the light given off by a more typical light source (which is a light-emitting surface, not a point) or an illuminated surface. The luminance is the luminous intensity per unit area of the light-emitting surface. It's measured in *candelas per square meter*, which is sometimes also known as the *nit* (from the Latin *nitere*, to shine). Luminance is the quantity represented by Y in CIE equations, and in color management we most often encounter luminance as a measurement of the photons emitted from a display.

Finally, the *illuminance* refers to the amount of light arriving at an illuminated scene. It's just the luminous flux per unit area of the illuminated surface, and is measured in *lumens per square meter*, or *lux*. (A non-metric unit is the *footcandle*, which is one lumen per square foot, or about 10.76 lux.) Typical supermarket lighting has an illuminance of about 1000 lux. Public areas like hotel lobbies have an illuminance of around 300 lux, while the full

moon produces an illuminance of about 0.4 lux.

In the definitions for the lumen and candela units above, we mentioned a *reference light source*. This reference has an interesting history. Much of photometry stems from an early unit called the *candle*. This was the perceived intensity of light in one direction from a specified standard candle (1/6-pound spermwhale wax burning at the rate of 120 grains an hour).

This reference candle was later replaced by specific types of oil lamps, then carbon filament lamps, and in 1948 by a black-body radiator at a specific temperature (to be precise, the freezing point of platinum— about 2042 K). Because black-body radiators are a pain to construct, the reference light source was redefined in 1978 as a light source with a specific frequency (equivalent to a wavelength of about 555 nm, which is where our brightness sensitivity hits its peak) and a specific radiant energy (1/623 watts per steradian). In all cases, this seemingly arbitrary definition is just the standards people's way of coming up with a definition that produces about the same unit quantity that people are already using—in this case tracing all the way back to that whalewax candle.

Tip: Use a Monitor Hood. You can increase the apparent contrast of CRT monitors significantly by using a hood to shield the face of the monitor from the ambient light. High-end CRTs often include a hood, but if yours didn't, you can easily fashion one for a few dollars from black matte board and adhesive tape—it's one of those investments whose bang for the buck is simply massive. It's also a good idea to wear dark clothing when you're evaluating color on a monitor, because light clothing causes reflections on the screen that reduce the apparent contrast.

Hard-copy viewing light. All the color science on which ICC profiles are based is designed to create color matches under D50 lighting, so for your critical viewing light D50 illumination would be ideal, but as we've already pointed out, there's no such thing as an artificial light source with a D50 spectrum. So-called D50 light boxes are really "D50 simulators." The minimum requirement is a light box with a 5000 K lamp and a Color Rendering Index (CRI) of 90 or higher. The best available solution is a 5000 K light box that lets you vary the brightness of the light, so that you can turn it up when you're comparing two hard-copy samples and turn it down to match the brightness of the monitor when you're comparing hard copy with the monitor image.

Tip: Tailor the Profile to the Light Source. A few packages (such as GretagMacbeth's ProfileMaker Pro 4.1) let you build profiles tailored to the spectral power distribution of specific physical light sources—they include spectral measurements for some common light boxes and also let you define your own. So instead of D50 LAB, you can end up with "GTI Lightbox LAB." This lets you make very critical color judgments under your viewing light, the trade-off being that those judgements may not translate perfectly to other viewing conditions. If you use this feature, use some other light source as a reality check—we really like filtered daylight!

A variable-intensity 5000 K light box is a fairly expensive piece of equipment, but if you're serious about color management, it's a worth-while investment. But it's not the be-all and end-all, either. As previously mentioned, many artificial light sources have spectra with more pronounced spikes than the relatively smooth spectrum our sun produces, and with some inksets, such as the pigmented inks used in some inkjet printers, which *also* have fairly spiky spectra, you may see significant differences between two 5000 K light sources, though you're unlikely to see differences with press inks.

Bruce always uses daylight, preferably filtered, indirect daylight, as a reality check. Whenever he's measured daylight anywhere close to sea level, it's come in significantly cooler than D50—typically between 6100 K and 6400 K—but the smoother spectrum eliminates some of the stranger behavior that can result from the combination of a light source with a spiky spectrum and an inkset with a spiky spectral response curve.

Tip: Use a Viewing Light Checker. Viewing light checkers are ingenious little color targets printed with two colors that match under D50 but show different colors under other light sources. One such is the GATF/ RHEM Light Checker—we've included one on the inside-back cover of the book. Place the checker on top of the sample you're evaluating. If you can't see stripes, your lighting *may* be good enough for all but the most critical color matches. If you *can* see obvious stripes, you definitely need to improve your lighting situation—these test strips don't validate good lighting conditions, they simply identify bad ones.

Monitor-to-print comparisons. CIE colorimetry wasn't designed to handle monitor-to-print comparisons—color monitors didn't exist when the models on which color management is based were being developed. Nevertheless, it's capable of doing a surprisingly good job.

Some pundits will tell you that it's impossible to match a monitor image and a printed one, because the experience of viewing light reflected from paper is simply too different from that of viewing light emitted from glowing phosphors. In a very narrow sense, they may be right—one important difference between hard-copy and monitor images is that with the former, our eyes can invoke color constancy (also known as "discounting the illuminant"—see "Color Constancy" in Chapter 1, *What is Color?*), whereas with the latter, we can't since the illuminant *is* the image.

This may help to explain why so many people have difficulty matching an image on a monitor calibrated to a 5000 K white point with a hard-copy image in a 5000 K light box. There may be other factors, too—a lot of work remains to be done on cross-media color matching—but whatever the reason, the phenomenon is too well reported to be imaginary.

We offer two pieces of advice in achieving monitor-to-print matching:

▶ Match the brightness, not the color temperature.

▶ Don't put the monitor and the light box in the same field of view.

When given a choice between 5000 K and 6500 K, we calibrate our monitors to 6500 K because it's closer to their native white point; we can obtain a better contrast ratio than we can at 5000 K, which requires turning down the blue channel. We dim the light box to match the contrast ratio of the monitor—a sheet of blank white paper in the light box should have the same apparent brightness as a solid white displayed on the monitor. If you're happy working with a 5000 K monitor, by all means continue to do so, but no matter what the white point, it's critical that you throttle back the light box to match the brightness of the monitor.

The second trick is to place the light box at right angles to the monitor so that you have to look from one to the other. This accomplishes two goals: it lets you use your foveal vision—the cone-rich area in the center of your retina where color vision is at its most acute—and it allows your eye to adapt to the different white points. (Short-term memory has been shown to be very accurate when it comes to making color comparisons.)

We've been using these techniques to do monitor-to-print matching for several years, and we find them very reliable. Does the monitor image perfectly match the print? Probably not. But frankly, short of a press proof, we're not sure that we've *ever* seen a proof that matched the final print perfectly. Laminated proofs, for example, tend to be a little more contrasty, and perhaps a shade pinker, than the press sheet—not to mention their inability to predict wet trap or print sequence—but we've learned to filter out these differences. You have to learn to interpret any proofing system, and the monitor is no exception.

Evaluating Profiles

Once you've ironed all the kinks out of your viewing environment, you can safely start evaluating your profiles. One of the trickier aspects of profile evaluation is being sure which profile is responsible for any problems you might see, because most of the color-matching exercises we go through need at least two profiles, sometimes more.

Anything that you view onscreen goes through your monitor profile, so the monitor is the first device to nail down—once you know you can rely on your monitor profile, you can use it as a basis for comparison. If you just trust it blindly, and it's flawed, you'll create a huge amount of unnecessary work for yourself. Once you've qualified your display profile, it's much easier to use it as an aid in evaluating your input and output profiles.

Checking the Display

Your display is not only the first device you need to nail down, it's also the one type of device where calibration and profiling are usually performed as a single task. Since it's much more common to find problems with the calibration than with the profile, you need to check the calibration first—if it's bad, the resulting profile will be, too.

Monitor Calibration

The two most common problems with monitor calibration are incorrect black-point setting and posterization caused by trying to apply a gamma that's too far away from the monitor's native gamma for the 8-bit tables in the video card to handle.

To check the calibration, you need to take the profile out of the display loop and send RGB values directly to the display. To do so, set your monitor profile as the default RGB space in the application of your choice so that RGB is interpreted as monitor RGB, and hence sent directly to the screen with no conversions.

Tip: Use Proof Setup in Photoshop. In Photoshop 6 or later, choose View>Proof Setup>Monitor RGB to send the RGB values in the file directly to the monitor. When you choose Monitor RGB, Photoshop automatically loads the Monitor RGB profile in Proof Setup and checks "Preserve Color Numbers," effectively taking your monitor profile out of the loop.

We generally use Photoshop for this kind of testing, though almost any pixel-based editing application should serve.

Black-point check. Setting the correct black point is the biggest challenge for monitor calibrators for two reasons:

▶ The monitor output is relatively unstable at black and near-black.

▶ Most of the instruments used for monitor calibration are relatively inaccurate at black or near-black—they attempt to compensate by averaging a lot of measurements.

Be warned that the following test is brutal at showing the flaws in most monitor calibration and can lead to significant disappointment! (See Figure 9-1.)

Figure 9-1
Black-point test

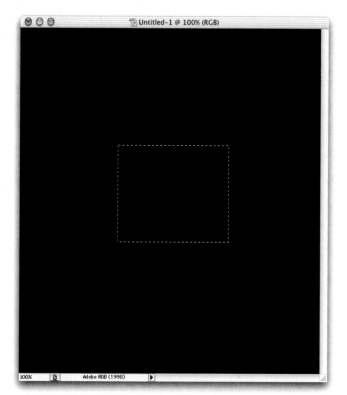

In Photoshop (or the pixel editor of your choice), create a solid black image, and make a selection in the center of the document with the marquee tool.

Figure 9-1
Black-point test,
continued

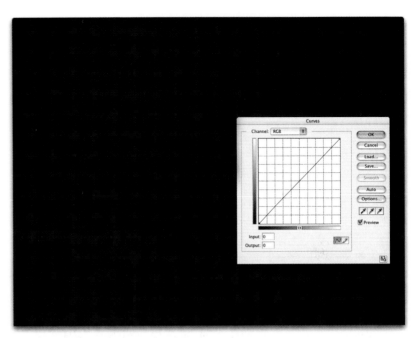

Hide all palettes, switch to full-screen mode with no menu bar, then hide the "marching ants." Open Curves or Levels, and target the 0,0 point in Curves.

Drag the dialog box off the screen, leaving only its title bar showing (the flare from the dialog's large expanse of white can prevent you from seeing small differences, which is what this test is about).

Figure 9-1
Black-point test,
continued

Use the up arrow to raise the level of the selected area—each press raises it by one level.

With excellent calibration systems, you may see a difference between level 0 and level 1. More typically, you won't see a change until somewhere around levels 5 to 7, or sometimes even higher. If you don't see any change when cycling through the first twelve levels, your black point is definitely set too low and you should recalibrate, requesting a slightly higher black point.

If the first few levels that are visible have a color cast, you may have set the bias controls incorrectly (if your monitor has them). Try making a small adjustment to the bias—for example, if the first few levels are red, try lowering the red bias slightly. Then recalibrate.

Gamma check. To refine the gamma setting, display a black-to-white gradient. We usually flip the top half of the gradient horizontally to produce a test image like the one shown in Figure 9-2.

If your application allows it, display the gradient in full-screen mode, hide all other user interface elements, and then look at the gradient closely. In an ideal situation, you'll have a perfectly smooth, dead-on-neutral gradient, and black will fade smoothly into the non-picture area of the monitor.

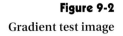

Figure 9-2

Gradient test image

Display the gradient test image in full-screen mode, with all user interface elements hidden, for best results.

In practice, this rarely happens. You'll almost certainly see some slight banding or posterization in the shadow areas, and you may see some color where you should see neutral gray. Make sure that you're looking at raw RGB sent straight to the monitor—at this point, you're checking the calibration, not the profile.

Color crossovers in a raw RGB gradient almost always indicate a fatally flawed calibration tool. If you've adjusted the R, G, and B bias controls on your monitor, it's possible to introduce color crossovers, so if you see them, the first thing to try is to reset the bias controls to the factory defaults. If you still see color where you should see grays, and you're absolutely sure that you aren't looking at the gradient through a profile, you need to toss your calibration tool and get one that works—this isn't something that you can fix with any amount of recalibration or profile editing.

More commonly, you'll see some slight amount of posterization in the shadows and three-quarter tones. Until the video card manufacturers decide that higher-precision videoLUTs are more important than the number of shaded polygons the card can draw per nanosecond, we'll all have to live with some slight irregularities in tonal response, but you can often improve the smoothness of the calibration by recalibrating, and by changing the requested gamma to something closer to the native gamma of the display system. Color management needs to know your monitor gamma, but it doesn't really matter what the absolute value is, only that it's known—so feel free to experiment with different gammas between 1.8 and 2.4 or so, and choose the one that gives you the smoothest gradient.

There are so many combinations of monitor and video card that we can't give you any magic numbers. Try raising the requested gamma by 0.1. If the posterization gets worse, try lowering it by 0.1. Eventually, you'll find the best compromise. When you've done so, don't forget to generate a new profile!

Monitor Profile

Monitor profile problems are relatively rare—flaws are usually either in the monitor calibration, or, in cases of gross mismatches between screen display and printed output, in the printer profile that serves as the source in the conversion from print RGB or CMYK to monitor RGB. Nevertheless, some monitor profiles may work better than others. If your profiling tool offers the ability to build different types or sizes of profiles, you may find that one type works much better than another.

Repeat the gradient test shown in Figure 9-2, but this time, set your working space to a gamma 2.2 profile such as sRGB or Adobe RGB, or simply assign one of these profiles to the gradient image, so that you're displaying the gradient through the monitor profile. If you see color crossovers that weren't visible in the raw display test, it's possible that your profile contains too much data—we often see LUT-based monitor profiles producing poorer results than simpler matrix or gamma-value profiles, so don't assume that bigger is always better.

Reference images. Of course, you'd probably rather look at images than at gray ramps. But the classic mistake many people make when evaluating a monitor profile is to make a print, then display the file from which the print was made, and compare them. The problem is that the display of the print file is controlled as much by, or even more by, the printer profile used to make the print as it is by the monitor profile, so you can be fooled into trying to fix problems in the printer profile by editing the monitor profile—which is like trying to fix the "empty" reading on your car's gas gauge by tweaking the gauge instead of putting gas in the tank.

When it comes to comparing a monitor image with a physical reference, the only reliable way to make sure that the monitor profile is the only one affecting the image is to compare an image in LAB space with the actual physical sample from which the LAB measurements were made. There are very few sources for a physical sample and a matching colorimetrically accurate digital file—Kodak's ColorFlow Profile Editor supplies a stringently manufactured photographic print with an accompanying digital file, but we don't know of any other vendor who does this. So unless you own ColorFlow (and we wouldn't recommend buying it solely for this feature), you'll need to use a little ingenuity. Here are some of the techniques we use.

The Macbeth ColorChecker. The Macbeth ColorChecker, made by GretagMacbeth, has long been used by photographers to check colors, and is available from any decent camera store. GretagMacbeth has never published LAB values for the 24 patches, but the LAB values shown in Figure 9-3 are ones that Bruce has collected and averaged over the years from various Macbeth targets in various stages of wear (with considerable help from Bruce Lindbloom and Robin Myers). Or you can simply measure the 24 patches yourself.

Figure 9-3
The Macbeth
ColorChecker

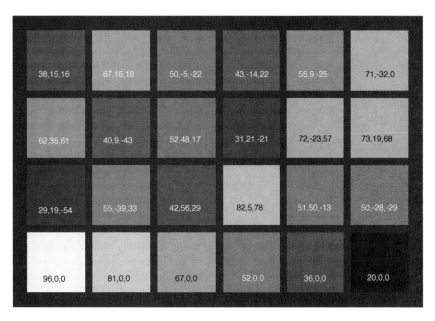

The Macbeth ColorChecker with its associated LAB values

Then, create a LAB image in Photoshop (or any other application that lets you define LAB colors), and compare the physical color checker, appropriately illuminated, with the image on screen. With CRT monitors, the saturated yellow patch (row 3, column 4) is outside the monitor's gamut, so you'll likely see a slightly more orangey-yellow. LCD monitors can hit the yellow, but may miss the sky-blue patch in row 3, column 6. But in either case, both the color relationships and the tonal values of the gray patches should be preserved reasonably well.

Scanner targets. If you have a scanner target, then you have a physical target and the LAB values of the colors it contains. All you need to do is create an image of the target containing those LAB values. Creating hundreds of LAB patches in Photoshop, though, is too much pain even for us, but fortunately, there's a solution, and it's free—see the sidebar, "Measurements to Pixels and Back," on the facing page.

Use the procedure outlined above for the Macbeth Color Checker to compare the physical target to the LAB image on screen. You'll likely have more out-of-gamut colors than you would with the Macbeth target, but the relationships between all but the most-saturated colors should be preserved.

Printer targets. Leverage your printer target! You've printed a target and measured it. Turn the measurements into pixels—see the sidebar, "Measurements to Pixels and Back" on the facing page—and compare the onscreen image with the printed target under appropriate illumination.

Your printer target will likely contain more patches than a scanner target, and fewer of them will lie outside the monitor's gamut, so it can give you a good idea of your monitor profile's color performance.

We don't advocate editing monitor profiles. It's not a philosophical objection—we simply haven't found it effective. If you find a display problem that you can more effectively solve by editing the monitor profile rather than by recalibrating and reprofiling, please let us know—we'll gladly eat our words, if not our hats!

Measurements to Pixels and Back

Logo ColorLab is an undocumented and unsupported free tool that you can download from GretagMacbeth's Web site. We don't pretend to understand all the things it does, but it has one very useful capability we've come to find indispensable. It lets us take measurement files in LAB, or target definition files in RGB or CMYK, and turn them into TIFF images in which each color patch is represented by a single pixel.

Since the color patches are solid colors, you really only need one pixel per color—you just print and display them at very low resolutions.

ColorLab can also go the other way, turning pixels into target files (RGB or CMYK) or measurement files (LAB), the only catch being that the image files need to be in 1-pixel-per-color format. If the target consists of solid patches with no borders, you can usually just downsample to one pixel per color using Nearest Neighbor interpolation in Photoshop. If the patches have borders, you need to do some work getting rid of them first.

ColorLab's requirements for measurement or target files are pretty straightforward. They need to be in Tab-delimited text format with a header that looks like the following:

```
LGOROWLENGTH        24
BEGIN_DATA_FORMAT
LAB_L LAB_A LAB_B
END_DATA_FORMAT
BEGIN_DATA
```

The first line tells ColorLab how many patches per column (even though it says row), and the number is separated from the rest of the line by a single space. LAB_L, LAB_A, and LAB_B on the third line are separated by tabs. After BEGIN_DATA, you simply record the three LAB values for each color, separated by tabs, and separate each color by a Return (so each color appears on a new line).

At the end of the data, you need a final line that says

```
END_DATA
```

We usually use a spreadsheet like Microsoft Excel to massage measurement files into the shape ColorLab needs—when you save an Excel file as Text, each column is separated by a Tab and each row by a Return.

We keep the header in an otherwise-blank Excel doc, and simply paste the measurement values from measurement files into it. ColorLab can tolerate other information in the file, so try simply opening your measurement files in ColorLab first. But if you get a "format error" message, the foregoing header always works.

Input Profiles

Scanner profiles are, as we noted in Chapter 7, *Building Input Profiles*, relatively easy to build. Scanners have a fixed, reasonably stable light source, and as long as you make sure the software settings remain consistent, they usually behave quite predictably. Digital camera profiles are much, much harder, both because cameras function under a huge variety of light sources, and because they have to capture photons reflected from a much wider variety of objects than do scanners. That said, there are a few tests that you can apply to either one.

Basic Test for Input Profiles

The first simple test is to open the scan or digital-camera capture of the profiling target in Photoshop, and assign the input profile to it. Then compare the image on your calibrated monitor with the appropriately illuminated physical target. If assigning the profile doesn't improve the match, you should probably just start over, double-checking your methodology. If the match is improved (as we hope it is), you may want to use a more objective test.

Objective Test for Input Profiles

This test uses a simple principle: we check the profile by comparing the known LAB values in the profiling target with the LAB values predicted by the profile. In an ideal world, they'd be identical, but in our experience, this never happens. If you care why, see the sidebar, "Objective Objectives," on the facing page. The reasons we do objective tests on input profiles are to help us understand and optimize our capture device's behavior, to identify problem areas in the profile that may respond to editing, and to help us understand what we see when we do subjective tests with images.

To accomplish this, we turn to the ever-useful Logo ColorLab (see the sidebar, "Measurements to Pixels and Back," earlier in this chapter). To make the comparison, we need two TIFF images of the target with one pixel per color patch. We can create the LAB image of the target values by simply opening it in ColorLab, but getting the image containing the LAB values predicted by the profile can be a little trickier.

Some profiling tools let you save the RGB values they capture from the target scan as a text file, which you can then open in ColorLab. Others, including those from GretagMacbeth and Heidelberg, store the captured RGB values right inside the profile as a "private" tag—private in name only, because you can extract the data by opening the profile with a text editor, then open the text file in ColorLab.

For those that do neither, you can downsample the target scan or digital camera capture to one pixel per patch using Nearest Neighbor interpolation in Photoshop, or build a 1-pixel-per patch image manually in Photoshop. Building the target by hand is fairly time-consuming, but produces more accurate results than resampling. A third alternative is to create a text file by hand, sampling the RGB values and entering them into the text file—we generally use Excel to do so.

Objective Objectives

You can lead yourself down all sorts of fascinating rabbit holes looking at numerical evaluations of profiles—we know because we've been there. So let's make something very clear. We don't do objective tests to come up with some unambiguous benchmark of profile quality, for two reasons:

▶ It's impossible to determine a profile's absolute accuracy unless you're willing to sample and measure every possible color combination in the profile's space, which is, to put it mildly, impractical—you'd need 16 million-some measurements in RGB, and four billion-some measurements in CMYK. The objective tests we do really only measure the profile's ability to predict or reproduce the colors in the test target we use. Different targets will return different average and maximum delta-e values.

▶ Accuracy isn't the only factor in determining a profile's quality. All CMMs operate at finite precision, making calculations from limited data, and a highly

accurate profile can very easily produce posterization and color-banding where a less-accurate one will produce smoother transitions. We often sacrifice absolute accuracy for smoothness, because our eyes are a lot more forgiving on small discrepancies in hue, saturation, or lightness than they are when they encounter sudden obvious discontinuities.

So what's the point of objective tests? Simply, they help us understand how the profile behaves, and why we see the results we do in our subjective tests. They help us understand the limitations of our devices, and they point us to areas in the profile that may respond to profile editing.

You may be tempted to use objective testing to compare profiling packages. The single best word of advice we can give you is, *don't*.

What the tests we've described here study is the profile's ability to predict and reproduce the colors in the target from which the profile was built. These tests

fail as an objective comparative benchmark for two reasons:

▶ They give an unfair advantage to profiles that were actually built from this target.

▶ They tell you nothing about the reproduction of colors that aren't in the target.

You can use these types of comparison to gauge the relative accuracy of profiles built from the same target, and as a *very* rough comparison between profiles built from different ones—but you'll get different numbers, though generally heading in the same direction, if you use different targets.

So you can't use these tests to say that profile *foo* has an overall delta-e of 1.28 while profile *bar* has one of 1.69, except in the context of the specific set of colors in the target. (Again, if you were willing and able to measure 16.7 million RGB patches, or 4.3 billion CMYK ones, you might be able to make such a statement. If you get around to it, let us know!)

If you're building either a text file or an image by hand, it's easier if you start out with a template. For text, open the target description file in Excel, and replace the LAB values with your captured RGBs (don't forget to change the Data Format definition). If you want to build an image, open the target description file in ColorLab, then save it as an image. Figure 9-4 shows the steps required to make the comparison.

Figure 9-4

Comparing actual and predicted LAB values

Step 1: Capture the RGB values from the scanned or photographed target.

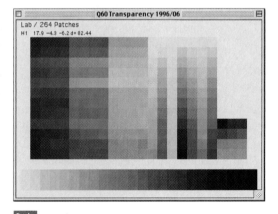

If your profiling tool includes the RGB data in the profile, you can open the profile with a text editor, then copy and paste the RGB values into a new text document. Start at the "BEGIN DATA FORMAT" line, and finish at the "END DATA FORMAT" line.

If your profiling tool doesn't capture the RGB numbers in a way you can access easily, you'll need to use one of the following methods. You need to wind up with either a text file formatted like the one above, or an image with one pixel per color patch. To create an image, it's easiest to use Colorlab to create a template from the target description file.

In ColorLab, choose Open from the File menu, and open the target description file. You'll get something that looks like the image at the right. You'll need this file anyway to make the comparison.

Since the IT8 target is non-rectangular, you need to choose IT8 to Rect Format from ColorLab's Tools menu to fill the rest of the target with neutral gray.

Figure 9-4

Comparing actual and
predicted LAB values,
continued

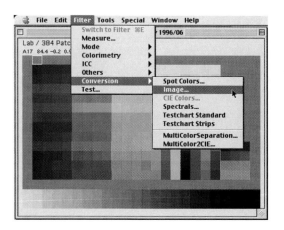

*To convert the file to a
TIFF that you can open
in Photoshop, choose
Image from the
conversion submenu
on ColorLab's Filter
menu. Then save the file
(at the time this was
written, you need to
change the extension
to .tif manually.)*

*Open the newly saved file in Photoshop, zoom in to 1600% so that you can see what you're doing,
convert the image to RGB (any old RGB—it doesn't matter because you'll be replacing all the RGB
values with ones from your target capture), and save it with a name like "Scannername RGB."*

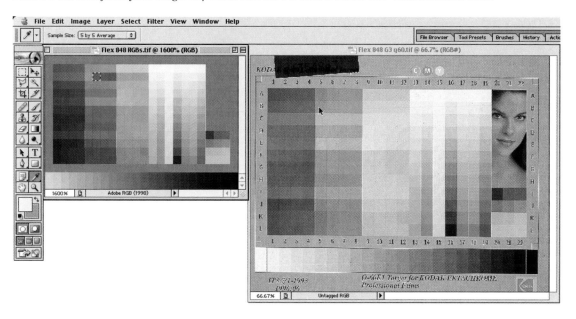

*To transfer the RGB values from the target capture to the Scannername RGB file, open the target scan,
and arrange the files side by side. Set the marquee tool to Fixed Size, 1 pixel by 1 pixel, and select the first
patch in Scannername RGB.*

*Then select the eyedropper tool, set it to 5×5 average, and option-click on the first swatch in the target
capture image to set that color as the Background color. Press Delete to fill the selected pixel in
Scannername RGB with that color, press the right arrow key to advance the selection to the next pixel,
option-click the next swatch in the capture target, and repeat until you've filled all the patches in
Scannername RGB with the values from the capture target.*

Figure 9-4

Comparing actual and predicted LAB values, *continued*

Step 2: Convert the captured RGB values to LAB (Photoshop), or ...

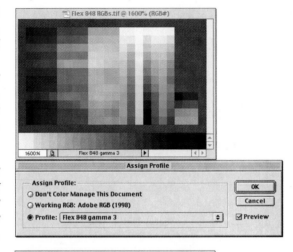

If you built the RGB file by hand in Photoshop, do the conversion to LAB there as well.

Assign the capture profile by choosing Assign Profile from the Mode submenu of the Image menu.

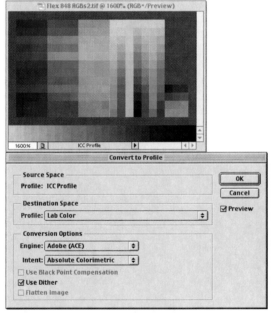

Convert the image to LAB by choosing Convert to Profile from the Mode submenu of the Image menu. Use Absolute Colorimetric rendering.

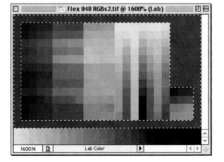

After conversion, fill the background with neutral gray, LAB 50, 0, 0.

Figure 9-4

Comparing actual and predicted LAB values, *continued*

Step 2: Convert the captured RGB values to LAB (ColorLab).

If you have an RGB text file, do the conversion to LAB in ColorLab

Open the RGB text file in ColorLab.

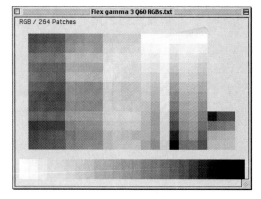

Choose LogoSync from the ICC submenu of ColorLab's Filter menu.

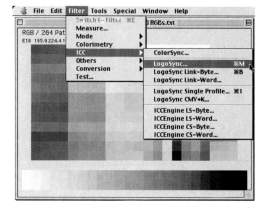

In the ensuing dialog box, set the capture profile as the Source profile, LAB as the Destination profile, and Absolute Colorimetric as the rendering intent.

Finally, choose IT8 to Rect Format from ColorLab's Tools menu.

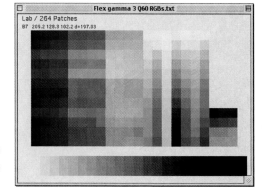

Figure 9-4

Comparing actual and predicted LAB values,
continued

Step 3: Make the comparison.

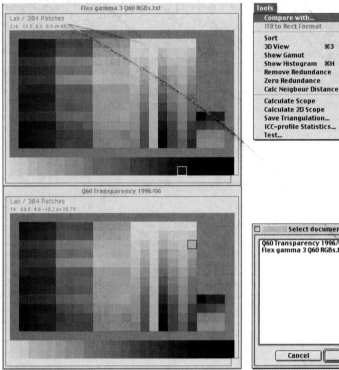

Open both the target description file and the file containing the LAB values you obtained by converting the capture RGB numbers through the profile. Make sure that both files are converted to rectangular format using Colorlab's IT8 to Rect Format command. Then choose Compare With from ColorLab's Tools menu, and choose the file you want to compare with the current one from the ensuing Select Document dialog box.

ColorLab generates a comparison that shows you the difference between the actual LAB values in the target and the LAB values that the profile predicts. It shows you the average overall delta-e, the average delta-e for the best 90% and worst 10% of patches, and the maximum delta-e for the best 90% and worst 10% of patches. The worst 10% patches are outlined in yellow, and the worst patch is outlined in red. You can check any patch's delta-e by clicking it.

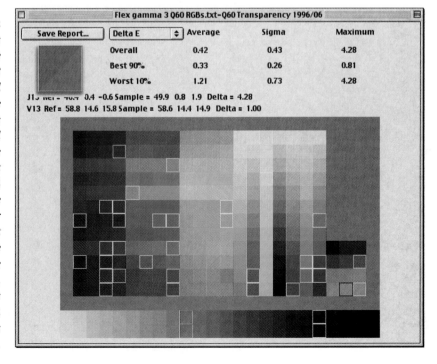

This test provides a decent metric for comparing input profiles built from the same target. For example, your profiling tool may provide several options for profile size. This test lets you determine which option gives the most accurate profile (see Figure 9-5).

Figure 9-5

Comparing large and small profiles

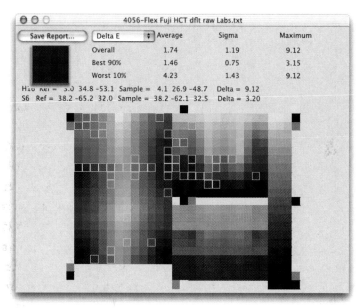

A comparison of small (above) and large (below) profiles built from the same scan shows that the large profile offers a clear improvement in accuracy over the small one.

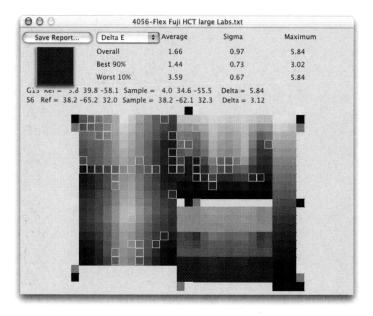

Figure 9-5

Comparing large and
small profiles,
continued

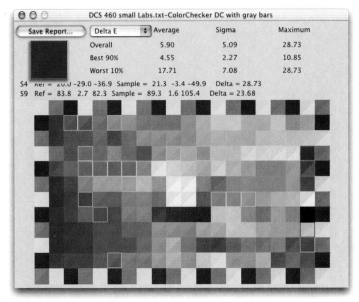

With this pair of small (above) and large (below) digital camera
profiles, we find that the reverse is true—the smaller profile is
slightly more accurate than the large one.

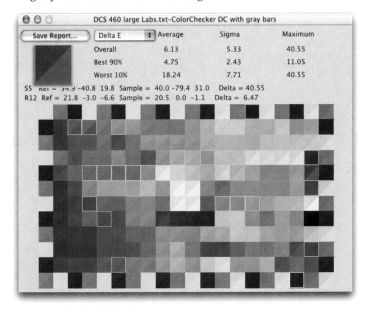

Colorimetric accuracy is important, but it's not the only concern.
Sometimes we have to sacrifice accuracy for smoothness, for example. A
profile that renders many colors very accurately at the cost of heavily
posterized images is usually less useful than one that distorts colors
slightly but produces smooth transitions between tones and colors.

Figure 9-6 shows a typical scanner profile evaluation. Note that we decided to improve shadow detail by raising the scanner gamma and reprofiling, rather than editing the profile.

Figure 9-6

Scanner profile evaluation

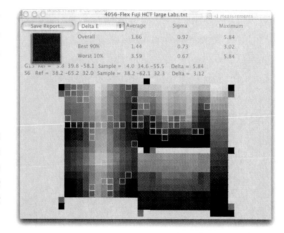

Default gamma (2.20)

Here we see a comparison of profiles built by scanning the target at different scanner output gamma settings.

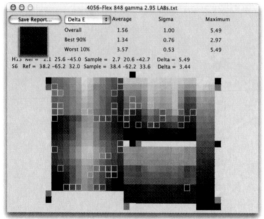

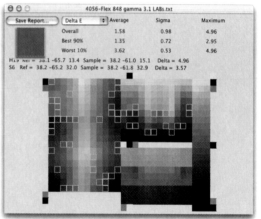

Gamma 2.95

Gamma 3.1

With this scanner, a gamma of 3.0 produces the most accurate profile, but there are always trade-offs. Some colors, such as the S6 patch in this case, may reproduce more accurately at different settings, but the gamma 3.0 setting produced the best overall results with the smallest errors.

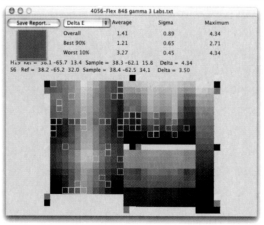

Gamma 3.0

Subjective Tests for Input Profiles

Any test that looks at the rendering of images is necessarily subjective. The key in evaluating an input profile is to select a representative sample of images, with low-key and high-key elements, pastels as well as saturated colors, and neutrals. Profiling involves a series of trade-offs, and if you judge the trade-offs on a single image, you're likely to regret it later. Of course, you need to use some common sense as well. If you are scanning or photographing only people, then you'll be more concerned with skin tones and you'll want a suitable set of test images to reflect a variety of skin tones.

It's also helpful to include a few synthetic targets as a reality check: they can often show you problems that natural images may mask or miss. Two such images that we use regularly are the Granger Rainbow, developed by Dr. Ed Granger, and the RGBEXPLORER8, developed by Don Hutcheson, both of which are shown in Figure 9-7. Note that we're constrained by the limits of our printing process in how faithfully we can reproduce these targets—the RGB versions will look quite different on your monitor!

The point of looking at synthetic targets like these isn't to try to get them to reproduce perfectly—that ain't gonna happen—but rather to provide clues as to why your images behave (or misbehave) the way they do. Sudden jumps in tone or color on the synthetic targets may happen in color regions that are well outside anything you're likely to capture, or they may lie in a critical area. It's up to you to decide what to do about them, but we believe that you're better off knowing they're there.

In the case of RGB input profiles, we use the synthetic targets by simply assigning the profile in question to the target and seeing what happens. Often, the synthetic targets make problem areas very obvious. We always make our final decisions by evaluating real images, but synthetic targets can be real time-savers in showing, at a glance, *why* the profile is reproducing images the way it does. Figure 9-8 shows a good example of this. One digital camera profile, applied to images, seemed a little weak in the reds and muddy in some yellows, but simply looking at a collection of images made it hard to pin down the specific flaw that one profile had and another did not. A single glance at the Granger Rainbow, with each profile applied, makes it very clear where the deficiencies lie!

Figure 9-7

Synthetic targets

The Granger Rainbow. You can easily make this target in Photoshop. Make a horizontal rainbow gradient, add a layer, make a black-to-white vertical gradient, and set the layer blending to luminosity.

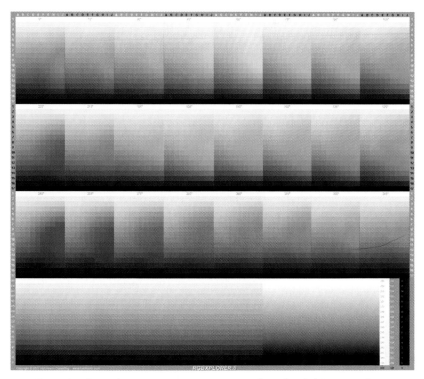

Don Hutcheson's RGBXPLORER8. You can download this target from www.hutchcolor.com—click the Free link.

Figure 9-8
Synthetic target
evaluation

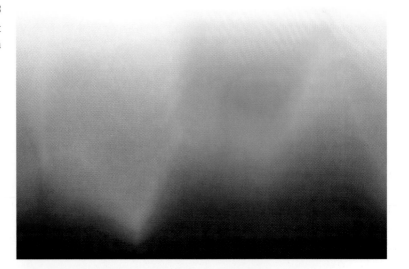

When we simply look at images, the digital camera profile whose effects are shown on this page seems to behave quite similarly to the one whose effects are shown on the facing page.

A close examination of the images points to the profile on the facing page having a problem with saturated orange-reds, but it's quite hard to spot in these images, even though they contain a lot of reds.

Figure 9-8
Synthetic target
evaluation,
continued

*When we assign the
respective profiles to
the Granger Rainbow,
we can see at a glance
that the profile on the
previous page has a
reasonably smooth
response throughout the
reds, while the profile
on this page has a huge
"hole" in the reds.*

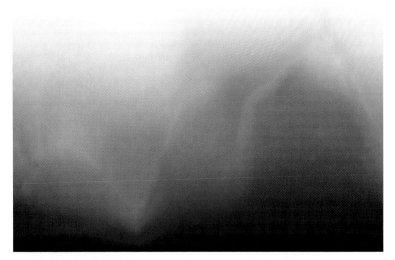

*This area of the image
hints at the problem,
but the Rainbow makes
it clear at a single
glance.*

Editing Input Profiles

With good scanners, we find we rarely need to edit the profile—the key parameter is finding the "ideal" gamma or tone curve for the scanner—but with low-end scanners that don't provide sufficient control, or sufficiently consistent control, we may resort to profile editing.

The simplest way to edit input profiles globally—that is, all rendering intents simultaneously—is to edit the capture of the profiling target. The only catch is that you have to make edits in the opposite direction from the behavior you want in the profile. If the profile's results are too dark, you need to darken the target; if there's a red cast, you need to add red, and so on.

This is very much a seat-of-the-pants procedure that absolutely requires a well-calibrated and profiled monitor, but it has the advantage that it doesn't require profile editing software, just an image editor. Small changes can make big differences to the profile—with practice you can be surprisingly precise in edits to tone, saturation, and even to hue in selective color ranges—but it's a fairly blunt instrument, and it affects all the rendering intents. So if you go this route, proceed with caution (see Figure 9-9).

For more precise edits, or for edits to a specific rendering intent, you need some kind of profile-editing software. Most of the high-end profiling packages offer editing in addition to profile creation. They all have different user interfaces, but they work in generally the same way: they let you open an image that's in the profile's space, and use it as a reference to make edits. It should go without saying (but we'll say it anyway) that for this to work, your monitor calibration and profile need to be solid.

Edit order. There's a classic order in which to make profile edits—it's the same order that traditional scanner operators use for image corrections—and we generally advocate sticking with it, with one exception, which is: *fix the biggest problem first!* Because if you don't, it often covers up other problems that suddenly become visible after you've done a lot of work.

The classic order for profile edits is:

▶ global lightness and contrast adjustments

▶ tone curve adjustments

▶ gray balance adjustments

▶ global saturation adjustments

▶ selective color adjustments.

Figure 9-9

Editing the target

The capture of the target, with the camera profile assigned, is shown above. It's quite good, but a little unsaturated.

To increase the saturation in the profile, we desaturate the capture of the target, then build a new profile from the desaturated target.

The capture of the target, with the new camera profile assigned, is shown above. It's noticeably more saturated than the original.

The order isn't arbitrary: it's designed so that the likelihood of an edit undoing the edits that went before is reduced, if not completely eliminated, so unless there's a huge problem staring you in the face that you need to correct before you can make any sensible decisions about other issues, stick to it.

Figure 9-10 shows typical editing sessions for a good midrange scanner. The scanner profile requires only minor tweaks, which is typical.

Digital camera profiles are more difficult to handle than scanner profiles, for three reasons:

▶ They don't use a fixed light source.

▶ They're more prone to metamerism issues than scanners.

▶ There's often no target reference against which to edit them.

If your work is all shot in the studio, you can and should control the lighting. If you have controlled lighting, and you gray-balance the camera, you shouldn't have many more problems than with a scanner profile. Ideally, you should edit the profile in the studio, with a reference scene set up, so that you can compare the digital capture to a physical object.

One problem you're unlikely to find in a scanner is camera metamerism, where the camera either sees two samples that appear identical to us as different, or more problematically, where the camera sees two samples that appear differently to us as identical. (Scanners aren't immune to this either, but if you're scanning photographic prints or film, you're scanning CMY dyes—digital cameras have to handle the spectral responses of real objects, which are a lot more complex.)

This isn't something you can fix with profile editing—you'll simply have to edit those images in which it occurs. So if a color is rendered incorrectly in a single image, check other images that contain similar colors captured from different objects to determine whether it's a profile problem that you can fix by profile editing or a metamerism issue that you'll have to fix by image editing.

With field cameras, you have no way of knowing the light source for a given exposure. Gray-balancing is the key to keeping the variations in lighting under reasonable control. You also have the problem of what to use as a reference when editing the profile.

Figure 9-10
Scanner profile editing

The first step in editing a profile is always to figure out which part of the profile you want to edit. Input profiles are almost always one-way, so we edit the RGB to LAB side. We usually start with the relative colorimetric intent, then apply the edits to the other intents when saving.

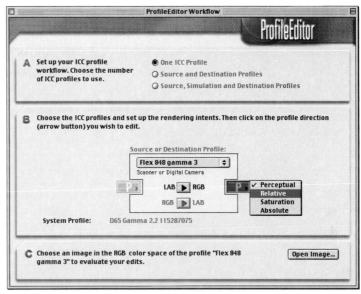

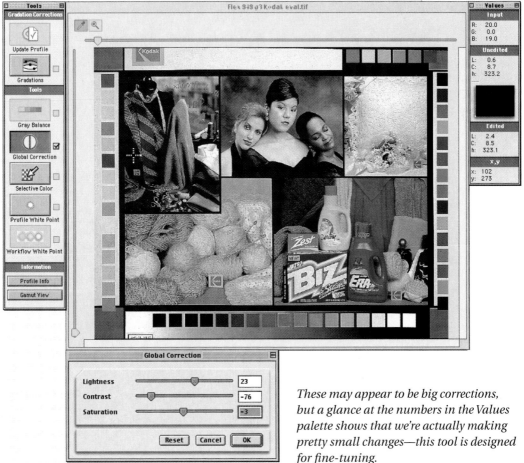

These may appear to be big corrections, but a glance at the numbers in the Values palette shows that we're actually making pretty small changes—this tool is designed for fine-tuning.

You can include a few images that contain a known target such as the Macbeth ColorChecker, but resist the temptation to edit the profile so that it reproduces the color checker perfectly without checking what it does to other images. We find that the best approach is to create a reference image by combining a wide variety of image types shot under varying conditions, and aim for a profile that helps them all more or less equally. Figure 9-11 shows a typical field camera profile editing session.

Figure 9-11

Digital camera
profile editing

Our first task is to assemble an image containing a selection of different image types. With the exception of the gray ramps, all the images we used here were shot with the camera whose profile we're editing. We gray-balanced each image, using the camera software's click-balance feature, before assigning the profile.

Figure 9-11 Digital camera profile editing, *continued*

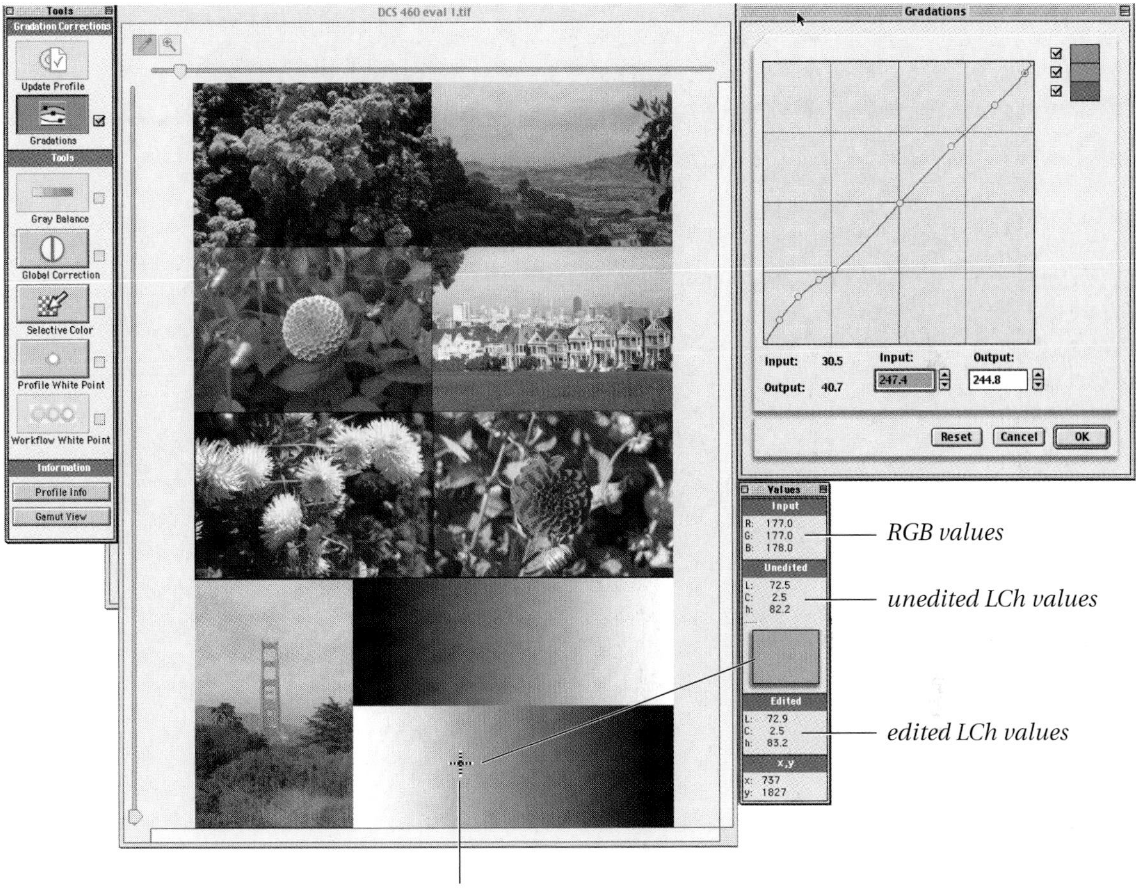

eyedropper sample point

Our first set of edits attempts to smooth out the rather abrupt transitions in tone, as evidenced by the gray ramp. We include the gray ramp because it lets us define the problem areas exactly. Clicking the eyedropper in the image loads that color into the Values palette, where we can track the unedited and edited LCh values of the color in question, as well as the RGB values.

Using the numbers as a guide, we are able to identify sharp transitions around level 60 and level 184. The curve shown above helps to smooth the sharp transitions while opening up the shadows and closing down the highlights.

While we edit, we pay close attention not only to the effect our edits have on the gray ramp, but also to what they're doing to the other images. We compare the edited and unedited versions after making each move.

Figure 9-11   Digital camera profile editing, *continued*

RGB values

unedited LCh values

edited LCh values

eyedropper sample point

Our second set of edits attempts to improve the gray balance, removing the yellow cast in the midtones, quartertones, and highlights, also shown by the gray ramp. Again, we make use of the eyedropper to load colors into the Values palette, where we can track the unedited and edited LCh values.

This time, we pay particular attention to the unedited and edited values for C (Chroma). We adjust the individual red, green, and blue curves to obtain the lowest possible values for C throughout the gray ramp—the lower the value of C, the closer we are to a neutral gray.

In this case, most of the work consists of fine-tuning the upper portion of the blue curve, but we also make a small tweak to the midpoint of the green curve to improve midtone neutrals.

Figure 9-11   Digital camera profile editing, *continued*

Our final set of edits make small tweaks to contrast and lightness. We resist the temptation to boost saturation because we'd rather fine-tune saturation as part of image editing. It's always easier to add saturation than to take it out, so we let our capture profiles err on the side of less, rather than more, saturation. The purple flowers in the top left image turned out to be a camera metamerism issue. Our attempt at selective color correction, to bring them closer to the cornflower blue that our eyes see, failed dramatically!

Output Profiles

We never edit monitor profiles, and we try to edit input profiles as little as possible, but we almost always wind up editing output profiles. Output devices tend to be less linear than capture devices or displays, they often use more colorants, and their profiles must be bidirectional so that we can use them for proofing as well as for final conversion—so they're by far the most complex type of profile.

That said, the techniques we use for evaluating output profiles are very similar to those we use for input profiles. Unless our evaluations reveal gross flaws, we tend to be cautious about editing the LAB-to-device (BtoA) side of the profile, except possibly to make slight changes to the perceptual rendering intent or to make a very specialized profile. But we find that we often have to make some edits to the device-to-LAB side to improve our soft proofs.

Before doing anything else, we always recommend looking at a synthetic target such as the Granger Rainbow or the RGB Explorer (see Figure 9-7), with the profile assigned to it in the case of RGB profiles, or converted to the profile in the case of CMYK profiles.

You'll almost certainly see some posterization somewhere—bear in mind that real images are very unlikely to contain the kinds of transitions found in these targets—so that shouldn't be a major concern. But if you see huge discontinuities, areas of missing color, or the wrong color entirely, stop. The problem could lie in the printer calibration or media settings, in your measurements, or in the parameters you set while building the profile. Whatever the cause, go back and recheck all the steps that went into building the profile, because you won't get good results from this one. Figure 9-12 shows typical appearances for the Granger Rainbow converted to output profiles. If what you see looks much worse than any of these, you need to back up and figure out where you went wrong.

Figure 9-12
Granger Rainbow
through profiles

It's common to see slight color-banding in some regions of the rainbow when you convert to an output profile, and equally common to see some color regions grow while others shrink.

However, if an output profile looks significantly worse than the examples shown here, something has almost certainly gone wrong!

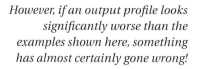

Objective Tests for Output Profiles

We do objective tests on output profiles not to provide an objective benchmark of profile accuracy, but to help us understand the profile's behavior, and to identify problem areas that may respond to profile editing—see the sidebar, "Objective Objectives," earlier in this chapter. (Bruce also does them for fun, but even he thinks that's weird.)

The fundamental principle for objective evaluations is to compare the device's known behavior with the behavior the profile predicts. We do that by comparing the actual measurements of the target—the color we *know* the device produces in response to a set of numbers—with the LAB values the profile predicts. We obtain the predicted LAB values by taking the target file, assigning the device profile to it, and then converting to LAB with absolute colorimetric rendering. This lets us see what's happening in the colorimetric AtoB1 (device-to-PCS) table.

But since output profiles are bidirectional, we go further. We take the predicted LAB values, print them through the profile, measure the print, and compare the measurements to the predicted LAB values. This lets us see what's happening in the colorimetric BtoA1 (PCS-to-device) table. We usually see higher delta-e values on this side of the profile because it's computed, whereas the AtoB table is based on actual measurements.

Lastly, we "close the loop" by comparing the original measurements with those from the predicted LAB image printed through the profile. Usually the errors in the AtoB and BtoA tables are in opposite directions, producing a lower delta-e between the two measurement files than between either measurement file and the values predicted by the profile. If you get higher delta-e values in this comparison than in the others, the errors are moving in the same direction on both sides of the profile—this may be a sign of bad measurements, so check them. If you're sure they're OK, you may want to edit both sides of the profile identically.

As with input profiles, we use Logo ColorLab to convert text to pixels and vice versa. You can use ColorLab to convert the RGB or CMYK device values to LAB, but we prefer to do that in Photoshop, since it lets us choose different CMMs easily. The CMM can make a big difference to the results—if your profiling package is designed to prefer a particular CMM, you can use this same test to determine whether the preferred CMM actually produces better results, and if so, how much better.

Figure 9-13 shows the steps needed to evaluate the AtoB colorimetric table, the BtoA colorimetric table, and the roundtrip result.

Figure 9-13

Output profile objective testing

In ColorLab, choose Open from the File menu, and open the target description file. You'll get something that looks like the image at the right. Choose Spot Colors from the Conversion submenu of the Filter menu, then click Enable in the dialog that appears.

Choose Image from the Conversion submenu of the Filter menu, click Enable in the ensuing dialog box, and then choose Export from the File menu and save the file as a TIFF.

Step 1: Obtain predicted LAB values.

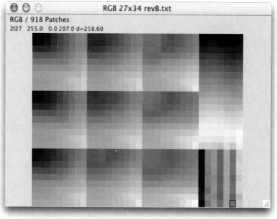

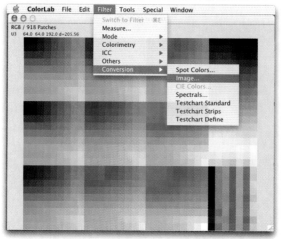

Open the TIFF in Photoshop, assign the profile being evaluated, then convert the TIFF to LAB with absolute colorimetric rendering to obtain the predicted LAB values. (The illustration shows an RGB output profile but the procedure is identical for CMYK.)

Figure 9-13

Output profile objective testing, *continued*

Make a duplicate of the "predicted LAB" file, convert it back to the profile using Absolute colorimetric rendering, print it, then measure the print to obtain the roundtrip LAB values.

Step 2: Obtain roundtrip LAB values.

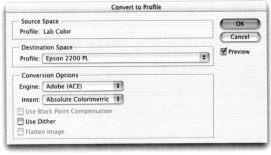

Step 3: Set up the comparison.

In ColorLab, open the original measurements from which the profile was built, the roundtrip measurements you just made, and the TIFF image containing the predicted LAB values.

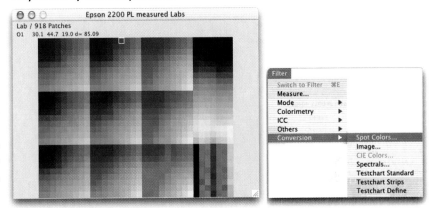

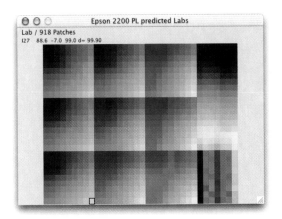

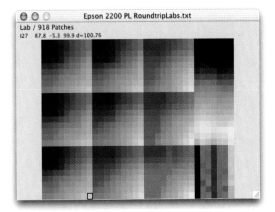

To ensure that all three files are available for comparison in ColorLab, choose Spot Colors from the Conversion submenu of ColorLab's Filter menu, then click Enable in the dialog box that appears. This tells ColorLab that each patch is a spot color and lets it generate a color-by-color comparison.

Figure 9-13

Output profile objective testing, *continued*

Step 4: Make the comparisons.

Select the original measurement file, choose Compare with ... from ColorLab's Tools menu, then select the predicted Labs file from the Select Document dialog box.

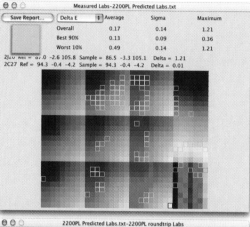

ColorLab generates a comparison of the measured LAB values with the ones predicted by the target. This provides a gauge of the accuracy of the AtoB (device-to-PCS) side of the profile.

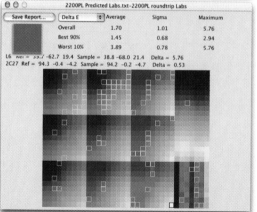

Repeat the process to compare the predicted LAB values with the roundtrip LAB measurements. This gives you an idea of the accuracy of the BtoA (PCS-to-device) side of the profile. You'll almost always get higher errors on this side of the profile.

Don't just look at the numbers. ColorLab does a good job of showing you the visual difference between the samples (if you have a good monitor profile), as well as the delta-e values.

A delta-e of 3 is much less significant in a color that's almost black than it is in one that's bright blue, for example.

Also, look for areas where the profile seems to have problems with a specific range of colors. They can help you spot possible candidates for profile editing.

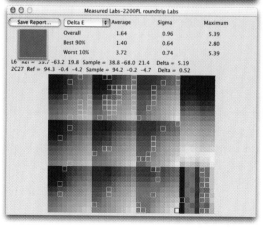

Close the loop by comparing the original and roundtrip LAB measurements. This gives you an idea of the overall accuracy of the profile. The errors are usually lower than those in the previous comparison.

If one profile or CMM seems to produce more accurate results than another, double-check by looking at the Granger Rainbow—accuracy often comes at the expense of smoothness. Don't make any hard-and-fast decisions yet—to fully evaluate the profile, you still have some work to do.

Subjective Tests for Output Profiles

Objective tests give you a good idea of a profile's overall accuracy—how much slop there is in the system—and the specific color areas where it has trouble. They're useful in determining the profile's ability to reproduce spot colors accurately, and to simulate other devices' behavior as a proofer. But they tell you very little about the profile's ability to print images. To do that, you need—you guessed it—to print images!

When you evaluate a profile's image-handling capabilities, you need to use a variety of image types with shadow and highlight detail, saturated colors, neutrals, skin tones, and pastels. The images must be in either LAB or a well-defined device-independent RGB space—such as Adobe RGB (1998) or ColorMatch RGB—to make sure that your evaluation isn't compromised by shortcomings in the input profile. (You can't use an original print or transparency to make the comparison, because the profiled print would then be the result of the input profile plus the printer profile.) Print your test images using both relative colorimetric and perceptual renderings.

You need to carry out two comparisons for each rendering intent. Compare the printed image, under suitable lighting, with the original image you were trying to reproduce (if you're evaluating a CMYK output profile, look at the original RGB image) on your calibrated and profiled monitor. This comparison looks at the colorimetric and perceptual BtoA (PCS-to-device) tables, which control the way the output device renders color.

Then convert the images to the profile you're evaluating, and compare its appearance on your calibrated and profiled monitor—this looks at the colorimetric AtoB (device-to-PCS tables), which control the soft-proof of the printed image on your monitor.

If you're happy with both, you're done, and you can skip the rest of this chapter. It's more likely, though, that you'll find flaws with one or the other. The two key questions you need to ask are, in this order:

► Does the screen display of the image converted to the profile match the print?

If the answer is yes, we recommend that you don't try to edit the profile, but instead soft-proof images and make any necessary optimizations as edits to individual images (see "Soft-Proofing Basics" in Chapter 10, *Color-Management Workflow*). It's a great deal easier to achieve predictable results editing images than it is editing profiles.

If the answer is no, we suggest that you edit the AtoB tables to improve the soft-proof before you even think about editing the BtoA tables. Most profile editors work by displaying your edits on an image that's displayed through the profile, so fixing the display side of the profile is pretty much essential before you can turn your attention to the output side.

► Does the print provide a reasonable rendition of the original image?

If the answer is yes, fix the AtoB tables if necessary or just use the profile as is. If it's no, do you see problems with both rendering intents, or just with one? If you only see problems with perceptual rendering, and your profiling package allows you to change the trade-offs between hue, saturation, and lightness in the perceptual intent, you may want to generate a new profile with different perceptual rendering parameters rather than editing. If you see real problems with the relative colorimetric rendering too, it's a candidate for editing.

Editing Output Profiles

Output profile editing isn't for the faint of heart. You're standing ankle-deep in a bog, you've decided that the map needs fixing, and all you have to fix it with is your eyeballs and a laundry marker. With care, practice, and skill, it's possible to make profiles more useful by editing them, but it's a great deal easier to screw them up beyond recognition.

With that cautionary note in mind, here are the types of edits that we think are rational to attempt:

► Globally editing all the AtoB tables to improve soft-proofing. We typically make *small* changes to white point, overall contrast, and saturation (see Figure 9-14).

Figure 9-14

Editing the AtoB
white point

*The paper-white
simulation of images
rendered to the screen
with absolute colorimetric
rendering is often too
drastic to be visually
useful. We address this
by slightly reducing
the color cast and
increasing the lightness.
Note that this adjustment
also affects absolute
colorimetric rendering
to hard-copy proofers.
Test both.*

▶ Making small changes to selective colors in all the AtoB tables to
improve soft-proofing (see Figure 9-15).

Figure 9-15

Selective color in
the AtoB tables

*Here, we made small
changes to the soft-
proofing of a small
range of yellow-greens
to make the soft proof
match the printed piece
more closely.*

▶ Making small changes to the BtoA0 (perceptual) table only, to improve the printed output of out-of-gamut colors, but only after you've finished editing the AtoB tables—unlike the first three types of edit, this one actually changes the printed output. Consider whether you'd be better off generating a new profile with different perceptual mapping—if your profiling package lets you control this, you're almost certainly better off making a new profile than editing this one.

You can also edit the colorimetric BtoA table to try to reduce the maximum errors, or to improve the reproduction of specific colors, but be warned—it's like trying to adjust a cat's cradle. You pull on one part of the color range, and another part moves. It's possible to reduce the maximum error, or improve the reproduction of specific colors that concern you, but only at the cost of increasing the overall average error. Within limits, this may be a perfectly sensible thing to do.

If your goal is to reduce maximum error, consider where in the color range it's happening. A LAB delta-e of 10 is a great deal more obvious in a light blue than it is in a light yellow, for example. So look at where the errors are showing up, and decide if they're visually objectionable enough to justify compromising the color in other areas (see Figure 9-17).

Edit, Reprofile, or Update?

When you're new to profile editing, you'll be tempted to edit the profile to fix problems that are really better addressed by either adjusting the device's behavior (perhaps by linearizing) and reprofiling, or reprofiling with different profile parameters. Going all the way back to the beginning and starting over may seem like a lot more work than editing the profile, but in the long run it's usually the easiest course.

Remember that a profile is the result of a lengthy process that's subject to all the variables we discussed in Chapter 5, *Measurement, Calibration, and Process Control*. Small changes in the variables early in the process tend to get amplified in the profile creation process.

If your profile has problems that are big enough to make you contemplate editing them, take a moment to reflect on all the steps that went before. Are both the device and the instrument correctly calibrated? Did you let the printer target stabilize? Are all your measurements correct?

Figure 9-17.

Reducing maximum
delta-e errors

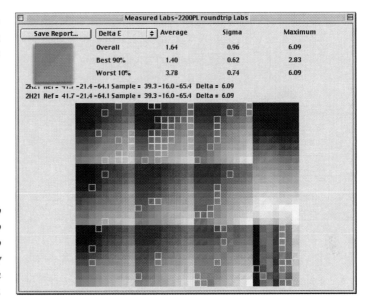

*This roundtrip
comparison led us to
edit the cyans to try to
improve the visually
obvious delta-e on
the cyan patches.*

*After editing, we
compared the new
roundtrip values. We
did indeed improve the
cyans, but only at the
expense of slightly
higher average and
maximum delta-e
values. Nevertheless,
we consider the effort
successful because the
increase in errors is very
small, and the worst
delta-e has shifted to a
color region where it's
visually much less
noticeable.*

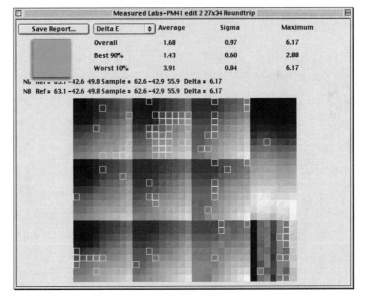

Did you set the separation parameters for your CMYK profile optimally?
All these factors can have a surprisingly large impact on the resulting
profile.

If the device has changed in a way that defies recalibration, or
calibration isn't an option with your particular device, *and* the result is
a shift in tone reproduction, you may be able to update the profile. Some
packages offer the ability to reprint a linearization target (or in the case

of GretagMacbeth's ProfileMaker, a calibration target), and update an existing profile. If the magenta in a color laser printer is printing heavier today, for example, updating may be adequate. But if you've changed to a new magenta inkset on press or in an inkjet, you'll most likely have to make a new profile. Subtle changes in paper stock can often be addressed by profile updating. The way to find out is to give it a try— updating a profile is quicker and easier than either editing the profile or making a new one.

Profiling is Iterative

Getting good profiles requires rigorous attention to detail, a reasonably stable device, a reasonably accurate instrument, and a reasonably good profiling package. Getting *great* profiles takes a good deal more work. We often go through multiple iterations of calibrating the device, measuring, profiling, evaluating, editing, evaluating again, going back and adjusting the device, and then repeating the whole process. Eventually, you'll reach the point of diminishing returns no matter how picky and obsessive you are, but just where that point occurs is a subjective call that only you can make.

Where Do We Go From Here?

We've just about run the analogy of profile as map into the ground, but it still has a little life left in it. In this chapter, we've shown you how to determine the accuracy of the map, and how to improve at least some aspects of its accuracy. In the next section, we'll talk about how to use the maps to get to where you need to go.

PART III

Applications and Workflow

Color Management Workflow

Where the Rubber Meets the Road

We've been straining the analogy of profile as map throughout this book, so let's give it one more good hefty yank. A few of us appreciate profiles, or maps, as works in their own right, but for most of us, they're simply tools, and maps aren't all that useful if we never *go* anywhere.

At this point, you probably know slightly more than normal people need to know about profiles. In this chapter, we look at where the rubber meets the road—how you *use* profiles with your various devices and applications to drive your color where you want it to go.

We give you the holistic overview of how your color management components interact, and describe the major principles that govern how you configure your applications to let color management make your color flow smoothly and predictably—from capture, through editing, to document assembly, to proofing, and to final output (or outputs).

You may be tempted to just skip ahead and delve into the chapters that describe *your* applications. Instead, we beg you to take the time to digest the material we present here, because while the application-specific material will tell you which buttons to push, vendors have a tendency to move and rename those buttons each time they revise the applications. If you understand the bigger picture we paint here, you'll know what kinds of buttons to look for, and you'll understand how, why, and when to press them to make your applications handle color the way you want them to.

What Is Color-Management Workflow?

"*Workflow*" is one of those slippery words like "quality," "art," or "postmodernism," where every expert claims to know what he's talking about, but no two can agree on its definition. We won't try to provide a comprehensive definition of workflow. Instead, we'll just tell you what *we* mean when we talk about color-management workflow.

In a nutshell, color-management workflow is the art and science of defining what colors the numbers in your documents represent, then preserving or controlling those colors as the work flows from capture, through editing, to output. In this chapter we'll look at how color-management workflow applies to three different areas:

▶ **The flow of documents or objects *within* a program.** For each application, how do we configure it for color management, and what procedures should we use to open and save documents, import objects into the program, and copy and paste colors between windows in the program?

▶ **The flow of documents *between* programs.** As we move color documents from program to program, or even from person to person, how do we keep colors looking right, and when and how do we convert to different forms for output?

▶ **The flow of materials into or out of a color-managed environment.** How do we bring in documents and objects from non-color-managed devices or applications, and integrate them with our color management documents? How can we get maximum benefit out of our color management efforts before sending our jobs off to environments where other non-color-managed steps may happen?

We color-manage two types of things: *documents*, and *objects* in documents. One program's document may be another's object. For example, a *document* in Photoshop consists of a raster image, but in Illustrator, QuarkXPress, or InDesign, this very same raster image may be just one *object* among many in an assembled document. And each one of these objects may have a different profile assigned to it (see Figure 10-1).

Figure 10-1

Documents and objects

assumed profile used in Illustrator

digital camera profile

profile from designer's monitor

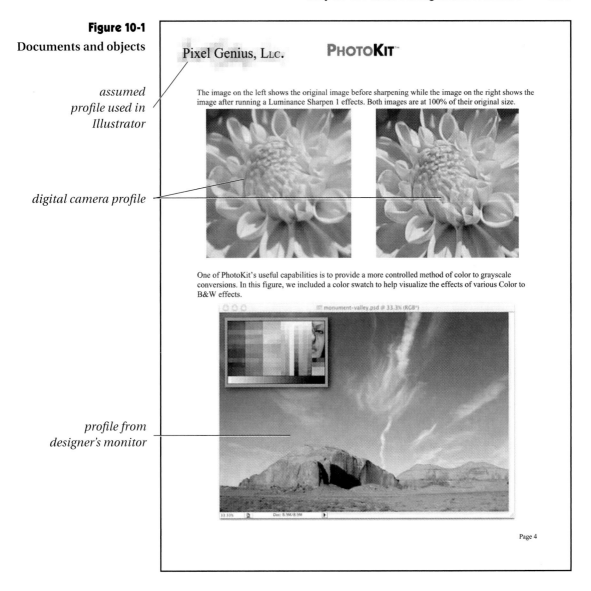

Ultimately, all these elements will wind up being converted to the same output space. There are really only two variables that differentiate the very large number of possible color-management workflows:

▶ When the conversions occur

▶ How the color meaning is conveyed.

As we told you way back in Chapter 3, these are the only two things that color management systems do. Applications may dress color management up in fancier clothing, but all color-management features ultimately break down into some combination of these two basics.

But timing conversions and conveying color meaning raise different types of issues. When to convert is a *strategic* decision that is in considerable part dictated by the type of work you do, while the way color meaning is conveyed is largely a *tactical* decision that's dictated by the capabilities of your applications. So we'll look at the bigger, strategic question first. But before doing so, we need to address one other issue.

Display Conversions

It may not be immediately obvious, but almost every time you display an image in a color-managed application, there's a conversion going on from the document's space to your monitor's space—the only exception is if the document is already in monitor RGB. If this conversion didn't happen, all your color would be displayed inaccurately.

From a workflow standpoint, however, the display conversion is out of the loop. Color-managed applications apply the display conversion on the fly to the data that gets sent to the video card—it never touches the documents themselves.

The beauty of this approach is that it allows color management to account for the quirks of each individual's display, transparently and automatically, without affecting any of the actual data being pushed through the workflow (see Figure 10-2).

Figure 10-2
Monitor compensation

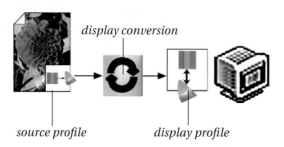

display conversion

source profile   *display profile*

Color-managed applications perform a conversion on the data sent to the monitor, from the document's source profile (or profiles) to the display profile. This conversion happens outside the main color reproduction loop and never touches the document data itself, so the same document can be displayed correctly on many different monitors without undergoing conversions to the source data.

When to Convert

Back in the 1990s, workflow was a hot topic that allowed consultants to earn large sums of money, mostly by telling their clients what they already knew and wanted to hear. But one useful distinction that dates from those halcyon days is the distinction between a *late-binding* and an *early-binding* workflow:

▶ Early-binding workflow converts all the color into final output space as soon as possible—traditional prepress workflows that took output CMYK right from the scanner are a classic example.

▶ Late-binding workflow delays the conversion to final output as long as possible. In-RIP separations in the platesetter's or imagesetter's RIP represent an extreme late-binding workflow.

However, late binding versus early binding isn't a binary, either/or choice. Rather, late binding and early binding define two ends of a continuum. Most color-management workflows fall somewhere between the two extreme examples cited above.

Early Binding Advantages

The biggest advantage of early-binding workflows is simplicity. Early in the workflow, everything gets converted to a single output space. As long as they stay in this closed-loop environment, there's no ambiguity about the color meaning of the device values in each document and object.

A second advantage is that it's easy to introduce color management gradually into existing early-binding prepress workflows. The only changes that color management brings are that operators see accurate color on their monitors instead of being forced to rely strictly on the numbers, and it becomes possible to pull intermediate comps and preproofs from inexpensive inkjet printers. The basic workflow doesn't change at all.

A third early-binding advantage is that it prevents designers from using non-reproducible colors in their designs. If everyone works in final output space, it's impossible by definition to create out-of-gamut colors.

Early Binding Disadvantages

The huge disadvantage of early-binding workflows is their inflexibility. Everything in the workflow is targeted to a single output process—all the color is squeezed into the output gamut and optimized for the output's tonal response. So early binding is practical in situations where the output process is always the same—a daily newspaper or monthly magazine, for example—but it's pretty useless for a freelance designer who may have to work on jobs where the output process isn't even known yet.

A second disadvantage when the output is CMYK is that many creative effects, such as a large number of Adobe Photoshop filters, are only available in RGB. And even those available in CMYK often make terrible assumptions about CMYK behavior, resulting in poorer quality effects.

A third possible disadvantage is that output files are usually CMYK, while most capture devices produce smaller RGB files (they only have three channels, as opposed to four-channel CMYK), so early binding means larger files, hence slower performance when opening, saving, or copying files across a network. While workstation storage is reasonably cheap, an additional 33 percent on a network, over the Internet, or in asset-storage requirements, is not insignificant.

Late Binding Advantages

The great advantage of late-binding workflows is flexibility. Maintaining the color gamut of the originals means that the work is easily repurposed for conditions as different as sheetfed printing, newsprint, or the Web.

Late binding also allows you to do a great deal of useful work before the final output conditions have been determined, and it's well-suited to situations where the color is assembled from many different sources.

Late Binding Disadvantages

The major disadvantage of late binding is its inherent complexity, not in the sense that it's difficult, but in the sense that there are many more places for things to go wrong. A single incorrect application setting can wreck one or more elements in the job.

A second disadvantage with extremely late-binding workflows such as in-RIP separations is that you don't have a chance to evaluate the final output data until very late in the game. In early-binding workflows, particularly those based on an established traditional prepress workflow, color management can be reasonably called a luxury, albeit a very useful one. But in a late-binding workflow, it's a mission-critical necessity.

Avoiding Extremes

The late binding/early binding distinction is a useful one to keep in mind, but it's important to remember that the terms represent two extremes. Most real color-managed workflows fall somewhere in the continuum that stretches between the two extremes.

It's also tempting to think of early binding as an all-CMYK workflow and late binding as an all-RGB one, and in a great many cases, you'd be right. But bear in mind that while all capture devices capture RGB (even the big prepress drum scanners that produce CMYK output scan in RGB, then convert the data), not all outputs are CMYK, so the distinction really does revolve around when you commit all your color to output space, which may or may not be CMYK.

There's one more important issue to factor into this equation. Most capture spaces and most output spaces aren't that well-suited to editing color, so many color-management workflows use an intermediate space between capture and output spaces to avoid the worst extremes of early or late binding, and to simplify the workflow.

Intermediate Spaces

If color reproduction were simply about reproducing original imagery or artwork as exactly as possible, it might make sense to keep all our color imagery in the RGB space in which it was captured until it was time to convert to final output space, as shown in Figure 10-3.

Figure 10-3
Scan to print

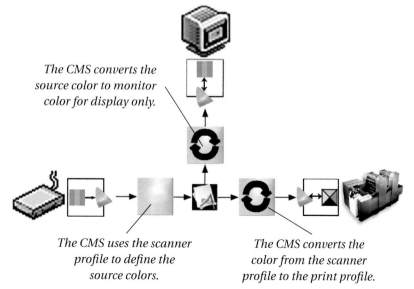

The CMS converts the source color to monitor color for display only.

The CMS uses the scanner profile to define the source colors.

The CMS converts the color from the scanner profile to the print profile.

But, in the real world, things are rarely that simple. Our originals almost always have a wider gamut than our output, and even the best profile with the best perceptual rendering is unlikely to do equal justice to all images—we typically need to make different compromises to a picture of a black cat in a coal cellar and one of a polar bear in the snow, to cite a couple of extreme examples. So we almost always need to edit our images, even if they were captured perfectly.

Input device spaces describe the behavior of capture devices, and as a result they usually have two properties that make them less than ideal as image-editing spaces:

▶ Input spaces are rarely gray-balanced.

▶ Input spaces are hardly ever perceptually uniform.

In a gray-balanced space, equal values of R, G, and B always produce a neutral gray, which simplifies one of the most powerful techniques for correcting color: pull the neutrals into place and the rest of the color follows. In a non-gray-balanced capture space, this is a lot more difficult to accomplish.

In a perceptually uniform space, the same incremental change in the numbers produces the same degree of change in the appearance, no matter where in the color gamut and tonal range it takes place. Capture spaces generally lack this property, which again makes them more difficult to use for editing.

Device-independent RGB. One solution, embodied in Adobe Systems' applications but usable by others, is to use a device-independent, gray-balanced, perceptually uniform space such as Adobe RGB (1998) for editing. This approach has proven sufficiently popular to spawn a plethora of editing spaces—often named for their developers—and debating the merits of each is decidedly outside the scope of this book. Instead, we'll simply say that the main criterion in choosing an editing space is its gamut.

Bigger isn't necessarily better. The trade-off is between finding an editing space that won't clip colors in either your capture or your output, and finding an editing space that doesn't waste huge numbers of bits describing colors that you can't capture, display, print, or in some cases, even see. In practice, it's pretty much impossible to find a space that contains all your colors yet doesn't waste bits, so you simply have to pick the best trade-off for your particular purposes.

CIE LAB. Why not simply use LAB as the intermediate space? It is, after all, gray-balanced and reasonably perceptually uniform. LAB-based workflows are quite popular in Europe, but less so in the USA. LAB-based workflows can be very predictable and productive, with two caveats. First, LAB is not a particularly intuitive space in which to edit: most LAB-based workflows use editing applications, such as Heidelberg's NewColor, that put an LCh interface between the user and LAB. Second, LAB is a very large space indeed, since by definition it contains every color we can see. As a result, it wastes an awful lot of bits on non-reproducible colors, so all major editing should be done at the capture stage on high-bit data—an 8-bit-per-channel LAB file is a fairly fragile thing that doesn't respond well to big moves in tone or color.

So a more typical color-management workflow might look like that shown in Figure 10-4, where captures from multiple sources are converted early on into an intermediate editing space.

Figure 10-4

Capture to edit to print

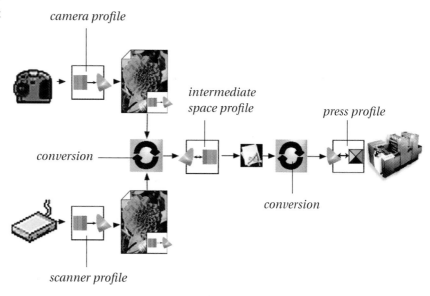

Scanner RGB and camera RGB both get converted to intermediate space RGB when the application opens them. Editing is done in intermediate space RGB, and the color is converted to press CMYK at print time.

The Intermediate Space Advantage

Intermediate-space workflows combine most of the simplicity of early-binding workflows with all of the flexibility of late-binding workflows. Early in the process, all imported color gets converted to the intermediate space, and all new colors get defined in the intermediate space, so there's little room for ambiguity. And as long as the intermediate space encompasses the gamuts of all likely output processes, or at least the colors likely to be output, it's easy to repurpose the work for different outputs, or to do most of the work before the output process has been decided. Adobe's applications use the term "Working Space" to define an intermediate editing space—see Chapter 12, *The Adobe Common Color Architecture.*

Conveying Color Meaning

Even though we're discussing it second, conveying color meaning is really the first part of the color management puzzle. You can't ask the CMS to match a color if you can't tell the CMS what that color is by supplying a source profile. And there are only two ways to supply the source profile:

► We can tell the CMS explicitly by embedding a profile in the document or object (or assigning a profile—see the sidebar "Terminology: Tagging, Assigning, Embedding, and Assuming," later in this chapter).

► We can tell the CMS implicitly by configuring applications to assume that, absent any indication to the contrary (such as an embedded profile), all RGB content is in ProfileX space, and all CMYK content is in ProfileY space.

The two options aren't mutually exclusive—many color-management workflows, including the one we used to produce this book, make use of both embedded and assumed profiles.

Embedded Profiles

The least ambiguous and most robust way to tell the CMS what colors the numbers in the document represent is to embed the profile that describes them. In an *embedded-profile workflow*, the profile always travels with the object to which it applies, and is always available to serve as the source profile for any conversion (see Figure 10-5).

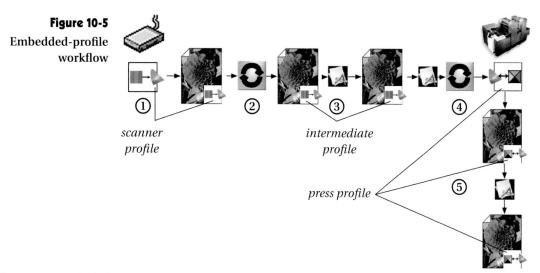

Figure 10-5
Embedded-profile
workflow

scanner
profile

intermediate
profile

press profile

1) *The scanner embeds the scanner profile in the image.*

2) *The receiving application converts from scanner RGB to intermediate-space editing RGB.*

3) *The application embeds the intermediate-space editing RGB profile.*

4) *The next application converts to press CMYK, and embeds the press CMYK profile.*

5) *Final editing is done in press CMYK. The edited image is saved with the press CMYK profile embedded.*

Premature Binding

We think it should be self-evident that it's technically impossible, and practically less than rational, to convert your color to output space before the output process is known, but every day we see people proving us wrong. People work on jobs with no idea whether they're going to be printed on a direct-to-plate sheetfed press or on newsprint with plates imaged from film, but they go ahead anyway and convert their color to some "middle-of-the-road" CMYK long before they need to, and hope for the best. Bruce wryly terms this the "premature-binding workflow," and points out that the middle of the road is generally where you find roadkill.

Sometimes you'll be forced to convert to CMYK for an unknown output process, and you'll be forced to use "middle-of-the-road" CMYK. But even then, if you want to avoid having your job look like roadkill, you should try to find out as much as you can about the likely output process—such as ink limits and dot gain, for example. See "Preparing Materials for a Non-Color-Managed Print Environment," later in this chapter.

Terminology: Tagging, Assigning, Embedding, and Assuming

One of the less-delightful aspects of color management is the great variety of terminology that different vendors use to describe the same thing. A good example is the set of terms mentioned above: all relate to associating a source profile with a document or object, and often their meanings overlap.

Tagging is simply a generic term for the act of associating a source profile with an object or document. A tagged document is one that has a source profile permanently associated with it, as an embedded profile or an assigned profile. An untagged document is one that lacks a source profile.

Assigning a source profile is a term that Adobe applications use to describe the act of tagging a document. Hair-splitters should note that assigning a profile is a distinct process from embedding a profile—you can assign a profile at any time, but you can only embed a profile as part of the Save process.

Embedding a source profile describes the act of saving a document with the source profile included as part of the file data. One example that makes the distinction between assigning and embedding more than mere hair-splitting is that if you assign a profile to a document, and your machine crashes before you save, when you reopen the file, it won't have the assigned profile associated with it, whereas if you embed a profile, and the machine crashes, the profile will still be associated with the document when you reopen it.

Assuming a source profile is a way to configure applications' behavior toward untagged objects. Typically, you set a source profile, sometimes called a default profile, for RGB, and another for CMYK. (Some applications let you set different default profiles for pixel-based data and vector-based data.) When the application encounters an untagged document or object, it uses the assumed profile as the source for any requested conversions, including the one that converts the color to monitor RGB for display.

Assuming a profile results in a different behavior from assigning a profile—if you change the default profile, all open untagged images change appearance, since they're now being interpreted with the new default profile as the source. But if you assign a profile, the image is no longer untagged as far as the application is concerned, and keeps its assigned profile no matter what you do to the default profile settings.

When you embed a profile, you literally write a copy of the profile into the document. All color-managed applications know how to interpret embedded profiles in TIFF, JPEG, and, on the Macintosh platform, PICT documents. Some applications also offer some degree of support for profile embedding in EPS and PDF documents, but it's sufficiently variable that we'll discuss it fully in the individual application-specific chapters that follow this one.

Embedded-profile workflows are by far the safest choice when your production chain takes inputs from multiple sources and converts them to outputs for multiple destinations, such as a service bureau operation.

When you always embed profiles, there's never any ambiguity as to the color meaning of the numbers in your documents. Many production people will argue the safest choice is one without any profiles that deals with color problems through an iterative proof-then-color-correct process. It's only safe because it's familiar, and it's extremely inefficient to use human skill to solve the problem of various devices having their own peculiar behavior. Such use of skill and craft is often necessary even in a color-managed workflow, but to nowhere near the same degree as in a traditional one.

One major disadvantage of embedded-profile workflows is that they increase file size, sometimes by a little, sometimes by a lot. Matrix-based RGB editing space profiles are relatively tiny—less than a kilobyte—but if you're uploading 30 images to a Web page, and embedding the same profile in each one, you're uploading 30 kilobytes of redundant data. CMYK output profiles can be quite large—the ones we used to make this book weigh in at 2.4 megabytes apiece—and if we chose to embed a profile in every single graphic in the book, we'd be shoving an extra one or two gigabytes through the production chain.

Assumed Profiles

The key feature of the *assumed-profile workflow* is that, instead of relying on embedding profiles in all our documents, we agree on a single profile to use for untagged documents that we push through the production chain, and we configure all our applications to assume that untagged documents have this profile as their source (see Figure 10-6).

Figure 10-6
Assumed-profile
workflow

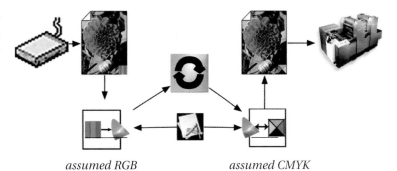

assumed RGB   assumed CMYK

In an assumed-profile workflow, RGB and CMYK values are always interpreted as assumed RGB and assumed CMYK, respectively. Profiles aren't embedded, and conversions are always between the assumed profiles' spaces.

Of course, an assumed-profile workflow puts all the onus on the user to disprove the old saw that "when you assume, you make an ass out of u and me"—you don't have the safety net offered by embedded profiles, so you have to make sure that the untagged objects were brought correctly into the assumed profile space to start with, and you also have to make sure that the assumed profiles are set correctly in each application so that, if conversions do occur, they're the right conversions.

As a result, assumed-profile workflows require a great deal more coordination between programs and people than do embedded-profile workflows, so they're best suited either to situations where a single individual is in control of all the work, or where a group with good communications is working towards a single output, such as a book or a periodical. In situations such as these, many people find an assumed-profile workflow makes it simpler to keep things straight. All programs that deal with any RGB color values use the same assumed RGB profile. All programs that deal with any CMYK color values use the same assumed CMYK profile, and all conversions from RGB to CMYK use the same source and destination profiles.

Hybrid Workflows

In practice, most real color-management workflows are hybrids, using embedded profiles and assumed profiles either for convenience, or because applications or devices force one or the other.

For example, Adobe Illustrator can assign profiles to EPS files, but it can't embed them. So when you transfer Illustrator EPS files to another application, you have three options: use an assumed profile in the receiving application, manually assign a profile in the receiving application, or consider the EPS "print-ready." The last case means that all color management must occur prior to saving the EPS file, and the values in the file will be sent to the output device.

It's also important to note that embedded-profile workflows, while robust, aren't bulletproof. (The first person to make a bulletproof workflow will get very rich, very quickly!) If one person opens an image in a non-color-managed application (such as Adobe Photoshop 4), does some minor editing, and resaves the file, the embedded profile is gone. In this scenario, if you spot what happened quickly, you can save the situation by simply re-embedding the profile with a suitable application.

But here's a worse scenario. If someone opens the image in Photoshop 5, and the application is configured to convert images to her working space and to save without embedding profiles, not only will the embedded profile get stripped out, but the numbers in the image will have changed drastically and no profile will be embedded upon resaving the image. So simply re-embedding the profile won't work—you'd have to find out what working space Photoshop 5 was set to use, then embed that profile to retrieve the correct color meaning for the new set of numbers in the image, which may be difficult for those of you who aren't mind-readers.

The lesson here is that profile embedding is a useful tool for communicating color meaning, but it isn't a substitute for clear communication between the people in the production chain.

Workflow Within a Program

Workflow within a single program can be broken down into two aspects:

▶ How the program handles untagged documents

▶ How the program handles tagged documents.

Remember, color management only does two things—convey color meaning and convert numbers to preserve that color meaning. So there are really only three possible things the application can do in either case, though the implications are slightly different in each.

Opening Untagged Documents

Any color-managed application has to make some assumption about the source profile for untagged documents. It needs a source profile so that it can display the document on your monitor and convert it to other profiles' spaces on request. So when the program encounters an untagged document, whether by the Open command or by commands like Import, Place, or Get Picture, it can only do one of three things:

▶ Assume a profile

▶ Assign a profile

▶ Assign a profile, and do a conversion to some other profile.

Some applications allow you to do only one of these things, while others may allow you to choose between two or three alternatives, but these are the only three possibilities—see the sidebar, "Terminology: Tagging, Assigning, Embedding, and Assuming," earlier in this chapter, for the subtle distinction between assuming and assigning a source profile.

The other factor to consider is that some applications only allow you to set a default behavior that applies to all untagged documents automatically, whereas others offer the option of choosing the behavior on a case-by-case basis by presenting a warning dialog like the one shown in Figure 10-7.

Figure 10-7

Photoshop's Missing
Profile warning

Note that in all cases, the question is fundamentally one of supplying a source profile for the untagged document. Once the application has done so, the only difference between tagged and untagged documents is that if you change the default profiles in the application, untagged documents take the new default profile as their source, whereas tagged documents keep their source profile until you explicitly change it by doing an assignment or conversion.

Note that the "assume profile" possibility is the only one which leaves the document/object untagged. In all other cases the document effectively becomes tagged—Macromedia FreeHand and CorelDRAW, for example, always assign the default profile rather than assuming it. However, the assumed-profile workflow, where documents/objects remain untagged, is the most common workflow.

Opening Tagged Documents

As with untagged documents, applications can only do one of three things when they encounter a document—whether by the Open command or by commands like Import, Place, or Get Picture—that contains an embedded profile:

▶ Use the embedded profile as the source profile.

▶ Use the embedded profile as the source profile, then convert from that source profile to another profile.

▶ Ignore the embedded profile and assume or assign a different profile.

Some applications only offer one of these alternatives, while others may offer two or three, but these are the only three possibilities. And some applications only let you choose a single behavior to apply to all documents automatically, while others may again let you choose on a case-by-case basis by presenting a warning dialog like the one shown in Figure 10-8.

Figure 10-8

Photoshop's Profile Mismatch (Open) warning

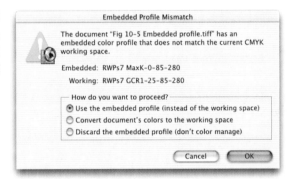

Color Management Between Documents

When you move objects between documents in color-managed page-layout or illustration applications, where a document may comprise multiple objects, each with its own source profile, you have exactly the same three options you have when you open, import, or place tagged documents:

▶ Use the embedded profile as the source profile for the object.

▶ Use the embedded profile as the source profile for the object, then convert from that source profile to another profile.

▶ Ignore the embedded profile and assume or assign a different profile to the object.

Some applications, such as QuarkXPress 4 and 5, allow you to set these options on a per-document basis as well as setting an application default, which is potentially powerful, but also potentially confusing.

So you need to pay attention to the color-management settings for each document, or decide to standardize your settings for all documents (in which case, make sure that you know what you're doing when you open a document that was created by someone else, because she may have set the color management preferences differently).

A different choice arises in applications such as Adobe Photoshop, where each document has a single profile governing all elements. When you move pixels (whether via copy and paste, or drag and drop) from one document to another in Photoshop, and the two documents have different source profiles, you have only two choices:

▶ Move the numerical values of the pixels (which means that their appearance will change because it will be governed by the source profile of the receiving document).

▶ Move the color appearance of the pixels (which means that the numerical values will change to recreate the original appearance in the different profile space of the receiving document).

A less-wordy description of the choice is: convert, or don't convert (as the dialog box shown in Figure 10-9 indicates).

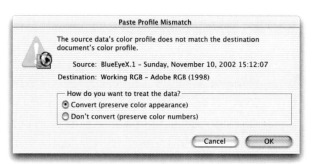

Some applications will always do one or the other without giving you a choice, in which case you need to figure out which one the application in question is doing. But these are the only two possibilities.

Assigning, Converting, and Soft-Proofing

So far, we've looked at what applications let you do when you open or import a document or object, transfer an object between documents, or combine different objects into a single document. But most color-managed applications also let you do profile assignments, profile conversions, and *soft-proofs*, which are really sets of conversions that are applied temporarily to let you use your monitor to simulate final output—see the sidebar, "Soft-Proofing Basics," later in this chapter.

In the case of applications like Photoshop, where a document can only have one profile, these options are relatively straightforward. You can assign a source profile to a document, you can convert a document to another profile's space with a choice of rendering intents, and you can set the monitor to provide a live preview of how the document would appear after a conversion to some other space—so you can, for example, work on an RGB document while previewing the effects your RGB edits would have on the file if it were converted to output CMYK.

With applications whose documents may contain multiple objects in different color spaces, such as page-layout applications, profile assignment becomes trickier. The main factor is that objects native to the layout application are handled differently from linked objects such as imported graphics. (By native objects, we mean text, lines, shapes, backgrounds, and so on, that were created inside the application.)

Native objects inherit the assumed or assigned profile that applies to the document in which they are placed—the key point is that you don't assign profiles to native objects directly. If the document has ProfileX assigned to it, all native objects assume that profile as their source. If you change the document profile, you change the source profile for all native objects.

For linked objects, however, a newly assigned profile only applies to the specific instance of the object in that page-layout document. It doesn't affect the original file—to do so, the page-layout application would need to be able to go out and rewrite the linked file, which the major page-layout applications can't do.

Essentially, the assigned profile acts like an assumed profile inside that specific page-layout document, and only to the specific instance of the object to which it's applied—if you import the image again, and place it in a different part of the page-layout doc, it'll use either the embedded profile or the default profile. We think that assigning profiles other than the true source profile to linked objects in a page-layout application is a dangerous practice, and avoid it in all but the direst emergency. We'd rather go back to the application that originated the object and assign a new profile there, then update the link in the page-layout application.

Conversions in page-layout applications generally apply only to native objects, not to linked or imported ones. We almost always try to create everything in our layout applications in final CMYK from scratch, but when this is impossible (because, for example, the final CMYK isn't known when we start creating the document), we use the page-layout applications' conversion features to convert the native objects. Then we make sure that all the linked objects are in the correct space, and if necessary, do any conversions in the applications that originated them.

Simulations always apply to the entire document, whether it's a single image in Photoshop or a whole book in a page-layout application. In some applications, such as QuarkXPress or Adobe PageMaker, the simulation controls are presented as part of the color-management preferences (see Figure 10-10).

Figure 10-10

Monitor simulation

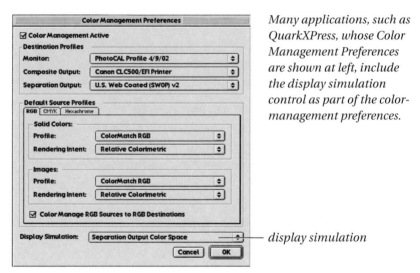

Many applications, such as QuarkXPress, whose Color Management Preferences are shown at left, include the display simulation control as part of the color-management preferences.

— *display simulation*

In other applications, such as Adobe Photoshop, Illustrator, and InDesign, simulations are controlled by commands accessed from the main menu bar (see Figure 10-11).

However they're presented, the soft-proofing simulations do the same thing. They convert all the supported objects in the document—on the fly, for display only—to the designated output profile space, then they convert that simulation to monitor RGB to display the predicted output correctly on the monitor. (Formats such as EPS or DCS EPS don't allow page-layout applications to change their preview, so you can't do soft proofs of objects in these formats.)

Soft-Proofing Basics

The naïve view of color management, as presented in all too many vendors' marketing spiels, is that it will make your prints match your monitor. If you've read this far, you know that the laws of physics make it impossible to do so.

What color management *can* do, however, is to show you on your monitor how your color will appear when it's reproduced in print. This technique is known as *soft-proofing*, and we think it's one of the most valuable capabilities that color management brings to the table.

Soft-proofing first converts the document's colors to the final output, then renders those colors back to the display, on the fly, without actually changing the values in the document. It's basically a preview of the final output.

Soft-proofing has limitations. Your display has a fixed color gamut, and it can't show you colors that lie outside it, so some saturated cyans and orange-yellows that are readily achieved in print can't be displayed, though the clipping is very slight.

But there are different ways to render a simulated print back to the display, and each one has its strengths and weaknesses.

Relative colorimetric rendering.
This is the way most applications render color, including simulations, to the display. White in the simulation—paper white—gets translated to monitor white, and all the other colors are shifted to match that white. This type of soft-proof doesn't show the effect of the paper white on the overall color, but since our eyes adapt to the monitor white, it's still a very useful view.

Absolute colorimetric rendering.
In theory, absolute colorimetric rendering, which shows the actual color of the paper white, should offer a more accurate soft proof than relative colormetric rendering, but in practice, you immediately encounter two problems:

▶ To show the color of paper white, the monitor has to display white as something less than RGB 255, 255, 255, so you immediately lose some

dynamic range, making the color appear flat.

▶ To make this view work, you *must* hide any white user interface elements, otherwise your eye adapts to that white instead of the simulated paper white, and the color seems to have a color cast.

You may be tempted to conclude from the above that accurate soft-proofing is impossible. In the strictest sense, you'd be right, but the truth is that we've never seen *any* proof that matched the final product exactly, except perhaps for press proofs, which are prohibitively expensive for most real-world jobs.

We learn to interpret hard-copy proofs, whether film-based or digital, and we simply have to do the same with soft proofs. Once you've learned to interpret what your display is telling you, we believe you'll find that a correctly configured soft proof is just as reliable as any other proofing system short of an actual press proof, and it's not only a great deal cheaper, but also a great deal faster.

Some applications offer per-object control over the rendering intent from the object's space to the simulated output space, some apply perceptual rendering to raster images and relative colorimetric rendering to vector graphics, and some simply use the profile default rendering in all cases. Most applications do relative colorimetric rendering from the simulation space to monitor RGB, though a few offer control over the rendering from simulation to monitor space. We'll look at these details in the application-specific chapters that follow this one.

Figure 10-11

Proof Setup

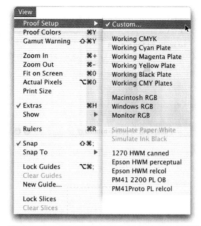

Applications such as Adobe Photoshop, whose display simulation controls are shown here, let you change the soft-proof settings without changing the color-management preferences.

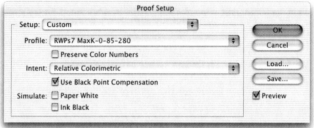

Printing and Proofing

The last set of color-management controls that work inside individual applications are those that deal with printing both final color and proofs of final color.

All the color-managed applications we know of allow you to perform a conversion from the source profile or profiles in the document to a single target output profile, as part of the print stream. The document itself remains unchanged—the conversion only applies to the data that gets sent to the printer driver.

Tip: Disable Color Management in the Printer Driver When You Use Application Color Management to Print. At the risk of belaboring the obvious, if the application performs a conversion to the data being sent to the printer driver, you almost certainly don't want the driver itself to do a conversion on top of the application's conversion—so when you use this feature, make sure that you turn off any color management in the printer driver itself.

In applications whose documents contain multiple objects with individual profiles, the rendering intent controls are the same as the ones offered for soft-proofing. Applications such as Adobe Photoshop, whose documents contain only one source profile, may allow you to choose a rendering intent (see Figure 10-12).

Figure 10-12
Printing Controls

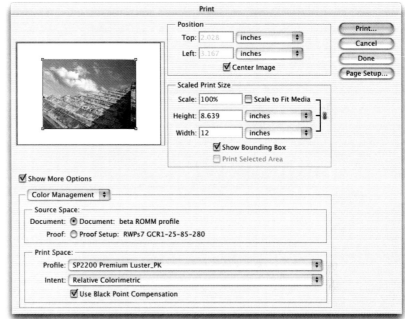

Photoshop's printing controls let you select a printer profile and rendering intent. When you do so, Photoshop performs a conversion on the data that gets sent to the printer driver.

In addition, most color-managed applications allow you to print a simulation of the final output to a composite printer such as a desktop inkjet or color laser.

In some applications, such as Adobe Photoshop, Illustrator, and InDesign, this feature is tied to the soft-proof setting, so that instead of choosing the document space as the source profile, you choose the soft-proof space. This makes the application perform the conversion(s) from object spaces to the soft-proof space as part of the print stream. You then choose an output profile and rendering intent to *cross-render* this simulation of the final output to your desktop printer, which makes the application do one more conversion from the output simulation to your desktop printer space using the selected rendering intent (see Figure 10-13).

Figure 10-13

InDesign and Photoshop
cross-rendering

*Source Space set to
Proof*

*Source Space set to
Proof*

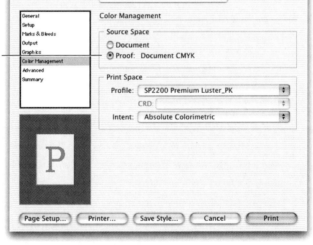

*Adobe Photoshop and InDesign both tie cross-rendering to the soft-proof.
When you choose Proof Setup (Photoshop) or Proof (InDesign) as the source
space, the application first converts the color using the destination profile
specified in the Proof Setup dialog box. Photoshop also uses the Proof Setup
rendering intent for this conversion—rendering intents in InDesign are
applied separately to each object. Then the application does a second conversion
using the destination profile and rendering intent specified in Print Space.*

Other applications may force you to actually convert every element to final output space as the only way to cross-render to a composite printer, in which case the conversion is simply one from document space to printer space.

Workflow Between Programs

You can convey color meaning between programs by either, or both, of two methods:

▶ Embedding profiles in any objects that travel between programs

▶ Ensuring that both the originating and receiving application use the same assumed profiles.

Our tendency, which is by no means a hard and fast rule, is to embed profiles in RGB, and assume profiles in CMYK, for two reasons:

▶ RGB profiles are typically small and add little to the file size, while CMYK profiles are often larger than the actual files themselves.

▶ At least two important CMYK formats—CMYK EPS and CMYK DCS EPS—don't reliably support profile embedding, and are often treated as "output-ready" formats, both by people and applications.

However, when we don't embed profiles in CMYK, we always leave some kind of audit trail that tells us what flavor of CMYK the numbers in the file represent. We may archive the files in a specific folder that also contains the profile, or we may include the profile name in the document name, in the file information, or in whatever form of metadata the file format permits.

Workflow between applications is perhaps the one aspect of color management where common sense applies. All applications that deal with color have to make some assumption about the colors represented by RGB and the colors represented by CMYK. Color-managed applications can only get those assumptions from one of two places, a default profile or an embedded profile. If you make sure that your default profiles are synchronized across all your applications, and you set your applications to deal with embedded profiles the way you want them to, your color will flow reliably and predictably from one to another.

Workflow Into and Out of Color Management

Even though this is a book about color management, we can't deny the fact that large chunks of the world aren't color managed. What we call the "color-management workflow" may be just a small piece of the overall workflow. We constantly bring materials in from devices, software, and people who don't use profile-based color management. At the other end, we prepare documents for further non-color-managed stages. For example, with some workflows, as soon as someone converts color to CMYK, he employs more-traditional CMYK correction, targeting, and output techniques that don't involve profile-based color management.

There's a widespread and totally incorrect assumption that color management is an all-or-nothing proposition—unless you have profiles for all your inputs and all your outputs, and you use them religiously, you can't do color management. If that were true, color management would be a great deal less useful than it is.

We routinely bring color from non-color-managed sources into a color-managed workflow, and we equally routinely export color from a color-managed workflow into The Great Non-Color-Managed Unknown.

Bringing Color Into a Color-Managed Environment

The first question we always ask when we're confronted with bringing non-color-managed documents into the color-managed workflow is, "Can we deduce the source profile?"

Known sources. If the source profile is known, or, with a little deductive reasoning, knowable, we can simply assign it, and from then on, the offending document is color-managed. A trivial example would be an image from a scanner whose software doesn't embed profiles, for which a profile is available. We'd simply open the scan in Photoshop and assign the scanner profile (and then we'd very likely convert it immediately to an intermediate editing space for further work).

A less-trivial example would be an untagged image sent by a peer who is reachable by that most-overlooked color-management tool, the telephone. Usually, a few questions could determine which space the image was saved in, and again, we'd assign the correct profile.

Unknown sources. In many cases, however, the source profile is simply unknowable, either for technological reasons—the image was shot on an unprofiled digital camera, or scanned from a color negative—or for human ones—the person who created the material is either unreachable or is sufficiently clueless about color management that asking questions is an exercise in futility. In that case, you have what Bruce fondly calls "mystery meat." We recommend different strategies for RGB mystery meat and CMYK mystery meat:

▶ In the case of RGB, we usually try a few different editing-space profiles to see if one produces a more reasonable appearance than another—there's an element of guesswork or mind-reading in this, so we don't hope for miracles. It's overwhelmingly likely that the color was created in either a monitor-like space such as ColorMatch RGB or sRGB, or an editing space such as Adobe RGB, so those are the ones we generally try. If the image appears dark in a gamma 2.2 space, we try a gamma 1.8 space. If it appears washed out in a relatively large-gamut space such as Adobe RGB, we try a smaller one such as sRGB. We then assign the profile that produces the most reasonable appearance (yes, this is a very subjective criterion), and use it as the basis for any editing and subsequent conversions (see Figure 10-14).

▶ In the case of CMYK, we lean to the view that guessing games are pointless because there are simply too many possibilities to address. We take the not-entirely-unreasonable position that if someone sends us a CMYK file, he expects us to print it, so we assign the CMYK profile for the project to which the document is related, and use that profile as the basis for any necessary editing. If the on-screen result is truly disgusting, we may try assigning some different output spaces to see if we can find a suitable match, and then convert to *our* CMYK, or we may simply edit the file, trusting our calibrated and profiled display as an additional aid to the process.

When Color Management Starts

The details of the recipes we gave above for turning mystery meat into something more palatable are ones we find useful, but what's really important is *why they work*. And the simple reason why they work is that,

Figure 10-14

Mystery meat

This mystery meat image appears both dark and oversaturated when we open it in our Photoshop working space, Adobe RGB (1998). A lower gamma value will lighten the image, and a smaller gamut will make the same numbers produce less-saturated colors.

Colormatch RGB has a lower gamma than Adobe RGB (1998)— gamma 1.8 as opposed to gamma 2.2— and it also has a smaller gamut than Adobe RGB (1998). When we assign the Colormatch RGB profile, the image appears less dark, with more natural-looking saturation.

as soon as you open a mystery meat document in a color-managed application, you're using a known source profile to look at the color. *Any* application that can convert color from one color mode to another—from RGB to CMYK, for example—has to make assumptions about the color appearance represented by both the RGB and CMYK numbers. One of the things that makes color management a cool tool is that, in color-managed applications, you can easily see and control those assumptions.

All color-managed applications let you set default profiles, which they use to interpret the numbers in untagged documents, so when you open an untagged document, you *know* which profile the application is using as the document's source profile, and you *know* what color that profile makes the document display on your calibrated monitor.

It may not be a source profile that represents the intent of the person who sent it to you, but you've gone from knowing nothing about the color to knowing how it looks in, say, Adobe RGB. Color-management purists might blow a gasket at the notion, but we'd say you've already started to color manage the document.

The purist (Bruce says "fascist") view of color management is that its goal and purpose is to take an original image, and represent it as faithfully as possible on various outputs. Purists see color management as a scalpel. We liken it more to a Swiss Army Knife—it's neither as precise nor as specialized as they claim. But it's a lot more useful.

In fact, it's impossible to *not* use color management in any application that does color conversions. All you can do is hide the assumptions the application makes when it does so, which we think is pointless. So as far as we're concerned, color management starts as soon as you open a file in a color-managed application.

The Limits of the Knowable

Of course, when you're dealing with mystery meat, there's always an element of mind-reading—because the person who sent you the mystery meat hasn't (yet) learned to use color management to convey his color meaning clearly, which is bad, but he also hasn't learned any other way to do so, which is the real problem.

Color management lets you attach a specific color appearance to a set of RGB or CMYK numbers. Getting from that appearance to the appearance the originator intended is not something that color management can address—it's a people problem, not a technology problem. Color management can help by letting you try out various plausible and implausible alternatives, but if people give you untagged files with no other information, you simply have to use your best judgement. Of course, you can always try asking why you're being given untagged files— see the sidebar, "Fear of Embedding," on the facing page.

Tip: Always Send Hard-Copy References. If you're dealing with someone whose workflow is obviously non-color-managed, and you're going through multiple edit rounds, *always* send a hard-copy reference such as an inkjet print, cross-rendered to the output space, that clearly indicates *your* color meaning. It's unlikely that the other person will see the same appearance you do when she opens your edited file, so the hard copy provides a less ambiguous reference.

If we have an agenda in writing this book, it's to make mystery meat go away. Lack of clear color communication is never a good idea—it simply creates extra work for all concerned. Embedding profiles is one simple way to remove ambiguity, but it's not the only way, and if you're dealing with someone who is seriously terrified of color management, it may not be the best way. So do whatever you can to eliminate mystery meat, but remember that gentle persistence almost always works better than wild-eyed evangelism, and in those cases where mystery meat is just a fact of life, use the guidelines we provided above to render it somewhat less mysterious.

Preparing Materials for a Non-Color-Managed Print Environment

There's no particular magic trick here. You simply have to find out as much as possible about the printing conditions, then convert to a CMYK profile that bears some reasonable resemblance to those conditions.

If the job is large or critical, and you have profiling capabilities, you may want to consider profiling the proofing system—just have the printer print the profiling target the same way they'd print your job, then measure it and build a profile.

Failing that, try to find out the ink limits and anticipated dot gain on press, and create your CMYK document using a profile that matches those conditions. Basically, you're aiming at the side of a barn—you want to try to hit it somewhere close to the middle.

Fear of Embedding

Very often, the reason people send mystery meat is because they're afraid to do anything else—specifically, they have an irrational fear of embedding profiles. This fear can stem from many sources, but some of the most common ones are:

Embedding profiles will change my color. Many people have had this experience when they sent a job to someone who had color management configured incorrectly, or who misunderstood its purpose. Of course, when color management is set to work right, embedding a profile makes it much *less* likely that the color will change. Remember—a single profile simply describes. It doesn't *do* anything to the file.

My service provider/color guru/ IT guy/drinking buddy told me not to. People generally fear what they don't understand, and try to make sure that no one else

understands it, either. In some workflows, it makes absolute sense to *not* embed profiles, but if you're receiving mystery meat, *this* workflow obviously isn't one of them.

I don't know how to embed profiles, or which profiles to embed. It's hard to argue with this one.

Very often, though, you'll find that people simply want to be told what to do with color management. Most applications make it difficult to embed the wrong profile, and easy to embed the right one. So if you're tired of cooking with mystery meat, it's always worth asking the question, "Why would embedding profiles make things worse than they are now?" If no good answer is forthcoming, gently suggest that profile embedding might be a good idea in this workflow. (If you're at the bottom of a long food chain, it may take persistence to make

the question percolate to a place where it can do some good.)

Don't make promises, or offer any guarantee other than that profile embedding won't make things any worse. Just be gently persistent. If the document originator obviously needs help figuring out how to embed profiles, decide if it's worth providing that help—you probably don't want to wind up giving endless hours of unpaid tech support unless it's to a very important client.

Sometimes it's easier to simply find out what profile the originator uses for his CMYK or RGB working space, and simply apply it yourself to incoming work. Profiles aren't the only way to convey color meaning, just the simplest and most automatic. But any small steps you can take to reduce the amount of mystery meat in your diet will make you a healthier and happier color-management user.

Convert all your color to final CMYK, don't embed any profiles, and submit the job. You may have to go through some rounds of proofing and correction—that's the normal, expected workflow—but your first submission will likely be in the ballpark.

Some non-color-managed shops will claim that they can accept RGB files and convert them to CMYK themselves. We usually treat such claims with suspicion, to say the least. If the shop can tell us what flavor of RGB they expect, we may at least go ahead and try a test. But if the response makes it clear that multiple flavors of RGB is a concept they've yet to entertain, we'll walk away.

However, if you submit RGB, with embedded profiles, on a CD or other non-rewriteable medium, there can be no argument about what you've submitted—and by accepting RGB files, the printer has taken the responsibility for the RGB-to-CMYK conversions. So if things go badly, you've at least covered your bases.

Preparing Materials for the Non-Color-Managed Internet

The vast majority of Web browsers simply take the RGB values in files and send them unmodified to the screen. So unless you go and calibrate the monitor of every user who is likely to look at your site, you have no way of knowing exactly what they're going to see.

Various vendors have touted schemes for managing color on the Internet. They all work, up to a point, but they all do so by forcing the viewer to do some kind of visual monitor characterization, which they then use to alter the information that gets sent to that particular Web browser. Most of these solutions are sufficiently complex and expensive that they can only be implemented at the enterprise level, and by all accounts, no one is making huge amounts of money doing so.

One day, all monitors will be self-calibrating and self-characterizing, and all operating systems will use display compensation as a system-wide feature. Until that lucky day arrives, we suggest that the only practical solution is to aim for the lowest common denominator. Fortunately, that lowest common denominator is exactly what the sRGB space was designed to represent—it purports to represent the "average" uncalibrated Windows monitor. So our simple recommendation is to convert all your color to sRGB, and then save without embedding a profile, before uploading it.

The only color-managed browsers we know of exist on the Macintosh. For Mac OS 8, 9 and X, it's Microsoft Internet Explorer. If you enable ColorSync in Explorer's Preferences, it will assume sRGB for untagged images and use the embedded profile in all other images, using your monitor profile as the destination profile. And on Mac OS X only, it's OmniGroup's OmniWeb, which currently always assumes images are sRGB and uses display compensation.

So Macintosh users who use a display gamma of 1.8 will at least have a chance of seeing correctly. For most Windows users, sRGB is at least in the ballpark. And while gamma 2.2 images will seem dark and muddy on an unmanaged Macintosh gamma 1.8 display, the Mac users should be used to that.

Internet Color Workflow

When you prepare materials for the Internet, you'll probably have to use a mixture of color-managed and non-color-managed applications. If you aren't bothered by the color appearing different in color-managed and non-color-managed applications, you don't need to do anything, but if you're at all like us, you may find that disconcerting.

There are really only two solutions to the problem that make sense to us:

▶ If your work is exclusively for the Internet, calibrate your monitor to sRGB—most monitor calibrators offer sRGB as a preset, and for those that don't, use 6500 K as the white point and 2.2 for gamma. Then, do everything in sRGB. Your calibrated color in the color-managed applications will closely match your uncalibrated color in the non-color-managed ones.

▶ Use monitor RGB as the source profile for all your Internet work. Color-managed applications will see that your RGB is already monitor RGB, so they'll just send the values in the file to the screen, the same way non-color-managed applications do. Then, when the work is complete, convert it to sRGB.

If you expect your target audience to be primarily Macintosh users, you may consider targeting Apple RGB instead of sRGB. Neither solution is ideal, but until such time as the Internet becomes something other than a very large collection of random output devices, they're the best we have to offer.

Understanding Workflow

In this chapter, we've tried to present the essential workflow concepts and features that all color-managed applications share, no matter how they're presented, while relating them to the fundamental concept that color management does only two things—convey color meaning, and convert device values to preserve that color meaning.

Once you grasp these basic concepts, you'll find that you can look at just about any application and figure out what each color-management feature does, because they *always* boil down to some combination of the two fundamentals. In the following chapters, we'll look at the specific ways color management is presented in some of the most common color-managed applications, but we can't cover them all, and it's often all too easy to get bogged down in the details. So use this chapter, and the concepts it presents, to keep the bigger picture in mind when you're grappling with the minutiae of this or that application—the answer is almost always simpler than it might first appear.

Color Management in the Operating System

Who Does What to Whom, When?

Operating system vendors like Apple and Microsoft tend to paint an overly rosy picture of color management as a panacea that will make whatever comes out of your desktop printer match your monitor, automatically. Anyone who has ever printed from a desktop computer, or has a passing knowledge of the laws of physics, knows otherwise. The truth is that OS-level color management does less than the marketing hype, but it also does much *more* than the marketing hype.

It does less in that OS-level color management can't change the gamut of your printer to match that of your monitor—it can come reasonably close, but there's simply no way you'll get that R0, G0, B255 blue out of your printer (or, for that matter, on any other reflective hard-copy medium).

But it does more in that it's not just a color management system—it's a whole architecture for color management systems to live in. OS-level color management provides a whole slew of services that applications can call to do all sorts of useful things.

Application-Level and OS-Level Color Management

One of the more confusing aspects of color management lies in figuring out who does what to whom, when. But doing so is critical if you want to ensure that color conversions happen correctly, at the right time, and only at the right time. Color-managed applications aim for cross-platform parity, so they generally make minimal use of OS-level color management, using built-in color management instead. But since printer, scanner, and digital camera drivers can't make assumptions about the applications with which they'll be used, they typically rely on the OS for all their color-management features.

On a basic level, two things can "make" color management happen:

▶ Applications written to perform explicit color-management tasks, or

▶ Applications and device drivers, such as scanner and printer drivers, that implicitly use OS-level color management (sometimes without being aware that they do so).

One of the keys to successful color management lies in making sure that OS-level color management in the various device drivers cooperates with the application-level color management done by color-managed applications, rather than injecting unexpected extra conversions into the color production chain.

From the color management perspective, applications come in two flavors:

▶ Color-managed applications have, at the minimum, settings and functions that allow us to specify source and destination profiles and perform conversions.

▶ Non-color-managed applications rely on device drivers to perform color management on capture and output.

With color-managed applications, you can use either application-level color management or driver-level color management, though we recommend using the application controls to manage color rather than relying on limited printer driver options. You usually want to avoid using application-level and driver-level color management at the same time. With non-color managed applications, driver-level color management is all you've got. Much of this chapter is devoted to understanding how OS-level color management functions, so that you can make sure that it doesn't do anything you didn't expect.

ColorSync and ICM

Apple's ColorSync and Microsoft's ICM (Image Color Management) are the technologies that provide color management services as part of the Macintosh and Windows operating systems, respectively. As previously noted, they're both less than and more than color management systems.

What Are They? What Do They Do?

The overwhelming bulk of both ColorSync and ICM is comprised of APIs, or Application Programming Interfaces. These are chunks of code that developers can exploit using relatively simple calls to the operating system. They provide a way for developers to include color-management capability into their applications without having to write their own color management system from scratch, and they also provide an architectural framework in which third-party CMMs can live.

For example, a programmer might use CMConvertXYZToLab to ask ColorSync to convert CIE XYZ-based data into CIE LAB. There are APIs for almost anything you can think of: support for all of the profile classes, conversions, status of conversions, reporting of profile locations and profile information, and ways for applications to request user settings related to color management—pretty much all the basic housekeeping services related to dealing with profiles and conversions. ColorSync and ICM are primarily useful for programmers, whose lives are made easier by using APIs instead of having to write the code themselves.

Users need relatively little interaction with ColorSync and ICM. The one user setting everyone needs to make is the display profile—most color-managed applications ask the OS-level color management for that single piece of user-supplied information. Other ColorSync and ICM user interface elements have less obvious effects.

Mac OS 9

On Mac OS 9, ColorSync 3 exists as two pieces—a system extension called "ColorSync Extension" and a control panel called "ColorSync." The only part of the ColorSync Extension that might concern users is the AppleScript dictionary it contains, accessed by the ScriptEditor. (See Chapter 17, *Automation and Scripting*.)

The control panel, on the other hand, is exclusively for users to manipulate (see Figures 11-1 and 11-2). The control panel is misleading because it implies that it will universally use profiles specified under "Profiles for Standard Devices" and "Default Profiles for Documents." Nothing could be further from the truth. In fact, applications must be specifically written to request this information from ColorSync. A few of the major applications offer the option to use the "Default Profiles for Documents" profiles, but we can't think of any that do so by default, and we don't know of any that use "Profiles for Standard Devices."

Figure 11-1

ColorSync control panel:
Profiles for Standard
Devices

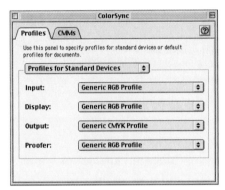

The only software we know that uses these settings is AppleScript, specifically the scripts that live in the ColorSync Extras:AppleScripts folder. Some of these scripts let you use the default profiles for devices as variables, so you can quickly change the profiles used by a script by changing them here rather than editing the script.

Figure 11-2

ColorSync control panel:
Default Profiles for
Documents

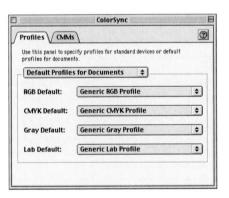

The "ColorSync Workflow" option offered by Adobe Photoshop, Illustrator, and InDesign uses these profiles, as do the aforementioned AppleScripts. We don't know of anything else that does so.

The ColorSync control panel represents a laudable attempt to create a single point of access and consistent user interface for configuring color management for all applications. It was great in theory, but since all the major applications aim for cross-platform parity, and ICM lacks any comparable features, it didn't work out in practice. So you can safely ignore the Profiles tab of the ColorSync control panel entirely. However, two OS-level settings *are* important.

ColorSync control panel settings. In the ColorSync control panel, under the CMMs tab you'll find a single setting for the Preferred CMM (see Figure 11-3). The default is Automatic, which is functionally equivalent to "random." If you want subtly random results, use this setting. Otherwise change it to something else. We've found the Apple CMM to work well, and with the exception of black point compensation, it provides similar results to the Adobe Color Engine (ACE) found in Adobe applications.

Figure 11-3
ColorSync control panel: CMMs tab

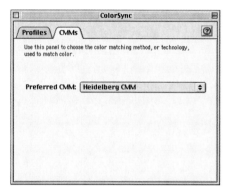

The CMM you specify here is used by all software that uses, or is set to use, OS-level color management to perform conversions.

If you're working in a cross-platform environment without the exclusive use of the Adobe applications (which can use ColorSync, ICM, or their own ACE engine), you may want to standardize on a single CMM for all systems. Since the Apple CMM doesn't exist on Windows, but the Heidelberg CMM exists on both, you can standardize on the Heidelberg CMM.

Likewise, if you have an important application or profile that uses the Kodak Digital Science Color Management System, you can standardize on the Kodak CMM.

Monitor settings. In the Monitors control panel, click on the Color button and you'll be presented with a list of ColorSync profiles (ICC profiles) to select (see Figure 11-4). Each display connected to your Macintosh can have a separate display profile selected, but don't count on applications performing display compensation on anything other than the primary display. (Adobe Photoshop 6 and 7 are the only applications we know of that can perform display compensation to multiple displays.)

Figure 11-4

Monitors control panel

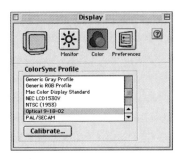

The Color panel of the Monitors control panel lets you specify the profile for each display.

This setting does two things.

▶ If the profile contains the vcgt tag, which most do, the Display Manager updates the video card LUTs with the correction needed to place the monitor in the calibrated condition defined in the profile.

▶ The selected profile becomes the display profile for the current display.

The effect of updating the video card LUTs happens immediately and is usually visually obvious. Changing the display profile may have no visible effect, but applications that query the system for the display profile use the one you specify here for display compensation. Adobe applications are well behaved in asking the system for the display profile, but most other applications require you to specify the display profile in their settings manually—watch out for this potentially major pitfall.

Profile locations. Profiles are usually stored in Hard Drive:System Folder:ColorSync Profiles. However, some older applications and printer drivers insist on finding profiles in the old location, Hard Drive:System Folder:Preferences:ColorSync Profiles. Other applications may store profiles in subfolders in the Hard Drive:System Folder:Application Support folder, though the ones of which we're aware always place an alias in the ColorSync Profiles folder to let other applications use the profiles. Since some applications don't resolve aliases, and others don't look deeper than the root level of the ColorSync Profiles folder, this doesn't always work, so if you have a profile that appears in some applications but not others, try placing a copy in the root level of the ColorSync Profiles folder.

Location for CMMs. CMMs are system extensions and live in Hard Drive:System Folder:Extensions.

Mac OS X

ColorSync 4 is the latest version of ColorSync and is only found on Mac OS X. ColorSync 4 is a framework buried quite deeply within the ApplicationServices.framework bundle. Fortunately, this isn't a problem since, again, it's intended for programmers.

Color is handled in a very different way on Mac OS X than on any other operating system, and, like much of Mac OS X, is a work in progress. The major applications still work as expected, but this operating system blurs the lines between what is and is not a color-managed application. It doesn't blur them heavily, but over time it will become increasingly easy for developers to implement color management in their applications and printer drivers, and increasingly hard for them to avoid doing so.

Mac OS X's color management rests on the premise that every window is color-managed, whether the application that requests the window to be drawn knows anything about ColorSync or not. This is currently achieved through assumptions, though the plan seems eventually to make it a matter of user preference settings.

For those of you using the major applications, Mac OS X will behave as you would expect. But it's interesting to imagine the possibilities for traditionally non-color-managed applications, which on OS X gain some color-management ability automatically.

Mac OS X's color-management behavior is in flux, and while we're sure Apple has a plan to stabilize it into something we can write about with authority in the future, we aren't fully privy to the plan. So we'll just report what we know at the time we're writing this chapter as it applies to Mac OS X 10.2.2.

ColorSync panel settings. The settings for ColorSync are in the ColorSync panel of the System Preferences application, and they've been greatly simplified compared to Mac OS 9 (see Figure 11-5 and 11-6). Here, you can specify default RGB, CMYK, and grayscale profiles for documents that don't contain embedded profiles.

Figure 11-5

Mac OS X
ColorSync panel:
Default Profiles tab

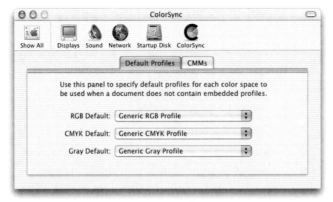

Figure 11-6

Mac OS X
ColorSync panel:
CMMs tab

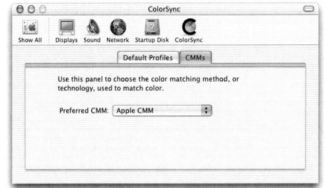

You may be tempted to conclude two things from these settings: embedded profiles are recognized system-wide, and documents without embedded profiles will have the default profiles assumed as source profiles. You'd be wrong on both counts.

Mac OS X, like OS 9 and Windows, still requires developers to specifically write code into their applications to make them recognize embedded profiles. An application that doesn't know what an embedded profile is opens the image as though it were untagged.

You might then conclude that untagged documents get their source profiles assumed by the specified default profiles. While this may be intended by Apple at some point, it's not the case in 10.2.2. As in OS 9, only applications written to request these settings make use of them.

The advice we gave under Mac OS 9 for the setting of the Preferred CMM applies here as well. If you like random results, use the Automatic option. Otherwise, pick something else.

Displays panel settings. This panel, also found in System Preferences, is functionally equivalent to the Monitors control panel on Mac OS 9. Click on the Color tab, and select the profile for your displays here. As on Mac OS 9, multiple displays are supported by the operating system, but also as with OS 9, you'll need to determine whether or not your specific application supports color management for two separate displays.

Profile locations. Mac OS X stores profiles in a variety of locations, and in order for it to make any sense, a bit of background on Mac OS X is necessary. Mac OS X is designed as a multiuser operating system. You may only have one user, but the system is still designed for more than one. Thus, the locations for profiles follow the general rule that there are five possible "domains": Apple only, all users, a specific user, a specific application, and network. For practical purposes we list just the first three:

▶ **/System/Library/ColorSync/Profiles**—all users can use profiles stored here, but they can't be removed or supplemented unless you have a special set of keys. Since this is Apple's domain, nothing except the Mac OS installer should remove profiles from or add profiles to this location.

▶ **/Library/ColorSync/Profiles**—all users can use these profiles, but only Admin users and authenticated installers can add profiles to or remove profiles from this location. The preferred location for display profiles is in the Displays folder contained within this location, although they'll work if placed in the other legitimate locations.

▶ **/Users/<username>/Library/ColorSync/Profiles**—profiles in this location are only available when this user is logged in, and aren't available to other users; only this user can add profiles to or remove profiles from this location.

More than likely you'll want profiles available to everyone, so we recommend placing them in the /Library/ColorSync/Profiles folder. If you're working in an administered environment where you don't have permissions for this location, place them in your user ColorSync Profiles folder instead.

Another major difference with Mac OS X, is that manufacturer-supplied "canned" printer profiles don't normally go in any of the above locations. Instead, they're stored as resources within the printer module bundle and as such aren't directly accessible by users. However, they *are* available to all applications just as if they were stored in /Library/ColorSync/Profiles, but they don't clutter the various Profiles folders with profiles for which professional users may have no use.

Locations for CMMs. CMMs live in /Library/ColorSync/CMMs.

Windows

ICM 2.0 (Image Color Management) is built into Windows 98 and higher, including Windows XP. Like ColorSync, ICM is a set of APIs intended for use by programmers. Outside of printer drivers, and applications specifically written to use ICM 2, there's only one user setting, but it's an important one to which you should pay special attention.

Setting the active color profile for the display. Each device on Windows can have multiple profiles associated with it, as well as a default profile. Only the default profile is the active profile for that device and is the one that gets used. To associate profiles with a device, and to set the default profile, go the device's Properties panel, click the Advanced button under Settings, then click on the Color Management tab. In that window, you can associate profiles with the device and also specify one of them as the default profile.

For example, to set the display profile, first associate a profile with the display by going to the Display control panel, clicking on the Settings tab, then clicking the Advanced button. In the resulting window, click on the Color Management tab and click Add to open the Add Profile Association dialog box. Locate the profile you want to associate with the display and click Add. To set a profile as the default, select the desired profile in the Color Management tab, and click Set As Default (see Figure 11-7 and Figure 11-8).

On Windows, you need to be extra careful in setting the active display profile. Unlike the Mac OS, Windows doesn't get calibration information from the profile to update the video card LUTs, so it's all too easy for the monitor to behave differently than the way the active profile describes.

The Generics

Mac OS 9 and X come with several generic profiles: Generic RGB, and Generic CMYK. Make a special note wherever it will stick, because they are different!

On Mac OS 9, Generic RGB is based loosely on the P22 phosphor set, a 9300 K whitepoint and a 1.8 gamma—the venerable Apple 13-inch RGB display.

On Mac OS X, Generic RGB is based exactly on P22 phosphors, a 6500 K whitepoint, and a 1.8 gamma.

On Mac OS 9, Generic CMYK is based on the Apple Color Laserwriter. Ever wonder why you'd get such disgusting results using it as source or destination for a press or inkjet printer? Now you know! On Mac OS X, Generic CMYK is based on sub-sampled TR 001 measurement data, so it's essentially SWOP. Don't expect it to do a great job on a CMYK inkjet or color laser printer though, as the output will likely look washed out. For press work, it's marginally acceptable, but we recommend using the U.S. Web Coated (SWOP) v2 profile that comes with Adobe Photoshop, InDesign, and Illustrator. Or visit www.profilecentral.com for more profiles based on TR 001.

Figure 11-7

Display Properties: Settings tab

Figure 11-8

Display Properties, Advanced: Color Management tab

Display calibration/profiling packages should set the display profile automatically when it's created, but if in doubt, double-check to make sure that it has in fact done so.

Locations for profiles. Where your profiles live depends on what version of Windows you're using, and whether or not you chose the most typical installation (on a C: drive). You don't need to worry about these locations except for doing housecleaning, because you can right-click on a profile in any location to get a contextual menu containing an option to "Install Profile," which will place it in the appropriate directory.

▶ **Win98, Win98SE, WinMe**—C:\Windows\System\Color

▶ **Windows 2000, XP**—C:\WinNT\System32\Spool\Drivers\Color

▶ **Windows NT**—C:\WinNT\System32\Color

NOTE: Windows NT doesn't support ICM 2, and has no built-in color management at all. Any color management happening under Windows NT is done entirely by applications, and is hardwired into them. So the location for profiles under Windows NT is merely for reference.

Color Management in Applications

In the introduction to this chapter, we mentioned that color management can be requested by either applications or printer drivers. This section looks at color management strictly from an application point of view, covering both color-managed and non-color-managed applications.

Color-Managed Applications

Color-managed applications know what ICC profiles are, and use them to at least some degree. Most of these applications use either ColorSync or ICM to do color-management tasks such as color space conversions.

Some color-managed applications implement their own color engine, such as the Adobe applications, all of which use ACE (the Adobe Color Engine). Within each application, ACE produces the exact same results between its Macintosh and Windows counterparts. However, even when using ACE, they still make minimal use of ColorSync and ICM to request the current display profile and to find profiles on the system. All conversions are performed, by default, by ACE. It's possible to select ColorSync or ICM (and thus any available CMMs) in lieu of ACE in most Adobe applications. More detail on this can be found in Chapter 12, *The Adobe Common Color Architecture*.

QuickDraw, GDI, and Quartz

Each of the three operating systems discussed in this chapter, Mac OS 9, Mac OS X and Windows, has its own display and print engine. On Mac OS 9, this is QuickDraw, on Mac OS X it's called Quartz, and GDI is for Windows.

QuickDraw and GDI have something in common. They have no idea what CMYK is all about, so non-PostScript printer drivers for these operating systems must receive RGB data.

Quartz is different. It's PDF-based, and as such it knows about CMYK and LAB as well as RGB. There's been some speculation that Mac OS X printer drivers could accept either RGB or CMYK data. It's theoretically possible, but even though Quartz can accept CMYK data, the Quartz PDF to raster RIP doesn't, at least not yet. And even if it did, various printer drivers that convert raster data into printer commands for generating droplets of ink (screening algorithms) still expect to receive RGB data. That may change in the future, but if you're holding your breath, we suggest you exhale now.

Note that color-managed applications don't all have identical capabilities. While they'll support color conversions in one way or another, not all of them support color management to the display (such as many scanner drivers) or fully support embedded profiles.

The sure way to distinguish a color managed application from a non-color-managed application is to snoop around in the program itself. All color-managed applications have preferences for configuring source, destination, and possibly display profiles (if they don't request the display profile from the operating system).

So where is the color management actually happening? From a programming point of view, it's in the application. While ColorSync or ICM may actually be doing the work, they're APIs, not standalone programs. Think of it like this, if you drive a friend to the airport, did you or the car do the work? Well, both.

Source profiles. Color managed applications can use the OS-level APIs to hand off the source profile for your document to the operating system at print time along with the data to be printed, but with the exception of the Adobe applications, this seems to be fairly rare. The point of doing so is to provide the source profile(s), and let the printer driver and operating system do any subsequent color management. However, color-managed applications can already do the conversion to print space while producing the print stream, so many of them don't include source profiles in the print stream.

Non-Color-Managed Applications

Examples of non-color-managed applications are Microsoft Word, Excel, and PowerPoint, as well as most Web browsers. Those Web browsers that manage color (currently only on the Macintosh) do so only onscreen and don't pass off the source profiles into the print stream, which means the operating system or printer driver has to make an assumption (see "Color Management in Printer Drivers," later in this chapter).

Non-color-managed applications send the RGB values in the file directly to the monitor, so the sensible assumption for a source profile for files generated by these applications is the display profile, since it defines the color the monitor produces in response to the RGB values.

To color manage files from these applications, export them as TIFF, JPEG, or as a PostScript file produced by printing to disk, then import them into a color-managed application, assign the current display profile, and resave with the profile embedded. From that point onward, the files are color managed. This technique works for screen shots, too. (Mac OS X screen shots currently get the Generic RGB profile embedded, though the eventual goal seems to be to embed whatever profile the user specifies as RGB Default.)

Color Management in Printer Drivers

At first glance, it may seem that the printer driver is where all color management destined for print was *intended* to occur. Applications would manage color within the application and pass on a source profile for their documents at print time, then the printer driver would specify the destination profile and the operating system would do the necessary conversion.

The truth is that printer drivers have no knowledge of the application that's sending the data, so they have to handle both tagged and untagged files. However, the assumptions that different printer drivers make as to the source profile vary widely, and in our experience, they're usually incorrect.

Meanwhile, color-managed applications generally want to color manage the content of their documents completely before passing it off onto the operating system for printing. But the printer drivers still expect to do color management at their end, and to date there isn't a mechanism for the application to tell the printer driver, "Hey, buddy, don't do any more color management!" That means you, the user, have to ensure that when you print from applications that do their own color management, either the printer driver color management is turned off or the application doesn't convert to printer space before handing off the data to the printer driver.

With non-color-managed applications, you can use printer driver color management to perform the conversion to print space, but doing so involves some pitfalls that we discuss below.

Default Behavior

Each manufacturer seems to decide a different default behavior for their printer driver, and sometimes they decide on different defaults for different models or change the default behavior between versions of the driver. Most raster drivers default to some proprietary color management rather than to ColorSync or ICM.

PostScript printers also vary their default settings, but we know of none that default to ColorSync or ICM—at least not directly. Nearly all of them use PostScript color management when receiving RGB data, to convert it into CMYK. Some still use PostScript color management when receiving CMYK data. The printer driver option that controls this is usually called something like *color correction, color management,* or *simulation.*

When you use driver-level color management, the settings you use when you print the target to profile the device are very important. For example, when you use ColorSync or ICM in Epson printer drivers, what actually goes on under the hood is that the driver uses the "No Color Adjustment" setting, and asks ColorSync or ICM to do the conversion to the print space. If you print the profiling target using the "Photo-realistic" setting to take advantage of its better linearization and gray balance (putting up with the smaller gamut), the resulting profile won't work with printer driver color management, because the printer driver won't use the "Photo-realistic" setting when you choose ColorSync or ICM.

Source Profile Assumptions

When the application doesn't include the source profile in the print stream, and you use ColorSync or ICM in the printer driver, a source profile has to be assumed. Two things can make the assumption: the printer driver itself, or the operating system.

In Windows, the assumed source profile is always sRGB, whether the printer driver or Windows itself is doing the assuming. Applications that don't generate their own PostScript must use GDI, which has no idea what CMYK is. So the application must convert CMYK content into RGB for either display or for print. A few applications use GDI+, which will assume a default CMYK SWOP profile.

On the Macintosh, the operating system assumes the currently selected display profile, although an increasing number of printer drivers tell ColorSync to use sRGB as the source instead. To find out which assumption *your* printer driver makes, print an image with a display profile selected, then select a substantially different display profile (or perhaps even a non-display profile such as Wide Gamut RGB if you have Photoshop installed) and reprint the image. If the test prints look the same, something is being assumed over which you have no control, probably sRGB. If they're different, the driver is assuming the display profile. CMYK behavior is similar to Windows.

On Mac OS X, Generic RGB is assumed system-wide for untagged RGB. For CMYK, the waters are muddy because legacy applications still use QuickDraw, so they still convert their content to RGB at print time, and this conversion is up to the developer. However, applications using Quartz can send CMYK data for display or print. Currently Generic CMYK is the assumed source.

Raster Drivers

Using printer driver color management with raster printers and non-color-managed applications boils down to choosing a destination profile—the source profile is largely out of your control as it's assumed by either the application, printer driver, or operating system. Where you choose the destination profile depends on the operating system.

We can't possibly cover all printer drivers, so let's use the example of printing to an Epson Stylus Photo 2200 from Microsoft PowerPoint, a typical non-color-managed application. You should be able to find similar terminology in other printer drivers. If you don't find a ColorSync or ICM option in your printer driver, then it almost certainly doesn't support ICC-based color management.

Mac OS 9. When you open the printer driver, the default behavior is set to Automatic. To access the ColorSync option, you must select Custom in the Mode portion of the driver, and click the resulting Advanced button (see Figure 11-9).

Figure 11-9

Mac OS 9 Epson Stylus Photo 2200 Main Dialog

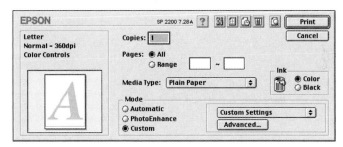

In the resulting dialog, look in the Color Management section. The default setting is for the Color Controls radio button, so select ColorSync here (when you're printing from an application that does its own color management, you'd select the setting you used when making the profile for this printer, usually No Color Adjustment). See Figure 11-10.

Figure 11-10

Mac OS 9 Epson Stylus Photo 2200 Advanced Dialog

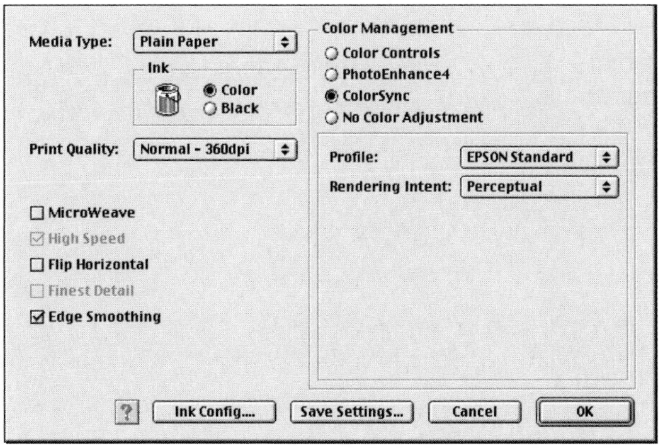

Epson drivers select a printer profile based on the media and resolution settings you've selected. Some printer drivers allow you to select a specific profile here manually, but in nearly all cases it must be the canned profile supplied by the manufacturer. We haven't had much success in getting custom profiles to appear in Mac OS 9 printer drivers, even by replacing the profile with an identically-named profile.

Mac OS X. Things are quite a bit different in Mac OS X, starting with the print dialog (see Figure 11-11). The third pop-up menu item lists different views, and the one you want is Color Management. Select ColorSync, and you'll see something like Figure 11-12.

Figure 11-11

Mac OS X Epson Stylus
Photo 2200 Print Dialog

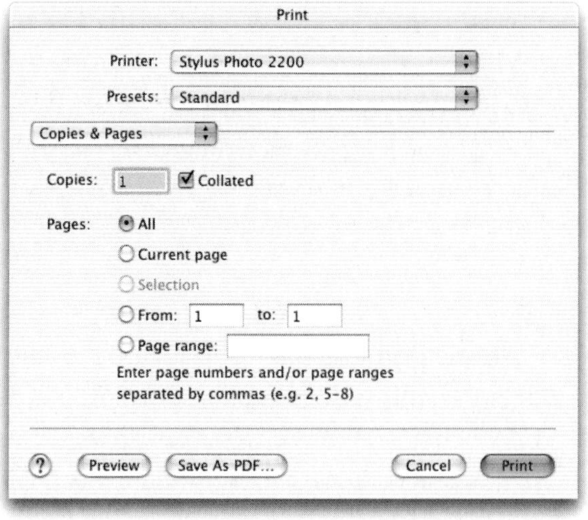

Figure 11-12

Mac OS X Epson Stylus
Photo 2200 Print Dialog:
Color Management
options

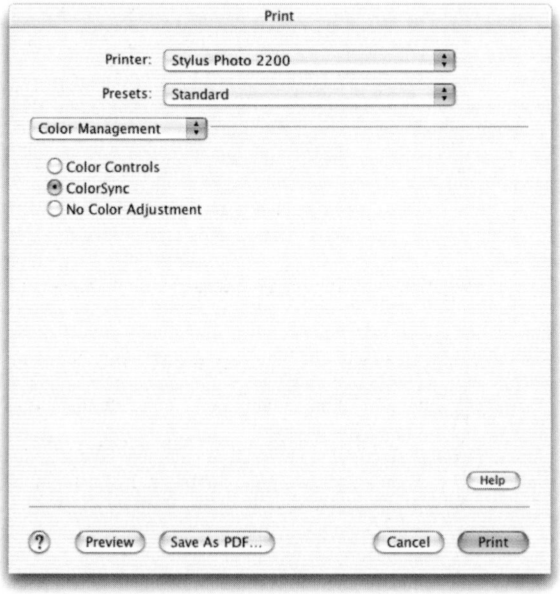

Where are the printer profiles? On Mac OS X, each device registers a device profile. Some printers, such as the Epson Stylus Photo 2200, register a profile for each media type they support. You don't need to do anything unless you don't want to use the registered profile for the media you're using.

Enter the ColorSync Utility application, found in /Applications/ Utilities. Click on the Devices panel option and you'll see something like Figure 11-13. Here we've selected Enhanced Matte, which happens to be one of the registered "behaviors" for the Stylus Photo 2200. Epson has chosen to register behaviors—profiles—for different media settings. Notice that lower on the list is Lexmark_Z22_Z32 which has no expand triangle, indicating there's only one registered profile for that device. No matter what settings you use for the media, it will always use the same profile, whereas the profile used by the Epson driver depends on the Media Type setting.

Figure 11-13

ColorSync Utility: Devices: Printers: Stylus_Photo_2200

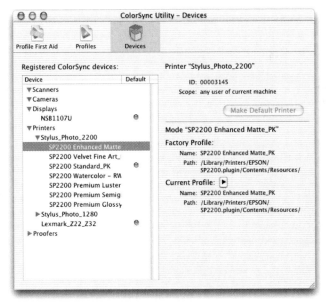

Continuing with the Epson example, when we click on a media type, the Factory Profile and its location appears to the right, as well as the Current Profile (which by default is the Factory Profile). If you click on the black triangle to the right of Current Profile, you are then presented with two options:

▶ Select any ICC profile, which will then be used with this device/media combination as the destination profile.

▶ Reset it to the Factory Profile.

For more information on the ColorSync Utility, see the sidebar, "ColorSync Utility."

The version of OS X that was current at the time of publication lacks any mechanism for selecting a rendering intent to use with printer driver color management. Once you've selected the desired profile for the intended media type in the ColorSync Utility, you simply print your document.

Windows 2000, XP. Windows printer drivers share similarities with both Mac OS 9 and Mac OS X drivers. Using the Epson 2200 as an example again, the main print dialog, like Mac OS 9, requires you to click on the Custom option in the Mode section of the dialog to access the Advanced button, which you then also need to click (see Figure 11-14).

ColorSync Utility

The ColorSync Utility, unique to Mac OS X, consolidates features found in various locations on Mac OS 9: Profile First Aid, (which was a standalone application on Mac OS 9); a Profiles tab to show you all installed ICC profiles and their location, along with some magic abilities we'll discuss below; and a Devices tab that takes the place of the "Profiles for Standard Devices" tab in the Mac OS 9 ColorSync control panel, and also lets us easily override manufacturer canned profiles with our own custom profiles.

Profile First Aid is a utility for verifying the integrity of ICC profiles stored on your system, and can repair most problems it finds. It looks for aspects of the profile that don't conform to the ICC specification. One of the most common side-effects of a non-conforming profile is that it doesn't appear in application pop-up menus, which, of course, means you can't use it.

Running a Repair session in Profile First Aid, then relaunching the application, frequently solves such problems. We recommend running a Profile First Aid Repair session regularly, because surprisingly enough, many profiles don't conform fully to the ICC specification. While most of the deviations are benign, it doesn't do any harm to run Profile First Aid periodically.

The Profiles tab doesn't seem to do much at first glance. It shows all installed profiles and where they're located. This is extremely helpful for hunting down profiles, since there are so many valid locations on OS X. But if you turn down the triangle-widget on a location to show profiles in that location, and then click on a profile, you'll get some nifty profile information, as well as a 3-D plot of its device's gamut. Click on the plot while dragging to rotate it, and hold down the Option key while click-dragging to zoom in and out. If you double-click on a profile, you can get even more information on the various tags it contains.

The resulting window contains a Color Management section where you select ICM (see Figure 11-15). As in Mac OS X, there are no options—they're determined from a list of associated profiles.

Figure 11-14

Windows 2000 Epson
Stylus Photo 2200
Print Dialog

CUPS

CUPS stands for the Common Unix Printing System. Apple has touted CUPS to the graphic arts community as a good thing, but hasn't done a very good job of telling us why we should care. The printing architecture designed for Mac OS X, as embodied in Mac OS 10.0 and 10.1, had, let's just say, lots of problems.

So it got gutted in favor of CUPS. CUPS is primarily a scheduling and queuing system, handing off print jobs from applications to appropriate filters, drivers, and printer modules. It's the center of the print architecture, and therefore defines it.

Now we have two kinds of printer drivers. We have the original architecture's Printer Modules, for which Apple created a bridge so that CUPS could use

them without requiring developers to rewrite their drivers from scratch. These Printer Modules can be ColorSync aware, and do driver-level color management. But now there are also CUPS printer drivers and filters.

Filters do conversions between formats. For example a PostScript to PDF filter converts PostScript into PDF, and a PDF to Raster filter converts PDF into something like a TIFF or other bitmap. A PostScript RIP filter would convert PostScript into a bitmap too, though we've yet to see one.

CUPS drivers are responsible for communicating with a particular printer in a language it can understand. An Epson Stylus Color 3000 printer driver would convert raster bitmap data into the language the printer needs,

accounting for media, resolution and other settings.

The good news? CUPS effectively turns any printer into a PostScript- and PDF-based printer. The plug-in filter-based architecture lets us insert different kinds of RIPs from various vendors, and immediately use these RIPs for any raster-based printer connected to the host computer. Stay tuned for more developments on this front as CUPS matures, and printer vendors decide to build CUPS drivers instead of Printer Modules.

The not-so-good news? CUPS and CUPS drivers thus far have no idea what ICC profiles are, and don't tie into ColorSync. So again, stay tuned for the ever-changing and maturing world of Mac OS X.

Figure 11-15

Windows 2000 Epson
Stylus Photo 2200 Print
Dialog: Advanced

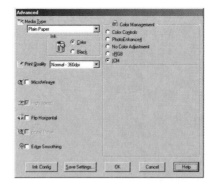

To associate profiles with a device, go to the Start menu>Settings>
Printers>yourprintername. Here we selected Epson Stylus Photo 2200, as
shown in Figure 11-16.

Figure 11-16

Epson Stylus
Photo 2200 queue

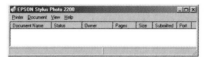

Go to the Printer menu and select Properties, as shown in Figure
11-17, which brings up the Properties dialog box shown in Figure 11-18.

Figure 11-17

Epson Stylus
Photo 2200 queue:
Printer-Properties option

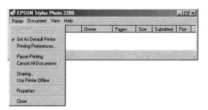

Figure 11-18

Epson Stylus
Photo 2200: Properties,
General tab

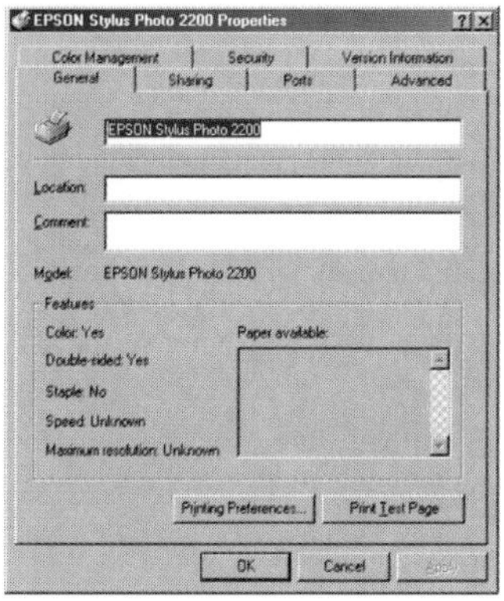

Here we click on the Color Management tab to open the dialog box shown in Figure 11-19. These profile associations, and the default profile, are device-specific, not media-specific.

Figure 11-19

Epson Stylus
Photo 2200: Properties,
Color Management tab

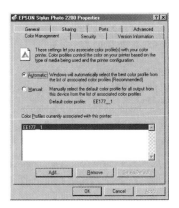

PostScript Drivers

ColorSync and ICM can affect PostScript output, even though neither actually knows what PostScript is. Non-color-managed applications don't generate PostScript themselves—they send drawing commands to the operating system, and the PostScript printer driver turns those QuickDraw, GDI, or Quartz commands into PostScript. The operating system can color manage QuickDraw, Quartz, and GDI/GDI+ routines, then produce the PostScript stream already color managed. The latest Mac OS and Windows operating systems can also produce CSAs (Color Space Arrays, which are PostScript source profiles). Note that applications that generate their own PostScript (which virtually every color-managed application does) aren't affected by ColorSync/ICM settings, so PostScript printer driver color management simply doesn't work with these applications.

Mac OS 9. The Mac OS 9 PostScript driver is a frequent and fruitful source of confusion due to the Color Matching section which contains ColorSync Color Matching (and, for some printers, PostScript Color Matching). See Figure 11-20.

Figure 11-20

Mac OS 9 Laserwriter 8:
ColorSync Color
Matching

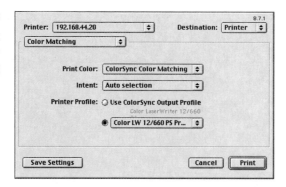

Both options only work with applications that don't generate their own PostScript. Why a mechanism was never developed for the application to better communicate its capabilities to the printer driver isn't something we can explain, so let us just stress that with all of the major applications we cover in later chapters, these printer driver options don't apply because all of them generate their own PostScript.

But if you're printing from an application like PowerPoint or a Web browser, you can use the ColorSync Color Matching option, which works the same as for raster printer drivers, with the exception that the current display profile is *always* the assumed source profile. You simply choose a destination profile, which normally should be the profile for your intended destination PostScript device.

PostScript Color Management is an option we don't recommend, both because we know of very few people who have made it work, and because there are precious few tools to help anyone do so. The way it's supposed to work is that the assumed source profile (the current display profile) gets converted by ColorSync into a PostScript CSA (Color Space Array). The selected destination profile gets converted into a PostScript CRD (Color Rendering Dictionary), and both are sent with the OS-generated PostScript print stream to the printer. The PostScript RIP uses the CSA and CRD as source and destination profiles, respectively, and makes the conversion. If you get it to work and it doesn't cause you confusion or misery, feel free to let us know.

Mac OS X (10.2). The PostScript driver on Mac OS X has absolutely no user options for color management, apparently by design. Applications that generate their own PostScript simply bypass any additional influence by the operating system, anyway. For all other applications, a PostScript CSA (a PostScript source profile) is placed in the print stream by the operating system based on the following conditions:

▶ **Tagged images.** The embedded profile is used as the source profile, so it becomes the CSA sent to the PostScript printer.

Tip: It's Only Tagged If the Application Knows It's Tagged. If the application being used to print doesn't know what an embedded profile is, the image isn't considered tagged by the operating system.

▶ **Untagged /DeviceRGB, /DeviceCMYK, /DeviceGray.** With applications that generate device-dependent color, a CSA is generated from the Generic RGB, Generic CMYK, or Generic Gray profiles. (In future versions of the OS, these will probably be replaced by the RGB Default, CMYK Default, and/or Gray Default settings in the ColorSync panel of System Preferences.)

▶ **Untagged /CalRGB or /CalCMYK.** Applications that produce calibrated color get a CSA generated from the calibrated color tables submitted by the application.

There are two gotchas inherent in printing under Mac OS X from applications that don't generate their own PostScript to a PostScript printer. First, there's no way to avoid sending a CSA to the printer, so there's no way to avoid PostScript color management (unless your RIP simply ignores CSAs, which is relatively rare). So don't print test files from such applications. Second, the destination profile is almost always the printer's built-in CRD, which is usually a generic placeholder rather than an actual description of the printer's behavior.

Eventually we expect Apple to provide a mechanism for sending CRDs based on ICC profiles, which should provide reasonable results from PostScript Level 2 or later RIPs. But for the time being, if you want good output from a PostScript device, print from an application that allows you to control the source profile, destination profile, and rendering intent.

Color Management in Scanner Drivers

Most scanner drivers don't implement their own color management, and instead tie into the operating system if they use color management at all. Moreover, scanner drivers that do offer color management exhibit a fairly wide range of behaviors and capabilities.

The best ones let you specify a source and a destination profile, convert the data from the source to the destination during the scan, and embed the destination profile in the scanned image on save, while also using the display profile to display the image correctly on the monitor. The worst ones have a single button marked ColorSync or ICM that converts from a hidden generic scanner profile to the display profile, and produces untagged RGB as output. Most fall somewhere between the two extremes, but the most common problem is the inability to let the user specify a custom scanner profile as the source profile.

In most cases, we find that the easiest course of action is to find out how to turn off both color management and any autocorrection features in the scanner driver, treat it as dumb and raw, bring the scans into Photoshop, and assign the scanner profile there. Some scanner drivers make this procedure more difficult than others, but it's rarely impossible.

If you decide to use scanner driver color management, you need to confirm whether the driver embeds the scanner profile, or uses it as a source profile for a conversion to some destination profile. If the latter, what is the destination? If there's no explicit setting for the destination, it's probably the display profile, which the scanner driver grabs automatically from the operating system. That means that all your scans get clipped to the gamut of your display, which is far from ideal.

Scanner drivers that operate as Photoshop plug-ins need special attention, because the API that lets the driver pass a source profile to Photoshop along with the pixels hasn't been implemented in any scanner software we've encountered, so the images always come in as either untagged or working space RGB. If the scanner driver actually converted the pixels to working space RGB, that's fine. If it didn't, you need to assign the scanner profile manually.

East Is East, West Is West

The old saw has it that, "East is east, west is west, and never the twain shall meet." It's generally a good idea to enforce a similar separation between OS-level and application-level color management as much as is feasible, and to ensure that when they *do* meet, they do so gracefully rather than colliding. It's not only possible, but distressingly easy to have *both* the application and the printer driver managing color behind each other's backs, so *you* need to keep track of who is doing what to whom. When you work with color-managed applications, the easiest course is almost always to turn off color management in the various device drivers and simply let the applications handle the color management.

The Adobe Common Color Architecture

Color Management in Adobe Photoshop, InDesign, and Illustrator

On our bleaker days, we wonder why all vendors that implement color management feel they have to do it *their* way, with their own unique user interface and their own unique terminology. So we derive a certain amount of comfort from the fact that Adobe Systems has at least attempted to standardize much of the user interface and most of the terminology between its three main color-managed applications, Adobe Photoshop, Adobe Illustrator, and Adobe InDesign.

We think that Adobe has done more than any other vendor in finding rational ways to present color-management options to the user, and the integration between the three applications generally makes life easier. However, since the three applications do rather different things, some of the apparent similarities are misleading—we'll point these out as they arise. And, sometimes, the more obscure consequences of some of the settings may not be particularly intuitive, so we'll likewise flag these when we get to them.

We'll start by looking at the settings that really do work identically in all three applications.

Color Settings—Command Central for Color

Adobe Photoshop, Illustrator, and InDesign all share a very similar and somewhat formidable-looking dialog box called Color Settings (see Figure 12-1).

Figure 12-1

Color Settings

*Photoshop's
Color Settings*

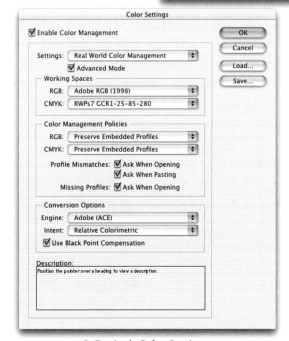

InDesign's Color Settings

Illustrator's Color Settings

For now, let's ignore the differences, and concentrate on the similarities. All three applications' Color Settings have areas labelled Working Spaces and Color Management Policies, though the options are slightly different in each one. Let's first look at what they have in common.

Settings

The Settings menu simply contains saved presets for the Color Settings dialog box. Settings files created in one of the three applications can be used by the other two, which makes synchronizing the behavior of the three fairly easy. However, Photoshop has more options than InDesign, which in turn has more options than Illustrator—so if you want to synchronize Photoshop's setting with either or both of the other applications, save the settings from Photoshop, and if you want to synchronize InDesign and Illustrator, save the settings from InDesign.

Saved settings *should* appear automatically in the Settings menu, and in the majority of cases, they do. If you find they don't, check the location of the settings files—the file extension is .csf. On Mac OS 9, they're stored in the Hard Drive:System Folder:Application Support:Adobe:Color: Settings folder; on Windows they're stored in the Program Files\Common Files\ Adobe\Color\Settings folder.

As we write this, the following locations apply to Mac OS X: Photoshop 7 defaults to saving them in the /Users/<username>/Library/Application Support/Adobe/Color/Settings folder, and can use .csf files saved in both the user Library and main Library location. InDesign 2 defaults to saving them in the /Users/<username>/Library/Application Support/Adobe/Color folder, not the /Settings folder, so once saved here *no* Adobe applications can detect them. It does, however, see .csf files saved in the Settings folder in both the user Library and main Library location. Illustrator defaults to saving .csf files in the /Library/Application Support/Adobe/Color/Settings folder, and only detects them here as well. The simplest solution is to save your settings to the desktop, then move them to the main Library folder.

Macintosh users get one extra preset, labeled ColorSync Workflow. When you choose this setting, the application uses the RGB, CMYK, and in the case of Photoshop, Grayscale profiles specified in the Default Profiles for Documents panel of the ColorSync control panel (Mac OS 9), or under the Default Profiles tab of the ColorSync panel (Mac OS X). Also, on both operating systems the application uses the CMM chosen in ColorSync—see "Engine," later in this chapter, for further ramifications.

Default Profiles—Working Spaces

The Working Spaces section lets you specify default profiles (called "Working Spaces" in Adobe's terminology) for RGB and CMYK. The exact role that these profiles play depends on the settings you enter elsewhere in the dialog box, but they always represent the default profile—either assumed or assigned—for untagged RGB and untagged CMYK, and for new documents.

When the "Advanced" checkbox is unchecked, your choices are limited to a recommended set of profiles for RGB and CMYK. But you can control which profiles appear in the lists when "Advanced" is unchecked. The lists simply show the profiles in the Recommended folder, so any profile you install there will show up in the list. This mechanism provides an administrator a convenient way to limit the choice of profiles in the three applications to "safe" ones.

On Mac OS 9, they're stored in the System Folder:Application Support:Adobe:Color:Profiles:Recommended folder, on Windows they're stored in the Program Files\Common Files\Adobe\Color\Profiles\Recommended folder, and on Mac OS X they're stored in the /Library/Application Support/Adobe/Color/Profiles/Recommended folder. (In all cases, the folder is aliased to the main Profiles folder, so any profiles you install in the Recommended folder are available to those other applications that search more than one level deep for profiles in both the main Library and the user Library.)

If you turn on the "Advanced" checkbox, the RGB Working Space menu lists all the installed bidirectional RGB profiles, and the CMYK Working Space menu lists all the installed bidirectional CMYK profiles—you can't use unidirectional input profiles that only convert from device values to PCS as working spaces. (In the case of RGB, you probably don't want to use a device space at all—see "Intermediate Spaces," in Chapter 10, *Color-Management Workflow*.)

Color Management Policies

The most critical choices you make in the Color Settings dialog box are the Color Management Policies, which control the applications' behavior when they open tagged and untagged documents, when you create new documents, and when you move selected elements between documents. They don't affect the handling of imported objects in InDesign documents, just native elements. The policies control the applications' default behavior for assuming or assigning profiles to untagged documents and for handling tagged documents by either honoring the embedded profile, converting from that profile to another, or ignoring the embedded profile and assuming a different one. All three applications let you set separate policies for RGB and for CMYK (Photoshop lets you set a third policy for Grayscale).

A complicating factor is that InDesign documents have two default profiles, one for RGB and one for CMYK elements, which can muddy the distinction between tagged and untagged documents. It's possible to have an InDesign document whose native RGB elements are tagged and whose native CMYK elements are untagged, or vice versa. We'll leave you to make the call as to whether such a document is half-tagged or half-untagged!

The three Warning options provide manual overrides to the policies by displaying dialog boxes that let you take an action different from the one dictated by the current policy. Before we look at the warnings, here's how the policies behave when the warnings are turned off.

Off. This is the probably the most misleadingly labelled option of the three. You can't turn color management off in these applications—they always convert from a source profile (either embedded/assigned or assumed) to the monitor profile for display, and they always use profiles to convert from RGB to CMYK.

For new documents, the Off policy makes the applications assume the working space profiles for all native RGB and CMYK elements, and treat the documents as untagged—if you change the working spaces, the documents take on the new profiles, and the appearance changes.

For documents that are tagged with a profile *other than the working space* profile, the applications discard the embedded profile, assume the working space profile, and treat the documents as untagged.

However, when the application opens a document that's tagged with the current working space profile, all sense goes out the window. It treats the document as tagged with the embedded profile, so any subsequent changes to the working space have no effect on that document. Effectively, a document with an embedded profile that matches the working space profile is treated with a "Preserve Embedded Profiles" policy (discussed next). We think this is counterintuitive, to say the least.

When you move native objects from a document in one space to another in a different space by copy and paste or drag and drop, the application simply moves the numerical values in the object.

Preserve Embedded Profiles. Unlike the previous option, this one does what it says. Tagged documents get opened in the embedded profile's space (in the case of InDesign documents, which can have both RGB and CMYK elements, each keeps its definitions). New documents use the current working space(s) and are treated as tagged. Untagged documents stay untagged—you can think of this as "preserving" their untagged status—and use the working space profiles as assumed profiles.

When you move native RGB objects from a document in one space to another in a different space by copy and paste or drag and drop, the application performs a conversion from the source to the destination and moves the color appearance. When you move native CMYK objects from a document in one space to another in a different space by copy and paste or drag and drop, the application transfers the numerical values in the object.

Convert to Working Space. This policy is best thought of as an automation feature. When the application opens a tagged document, it performs a conversion from the embedded profile's space to the current working space. When it opens an untagged document, it uses the working space as an assumed profile and keeps the document untagged.

When you move native RGB or CMYK objects from a document in one space to another in a different space, the application always performs a conversion from source to destination, preserving color appearance and changing the numbers.

As a general rule, we set all our policies to Preserve Embedded Profiles—that way, we at least get to evaluate the image in its profiled space before deciding what to do next.

Warnings—Manual Overrides

The Missing Profile warnings in Photoshop and InDesign and the Profile Mismatch warnings in all three applications let you manually override the default behavior dictated by the color-management policy currently in effect. The policies determine which radio button is checked by default in the warning dialogs, but the same options are available no matter which policy is in effect. However, since each of the three applications is designed to do different things, the warnings are presented slightly differently in each one.

The Missing Profile warnings appear when you open an untagged document, and offer the options listed below.

Missing Profile warning in Photoshop. The Missing Profile warning, when enabled, appears whenever you open an untagged document (see Figure 12-2).

Figure 12-2
Photoshop Missing
Profile warning

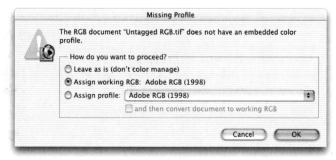

The warning offers four options:

▶ Leave as is (don't color manage) tells the application to assume the current working space profile and treat the document as untagged.

▶ Assign working RGB/CMYK/Grayscale tells the application to assign the working space profile and treat the document as tagged.

▶ Assign profile lets you tell the application to assign any profile that's applicable to the document's color mode (you can only assign RGB profiles to RGB documents and CMYK profiles to CMYK documents) and treat the document as tagged.

▶ Assign profile, then convert to "working RGB/CMYK" lets you tell the application to assign any profile that's applicable to the document's color mode, then convert from that profile to the Working Space for that color mode, and treat the document as tagged.

Missing Profile warning in InDesign. While Photoshop documents only exist in a single color space, InDesign documents can contain RGB and CMYK elements governed by different profiles, called Document profiles—so InDesign has not one, but two Missing Profile warnings, one for RGB, one for CMYK (see Figure 12-3). Note that this dialog only pertains to native InDesign content, not to placed objects. If the document has profiles embedded, but placed images do not, you won't see this dialog. However, it's also important to realize that untagged placed images will use the Document profiles (for RGB and CMYK) as assumed source profiles.

Figure 12-3

InDesign Missing Profile warnings

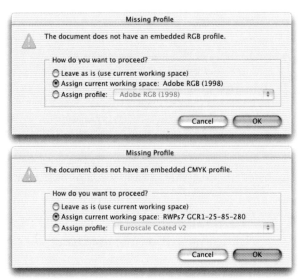

InDesign's Missing Profile warnings provide the same three options (with slightly different labels), first for RGB, then for CMYK:

► Leave as is (use current working space) tells the application to assume the current working space profile and treat the RGB or CMYK elements in the document as untagged.

► Assign current working space tells the application to assign the working space profile (which becomes the RGB or CMYK Document profile for this document) and treat the RGB or CMYK elements in the document as tagged. Untagged placed objects assume these profiles as source and remain untagged.

▶ Assign Profile lets you tell the application to assign any RGB profile in the first warning, and any CMYK profile in the second one. Untagged placed objects assume these profiles as source and remain untagged.

Missing Profile warning in Illustrator. Unlike the other two applications, Illustrator doesn't let you turn off the Missing Profile warning—it always displays the warning when you open a document without an embedded profile (see Figure 12-4). (This can be annoying, since Illustrator always looks for profiles in EPS documents, but can't embed profiles in EPSs on save.)

Figure 12-4

Illustrator's Missing
Profile warning

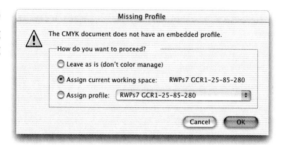

Illustrator's Missing Profile warning provides the same options as InDesign's—the only difference is that Illustrator documents are always defined as either RGB documents or CMYK documents, so you only get one warning:

▶ Leave as is (don't color manage) tells the application to assume the current Working Space profile and treat the document as untagged.

▶ Assign current working space tells the application to assign the working space profile and treat the document as tagged.

▶ Assign Profile lets you tell the application to assign any RGB profile to an RGB document, or any CMYK profile to a CMYK document.

The Profile Mismatch: Ask When Opening warning appears when you open a document with an embedded profile that's different from the current working space.

Photoshop's Embedded Profile Mismatch warning. When enabled, this warning displays the dialog box shown in Figure 12-5.

Figure 12-5

Photoshop's
Embedded Profile
Mismatch warning

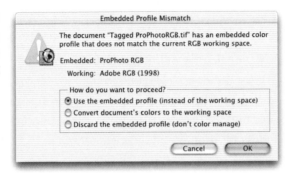

The warning offers the following three options:

▶ Use the embedded profile (instead of the working space) preserves the embedded profile and treats the document as tagged. The embedded profile is used as the source for all conversions.

▶ Convert document's colors to the working space tells the application to perform a conversion from the embedded profile to the working space profile, and treats the document as tagged with the working space profile.

▶ Discard the embedded profile (don't color manage) tells the application to discard the embedded profile, assume the working space profile, and treat the document as untagged.

InDesign's Embedded Profile Mismatch warnings. Again, since InDesign documents can contain both RGB and CMYK elements, it's possible to have a profile mismatch in either or both. If the Color Management Policies are set to anything other than Off, InDesign will embed the Document profile for that mode. If neither mode is set to Off, InDesign will embed both Document profiles (RGB and CMYK), regardless of the contents of the document. When enabled, this warning displays the dialog boxes shown in Figure 12-6.

Figure 12-6

InDesign's
Embedded Profile
Mismatch warnings

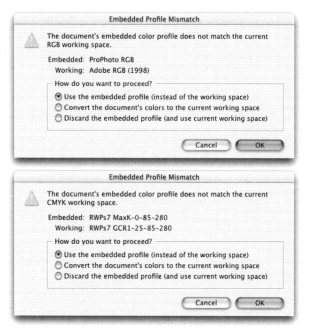

Both warnings offer the following three options:

▶ Use the embedded profiles (instead of the working space) preserves the embedded profiles and treats the RGB or CMYK elements in the document as tagged. The embedded profiles become the Document profiles for this document, which means they are used as the source profiles for all conversions of native objects, and as the assumed source profiles for untagged placed objects.

▶ Convert the document's colors to the working space tells the application to convert the color from the embedded profiles to the working space profiles (which become the Document profiles for this document), and treats the document as tagged. It doesn't convert placed objects, but untagged objects use the new Document profiles as assumed source profiles.

▶ Discard the embedded profile (and use current working space) tells the application to discard the embedded profile, assume the working space profile, and treat the RGB or CMYK elements in the document as untagged. Untagged objects use the working space profiles as assumed source profiles.

Illustrator's Embedded Profile Mismatch warning. Illustrator's warning is functionally identical and cosmetically very similar to Photoshop's (see Figure 12-7).

Figure 12-7

Illustrator's
Embedded Profile
Mismatch warning

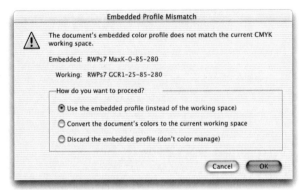

It offers the following three options:

▶ Use the embedded profile (instead of the working space) preserves the embedded profile and treats the document as tagged. The embedded profile is used as the source for all conversions.

▶ Convert document's colors to the working space tells the application to perform a conversion from the embedded profile to the working space profile, and treats the document as tagged with the working space profile.

▶ Discard the embedded profile (don't color manage) tells the application to discard the embedded profile, assume the working space profile, and treat the document as untagged.

Profile Mismatch: Ask When Pasting warning. The last set of warnings lets you override the default behavior when you move elements (or in the case of Photoshop, selected pixels) from a document in one space to another in a different space, by copy and paste or drag and drop. It only applies when both source and destination document are in the same color mode—RGB to RGB or CMYK to CMYK. If you move elements from one color mode to another, a conversion always occurs—you can't paste RGB values into a CMYK document or vice versa.

The warning offers the same pair of options in all three applications (see Figure 12-8).

Figure 12-8

Paste Profile
Mismatch warnings

Photoshop's Paste Profile Mismatch warning

InDesign's Paste Profile Mismatch warning

Illustrator's Paste Profile Mismatch warning

In this situation, the only choices are to move the RGB or CMYK values, in which case the appearance will very likely change, or move the color appearance, in which case the RGB or CMYK values will change.

▶ Convert (preserve color appearance) makes the application convert the object from the source document's assigned or assumed profile to the destination object's assigned or assumed profile, preserving the color appearance.

▶ Don't convert (preserve color numbers) moves the numerical values in the object to the destination document, where they will likely generate a different color appearance.

We usually leave all the warnings turned on—they provide a useful reality check. If we know that we'll be dealing with a large number of documents in a space other than our current working space, we'll change the working space rather than turn off the warning.

Advanced Options—Default Conversion Settings

When you enable the "Advanced" checkbox, new controls appear that let you control how the applications perform conversions, including not only the ones discussed above, but all other conversions that don't present a user interface with a choice of conversion options. This includes choosing a different mode from Photoshop's Image>Mode menu, Illustrator's File>Document Color Mode and Filter>Colors> Convert to RGB/CMYK, or InDesign's Color palette pop-out menu (see Figure 12-9).

Figure 12-9
Conversion Options

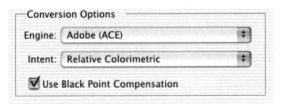

Photoshop's Conversion Options

InDesign's Conversion Options

Illustrator's Conversion Options

Engine. This option allows you to choose a specific CMM from the ICC-compliant CMMs installed on your computer. We're big fans of the Adobe (ACE) engine—it seems to be remarkably bug-free and accurate. Its only major downside is that it's only available inside Adobe applications, so if you need to make sure that you're getting *exactly* the same conversions inside and outside Adobe applications, you'll need to settle on a CMM that's installable as a standalone.

Most of the items on the menu are self-explanatory—it's simply a list of different CMMs—but Mac users get one extra item, Apple ColorSync, that's a bit more mysterious. When you choose Apple ColorSync, the application uses the CMM specified in the ColorSync control panel (Mac OS 9) or the ColorSync panel found in System Preferences (Mac OS X). If you choose Automatic, each profile looks for its preferred CMM, which then gets used for the conversion between that profile and the PCS. The positive aspect of this is that you ensure that any profiles containing "secret sauce" that's reliant on a particular CMM will get used to their fullest potential. The negative is that it's very unlikely that you'll know at any given moment which CMM is doing what to whom!

Intent. This option lets you choose the default rendering intent, which is used for all conversions that don't let you specify a rendering intent at conversion time. For those into trivia, it also affects the LAB values in the Info palette, so if you are wondering why the LAB values in the Info palette don't match up to actual measurements, it's because this setting isn't set to absolute colorimetric.

Note that the default rendering intent is relative colorimetric *with black point compensation*, which is not at all the same thing as relative colorimetric *without* black point compensation—see "Use Black Point Compensation," below. We leave this setting at the default, but if you find that you want to use some other rendering intent more than half the time, you may want to change it to the one you use most often.

Use Black Point Compensation. This proprietary Adobe feature plugs a hole in the ICC profile spec. It ensures that black in the source is always mapped to black in the destination, so that the entire dynamic range of the input is mapped to the entire dynamic range of the output (see Figure 12-10).

Figure 12-10
Black point compensation

black point compensation on   *black point compensation off*

Black point compensation ensures that black in the source is always translated to black in the destination, preventing the loss of shadow detail that's evident in the above right image.

When "Use Black Point Compensation" is turned off, it's possible to get either of two undesirable outcomes:

▶ If the source has a lower black point than the destination, all values in the source that are darker than destination black get clipped to black, destroying shadow detail.

▶ If the source has a higher black point than the destination, the converted color contains no true blacks, so the result appears washed out.

"Use Black Point Compensation" avoids both these problems. The only reason we can see for turning it off, other than to see what it does, is if your workflow depends on having exactly the same conversions available inside and outside the Adobe applications— and quite honestly, we find it so valuable that if you do have such a workflow, you may want to consider changing it.

Manual Assignments and Conversions

The Color Settings dialog box is mostly concerned with the behavior of newly opened or newly created documents, but the three applications also let you perform profile assignments and conversions while you're working on a document.

Like the Color Settings, the controls described in this section operate at the document level. They don't affect the behavior of linked graphics with embedded profiles in InDesign, although they *do* affect the assumed profile for linked untagged graphics.

Assign Profile

All three applications offer an Assign Profile command. It lets you do three things:

▶ Untag any document (don't color manage). Working spaces are assumed as source.

▶ Assign the Working Space profile to a document. If the document was untagged, assigning the profile turns it into a tagged one.

▶ Assign any profile to a tagged document, overriding the one that was previously in force, or to an untagged document, thereby turning it into a tagged one.

In Photoshop, Assign Profile is found on the Mode submenu under the Image menu. In InDesign and Illustrator, it's on the Edit menu. The Assign Profile dialog box is virtually identical in Photoshop and Illustrator. Since InDesign documents can contain both an RGB and a CMYK document profile, the InDesign Assign Profiles dialog box lets you make separate assignments for RGB and CMYK (see Figure 12-11).

Figure 12-11

Assign Profile(s) dialog boxes

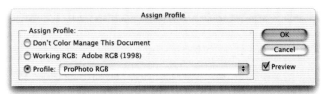

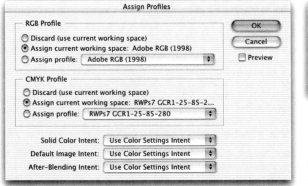

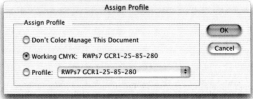

Clockwise from top: Photoshop's Assign Profile, Illustrator's Assign Profile, and InDesign's Assign Profiles dialog boxes.

Tip: Don't Trust Illustrator's Document Info Palette. One of Illustrator 10.x's more endearing bugs is that the profile information in the Document Info palette usually doesn't update until you close and reopen the palette. At the time of writing, the current version of Illustrator is 10.0.3, and the bug has persisted in all versions of Illustrator 10, so we aren't overly optimistic that it will get fixed anytime soon. The Document Profile display from the pop-up menu at the lower left of the document window, however, operates as expected.

InDesign's Assign Profiles command is different in other ways, too. The profile assignments apply not only to native objects, but also to linked, imported objects that are untagged. To make matters a little more confusing, the rendering intent choices apply to both native and imported objects, whether tagged or not, by default. You need to use the Image Color Settings option, discussed later in this chapter, to specify a different rendering intent.

Convert to Profile

Photoshop and InDesign both offer a command labeled Convert to Profile, but due to the different nature of the two applications, they do very different things.

Photoshop's Convert to Profile. Photoshop documents are always governed by a single profile, so assignments and conversions are both relatively straightforward. Photoshop's Convert to Profile command is found on the Mode submenu of the Image menu. The dialog box lets you choose a destination profile, a CMM (or Engine, in Adobe terminology), a rendering intent, and a "Use Black Point Compensation" checkbox (see Figure 12-12).

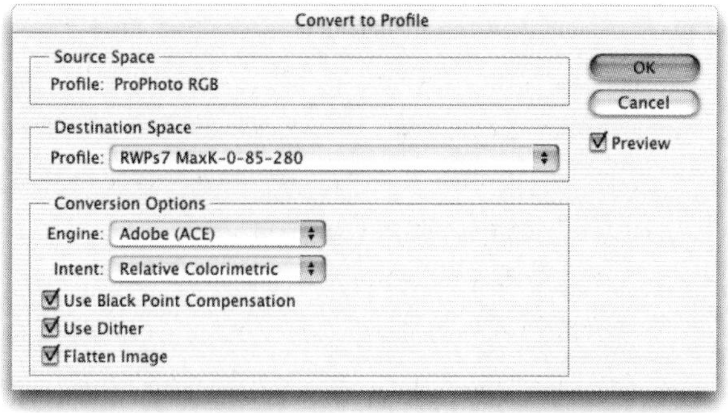

Figure 12-12

Photoshop's
Convert to Profile
dialog box

The conversion applies to the entire document. In the case of layered files, the dialog also offers the option to flatten the document—it's usually a good idea to do so, particularly when the conversion also includes a mode change, because layers may blend differently in the destination space, changing the document's appearance. The Preview checkbox lets you preview the result of the conversion.

InDesign's Convert to Profile. InDesign's Convert to Profile dialog box looks fairly different from Photoshop's, since InDesign documents have two embedded profiles—one for RGB, one for CMYK (see Figure 12-13).

Figure 12-13

InDesign's
Convert to Profile
dialog box

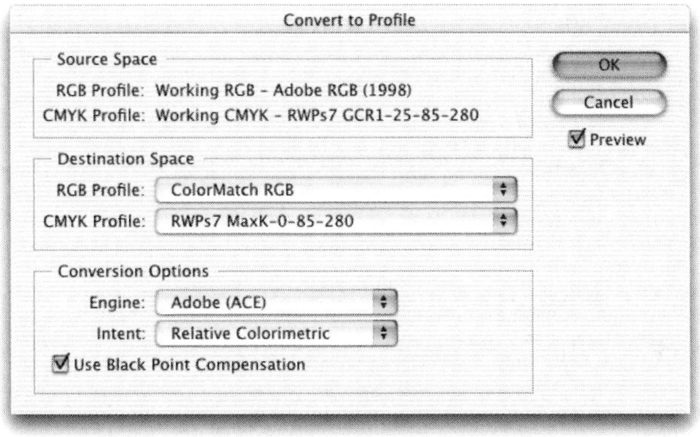

InDesign's Convert to Profile converts all native InDesign elements from the Document profiles (the current spaces) to the selected destination spaces. The destination spaces then become the Document profiles for that document. As a result, they also become the new assumed profiles for untagged placed objects. The operation has no effect on tagged placed objects.

Illustrator conversions. Illustrator only allows you to perform one type of conversion—a mode change between RGB and CMYK. The source profile is always the working space for the document's color mode in the case of untagged documents, or the Document profile (which may be the working space, or may be a different assigned profile) in the case of tagged ones. The destination is always the working space for the destination color mode.

The Document Color Mode command (on the File menu) lets you convert an entire document from RGB to CMYK or vice versa.

Color Managing Imported Graphics

All the controls we've discussed so far operate primarily on native objects in a document, not on imported graphics such as placed images. But we have to leave in the weasel word, "primarily," because the color-management policies *do* have an impact on how imported graphics are handled, and these interactions can be subtle and quite often counterintuitive. Moreover, all three applications have quite different controls.

Placed Graphics in Photoshop

Photoshop is pretty straightforward. It has a Place command, but any placed elements end up as part of the document, and are governed by the document's assigned or assumed profile. Photoshop always places the numerical values contained in the placed document, so its embedded profile is ignored. Basically, once an object is placed in Photoshop, it ceases to be a placed graphic.

Placed Graphics in InDesign

When you place a graphic in InDesign, the numerical values in the file are always preserved—InDesign never changes these numbers except as part of the print stream. It lacks the ability to go out and change the source file. All it can do is take the numbers in placed graphics and put different interpretations on them by assigning or assuming profiles. The profiles are used for display and for conversion to output space at print time (and for exporting to PDF, discussed in Chapter 16). InDesign also allows you to specify rendering intents for placed objects, both as defaults and on an object-by-object basis—the rendering intents are used only for the conversion to output. Conversion to the display rendering intent is controlled by Color Settings.

Placing tagged graphics. InDesign always honors embedded profiles in placed graphics, even if you choose the Color Management Off preset in Color Settings. To make InDesign ignore an embedded profile when you place a graphic, either uncheck "Enable Color Management" in the Color Settings dialog box, or check the "Show Import Options" checkbox in the Place dialog box, then turn off the "Enable Color Management" checkbox in the Color Management Image Import Options (see Figure 12-14).

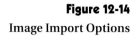

Figure 12-14

Image Import Options

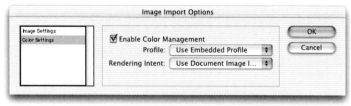

Since this is a book about color management, we assume that you're unlikely to disable color management by either of the aforementioned methods, but if you do, note that placed objects aren't color managed at all, even to the monitor. There's *no* display compensation, and CMYK images typically look hideous. If you subsequently enable color management for that object, InDesign will revert back to the embedded profile if present; otherwise it will assume the Document profiles, if present, and the working spaces if not. We take the view that placing tagged files in InDesign, then trying to make it do something other than honor the embedded profile, is at best a recipe for confusion, and more likely a fast ticket to the funny farm (assuming you're not already there).

The key thing to realize here is that there's no way to make InDesign ignore an embedded profile in an image and assume some other profile in order to get on-screen previews. We feel this is a major oversight on the part of the InDesign 2 design team. We'd like the option of a workflow that let us place CMYK images with embedded profiles, but override them to see what they'd look like when printed to some other output. The only way to do so in InDesign 2 is by either manually reassigning every placed image's profile, or batch stripping the embedded profiles.

Placing untagged graphics. The key to understanding the behavior of placed untagged graphics in InDesign is knowing whether the host InDesign document is itself tagged or untagged. By default, placed untagged graphics always use the Document profile for their color mode as the assumed source profile.

▶ Tagged host documents have Document profiles assigned to them. Changes to the working spaces don't affect the document or the Document profiles, and therefore don't affect the placed graphic. If you change the Document profiles (by using Assign Profiles or Convert to Profile), then the placed untagged graphic is affected.

> ▶ Untagged host documents have Document profiles that aren't assigned to them, but are assumed from the working space profiles. If you change the working spaces, you also change the Document profiles, and therefore the behavior of untagged graphics.

Two corollaries of this behavior involve the Assign Profile and Convert to Profile commands. Remember, the default profiles for untagged placed graphics are the Document profiles: both Assign Profile and Convert to Profile change the Document profiles, and hence the source profiles for untagged placed graphics.

Image Color Settings. The Image Color Settings command lets you assign a different profile to placed graphics on an object-by-object basis (see Figure 12-15).

Figure 12-15
Image Color Settings

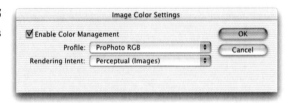

Image Color Settings lets you assign a specific profile and rendering intent to a placed object. If you assign a specific profile, it becomes the assigned profile for that instance of the placed object, and remains in effect until you change it by assigning a different profile through Image Color Settings. If you choose Use Document Default in Image Color Settings, you're in effect asking InDesign to treat the image as untagged, which means the Document profiles will apply.

Placed Graphics in Illustrator

We often finding ourselves wishing that Illustrator would decide what it wants to be when it grows up. It's true that it's an amazingly flexible tool that's used for everything from page layout to Web page design, but all too often the process winds up being a bit like doing brain surgery with a Swiss Army knife, and we've seen Illustrator's approach to color management reduce grown men to tears. This is particularly true in the case of images placed in Illustrator.

The first key point to understand is that Illustrator always includes a copy of the placed image in EPS files. Illustrator itself doesn't seem to be aware of this—if you don't specifically include the linked files when you save an EPS from Illustrator, and reopen the EPS in Illustrator, it looks for the linked file, and if it can't find it, it asks you to replace it. But if you place the EPS in a page-layout application, it will display and print correctly.

However, it doesn't do this with native Illustrator files—if you want these to be self-contained, you need to save using the "Include Linked Files" option, or uncheck the Link checkbox in the Place dialog when you place images.

The second key point to understand is that Illustrator color-manages either the copy that's always embedded in EPSs, or the copy that's embedded in native Illustrator files, either by explicitly embedding or by refreshing the link. Illustrator never does anything to the source image.

The third key point to understand is that Illustrator always converts placed images to the document color mode. If you place an RGB image in a CMYK Illustrator document, the copy that goes in the Illustrator file will be converted to CMYK, and if you place a CMYK image in an RGB Illustrator document, the copy that goes in the Illustrator file will be converted to RGB. You may get error or warning messages that would lead you to believe otherwise, but we've done enough testing to be pretty confident that they're bogus.

All conversions of placed graphics use the CMM and rendering intent specified in Illustrator's color settings, and the destination profile is always the document profile. So the only real questions are:

▶ Does a conversion occur?

▶ If so, what is the source profile?

Placing untagged files in Illustrator. When you place untagged files in an Illustrator document, one of two things happens:

▶ If the placed file is in the same color mode as the Illustrator document, the numerical values in the placed file are transferred to the Illustrator document with no conversion.

▶ If the placed file is in a different color mode from the Illustrator document, the copy in the Illustrator file is converted using the Working Space profile for that color mode as the assumed source profile.

For example, if you place an untagged RGB image in a CMYK Illustrator file, Illustrator will use the RGB Working Space profile as the assumed profile for the conversion to document CMYK.

Placing tagged files in Illustrator. If you consider placing images in Illustrator documents as a pasting activity, things make more sense, including the occasional Paste Profile Mismatch dialog box you get when placing images. If the placed file is in a different color mode from the Illustrator document, Illustrator always performs a conversion using the placed file's embedded profile as the source. If the placed file is in the same color mode as the Illustrator file, Illustrator works the same way as Photoshop's pasting behavior, which depends on the Color Management Policy selected.

▶ **Off:** The numerical values in the file get placed (pasted).

▶ **Preserve Embedded Profiles:** Placing (pasting) RGB in an RGB document preserves the color appearance (Illustrator converts using the embedded profile as the source and the Document profile as the destination). Placing CMYK in a CMYK document preserves the color numbers and doesn't do a conversion.

▶ **Convert to Working RGB/CMYK:** Illustrator always preserves (pastes) the color appearance—it converts from the embedded profile to the Document profile.

Of course, if the source and destination profiles are the same, no conversion occurs. If you've checked "Ask When Pasting" for Profile Mismatches in Color Settings, you'll only get a Paste Mismatch dialog to override the above default behaviors if the Link checkbox is unchecked in the Place dialog. If you choose to Link the file to be placed, you won't get a Paste Mismatch warning.

If you find this collection of paste behaviors counterintuitive, you're not alone! The only silver lining is that they're consistent in all three Adobe applications.

Simulations and Soft-Proofing

One of the most valuable capabilities of the Big Three Adobe applications is their ability to simulate, on the monitor, the result of conversions to other profile spaces, or, in the case of Illustrator and Photoshop, the result of sending the unconverted file to different outputs.

All three applications let you invoke a soft proof by choosing Proof Colors from the View menu. Soft proofs are window-specific, so you can view the same document with different simulations by opening multiple windows and assigning different soft proofs to each one.

The default simulation is for the CMYK working space, but you can change and control the simulation by choosing Proof Setup from the View menu. At this point, however, the applications diverge in the controls that they offer. We'll start with Illustrator, since it's the simplest.

Simulations in Illustrator

Illustrator's Proof Setup dialog box is relatively simple (see Figure 12-16).

Figure 12-16

Illustrator's Proof Setup

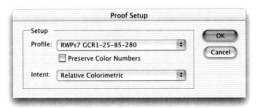

Illustrator's Proof Setup offers only three controls:

▶   The Profile menu lets you choose the destination profile for the simulation.

▶   The "Preserve Color Numbers" checkbox tells the application to simulate what would happen if you printed the numerical values in the file, so it's only available when the profile selected for the simulation is in the same color mode as the document—you can only send RGB numbers to RGB devices and CMYK numbers to CMYK devices. The visual result is the same as assigning the selected profile, but it's a simulation rather than a permanent profile assignment. If you enable the checkbox, the third item, Intent, becomes dimmed and unavailable—rendering intents aren't applicable since you aren't requesting a conversion.

▶ The Intent menu lets you choose a rendering intent for the conversion from document space to simulation space, allowing you to preview the effects of different renderings.

Illustrator doesn't let you control the rendering from the simulation space to the monitor space—it's always relative colorimetric, with black point compensation if it's checked in Color Settings, and without it if not. Note also that the Color Settings "Use Black Point Compensation" setting also affects the conversion from document to simulation space.

Simulations in InDesign

InDesign's Proof Setup dialog box is rather different from Illustrator's. In InDesign, rendering intents are applied to individual document elements rather than to the document as a whole, so the Proof Setup dialog box has no rendering intent control for the conversion from the various source spaces used by the document elements to the simulation space. Instead, each element is rendered according to its specified intent. As with Illustrator, the Color Settings "Use Black Point Compensation" setting applies globally to the conversions from all the source spaces to the simulation space.

Unlike Illustrator, InDesign offers control over the rendering from the simulation space to the display (see Figure 12-17).

Figure 12-17

InDesign's Proof Setup
dialog box

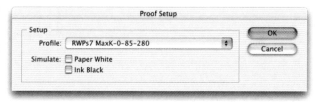

InDesign's Proof Setup dialog box contains three controls, the Profile pop-up menu, and two Simulate checkboxes:

▶ The Profile menu lets you specify the destination profile for the simulation.

▶ The Simulate checkboxes let you control the rendering from the simulation space to the monitor:

▶ "Paper White," when checked, produces an absolute colorimetric rendering from the simulation to the monitor, showing the color of the paper, and its influence on the rest of the color. When it's checked, the "Ink Black" checkbox is automatically turned on and dimmed.

▶ "Ink Black," when checked, turns off black point compensation for the rendering from simulation to the monitor, so if the simulation space black is lighter than the monitor black, "Ink Black" will show you the washed-out blacks you'd get on output—it's most noticeable when you're simulating low dynamic range processes like newsprint.

▶ When both "Ink Black" and "Paper White" are unchecked, which they are by default, the rendering from simulation to display is relative colorimetric with black point compensation, which means that the simulation white is displayed as monitor white, and the simulation black is displayed as monitor black.

For a more in-depth discussion on the pros and cons of the different renderings to the monitor, see "Soft Proofing Practices and Pitfalls," later in this chapter.

Simulations in Photoshop

Of the three applications, Photoshop offers the most complete set of soft-proofing controls. Photoshop's Proof Setup is shown in Figure 12-18.

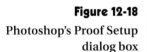
Figure 12-18
Photoshop's Proof Setup
dialog box

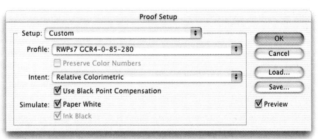

Photoshop offers the unique ability to name and save different proof setups for fast recall. The Setup menu lets you recall Proof Setups that you've saved in the special Proofing folder. (On Mac OS 9, this is the System Folder:Application Support:Adobe:Color:Proofing folder. On

Mac OS X it's the /Library/Application Support/Adobe/Color/Proofing folder, and in Windows, it's the Program Files\Common Files\Adobe\Color\Proofing folder.) You can save Proof Setups anywhere on your hard disk by clicking Save, and load them by clicking the Load button, but the setups you save in the Proofing folder appear on the list automatically. (Even better, they also appear at the bottom of the Proof Setup submenu, where you can choose them directly.)

Photoshop is also unique in offering a live preview—the window updates while the dialog box is open—when the "Preview" checkbox is checked. We find that this makes it much easier to compare the effects of different rendering intents.

The remaining controls operate like those in the other applications.

▶ The Profile menu allows you to choose the destination profile for the simulation.

▶ The "Preserve Color Numbers" checkbox tells the application to simulate what would happen if you sent the numerical values in the file, so it's only available when the simulation and document profile are in the same mode—RGB to RGB or CMYK to CMYK.

▶ The Intent menu allows you to choose a rendering intent for the conversion from document space to simulation space, letting you preview the effects of different renderings.

▶ The "Use Black Point Compensation" checkbox lets you choose whether or not to apply black point compensation in the rendering from the document space to the simulation space.

The Simulate checkboxes control the rendering from the simulation space to the monitor.

▶ "Paper White," when checked, produces an absolute colorimetric rendering from the simulation to the monitor, showing the color of the paper and its influence on the rest of the color. When it's checked, the "Ink Black" checkbox is automatically turned on and dimmed.

▶ "Ink Black," when checked, turns off black point compensation for the rendering from simulation to the monitor, so if the simulation space black is lighter than the monitor black, "Ink Black" will show you the washed-out blacks on output—it's most noticeable when you're simulating low dynamic range processes like newsprint.

▶ When both "Ink Black" and "Paper White" are unchecked, which they are by default, the rendering from the simulation space to the display is relative colorimetric with black point compensation, which means that the simulation white is displayed as monitor white, and the simulation black is displayed as monitor black.

Soft-Proofing Practices and Pitfalls

Using soft proofing successfully requires a little forethought and a little knowledge. First, it's useful to distinguish between "Preserve Color Numbers" simulations, and simulations of actual conversions. We use Preserve Color Numbers in two different scenarios:

▶ With RGB, we use Preserve Color Numbers in conjunction with Web graphics. Choosing the Windows RGB and Macintosh RGB settings lets us see approximately how Web graphics will appear on uncalibrated Mac and Windows systems.

▶ With CMYK, we use Preserve Color Numbers to see how existing CMYK files will work on different printing processes. For example, we may use Preserve Color Numbers to decide whether we can get away with using the same file for several slightly different printing conditions, or if we need to create a separate file for each one.

Most of the time, though, we use Proof Setup to preview conversions to final output space. But no matter whether you're previewing straight output or conversions, there are a few things you need to know about InDesign's and Photoshop's "Paper White" and "Ink Black" simulation settings.

You might expect the absolute colorimetric rendering of the simulation to the display that you get from checking "Paper White" to be the most accurate of the three possibilities. The problem, though, is that if you have any white user-interface elements—InDesign's Pasteboard, or any menus or palettes—displayed on the screen, your eye adapts to that white, so the simulated paper white looks wrong.

In Photoshop, it's relatively easy to hide everything except the image— we hide all the palettes, and use full-screen mode with the menu bar hidden—and get an honest absolute colorimetric soft proof. In InDesign, though, it's just about impossible to do so. Hence in InDesign, we only use paper white simulation when we're dealing with papers that are a long way from white or when we're comparing the screen display with actual hard copy. (See "Viewing Environment" in Chapter 9, *Evaluating and Editing Profiles*, for a thorough discussion of the pitfalls of screen-to-print comparisons.)

With both Simulate checkboxes unchecked (and always in Illustrator since it lacks them), the rendering to the screen is relative colorimetric with black point compensation, which means that paper white is mapped to monitor white and ink black is mapped to monitor black. We find that this is generally the most useful view for making overall judgements on tone and color. Its only flaw is that it provides a somewhat optimistic rendering of low dynamic range processes such as newsprint or inkjet on uncoated papers.

In those cases, we'll use the ink black simulation to make quick reality checks on shadow detail, but we still rely primarily on the other two settings to make critical judgements.

Tip: Change the Default Proof Colors From Working CMYK. The default setting when you choose Proof Colors is for Working CMYK, using the rendering intent and black point compensation settings specified in Color Settings, with (in InDesign and Photoshop) simulate paper white and ink black turned off. If you want to change the default, simply choose Proof Setup with no documents open, enter the settings you want as the defaults, and click OK. The application will use the new settings whenever you choose Proof Colors.

Although Proof Setup is primarily for on-screen simulations, it also plays into the applications' printing architectures, which are the last stop on our journey through Adobe's color-management features.

Printing

Photoshop, Illustrator, and InDesign can all perform a conversion on the data that gets handed off to the printer driver.

If you use these features—and we encourage you to do so—the one major pitfall to avoid is *also* having color management performed by the printer driver. It's quite easy to set things up so that the driver does corrections to the already corrected data, and the results usually aren't pretty. See Chapter 11, *Color Management in the Operating System.*

The features in these applications' printing controls allow you to do essentially four things.

▶ Send the numbers in the document directly to the printer driver.

▶ Send the numbers in the document, along with a profile that describes their meaning, to the printer driver (with the assumption that the printer driver will be able to interpret the profile and do something useful with it).

▶ Convert the numbers in the document to the printer space, and send the converted numbers to the printer driver.

▶ Convert the numbers in the document to the space you specified in Proof Setup, then convert those numbers to the printer space, so that the resulting print is a hard-copy simulation of the Proof Setup space—this is sometimes called *cross-rendering*. (This option is not available in Illustrator.)

Let's look at how the controls operate to let you accomplish these various ends. The layout of the dialog boxes is different in each of the three applications, but the controls have the same labels. In InDesign, they're in the Color Management panel of InDesign's Print dialog box. In Photoshop, they're in the Color Management section of Photoshop's Print with Preview dialog box. And in Illustrator, they're in Illustrator 10 options for PostScript drivers and as an extension to raster printer dialogs. The dialog boxes are shown in Figure 12-19.

Figure 12-19

Print Color Management
in Photoshop, Illustrator,
and InDesign

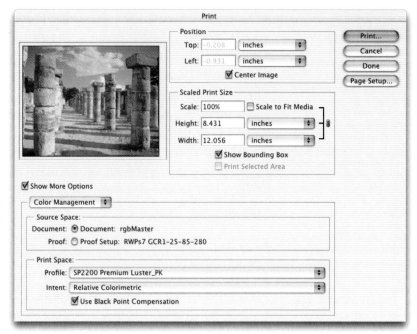

*Photoshop's Print
with Preview
dialog box*

*Illustrator's
application-specific
Print settings*

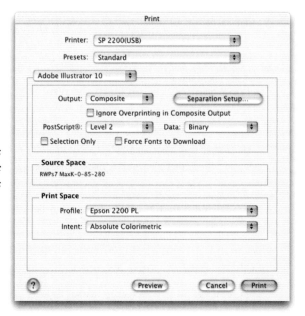

Figure 12-19

**Print Color Management
in Photoshop, Illustrator,
and InDesign,** *continued*

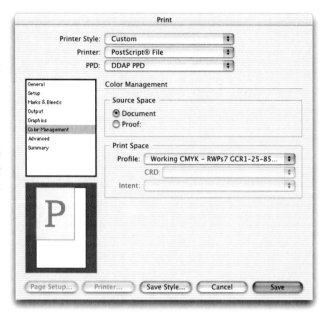

*The Color Management
panel of InDesign's Print
dialog box*

Each dialog has a section labeled Source Space and a section labeled Print Space. Source Space has only two options (except in Illustrator):

▶ Document uses the Document profile (or profiles, in the case of InDesign) as the source profile for any conversion specified in the Print Space section.

▶ Proof Setup (Proof in InDesign) makes the application perform a conversion from the document profile(s) to the profile specified in Proof Setup. In Photoshop, it uses the rendering intent specified in Proof Setup. In InDesign, each object in the document has its own rendering intent. The results of this conversion are passed to the Print Space section of the dialog.

Print Space has only three options:

▶ Same as Source passes the numbers that result from the choice made in Source Space to the printer driver (InDesign doesn't have this option).

▶ Printer Color Management/Postscript Color Management passes the numbers that result from the choice made in Source Space to the printer driver, along with the profile or profiles that describe the meaning of these numbers. The assumption is that the printer driver will then use the profile(s) as source space(s) for a conversion to the print space.

▶ Choosing a specific profile instructs the application to perform a conversion from whatever numbers result from the choice made in Source Space to the selected profile, using the rendering intent you've specified in Print Space.

InDesign has a couple of extra wrinkles. First, if you choose Document in the Source Space, you don't get to choose a rendering intent in Print Space—instead, each object in the InDesign document is rendered using its own specified intent. (If you choose Proof in the Source Space, you *do* get to choose a rendering intent, since the conversion is now from one single space—the Proof space—to another—the Print Space.)

Second, the choice of profiles in InDesign's Print Space is governed by the choices you make in the Color menu of the Output panel of InDesign's Print dialog box (see Figure 12-20). If you choose Composite RGB, only RGB profiles are available, while if you choose Composite CMYK or Separations, only CMYK profiles are available.

While the number of possibilities that exist is extremely large, the printing controls offer easy support for three fairly obvious workflow options:

▶ In an early-binding workflow, where all the color is already in final output space, setting the Source Space to Document and the Print Space to Same as Source lets you print the document values unchanged to the final output device.

You can also print proofs to some other device by selecting its profile in Print Space. If you choose absolute colorimetric rendering, the proofing printer will lay down ink in the paper white areas to match the paper white of the final output, while relative colorimetric will scale the final paper white to the paper white of the proofer.

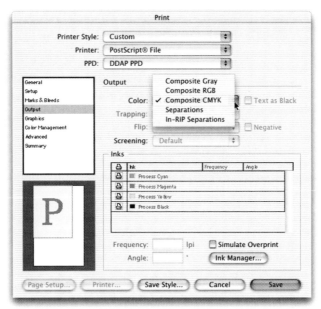

The choice you make in the Output pop-up menu determines which profiles become available in the Color Management panel shown in Figure 12-19.

▶ In a late-binding workflow, where the document is in a space other than the final output space, choosing the profile for the final output device in Print Space makes the application convert the color to the final output space—you'd use this when you're actually printing to the final output device.

▶ To generate proofs in a late-binding workflow, you can set Proof Setup to the final output space, then select Proof in the Source Space, and the profile for your proofing device in Print Space. This instructs the application to first convert the color from the source spaces to the final output space specified in Proof Setup, then to convert that color to the space you've specified in Print Space. The result is that the printer simulates the final output. Again, absolute colorimetric rendering makes the proofer simulate the final paper white, while relative colorimetric scales the color to the paper white of the proofer.

One caveat: InDesign only applies absolute colorimetric rendering to the contents of frames. It leaves the paper white areas paper white, which defeats the point of the excercise since our eyes promptly adapt to the blank paper white. An easy workaround is to place a blank frame on the background of the master page.

The Same, But Different

Adobe deserves kudos for at least attempting to provide a consistent and rational user interface for color across its main applications, but as we've pointed out throughout this chapter, sometimes the similarities are misleading. Part of this is an inevitable consequence of the different capabilities of each application; part is an example of good intentions gone astray. The moral is to make sure that you understand the often-subtle differences between apparently identical features in each of the applications, and use them wisely.

13

Color Management in Macromedia FreeHand 10

Capable but Quirky

Macromedia must have a whole bunch of customers with an interesting variety of legacy needs, because Macromedia FreeHand doesn't have just one color management system. Exactly how many it has depends on your point of view, but we'll concentrate on the ones that use ICC profiles, with a brief overview of the others—if only so that you can wonder, as we do, why they're even there.

FreeHand has many strengths, but we can't count color management as being among them. The main limitation of FreeHand's color management is that it only performs conversions on output, and it only supports one CMYK source profile at a time.

FreeHand honors embedded profiles in imported RGB images, and lets you assign profiles to imported untagged RGB images, but both imported and native CMYK elements are always assumed to be output CMYK. If your workflow is to design in RGB and convert to CMYK at output time, FreeHand's color management can serve you well. Likewise, if you do all your work in final CMYK, FreeHand can provide you with good on-screen previews, and pass the CMYK values unchanged to output.

For any other workflow, all bets are off. And even in these two simple workflows, FreeHand offers plenty of opportunities for mistakes—so in this chapter, we'll try to steer you clear of the shoals of confusion and guide you to the safe harbor of well-functioning color management.

FreeHand's Color Preferences

The Preferences dialog has a series of categories on the left-hand side. When you select Colors, a dialog box appears that looks like the one in Figure 13-1.

Figure 13-1

FreeHand Color Settings dialog box

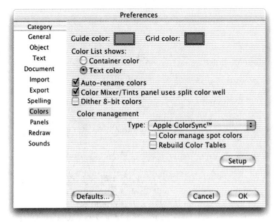

Color Management Types

On Windows systems, the dialog box offers four possibilities: None, Adjust Display Colors, Color Tables, and Kodak Digital Science. Mac OS offers the same four and adds is a fifth option, Apple ColorSync (see Figure 13-2) We strongly recommend that you ignore the first three options and choose either Kodak Digital Science or Apple ColorSync, which offer identical options and functionality in FreeHand But for those who must know, here are the ramifications of the first three options.

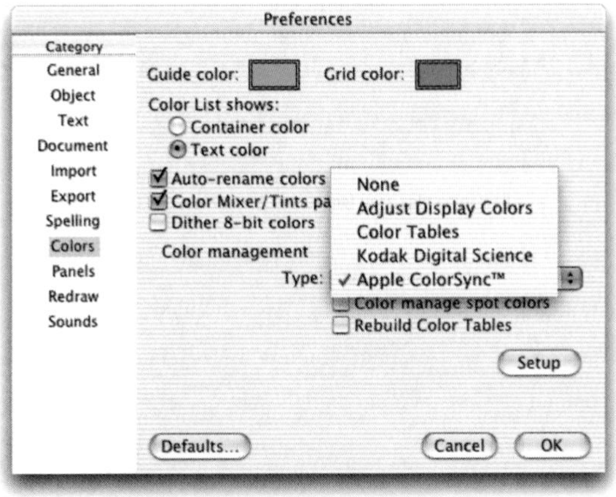

Figure 13-2

Color management types

None. This option offers no user control for either output conversions or on-screen previews. The conversion from CMYK to RGB for either display or for RGB output devices is controlled by a built-in and non-modifiable table, as is the conversion from RGB to CMYK output triggered by the "Convert RGB Colors to Process" option in FreeHand's print dialog (discussed later). Needless to say, we don't recommend this type of color management.

Adjust Display Colors. We have two problems with this option—one philosophical, one practical. It lets you change the behavior of your monitor, for FreeHand only, in an attempt to match printed output—the approach that Bruce calls "messing up your monitor to match the print" (though he usually uses a stronger term than "messing").

The philosophical objection is that it negates one of the major strengths of color management. Back in Chapter 3 we pointed out that color management reduces the number of device-to-device links from n×m to n+m. This approach goes back to the n×m method, because you need to mess up your monitor in a different way each time you change output processes.

The practical objection is that it simply doesn't work very well. Even when we adjust the display to match printed versions of the swatches, we find that the swatch colors are just about the only things that match between display and print—everything else is off, sometimes a long way off. And to add insult to injury, this method only compensates for native FreeHand elements—imported images preview inaccurately.

Color Tables. This type of color management is pointless. It depends on Kodak Digital Science or Apple ColorSync, and builds Color Tables based on existing ICC profiles. Since you have to base the tables on ICC profiles anyway, you might as well just learn to use ICC color management. We see no advantage to this method, and would be glad to see it removed from FreeHand.

Kodak Digital Science and Apple ColorSync

Referring back to Figure 13-1, we need to cover two checkboxes before getting to the Setup dialog, the meat and potatoes of this course.

▶ Color manage spot colors lets you color manage just their on-screen preview. You don't manage their CMYK values for output, because they're hardwired based on FreeHand's built-in Pantone tables. (In FreeHand 10, these are the older pre-May 2000 tables.) See "Named Colors" in Chapter 18, *Building Color-Managed Workflows*.

▶ Rebuild Color Tables uses the settings in Setup to build color tables for use with the Color Tables type of color management previously mentioned, but since we told you not to use this feature, let's move on to the contents of the Setup button.

The Color Management Setup dialog box offers seven options (see Figure 13-3). FreeHand isn't particularly assiduous in looking for profiles—on Mac OS X, it only looks in the /Library/ColorSync/Profiles folder. On other platforms, it ignores both subdirectories and aliases in the usual directories for profiles—so it doesn't, for example, find display profiles stored in the Displays subfolder in the Mac OS 9 ColorSync Profiles folder.

Figure 13-3

Color Management
Setup dialog box

Monitor. This is where you select your current display profile—FreeHand doesn't get this information automatically from ICM or ColorSync.

Monitor simulates. The options offered are None, Composite printer, and Separations printer. "None" literally means do *no* display compensation. If you use this option, neither embedded profiles nor assumed profiles get used for on-screen display, though they may be used for output.

If you use either of the other options, RGB images are displayed by converting from their embedded profile or the "Default RGB image source" profile to the Composite or Separations printer profile, (depending on which one you choose in the Monitor simulates pop-up), then to the display profile.

CMYK images, however, are always converted for display using the Separations printer profile as source, even if Monitor simulates is set to "Composite printer." If you set Monitor simulates to "None," FreeHand uses its built-in unmodifiable table as the source for display conversion of CMYK instead.

Separations printer. This setting lets you choose a CMYK profile, which becomes the assumed source profile for all CMYK content, including imported images, even if they have an embedded profile—FreeHand simply ignores embedded profiles in imported CMYK. As the CMYK source profile, it affects on-screen preview of CMYK native elements and placed objects. If you print from FreeHand to an RGB device, the profile you select here is used as the source profile for all CMYK content. The only CMYK-to-CMYK conversion FreeHand performs is to a composite CMYK printer when "Composite simulates separations" is turned on— again, the Separations printer profile is used as the source.

Intent. This pop-up lets you specify a rendering intent for all conversions. It affects RGB-to-CMYK conversions at print time, and also affects RGB-to-RGB and CMYK-to-RGB conversions when the Composite printer is an RGB printer (and the output device is non-PostScript). This is the *only* rendering intent control FreeHand offers.

Composite simulates separations. This checkbox only affects the output, not the on-screen preview. It makes the composite device simulate the separation printer by converting all non-CMYK content to Separations printer CMYK, assigning the Separations printer CMYK profile to all CMYK content, then converting the resulting Separations printer CMYK to the composite printer space.

All the conversions use the rendering intent you specify under intent, so it's impossible to use perceptual or relative colorimetric rendering to go from the source profiles to Separation printer CMYK, then absolute colorimetric rendering to go from Separation printer CMYK to the Composite printer space. If you want the composite printer to produce a reasonable simulation of the final separations, we recommend that you set the Intent to Relative Colorimetric.

Composite printer. Here you may select an RGB or CMYK profile for a composite printer. If you select an RGB profile, the "Convert RGB to process" check box in the FreeHand print dialog is ignored, though it isn't grayed out. But selecting an RGB profile here is quite dicey when it comes to printing—see "Printing," later in this chapter, for more information.

To select a profile here, you must check the "Composite simulates separations" checkbox previously described. There's no logical reason for this; that's just the way it is. You can temporarily check the box to change the profile, and then uncheck it to ensure separation simulation does not occur. Even though the selected profile is grayed out when this box is unchecked, it's still set as the Composite printer profile.

Default RGB image source. The profile selected here is *automatically assigned* to untagged imported RGB images rather than simply acting as the assumed profile. We make this distinction because images imported while profile "A" is selected will retain profile "A" as their source if you subsequently change the default RGB image source to profile "B." Only subsequently placed images will use profile "B."

If you choose "None," the display profile, set in the Monitor pop-up menu, is assigned as the source.

The profiles automatically assigned to imported RGB images are referenced in the saved FreeHand document, but not embedded. If you open the file on another workstation that doesn't have the profiles installed, you'll get a cryptic warning dialog listing the missing profiles when you open the document (see Figure 13-4). The dialog says that the default RGB image source will be used instead—that means whichever default RGB image source profile is selected in Preferences at the time the document is opened.

Figure 13-4

Missing Image Sources

If you get this warning dialog, the prudent thing to do is make a note of the missing profiles, click the Cancel button, then go find the missing profiles and install them. Upon relaunching FreeHand and reopening the document, the warning will no longer appear.

Note that this setting applies only to imported graphics. Native RGB elements are always treated as untagged in FreeHand, assuming the display profile as their source profile. This is annoying because the same native elements on two different workstations have different RGB source profiles assumed, and will print differently. To avoid major differences when printing native elements, you need to calibrate all monitors to the same standard. Even then, there's typically enough variation from display to display that you'll still get minor differences.

Imported images will display and print the same from multiple workstations, but native elements probably won't. It's a major gotcha and oversight by Macromedia.

Manual Assignments

FreeHand offers only one manual control, for assigning profiles to imported images, and it applies exclusively to imported RGB images.

Object Palette

The Object palette—which you open by choosing Object from the Inspectors submenu of the Windows menu—shows you the file type and color space, as well as a pop-up menu showing the source profile, of a currently selected imported RGB graphic (see Figure 13-5).

Figure 13-5
Object palette for RGB
TIFF and for CMYK TIFF

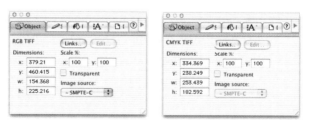

Notice that the Object palette example for RGB indicates the Image source is "- SMPTE-C." The "-" in front of the profile name indicates that this profile was embedded in the imported image. FreeHand always uses the embedded profile in supported RGB image formats unless you change it in this pop-up menu (which we don't recommend).

If you do change the profile associated with an object, FreeHand immediately forgets the embedded profile. If you later decide to use the embedded profile instead, you'll need to re-import that object.

Note that the Image source pop-up menu is grayed out for the CMYK example. Embedded profiles for CMYK images are ignored, and it's impossible to assign profiles manually. As previously discussed, the Separations printer profile specified in Color Management Setup is the assumed source profile for all CMYK elements, including imported images.

Exporting

The undocumented rules that govern how document content is converted by Freehand's Export command to various file formats cause Bruce to muse, "Where am I going, and why am I in this handbasket?" As far as we've been able to determine, they spell disaster. The export commands have few options pertaining to color conversions; everything else is controlled by the color management settings in Preferences. There are so many permutations that we confined our testing to just Apple ColorSync behavior as it pertains to EPS, PDF, and TIFF exporting. We expect the behavior when using Kodak Digital Science to be the same.

Tip: Create Output-Ready CMYK EPS Files. To create a CMYK print-ready EPS file, print a PostScript file from FreeHand to disk—which will make FreeHand color manage the output following the rules for printing (see "Printing," later in this chapter)—then process the PostScript file in Acrobat Distiller and make a PDF. Finally, open the PDF in Acrobat or Illustrator and export as EPS. Voila, output-ready EPS that you can place in your page-layout application.

But for the brave or foolish, we'll document what we've learned thus far in the hopes of shaming Macromedia into making FreeHand's Export features more rational in a future version of the application.

TIFF

TIFF export is always to untagged RGB. It doesn't matter if the entire content of your document is CMYK—it will end up as an RGB TIFF. The controls in the Export dialog box for TIFF are limited, and don't include options for CMYK export or profile embedding.

All CMYK elements and images get converted from the Separations printer profile to the display profile, using the rendering intent set in the Intent pop-up in FreeHand's Color Management Setup.

RGB behavior is controlled by the Monitor simulates setting. If it's set to "None," RGB objects aren't color managed on export—the raw RGB values are simply written to the TIFF. If it's set to "Separations" or to "Composite," RGB objects get converted to the Separations or Composite printer profile, respectively, then to something we've been unable to determine—perhaps a hardwired internal space—and finally, to monitor RGB.

EPS and PDF

Both EPS and PDF exporting have a Setup button to access their options, and both offer a "Convert colors to" pop-up menu containing three choices: CMYK, RGB, or CMYK and RGB. The similarities end there.

EPS. The three options produce EPS files on Export as follows:

▶ **CMYK.** This option produces an all-CMYK EPS. All CMYK objects, whether native or imported, simply have their raw values written into the EPS file. RGB native elements use the Monitor profile as the assumed source, and RGB imported images use their assigned profile. Both are then converted to an unknown CMYK destination. We haven't been able to figure out what it is, or get an answer from Macromedia, but it definitely isn't the Separations printer profile.

▶ **RGB.** This option produces an all-RGB EPS. Native and imported CMYK elements use the Separations profile as the assumed source, and are converted to an unknown RGB destination. Imported RGB images use their assigned profile as source, and are also converted to an unknown RGB destination. RGB native elements are left unconverted, and the raw RGB values are exported to the file.

▶ **CMYK and RGB.** This option produces a mixed-mode EPS. Imported CMYK images, as well as RGB and CMYK native elements, are left unmodified. Imported RGB images are converted to CMYK using their embedded or assigned profile as source, and an unknown CMYK destination profile.

PDF. The three options produce PDF files on Export as follows:

▶ **CMYK.** You get a mixed-mode PDF. Imported CMYK images and CMYK native elements are unmodified, so their raw values are exported. Imported RGB images are exported unmodified with raw RGB values intact. RGB native elements use an unknown source and unknown destination, and are converted to CMYK.

▶ **RGB.** You also get a mixed-mode PDF. Nothing is converted—raw values are exported for all images and elements.

▶ **CMYK and RGB.** Same as for RGB.

If anyone can provide a rational explanation for this set of Export behaviors, we'd love to hear it!

Printing

Printing from FreeHand using color management is relatively straight-forward. The main thing you need to do at print time is to tell FreeHand whether you're printing to the Composite printer or to the Separations printer (see Figure 13-6).

In the middle of the print dialog is an Output option with two radio buttons, Composite and Separations. If you click on Separations, the Separations printer profile you selected in Color Management Setup is used as the destination profile. If you click on Composite, the Composite printer profile you selected in Color Management Setup is used as the destination profile. To use the "Composite simulates separations" feature, you must select the Composite radio button here, and have previously checked the "Composite simulates separations" checkbox in Color Management Setup.

At the bottom of the print dialog is a Color Management button. This is just a shortcut to the Color Management Setup dialog. Even though clicking it brings up a dialog titled "Color Management Preferences," it's the same thing, and any changes made here will be reflected in the Setup version of the same dialog.

Figure 13-6
FreeHand Print Dialog

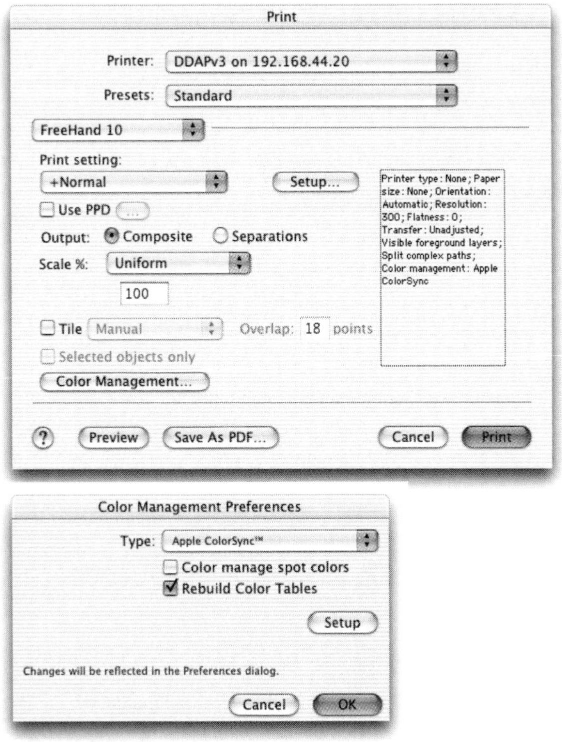

Gotchas

Didn't think it was going to be that simple, did you? Certainly not after the hell called Export.

► "Convert RGB to process" must be checked (it is by default), or else RGB content isn't converted to CMYK at output time. This checkbox has two locations—you can check either one. One is reached through Output Options on the File menu. The other is in the Output Options section of the Imaging panel in the Print Setup dialog box, which is reached by clicking the Setup button in the Print dialog (see Figure 13-7).

► When you print to a PostScript device, FreeHand wants almost everything to be CMYK. Even if you uncheck the "Convert RGB to process" option and select an RGB profile for the Composite printer, only imported RGB images get converted to the destination Composite printer profile. Everything else is CMYK, and there appears to be no way around this, so you may have significant problems printing to an RGB PostScript RIP.

Figure 13-7

Output Options and Print
Setup: Imaging tab

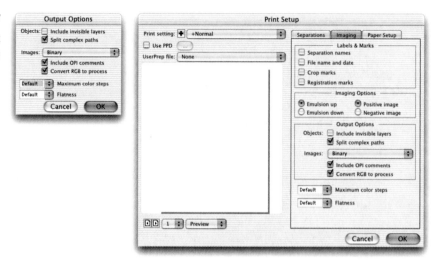

▶ On Mac OS X, the default printer, set in the Print Center utility, must be a PostScript printer. Otherwise, FreeHand assumes that you're printing to an RGB raster device and produces exclusively RGB PostScript, so you'll most likely end up with a mess.

Be Careful

If you're careful, you can produce good results using Freehand's color management. You can either work entirely in final CMYK, or work in RGB and separate to final CMYK on output. If you work in mixed RGB and CMYK, make sure that any imported CMYK is already in the final print space. If you need to export CMYK from FreeHand, the only way that works is to use the rather laborious process we describe in the Tip, "Create Output-Ready CMYK EPS Files," earlier in this chapter. FreeHand's Export features are—at least in the current version, FreeHand 10—unsafe at any speed!

Color Management in CorelDRAW 10

It Manages Everything But Its Own Files

CorelDRAW has a rather clever user interface for color management that makes the way it functions relatively obvious, but its use of icons instead of menu options makes it a little hard to describe in writing.

Like Macromedia FreeHand, CorelDRAW sees CMYK as press-ready, so it doesn't do any CMYK-to-CMYK conversions except when you make a composite CMYK printer simulate the Separations printer or you print CMYK content to an RGB output device. Also like FreeHand, CorelDRAW only performs conversions on output (with one exception—see "Manual Controls," later in this chapter) or on export. It supports embedded profiles in RGB images for import and export of TIFF, JPEG, and .PSD (Photoshop) formats, but it doesn't support profile embedding in its own document format, and it never embeds profiles in CMYK documents.

CorelDRAW settings are application-wide, so they apply to all open documents. CorelDRAW documents are always governed by only two profiles, one for RGB and one for CMYK, but the gaping hole in CorelDRAW's color management is that it doesn't embed these profiles in its own native files, and doesn't offer any other mechanism for recording the settings that apply to a specific document. So the only way to color manage native CorelDRAW files is to note the settings manually, and associate them somehow (text file, Mac OS Finder Info) with the document—a kludge at best.

Color Management Preferences

You access the Color Management Preferences by going to Color Management on the Edit menu in Mac OS 9 and X, and on the Tools menu in Windows. The resulting dialog box shows a series of icons and arrows representing workflow (see Figure 14-1).

Figure 14-1

CorelDRAW Color
Management dialog box

CorelDRAW's Color Management dialog box uses icons and arrows to represent the color management workflow.

This dialog works a little differently from most. As you move your mouse around, the cursor periodically changes into a hand. If you briefly pause, a description of what the hand is pointing to appears (see Figure 14-2). Each icon has a description, as does each of the arrows that serve to enable or disable color management in the direction of the arrow.

Figure 14-2

Mouse over in Color
Management dialog box

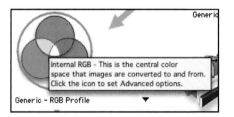

When you mouse over the icons and arrows, rollover help boxes appear.

To select a profile, click once on the black arrow below the icon for the device/feature you want to change, and a pop-up menu of available profiles appears—CorelDRAW finds ICC profiles in their usual locations on each platform. In addition, three of the icons have advanced options that are accessed by clicking once on the icon. If you click on an icon and nothing happens, that icon doesn't have advanced options.

At the very bottom is a Style pop-up menu. These are presets—once you've configured CorelDRAW to your liking, you can click the "+" button to save your settings as a preset. The ColorSync Workflow preset grabs settings from ColorSync, such as the RGB default, CMYK default, and the current display profile. At least on Mac OS X, we've found the behavior to be inconsistent, so don't rely on making changes in the ColorSync panel without also going into Corel's Color Management dialog to make sure the profiles you want are selected.

We'll describe each settings icon—including any advanced features—starting with the center icon, followed by the monitor, then clockwise from there.

Internal RGB

The center icon represents the RGB editing space used in CorelDRAW. By default it's effectively disabled since its profile is the same as the Monitor profile, so no display compensation is in effect, although import, export, printer, and scanner conversions can still happen.

It's important to understand that Internal RGB is the assumed RGB source profile for all RGB content, both native and imported. It doesn't get embedded into CorelDRAW documents when you save, so you need to pick a profile and use it consistently. If you share documents with others who also want to use color management, you'll need to tell them what profile you used for Internal RGB. If you change the Internal RGB profile while working on a document, the color behavior of all RGB content is updated immediately to reflect the new profile. This isn't a conversion, but a change to the assumed profile—so the numeric values for RGB content don't change—but their color meaning, and hence their appearance, does.

When you click once on the Internal RGB icon itself, you get an Advanced Settings dialog box (see Figure 14-3).

Figure 14-3
Internal RGB:
Advanced Settings
dialog box

The Advanced Settings dialog box for Internal RGB lets you set the rendering intent and CMM for all conversions.

Rendering Intent. Rendering Intent affects all conversions except those going to the display profile for on-screen preview purposes—Relative Colorimetric is probably the best choice considering the lack of per-object control.

Color Engine. Color Engine lets you choose a CMM. On Mac OS, if you choose ColorSync, CorelDRAW uses the CMM you've selected in the ColorSync control panel (OS 9) or System Preferences (OS X), and if you choose Kodak Digital Science CMM, CorelDRAW uses that CMM for all conversions. On Windows, the options are Microsoft ICM 2.0 CMM or Kodak Digital Science CMM.

Monitor

This is where you select the profile for your display. When you click on Monitor, the Advanced Display Settings dialog box appears (see Figure 14-4). If you have activated either of the arrows coming from the Composite or Separations printers, then the "Highlight display colors out of printer gamut" option becomes available. It does exactly what the name implies—if the color can't be printed on the output device the display is simulating, CorelDRAW superimposes a chosen warning color instead.

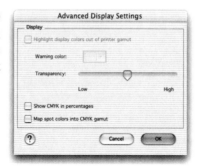

Figure 14-4
Monitor: Advanced
Display Settings
dialog box

The Advanced Display Settings dialog box lets you set the gamut warning and control the display of spot colors.

What determines whether the on-screen simulation is based on the Composite or Separations printer profile is whether the arrow to the Monitor icon comes from the Composite or Separations printer icon. If it comes from the Internal RGB icon, the software just performs display compensation from the Internal RGB profile to the display profile.

Map spot colors into CMYK gamut. This option displays spot colors using their Pantone-specified process equivalents (which are pre-May 2000 in CorelDRAW 10) piped through the Composite or Separations printer profile (used as the source profile), and then to the display profile (used as the destination profile), to show how those CMYK builds would output on the simulated printer. It doesn't create custom CMYK builds for Pantone colors—it's an on-screen simulation only.

Composite Printer

This can be either an RGB or CMYK profile. CorelDRAW supports full RGB-to-RGB and CMYK-to-RGB workflows. To make the Composite printer simulate the Separations printer, click on the large curved arrow at the bottom of the Color Management dialog, which then deactivates the arrow between Internal RGB and Composite printer.

Import/Export

By default, no profile is selected for this icon; click on it once and you'll get the Advanced Import/Export Settings dialog box (see Figure 14-5). Above all, note that this dialog pertains only to RGB. On CMYK import, CorelDRAW ignores embedded profiles and uses the Separations profile instead.

Figure 14-5

Advanced Import/
Export Settings
dialog box

The Advanced Import/Export Settings dialog box lets you control profile handling on import and export.

The first options in the import and export sections ("Use embedded ICC profile" and "Embed Internal RGB profile," respectively) are the settings we recommend. The others are potentially dangerous.

Import: Use embedded ICC profile. This option makes CorelDRAW use the embedded profile as the source profile for tagged RGB images, and the profile that you choose here as the source for untagged RGB images. From there, CorelDRAW converts images to the Internal RGB profile. If you choose "None" then it assumes the Internal RGB profile for untagged images, and no conversion occurs.

Import: Always convert using. This option ignores the embedded profile, substitutes the selected profile as the source profile, and converts the image to the Internal RGB space. Needless to say, we don't think this is a good idea. If there's a problem with the embedded profile in an image, correct it in the originating application.

Import: Ignore embedded ICC profile. This option ignores embedded ICC profiles, doesn't convert the image, and assumes the Internal RGB profile.

Export: Embed Internal RGB profile. This option embeds the Internal RGB profile in exported RGB files.

Scanner/Digital Camera

Select a profile here to be used as the source profile for acquiring images from the File menu's Acquire Image command. All images that come in through Acquire Image are converted to Internal RGB when Internal RGB and Scanner/Digital Camera are set to different profiles.

Separations Printer

This setting accommodates only CMYK profiles. The profile you choose here is used as the source profile for all CMYK content. It's also used as the destination profile for the conversion that takes place when you print to the Separations printer. (Which profile is used at print time—this profile or the Composite printer—depends on settings in the printer driver, which we discuss in "Printing," later in this chapter.)

Tip: Check Your Output Conversions. Make absolutely certain that the arrow between Internal RGB and Separations Printer is turned on, or CorelDRAW won't use ICC color management for its RGB to CMYK conversions. Instead, it will use a built-in table whose separations are uncontrollable and usually pretty hideous. For the Composite printer, make sure that either the arrow from Internal RGB, or the large curved arrow from the Separations printer is activated, for the same reason.

Importing

Importing files into CorelDRAW is fairly straightforward once you know the rules. The Import dialog box appears when you choose Import from the File menu (see Figure 14-6). When importing a file with an embedded profile, the "Extract embedded ICC profile" checkbox is ungrayed. If you check this box, then immediately after clicking the Import button for this dialog, you're presented with a Save dialog box that lets you save the profile embedded in the image.

Figure 14-6

Import dialog box

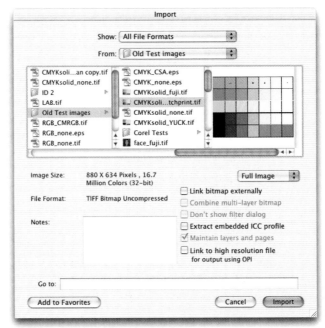

CorelDRAW *does* see embedded profiles in CMYK images, as the example figure shows, but it doesn't retain them upon import. Instead, it always assumes the Separations printer profile as the source for any imported CMYK, ignoring the embedded profile.

For RGB importing, CorelDRAW honors embedded profiles and uses them as the source profiles (if you've configured the Advanced Import/ Export Settings to use embedded profiles) in the following file formats: TIFF, JPEG, PSD, and CPT (Corel PHOTO-PAINT). We've tested TIFF, JPG, and PSD, and we're confident that those formats are reliable.

Tagged RGB images then get converted on import to Internal RGB. Untagged RGB images use Internal RGB as their assumed profile.

Manual Controls

CorelDRAW has no manual controls for per-object profile assignment. However, it does let you do mode changes on already-imported bitmap images, such as from RGB to CMYK, CMYK to RGB, RGB to RGB, and even from RGB or CMYK to LAB.

▶ To convert RGB to CMYK, select an RGB image, then choose CMYK Color (32-bit) from the Mode submenu on the Bitmap menu. The image gets converted from the Internal RGB profile to the Separations printer profile.

▶ To convert CMYK to RGB, select a CMYK image, then choose RGB Color (24-bit) from the Mode submenu on the Bitmap menu. The image gets converted from the Separations printer profile to the Internal RGB profile.

▶ To convert RGB to RGB, select an RGB image, then choose Apply ICC Profile from the Mode submenu on the Bitmap menu, which opens the Apply ICC Profile dialog box (see Figure 14-7). The profile you choose in the pop-up menu is used as the source profile for the conversion—the destination profile is always the Internal RGB profile.

Figure 14-7
Apply ICC Profile
dialog box

The Apply ICC Profile dialog box lets you choose a source profile for conversions to Internal RGB.

Exporting

The previously described Color Management Advanced Import/Export Settings dialog box implies that if you select "Embed Internal RGB profile," CorelDRAW will embed the Internal RGB profile in the supported formats, and this is true.

At export time, the Bitmap Export dialog box appears, which contains an "Apply ICC profile" checkbox (see Figure 14-8). This control has varying effects depending on just what you're exporting. When exporting RGB, it seems to have no effect.

Figure 14-8
Bitmap Export and
EPS Export dialog boxes:
Color Management
options

Color management in Bitmap and EPS Export

The EPS Export dialog box contains a Color Management section (see Figure 14-8). If you don't check "Apply ICC profile," you get a hardwired separation instead of one that's ICC based. You can choose the Composite or Separations printer profile as the destination using the radio buttons—CorelDRAW also displays the name of the specific profile.

When you select CMYK Color from the Color pop-up menu, the document is converted to CMYK using Internal RGB as the source and the Separations Printer profile as the destination—but only if "Apply ICC profile" is checked. Otherwise you'll get a remarkably ugly hardwired conversion to CMYK.

Profile Embedding

The documentation states that the supported export formats for embedding profiles are TIFF, JPEG, EPS, PDF, PSD (Photoshop), CPT (Corel PHOTO-PAINT), and CDR (CorelDRAW). However, EPS files only seem to contain a reference to the profile, not the profile itself.

The CDR format doesn't even appear as an export format option. Since we get no profile mismatch warning when opening an exported CDR file, even with an Internal RGB profile that doesn't match what should be embedded in the document, we can't tell whether or not a profile is really embedded.

The PDF format isn't an export format option, but CorelDRAW offers a Publish To PDF command on the File menu. CorelDRAW doesn't embed ICC profiles in PDF, at least as far as Photoshop and Enfocus PitStop Pro are concerned.

We can confirm that CorelDRAW does embed profiles in RGB TIFF, JPEG, and PSD files. It never embeds profiles in CMYK exports.

Printing

For color-management purposes, the options in the Print dialog are fairly straightforward. The first option selects the Composite printer profile or Separations printer profile as the destination for RGB-to-CMYK or RGB-to-RGB conversions at print time (see Figure 14-9). In the Print dialog, under the Separations tab, the first option on the upper left corner is "Print separations." When this is unchecked, the Composite printer profile is the destination, and when it's checked, the Separations printer profile is the destination. To produce simulations of the Separations printer on your composite printer, uncheck "Print separations," and select the large curved arrow that goes from Separations printer to the Composite printer in the Color Management dialog box. Piece of cake.

Figure 14-9

Print dialog box: Separations tab

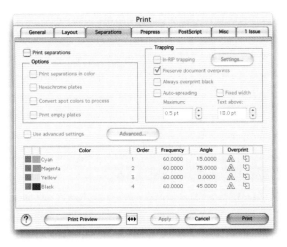

The "Print separations" checkbox controls whether print is converted to the Separations or the Composite printer.

The Misc tab of the Print dialog box contains two options that are easy to overlook.

First, the "Apply ICC profile" checkbox is available and checked by default in two situations:

▶ The arrow from Internal RGB to Composite printer is enabled in the Color Management dialog box, and the "Print separations" checkbox is unchecked.

▶ The arrow from Internal RGB to Separations printer is enabled in the Color Management dialog box, and the "Print separations" checkbox is checked (see Figure 14-10).

Figure 14-10

Print dialog box: Misc tab

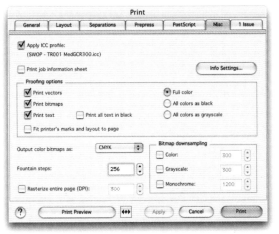

To Print RGB output, you must choose RGB from the "Output color bitmaps as" pop-up.

Second, you must pay attention to the "Output color bitmaps as" pop-up menu if you want RGB output. Even if you select an RGB profile for the Composite printer and it appears under "Apply ICC profile," if you don't select RGB from the "Output color bitmaps as" pop-up, your images get converted to CMYK or grayscale instead.

Strengths and Weaknesses

CorelDRAW lets you work entirely in CMYK, using color management for on-screen previews and proofing. It successfully color manages exports according to the Color Management settings and a simple set of rules for a limited set of file formats. You can print to RGB printers, but native elements built in CMYK may not turn out the way you want. The biggest plus for CorelDRAW is its Color Management dialog box user interface. The glaring weakness that it doesn't embed the profiles that define RGB and CMYK into its own documents. So it's relatively easy to export color-managed content from CorelDRAW, but the only way to manage CorelDRAW files themselves is to keep track, manually, of the RGB and CMYK profiles you used to create the document.

Color
Management
in QuarkXPress

Incremental Improvements

In print production, QuarkXPress is still very much the 800-pound gorilla, so we can't ignore it, but we find a certain irony in the fact that despite being one of the first applications to offer color-management capabilities way back in the early 1990s, those capabilities have improved surprisingly little in the intervening decade. In this chapter, we cover QuarkXPress 3.32r5 through QuarkXPress 5 because many sites still use older versions of it, and the third-party solutions we discuss work with all three versions.

QuarkXPress 3 effectively lacks built-in color management, and the QuarkXPress 4 CMS lies somewhere between almost-usable and totally maddening. QuarkXPress 5 offers color-management capabilities that are generally useful, with some annoying limitations. Nevertheless, we have effective solutions for all three versions.

So fear not. In this chapter we'll look at solutions for the most common QuarkXPress output workflows: CMYK output destinations, RGB output destinations, the Web, proofing, and miscellaneous—grayscale and duotone images, spot colors, and spot-to-process, simulating spot colors with RGB or CMYK builds.

Turning It Off

The simplest way of doing something is usually the safest, and often the most efficient. If you use early-binding workflows, the safe and simple way to handle color management in QuarkXPress is to turn it off.

All the elements you import into your QuarkXPress documents—images, vector art, etc.—must be "print-ready" and already converted to final output CMYK. You need to do this anyway with grayscale, duotone, tritone, and quadtone images, all of which must be targeted specifically for the output method in question before you place them into QuarkXPress.

Any CMYK colors specified in the Color palette must also be output-ready, because their actual color appearance depends on the output device—a CMYK build won't look the same on newsprint as it will in a magazine. Consider creating your CMYK builds in an application such as Photoshop or Illustrator, then simply using the same numbers in QuarkXPress, and not worrying about display discrepancies—they'll print the same even if they look different.

Note that with color management turned off in QuarkXPress, you can't use RGB images and native elements—because while they'll often look OK onscreen, they'll either separate poorly or wind up entirely on the black plate. CMYK images, on the other hand, print according to the numbers in the file, but often look like neon onscreen.

Turn Off QuarkXPress 3 CMS (Mac OS Only)

QuarkXPress 3.3.2r5, the most recent and last version of QuarkXPress 3, included a color management system called "EFIColor." It predated the ICC profile format, so it used its own proprietary profiles, never worked well, and is best avoided—try finding software for making EFIColor profiles if you enjoy exercises in futility.

Turning color management off is the only practical solution in QuarkXPress 3, unless you resort to a third-party XTension such as Compass Pro XT (which we discuss later in this chapter). To do so, you need to delete three components on the Macintosh: the EFIColor system extension, the EFIColor folder, and the EFIColor XTension.

Turn Off QuarkXPress 4 and 5 CMS

The first method is to close *all* documents, then go to the Edit:Preferences:Color Management Preferences window and uncheck "Color Management Active." It's *very important* that you do this while all documents are closed, otherwise you only turn off color management for the foreground document.

The absolute, sure-fire method of disabling color management in QuarkXPress is to physically remove the Quark CMS XTension from the XTensions folder, found inside the QuarkXPress application folder.

Built-in Color Management

We've already told you the bad news about EFIColor, the built-in CMS in QuarkXPress 3 for Macintosh—get rid of it before it hurts you. The Windows version has no built-in color management whatsoever. Essentially, there's no built-in color management in QuarkXPress 3.32 on either platform. In a way, this isn't a bad thing because you can be certain QuarkXPress 3.32 will send the RGB or CMYK values in the document as is, without massaging the data first.

QuarkXPress 4

QuarkXPress 4 includes the Quark CMS XTension, which brings a certain level of ICC support. It works in conjunction with ColorSync on Mac OS, and ICM 2 on Windows 98 and higher.

You need to be either brave or nuts before deciding to use the Quark CMS in this version of QuarkXPress. In theory, it will color manage any RGB or CMYK TIFF and native colors from the Color palette, and let you convert them to a CMYK or Hexachrome destination (with no control over rendering intents). It sounds limited, and it is, but the limitations aren't the issue. The real problem is that QuarkXPress 4.11 has enough bugs to qualify as a lifetime employment program for the Orkin man. QuarkXPress 4.04 and 4.1 don't have as many problems, but they still have enough to be considered dangerous.

Here's a short laundry list of QuarkXPress 4.11 CMS problems:

▶ QuarkXPress 4 sees, and claims to use, embedded profiles in RGB and CMYK images, but it doesn't actually use them. Instead, it uses the Default Source Profiles. To make matters a little more complex, when you change the Default Source Profile, imported images with embedded profiles (which QuarkXPress ignores) continue to use *the Default Source Profile that was in effect at the time they were placed* as their source profile. Untagged images, however, will use the new Default Source Profile.

▶ Separations from RGB to CMYK produce different results depending on whether the source profile is embedded, or manually selected in the Profile Information palette.

▶ In the Print dialog box, in the Profiles tab, the "Composite Simulates Separation" option implies that QuarkXPress can cross-render final CMYK to a composite printer for proofing. It can't. Whether the option is checked or not, it makes no difference in output.

A cautious person might be able to incorporate all of the limitations and bugs into an effective workflow using the Quark CMS, but we're hard-pressed to think of any real benefits to doing so, considering the potential for disasters. If you need built-in color management for specific features such as soft proofing, we recommend reading the next section on QuarkXPress 5's CMS, and the coverage of InDesign 2 in Chapter 12, *The Adobe Common Color Architecture*, then upgrading to either of those packages.

QuarkXPress 5

The Quark CMS in QuarkXPress 5 is, according to Chris, "nearly usable." It doesn't support color management of EPS and grayscale files, but neither do other page-layout applications—it's simply a limitation of which you need to be aware.

If you frequently use EPS or grayscale images, you can't really use the "Composite Simulates Separation" feature for proofing, because some content proofs correctly while other content is left untouched by QuarkXPress. For such workflows, a solution that effectively handles *all* content is needed—such as Compass Pro XT, discussed in this chapter, or some of the solutions we discuss in Chapter 17, *Automation & Scripting*.

The biggest question mark with the version 5 Quark CMS is in regards to RGB-to-CMYK conversions. Certain combinations of profiles produce discrepancies of 5-10% compared to using the same profiles, CMMs, and other settings in Photoshop. In our experiments, the most likely suspect to trigger this problem is when the RGB image uses a wide gamut RGB profile—such as Wide Gamut RGB, ProPhoto RGB, and some scanner profiles—as the source profile.

Because of the uncertainty that surrounds this particular issue, we can't recommend using the Quark CMS for RGB-based workflows. But at the same time, we can't *not* recommend using it at all. The following features all appear to work reliably:

▶ **Soft proofing:** The Quark CMS properly displays RGB and CMYK images, including the ability to simulate the output from the composite or separation printer onscreen.

▶ **Hard proofing:** The Quark CMS "Composite Simulates Separations" feature lets you produce proofs on a composite PostScript printer, but only using relative colorimetric rendering. The option isn't available for non-PostScript printers.

▶ **CMYK-to-CMYK conversions:** used for repurposing images for output processes other than the ones for which they were originally separated.

▶ **RGB-to-RGB conversions:** for RGB workflows with RGB source images outputting to RGB destinations. CMYK-to-RGB is also supported.

▶ **Embedded Profiles:** QuarkXPress 5 both recognizes *and* uses embedded profiles.

The most useful feature by far is soft proofing. With the caveat that only TIFF, JPEG, PICT, and native colors used in the Color palette are color managed, it can be helpful to many workflows. No third-party product is capable of bringing soft proofing to QuarkXPress.

Color Management Preferences

Pay particular attention to the behavior of the Color Management Preferences window. To set the application-level color-management preferences, you must choose Edit:Preferences:Color Management *with no documents open*. The title bar then reads, "Color Management Preferences." This application-level setting serves as the default settings for any newly created documents. If you have one or more documents open, the preferences apply only to the foreground document, and the title bar reads, "Color Management Preferences for <documentname>."

The Color Management Preferences window is where you configure the Quark CMS (see Figure 15-1). We'll now decode it for you:

Figure 15-1

QuarkXPress Color Management Preferences

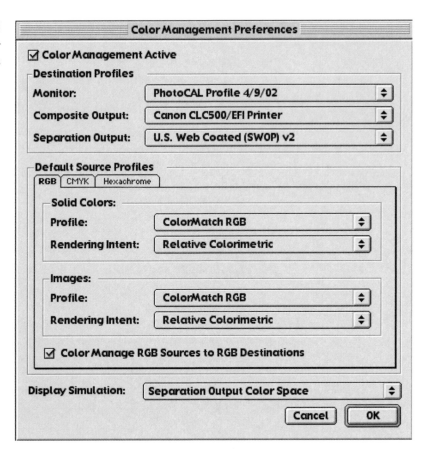

When you choose Color Management Preferences with no documents open, you set the global application-level color-management preferences. If you choose Color Management Preferences when one or more documents are open, you set the preferences for the foreground document instead.

▶ **Color Management Active checkbox:** This turns color management on and off.

▶ **Destination Profiles, Monitor:** This is where you set your current display profile. The Quark CMS doesn't grab your display profile from the operating system automatically. This may not sound like a problem, but if you open a legacy document three months from now, it will have its own color management preferences associated with it, including a display profile that probably bears no relationship to the current one.

▶ **Destination Profiles, Composite Output:** This is the profile for your composite printer. It can be an RGB or CMYK printer. In most workflows, it's the local color printer used for proofing, but in non-press workflows it may be your final output device.

In workflows with a contract proofing device that simulates the press, you'll want to specify the press profile here as well as in the Separation Output pop-up—proofing systems and presses are effectively the same device in these workflows.

▶ **Destination Profiles, Separation Output:** This is the profile for a separation device, such as a printing press. The only profiles that appear in this pop-up menu are CMYK and six-channel profiles. The way it's actually triggered for making conversions at print time, is by checking the "Separations" checkbox in the QuarkXPress Print dialog—see Figure 15-6. When unchecked, the Quark CMS uses the Composite Output profile.

▶ **Default Source Profiles, RGB, CMYK, and Hexachrome:** Within the respective tabs, you can select default source profiles for images and solid colors. By default, they affect untagged images and all solid colors. For images, you can use either the Get Picture dialog box or Profile Information palette to specify a profile other than the Default Source Profile. QuarkXPress doesn't let you select RGB output device profiles as Default Source Profiles.

The Rendering Intent pop-ups serve as default rendering intents when you use "Get Picture" to place images. We usually set all of the tabs to Relative Colorimetric for RGB and CMYK images, Relative Colorimetric for RGB Solid Colors, and Absolute Colorimetric for CMYK Solid Colors.

▶ **Solid Colors:** These are colors specified in the Color palette used for text, shapes, or backgrounds. The models affected are RGB, LAB, and CMYK only. If you add Pantone, Toyo, Trumatch, or DIC colors, color management doesn't apply—instead, you get the hardwired RGB or CMYK values specified in those palettes.

▶ **Color Manage RGB Sources to RGB Destinations/Color Manage CMYK Sources to CMYK Destinations:** These options let you allow or disallow RGB-to-RGB or CMYK-to-CMYK conversions. Checking the box lets you place images targeted for one kind of color space or device and repurpose them for a different output device. For example, placing all images separated for SWOP, then selecting a newspaper profile, repurposes the images for newsprint.

In another example, you could assume all CMYK images are "press ready." Unchecking the box in the CMYK tab prevents CMYK images from being converted by the Quark CMS. At the same time, RGB-to-CMYK conversions for output and onscreen simulations are still allowed to happen.

Conversely, in RGB output workflows, you can disallow RGB-to-RGB conversions, assuming all RGB content is output-ready, while still allowing CMYK-to-RGB conversions.

But, if you uncheck "Color Manage RGB Sources to RGB Destinations," it completely disables Display Simulation for those images as well. Therefore, they don't preview as they'll print to either RGB or CMYK output devices. The monitor *is* an RGB destination, but this checkbox would be a lot more useful if its effects were confined solely to RGB printers, rather than to any RGB destination including the monitor.

And there's an annoying bug. "Color Manage CMYK Sources to CMYK Destinations," when unchecked, passes CMYK values directly to CMYK output with no conversion, as one would expect. But they preview as though they *would* be converted, so the onscreen simulation is incorrect.

▶ **Hexachrome tab:** A couple of aspects of the Hexachrome tab are a bit misleading. First, it should be named "Six-Color" because it will actually use any six-color ICC profile—not just Hexachrome, which is a proprietary six-color ink set developed by Pantone. Second, we're confused by the presence of a Default Source Profiles tab to begin with since QuarkXPress doesn't color manage DCS 2.0 files, which are the only way we know of to save six-channel images and get them into QuarkXPress in the first place!

▶ **Display Simulation:** This option tells QuarkXPress how the display simulation should function. None means exactly that, don't simulate anything on the display. Monitor Color Space means convert from the source profile to the display profile for display only. Composite Output Color Space makes the display simulate the Composite printer. Separation Output Color Space makes the display simulate the Separations printer.

Note that Display Simulation isn't wired to the "Separation" checkbox in the Print dialog that controls whether the Quark CMS converts to the Separation Output or the Composite Output profile. So it's possible for the display to simulate one device when you actually intend to print to the other.

The Quark CMS only looks at the root level of the ColorSync profiles folder, so profiles stored in subfolders within the ColorSync Profiles folder aren't visible. This includes the Profiles and Recommended aliases to folders containing Adobe profiles such as ColorMatch RGB, Adobe RGB (1998), and U.S. Web Coated (SWOP) v2, among others. If you want access to those profiles from inside QuarkXPress, you need to put copies of them in the main ColorSync Profiles folder—aliases of ICC profiles don't work, either.

Manual Controls

QuarkXPress offers only two manual controls. The controls in Get Picture apply when you're opening images for import, while the Profile Information palette applies to images that have already been imported.

Get Picture

The Get Picture dialog box appears when you use the Get Picture command from the File menu (see Figure 15-2). When color management is active for the current document, an extra tab called Color Management appears at the bottom of the Get Picture dialog.

Figure 15-2

Get Picture dialog box

The Color Management tab lets you set the assumed source profile and the rendering intent for the image.

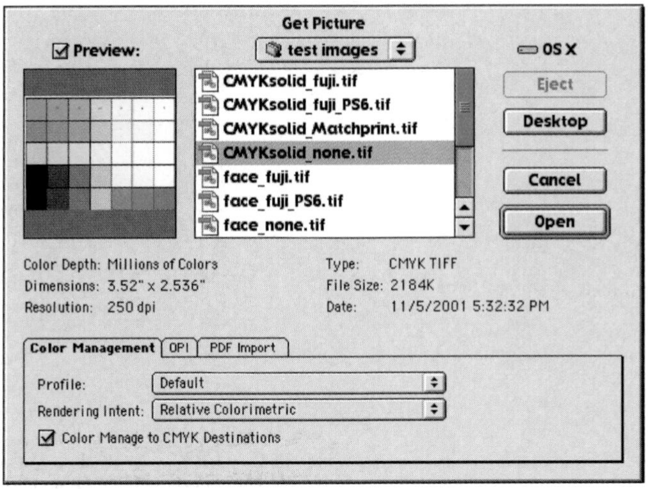

Perhaps it's a small bug or user interface oversight, but the Color Management tab contents remain grayed out unless you check the "Preview" checkbox in the upper left corner of the dialog.

The Profile pop-up menu snaps to Embedded if the image you select has an embedded profile, or to Default if the image is untagged. You can override these settings by selecting another profile from the pop-up list, which then becomes the assumed source profile for the image.

The Rendering Intent pop-up snaps to the intent specified under Default Source Profiles in Color Management Preferences. You can override this here, if you wish.

The "Color Manage to RGB/CMYK Destinations" checkbox reads RGB when you click on RGB images, and CMYK when you click on CMYK images. It has the same function as the checkbox found in Color Management Preferences in the Default Source Profiles section, and it uses the settings specified there as defaults. You can override this here, if you wish.

Profile Information

You open the Profile Information palette by choosing Profile Information from the View menu. Its controls offer identical functionality to the Get Picture dialog's Color Management tab (see Figure 15-3). It applies only to the currently selected image. As previously mentioned, the "Color Manage to RGB/CMYK Destinations" checkbox has some bugs. We recommend you review them, and be careful.

Figure 15-3
Profile Information palette

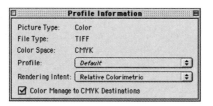

The Profile Information palette lets you change the assumed source profile and rendering intent for the selected image.

Printing

The Print dialog box, which you open by choosing Print from the File menu, has some settings that apply whether color management is active or not, and others that only become available when color management is active.

With or without color management. The Output tab of the QuarkXPress Print dialog box deserves a brief explanation (see Figure 15-4). When color management is inactive, the Print Colors pop-up menu only shows the supported modes for the currently selected printer. If it's a non-PostScript inkjet printer, for example, Composite CMYK isn't an option. If it's a PostScript printer, both Composite RGB and Composite CMYK are available options. This is normal.

Figure 15-4

Print dialog box: Output tab

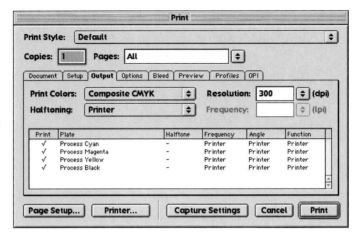

With color management active, the Print Colors pop-up menu only shows the mode that matches the profile specified for the Composite printer.

When color management is active, however, the Print Colors pop-up menu grays out either Composite CMYK or Composite RGB depending on the profile selected in the Composite Output pop-up menu. If you select a CMYK profile, Composite RGB is grayed out, and if you select an RGB profile, Composite CMYK is grayed out. This is also normal.

With color management. The Profiles tab of the Print dialog box is a shortcut to the Composite and Separation Output profiles, and is only available when color management is active (see Figure 15-5). If you change them here, they *only* change for the current document, and the change is reflected in the document's Color Management Preferences as well.

Figure 15-5

Print dialog box: Profiles tab

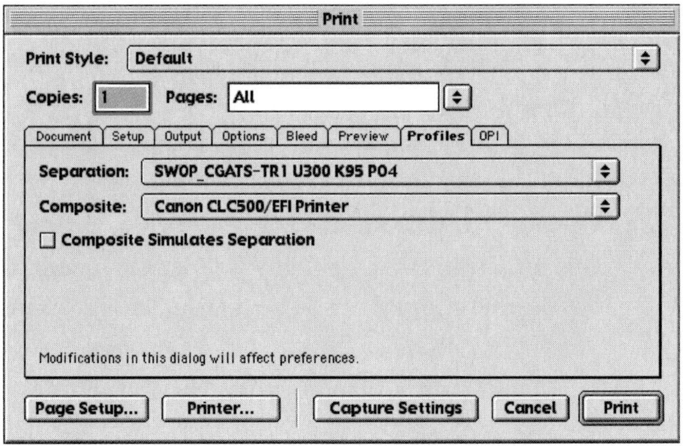

Profile selections you make in the Profiles tab of the Print dialog only apply to the current document, and the change is then reflected in the document's Color Management Preferences.

You invoke XPress's built-in hard proofing by checking the "Composite Simulates Separation" checkbox in the Profiles tab of the Print dialog box. It always uses relative colorimetric rendering, so simulating the source white on your proof isn't possible. The potential gotcha is the "Color Manage CMYK Sources to CMYK Destinations" checkbox associated with each image. When this is turned off, the CMYK image isn't color managed at all, including to the Composite Output device. The CMYK values in the image pass straight through to the composite printer, so no simulation takes place.

Last, and certainly not least, you may have noticed there are two possible output profiles: Composite Output, or Separations Output. Which one is used as the destination? In the Document tab of the Print dialog box is a "Separations" checkbox. When unchecked, the composite profile is used, and when checked the separations profile is used (see Figure 15-6). If you print composite PostScript to your imagesetter or platesetter RIP, you need to select your final output profile as Composite Output when it's time to print.

Figure 15-6

Print dialog box: Document tab

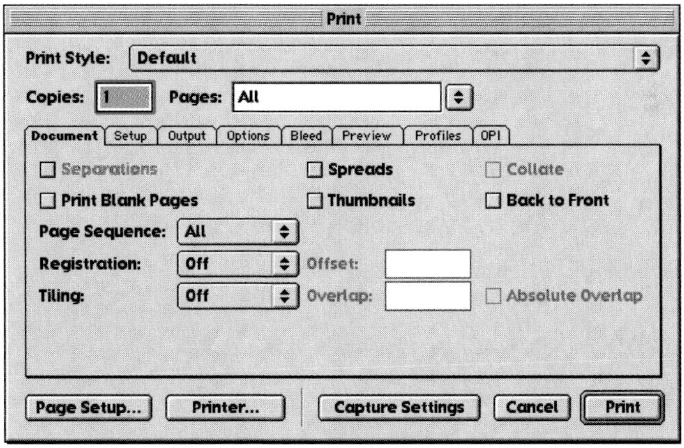

The "Separations" checkbox, shown in red for emphasis, above, controls not only whether you print composite or separated output, but also the destination profile for all conversions.

Hard Proofing

QuarkXPress 3 has no press simulation features, and the ones in QuarkXPress 4 don't work, so hard proofing using built-in color management isn't applicable. QuarkXPress 5's built-in method of producing hard proofs on composite devices has some limitations: if you use TIFF images only; can always use the "Color Manage CMYK Sources to CMYK Destinations" option; and don't need to proof Pantone, FocolTone, or other named color systems, the built-in method works quite well. But if your workflow relies on EPS files, or Pantone, Focoltone, or other named color systems, you'll need to look for a third-party solution.

Third-party proofing solutions come in several forms. Praxisoft's Compass Pro XT XTension, color servers, and self-contained proofing systems all have strengths and weaknesses, including cost, support, and deployment issues. We recommend you see a demo of any products you're interested in, to be sure that they'll meet your needs.

Praxisoft Compass Pro XT

Compass Pro XT, discussed in more detail below, is an XTension for QuarkXPress 3, 4, and 5 that lets you turn any profiled printer with a sufficiently large gamut into a proofing device, and offers an assortment of other useful features.

Pros. For individuals and relatively small organizations, this is probably the least-expensive way to produce proofs with existing equipment. If you can also exploit other features offered by Compass Pro XT, its value increases exponentially.

Cons. This product is feature-rich, and despite decent documentation and a fairly straightforward user interface, it has a learning curve—it's not a point-and-print kind of system. In larger organizations, even with the price breaks Praxisoft offers for purchasing multiple quantities, you'll quickly find yourself in a price range comparable to that of the other solutions.

Vector Pro. Compass Pro XT's companion application, Vector Pro, can simulate Pantone or Focoltone colors using hand-tuned RGB, CMYK, or multichannel builds. Vector Pro then outputs these customized, output-device-specific colors as Vector Pro palettes, which you can import into Compass Pro XT. Without Vector Pro, Compass Pro XT does a decent job of simulating solid colors, but if you're looking for an extra level of accuracy, you'll want Vector Pro.

Compass Pro XT

Compass Pro XT is an XTension exclusively for QuarkXPress. The currently-available versions are, v2.2 for QuarkXPress 3 and 4, and v5 for QuarkXPress 5. It's published by Praxisoft (www.praxisoft.com).

Compass Pro XT can convert documents for any RGB or CMYK destination, be it the Internet, a large-format inkjet, or a printing press. It can also convert documents for proofing purposes, so your lower-cost printer can simulate final output. It's flexible enough to be used in virtually any workflow calling for this kind of functionality from within QuarkXPress.

The file types it supports include not only the usual TIFF, JPEG, and PICT suspects, but also EPS (including Illustrator EPS). It also manages QuarkXPress Color palette colors (in RGB, LAB, and CMYK modes), as well as Pantone and Focoltone colors. It doesn't, however, support PDF.

Compass Pro XT offers three unique features:

▶ It's totally happy allowing multiple source profiles in a document: you can place images directly into your documents whether they're from Photoshop, digital cameras, scanners, or stock photography, each with its own source profile. You can mix and match RGB and CMYK images into the same layout, and Compass Pro XT converts *all* images (except for grayscale, which it leaves untouched) properly to the desired destination.

▶ It's the only way to color manage EPS files inside a page-layout program. Not only does it color manage RGB, LAB, and CMYK colors inside EPS files, but also Pantone and Focoltone colors. It even color manages EPSs or TIFFs embedded within an imported EPS file.

▶ It supports RGB output device profiles, so in an RGB-destination workflow, it lets you color manage content to RGB output devices in all versions of QuarkXPress, including both RGB final output devices and RGB proofers.

Another useful feature is the ability to make a duplicate of an entire QuarkXPress document, images and all, converted to a specific output profile—so you can rework those files instead of the originals, or send the press-ready duplicate back to the originator, to the service bureau, or to the printer.

One last note is that the features in Compass Pro XT are extremely customizable. Even hard-core CMYK-only output workflows going to known specific presses can take advantage of this XTension. For example, you can disable all CMYK-to-CMYK conversions, but enable RGB-to-CMYK conversions to catch the occasional RGB image that slips through. You can also take advantage of Compass Pro's solid-to-process conversions, which use builds calculated for your specific press condition instead of the generic ones published in the Pantone Solid to Process Guide. Get a copy for each workstation that does preflighting to weed out RGB images that haven't been separated yet, and rebuild solid-to-process colors correctly as a standard operating procedure.

The 800-Pound Gorilla

QuarkXPress still dominates the page-layout market despite some stiff competition from Adobe's InDesign 2.0, but its color-management capabilities, though greatly improved in version 5.0, still have rather more than their fair share of quirks. Nevertheless, as long as you're aware of the limitations and occasional oddities, you can make the Quark CMS work well in many workflows. For those workflows that need a more capable solution, XPress is well-supported both by XTensions such as Compass Pro XT and by external color servers.

Color Management and PDF

The Wave of the Future

"Once upon a time, there was a great … no wait, wrong story" is often Chris's initial thought when the subject of PDF arises. So much promise, so many problems (just like color management, sometimes), but anything worthwhile usually involves a fair bit of work. Over the years, PDF has been touted as the solution to so many different problems—as Bruce likes to say, "it's a dessert topping *and* a floorwax"—that it's often been hard to figure out just what it *is* good for.

PDF workflows can bring numerous benefits and numerous pitfalls, most of which we'll ignore in this chapter. We won't attempt to compete with the variety of excellent books and primers on PDF; instead we'll simply give you a status report on the interaction between PDF and color management. We can tell you a lot, but there are still a huge number of unknowns, so you're doubly on the bleeding edge when you deal with color management in PDF.

Why a chapter on PDF and not on Acrobat? First, PDF is much bigger than just Acrobat—many PDF workflows don't even use Acrobat—so the real story is about PDF. The Portable Document Format (which is what PDF stands for) is designed as a platform-neutral container for all types of digital content, allowing that content to be distributed without requiring the recipients to possess, or even have any knowledge of, the various applications that generated the various components in the document. This flexibility is a mixed blessing for print publishers, so much of the ongoing effort in developing standards for PDF workflows involves defining subsets of PDF features that define what is and is not allowable in PDFs designed for print workflows.

It's important to keep in mind that there are two halves to PDF: the file format half of PDF that gets most of the attention, and the equally important but often-overlooked usage half. We intend to focus primarily on the usage of PDF in a color management context, but to do so, we first need to talk about the various flavors of PDF that interest us.

The Flavors of PDF

Unlike PostScript, the Portable Document Format is an open one—Adobe publishes current versions of the specification so vendors can decide which aspects of each version they want to implement. Sounds like a recipe for chaos, and in some ways it is, but there's also a method to the madness.

PDF Versions

There are three basic versions of the PDF specification: we're primarily interested in only one of them, but we mention the others for the sake of completeness.

▶ **PDF 1.2.** This is the version of PDF produced by Acrobat 3, and it's completely ICC-unaware, lacking any mechanism for supporting ICC profiles.

▶ **PDF 1.3.** This is the highest version of PDF produced by Acrobat 4, and the default for Distiller 5. It supports the embedding of ICC profiles on a per-object basis. This is the version of PDF that's most interesting to the color management world.

▶ **PDF 1.4.** This is the version of PDF produced by Acrobat 5, and the highest version produced by Distiller 5. It too supports ICC profiles, along with transparency and a host of other features that lie outside the scope of this book.

Embedded profiles. PDF supports multiple objects (images—both vector and bitmap—as well as text, shapes, backgrounds, etc.). PDF can contain objects in different color modes, and each object can have an ICC profile associated with it as long as that mode supports ICC profiles. You could, for example, have multiple RGB, CMYK, and grayscale objects, each with a different source profile.

To minimize file size, each object references its source profile instead of having the profile embedded in the object—so six objects with Adobe RGB (1998) as their source profile don't cause six copies of Adobe RGB (1998) to be embedded in the PDF, but rather just one copy referred to six times. These objects have a color space called "ICC-Based," which means they're considered device-independent.

Any object that doesn't reference an ICC profile is device-dependent, denoted as: /DeviceRGB, /DeviceCMYK, and /DeviceGray, as the case may be.

Other noteworthy items. Rendering intent is set at the time the profile is embedded and is not related to the default rendering intent in the ICC profile. Also, destination profiles are not embedded in PDF documents, at least not yet.

PostScript Color Management

PostScript's color-management philosophy has affected PDF's color-management philosophy, and thus its behavior, so a little history is in order.

PostScript color management predates ICC-based color management, and is built-into RIPs with a version 2017.xxx and greater. PostScript profiles are always uni-directional, so there are always at least two profiles for an output device. One profile is used as a source profile (device to PCS) called a Color Space Array, or CSA for short. The other is used as a destination profile (PCS to device) called a Color Rendering Dictionary, or CRD for short. CRDs only contain a single rendering intent, so there's a separate CRD for each rendering intent.

Fundamentally, PostScript color management operates in the same way ICC-based color management does: CSAs and CRDs, like profiles, establish a relationship between device values and PCS values, and the color management system uses the information they contain to convert the device values, using a specified or default rendering intent.

Where do CSAs and CRDs live? The usual location is in the RIP itself, and it's all-too-common for built-in CSAs and CRDs to have no basis in reality as either assumed source profiles, or as descriptions of the behavior of the output device in question, so the resulting conversions are frequently hideous. Recent products—in particular, newer color laser printers—have more reasonable RGB CSAs and CMYK CRDs, so the printers can receive RGB graphics and convert them properly to printer CMYK. But that's still the exception rather than the rule.

The other location is in the PostScript print stream itself. The RIP then uses the CSAs and CRDs in the PostScript file instead of the built-in ones. If you create a PostScript stream that contains CSAs but not CRDs, the built-in CRDs are used.

In theory, each object gets its own CSA (source profile) and is also tagged with the CRD that should be used (because the CRD controls the rendering intent). Then the RIP uses each CSA and included CRD to perform color space conversions in the RIP. In practice, though, you quickly find out that some RIPs ignore CMYK CSAs altogether, others ignore CSAs in the print stream and use only built-in CSAs, and still others ignore CRDs as well. When it comes to implementing such a system, you usually end up with a mess (the fact that the most common page-layout program, QuarkXPress, can't produce either CSAs or CRDs doesn't help).

PostScript to PDF, PDF to PostScript. Enter PDF 1.3, which uses ICC profiles, not PostScript color management. Adobe created a mechanism whereby with PDF 1.3 and higher, profiles and CSAs can be interchanged when the document is converted from PostScript to PDF and vice versa. When you print a PDF to a PostScript printer, it's turned back into Post-Script, and all the ICC source profiles become PostScript CSAs. When you convert PostScript into PDF, all CSAs are converted into ICC profiles, and any CRDs are simply tossed into the bit-bucket.

You may have experienced Acrobat Distiller 3 and 4 converting CMYK images into LAB. This generally happens when those versions of Distiller encounter a PostScript CSA embedded in a CMYK EPS (probably from Photoshop with the "PostScript Color Management" checkbox selected). Distiller 5 either converts the CSA into an ICC profile or ignores it entirely, depending on the Distiller color settings.

With the possible exception of thoroughly-troubleshot proofing systems, we recommend avoiding PostScript color management unless you're one of the handful of people who've already gotten it to work reliably. If you have, congratulations—maybe you should write a book!

PDF/X

PDF supports many different types of digital content, but it doesn't really help your PDF print workflow at all when the PDF contains the sixth Brandenburg Concerto or the latest Star Wars movie. So the PDF/X format and usage guidelines were created to ensure that PDF/X compliant PDFs contained *only* the data required for print. PDF/X is rapidly emerging as the standard for PDF-based print workflows.

Did we say "standard?" Of course, life is rarely that simple, and while the PDF/X bandwagon continues to gather momentum, PDF/X isn't just one standard. Instead, it has several different conformance levels, predicated primarily on the PDF 1.3 specification, that fall under the umbrella of International Standard ISO 15930 as follows:

▶ **PDF/X-1:1999.** This early version is an ANSI standard, but it has a number of technical flaws and little vendor support, and is effectively obsolete.

▶ **PDF/X-1:2001.** This version, defined in ISO 15930-1:2001, is similar to PDF/X-1a:2001, but it exists for legacy reasons, allows encryption, and supports limited OPI. It too doesn't appear to have any support and isn't likely to gain any in the future.

▶ **PDF/X-1a:2001.** This version, defined in ISO 15930-1:2001, is designed for "blind transfer" of print data in press-ready form—the PDF itself contains all the elements needed to print. Color must be CMYK (plus optional spot) only, and all images and fonts must be embedded.

▶ **PDF/X-2[:2003].** This version, defined in ISO 15930-2, was at the time of writing awaiting completion of ballot approval, and is expected to be published around August 2003. It's functionally similar to PDF/X-3 but allows for externally-referenced data, so it isn't usable for blind transfers, and uses portions of PDF 1.4.

▶ **PDF/X-3:2002.** This version, defined in ISO 15930-3:2002, is similar to PDF/X-1a:2001, with the important difference that it allows device-independent color. As with PDF/X-1a:2001, it's designed for blind transfers, and hence all images and fonts must be embedded.

Gazing into our crystal ball, we expect that PDF/X-1a will become the dominant standard for blind transfers in the United States, PSD/X-3 will become the dominant standard for blind transfers in the European market, and PDF/X-2 will mostly be used as an internal format inside large enterprises.

Various third-party tools make creating PDF/X straightforward—we discuss some of them in "Third-Party Stuff," later in this chapter. You can't make PDF/X directly using Adobe Acrobat, so a third-party tool is necessary.

For more information on PDF and PDF/X, check out these resources:

▶ http://www.planetpdf.com/

▶ http://www.pdfx.info/index.html

▶ http://www.pdfzone.com/

OutputIntent. All PDF/X documents must have an OutputIntent specified. This can be an ICC-registered print condition name or an ICC profile. That means there's an implicit and an explicit possibility. The implicit one is really vague, in our opinion—check out the ICC registry at www.color.org/registry2.html, and you'll see what we mean. So we recommend setting the OutputIntent with an actual ICC profile, at least until the registry matures into something useful.

PDF/X-1a. By far, PDF/X-1a interests us the most since it's relatively straightforward and has strong vendor support. Objects must be device-dependent (CMYK plus spot) color—ICC-Based color isn't allowed. However, an OutputIntent is required. It's important to realize that while you can use an ICC profile for the OutputIntent—and hence effectively make the PDF device-independent, repurposable, and proofable—the objects in the document are still device-dependent because PDF/X-1a prohibits per-object ICC profiles.

The OutputIntent is the profile that was used for separation of the PDF's content, so it becomes the source profile for all CMYK content (which is everything except for spot color).

PDF/X-3. We'll discuss PDF/X-3 from a "sneak preview" point of view since it's still pretty green, with limited, though growing, vendor support. (It's too soon to even look for PDF/X-2 products.)

PDF/X-3 can contain device-dependent data (either untagged RGB or untagged CMYK, but not both in the same document), as well as device-independent data (tagged RGB, tagged CMYK, and LAB). Each device-independent object, by definition, has an ICC profile associated with it, and the actual color space is referred to as "ICC-Based."

For PDF/X-3, the OutputIntent is the source profile for the untagged device-dependent data, and is the intended destination profile for device-independent data. So the device-dependent data must be separated for the intended output already, as it won't be converted again. This is the only PDF/X variant that:

▶ Allows a destination profile to be included in the PDF for the explicit purpose of performing conversions

▶ Supports device-independent data

▶ Supports RGB output devices.

The biggest challenge with PDF/X-3 is making one. In subsequent sections of this chapter, you'll find that specifying per-object ICC profiles isn't for the faint of heart, and requires special workflow and software considerations. Once you have a PDF/X-3 document, printing or proofing it requires both faith and courage. You'll need to use products that specifically support PDF/X-3 documents to effectively proof and output them.

Distiller 5

Adobe Distiller isn't the only product capable of converting PostScript into PDF, but it's one of the most common, and it serves well as an example application—just look for similar features and settings in the application you use.

Compatibility

We previously mentioned the various versions of PDF. Distiller's Job Options dialog box is one of the places where they're directly relevant to color management. The Compatibility pop-up menu in the General tab of Job Options affects the options available in the Color tab. If you select "Acrobat 3.0 (PDF 1.2)," your only color management policy options are to leave colors unchanged or to convert them. Since PDF 1.2 doesn't support ICC profiles, there's no way to simply tag the documents. Unless you have good reasons to do otherwise, we recommend choosing "Acrobat 4.0 (PDF 1.3)," because that's what PDF/X is based on (see Figure 16-1).

Figure 16-1

Adobe Distiller
Compatibility settings

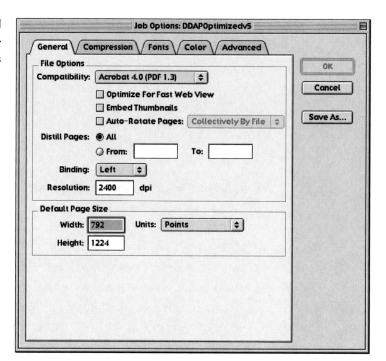

Color Settings

The Adobe Color Settings for Distiller, which you'll find under the Color tab of Job Options, look like those for other Adobe applications—but the similarity is misleading, because their behavior is unlike those other Adobe applications (see Figure 16-2).

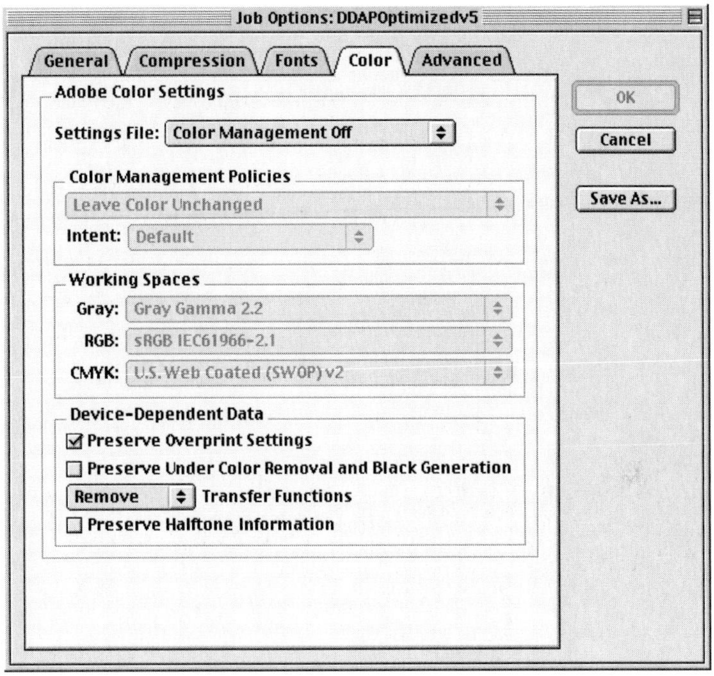

Figure 16-2
Adobe Distiller
Color settings

Figure 16-2
Adobe Distiller
Color settings

Settings File. Distiller uses .csf files created in other Adobe applications, and displays them in the Settings File popup menu, but it can't create them itself. When you choose a setting from the Settings File menu, the Color Management Policies menu is grayed out—the only way to enable Color Management Policies is to select the settings file called "None."

Possibly the best way to handle this is simply not to worry about creating settings files for Distiller, since Distiller has such unusual color behavior anyway. If you save a .joboptions file, any custom color settings are saved as well.

Color Management Policies. The color management policies in Distiller are quite different than in any other Adobe application, by necessity, since Distiller's job is to convert PostScript into PDF. Other Adobe applications open and display files, then let you edit them in some fashion. Distiller is just a completely different beast, and has policies to match.

- ▶ **Leave Color Unchanged**—this means preserve the numeric values in the PostScript file when converting it into a PDF. Ignore any CSAs in the PostScript file, and don't embed the Working Space profiles.

- ▶ **Tag Everything for Color Mgmt (no conversion)**—also means preserve the numeric values in the PostScript file when converting it into a PDF. CSAs associated with objects are converted into per-object ICC profiles. The selected Working Space profiles are embedded, and apply to all other objects. All objects are considered tagged.

- ▶ **Tag Only Images for Color Mgmt (no conversion)**—means the same as tagging everything, except that only images are tagged. So vector objects, including text, are untagged, and considered device-dependent.

- ▶ **Convert All Colors to sRGB**—any CSAs associated with objects are used as source profiles. Objects with no CSAs take the Working Space profiles as assumed sources. The destination profile is sRGB, so everything is converted to sRGB.

A brief note on the Intent pop-up. Rendering intents are chosen at the time of PDF creation, just as in PostScript, which seems backwards—we generally find that we can't tell which rendering intent will work best for a given object until we know the output destination. But that's the way it currently works.

The Default option is unclear—it's either the default PDF rendering intent (relative colorimetric), or it's the intent, set in the PostScript file, that points to the CRD that would have been used had the PostScript file been interpreted by a PostScript RIP rather than by Distiller. We suggest setting it to relative colorimetric—then you at least know what you're dealing with.

Working Spaces. The Working Space profiles are the ones that are used for tagging, depending on the color management policy selected.

For example, if your document contains a mix of RGB, CMYK and grayscale images, and you print a PostScript file, then distill with one of the "Tag for Color Management" color management policies, a single copy of each working space is embedded in the PDF document. The RGB Working Space profile becomes the source profile for all RGB images, the CMYK Working Space profile becomes the source profile for all CMYK images, and the Gray Working Space profile becomes the source profile for all grayscale images. Whether these embedded profiles apply to non-image objects depends on which color management policy you selected.

The key thing to note is that "Working Spaces" in Distiller really means the profiles that are embedded into the document. They start out as assumed profiles and become embedded profiles in the PDF.

Any objects in the PostScript stream that have CSAs associated with them don't use the Working Space profiles, but have their CSAs converted into ICC profiles which are embedded into the PDF along with the Working Space profiles. CSAs are the only mechanism that allows Distiller to specify profiles on a per-object basis. Distiller also ignores embedded ICC profiles in the PostScript print stream (which usually appear only when you print a document containing an EPS file with an embedded ICC profile).

Device-Dependent Data. As the name implies, these settings only affect device-dependent data, and prior to PDF generation typically only apply to EPS files, since the options are all based on PostScript functions. With the possible exception of overprint settings, ICC-based objects aren't affected by these options.

It's generally a good idea to preserve overprint settings. If they exist in the PostScript file, they have to be preserved in the PDF file if you want the document to print the way the originating application intended.

"Preserve Under Color Removal and Black Generation" exist mainly for legacy support. If your images have already been separated to CMYK, then placed into a page-layout application, and output to PostScript, the images are "press-ready" so PostScript UCR or GCR functions shouldn't exist to begin with, and preserving them is moot.

Transfer functions should almost always be removed unless you really know what you're doing, and have a specific reason for using them. It's usually counterproductive to use them on other people's equipment, and since a PDF could end up being printed anywhere, it's almost always best to remove them.

Unless you explicitly want an element to override RIP settings because you placed an EPS with specific halftone screens in your page-layout software, you usually want to remove halftone information too.

Making PDFs

Three main factors affect your ability to make decent PDFs whether you intend to use them for the Web, soft proofing, or final output (plain PDF, PDF/X-1a, or PDF/X-3):

▶ Proper preparation of all support files in their respective applications, especially the final application you use to print the PostScript file that Distiller will process. This includes page settings, font embedding, image preparation and linking, and so forth.

▶ Use of an appropriate PPD file for your PostScript printer driver (which includes making the application you're printing from aware of the PPD—something that may or may not happen automatically).

▶ Use of appropriate settings in Distiller, paying special attention to the color settings.

Output-only PDF—press. As previously mentioned, there are many resources on how to make good PDFs, so we'll stay focused on the color aspects. We've already discussed the first of the three factors mentioned above in the earlier application chapters.

The second and third factors mentioned above are workflow-specific, but very important. We've come to trust and recommend as a starting point the DDAP PPD, and their accompanying Distiller Settings Files, which are available for both platforms at www.ddap.org/tools/univppd/.

Note that the Distiller Settings File turns color management off, so you'll end up with a device-dependent PDF. This works as long as you produce output-ready PostScript prior to building the PDF. The resulting PDF won't have automatic soft-proofing or hard-proofing capabilities, since there's no source profile embedded in the document. (If you refer back to Figure 16-2, you'll see that it's based on the DDAPOptimizedv5 settings file for Distiller 5. Colors are left unchanged and untagged.)

From here, you can feed the PDF to an application such as Apago PDF/X-1 Checkup, or Enfocus Certified PDF (part of Pitstop Pro and Server, and Instant PDF), which preflights the PDF, fixes problems it can fix, and makes a note of those it can't. Assuming everything can be fixed, you end up with a PDF/X-1a document.

Color-managed PDF—desktop. This is a PDF that has profiles associated for all objects. While it's possible to produce a PDF that has profiles associated with some objects and not others, we recommend you avoid doing so unless you enjoy lessons in frustration.

Using Distiller, we recommend producing an "output-ready" PDF in your page layout application, as previously described in "Output-only PDF—press," only embedding the final output device's profile. Since all the color is already converted for one kind of output device, you can describe it all with a single device profile. Embed that profile, and Acrobat 5 and Acrobat Reader 5 use it automatically for on-screen preview, while other applications that can read color-managed PDFs may be able to repurpose the content for some other device (such as for proofing—see Figure 16-3).

Figure 16-3

Adobe Distiller Settings: color-managed PDF

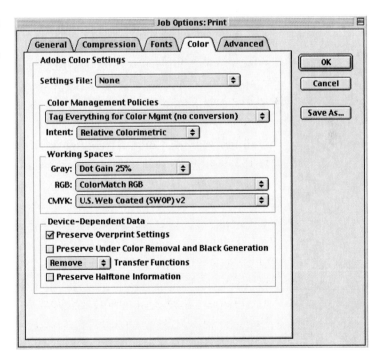

Be careful: as configured in Figure 16-3, Distiller won't convert anything in the document, so you must make sure that all the color is already converted for output before you feed it to Distiller. Distiller is just being used to tag objects with a source profile (and of course make a PDF file.)

Also, while you can effectively use such a PDF for soft and hard proofing, it isn't necessarily repurposable—since all objects, including things like black-only text, become device-independent, they won't be black-only if repurposed.

The real problem is that Distiller's options don't really offer enough flexibility. If you choose "Tag Only Images," non-image objects will only print correctly to the intended destination and will look wrong everywhere else, whereas if you choose "Tag Everything For Color Mgmt (no conversion)" and print to a destination other than the intended one, black text gets converted to rich black, which can create major problems.

PDF/X-3 addresses the problem by letting you define black text as device-dependent, so that it will print as black-only on any destination device, while tagging all objects that need color management to produce the correct appearance.

Color-managed PDF—Internet. The suggestions in the previous two sections generally provide the best results. But if you want to create the smallest possible files, and have the color display reasonably well on the random collection of uncalibrated monitors that serve as the delivery system for the Internet, you may want to try these settings instead.

In Job Options, Color tab, change the Settings File to None—the Web Graphics Default color settings file is useless with Adobe Distiller. Next, set the Color Management Policies to "Convert All Colors to sRGB." Finally, set whatever output profile you used to create the PostScript as the working space—if your document is entirely Adobe RGB (1998), for example, set that as the RGB Working Space so that Distiller uses it as the source profile when it converts everything to sRGB. Likewise if your document is CMYK, set the working space to the CMYK profile you used as the destination when you created the PostScript file (see Figure 16-4).

Acrobat 5

Compared to Adobe's other applications, Acrobat 5's color management capabilities are just as funky as Distiller's. While the Color Management Preferences dialog box looks familiar, its scope is limited compared to the other applications, and printing from Acrobat makes us wonder what in the world Adobe was thinking.

Figure 16-4

Adobe Distiller settings:
Convert to sRGB PDF

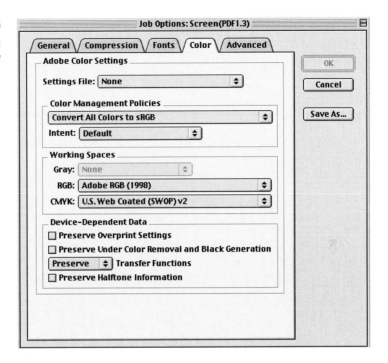

The redeeming feature of Acrobat is that color management really just happens without any configuration. Acrobat grabs the display profile automatically from the operating system, and uses embedded profiles automatically and seamlessly, regardless of the color management preferences. Setting up remote soft proofing is as simple as calibrating and profiling a monitor and installing Acrobat on the client side. (On the "server" side, of course, someone needs to embed the correct profiles into the PDFs.)

Color Management Preferences

To open Acrobat's Color Management Preferences click on "Color Management" in the list on the left of the General Preferences dialog box (see Figure 16-5). Like Distiller, Acrobat can use Color Settings files created in other Adobe applications as well, but it can't create them itself. Since Acrobat always uses either an embedded or assumed source profile, color management is always on, even though there's a "Color Management Off" settings file.

The Working Spaces are the assumed profiles—they apply to all untagged objects in PDF files. If you set the RGB Working Space to monitor RGB (your display profile), the numbers in untagged RGB images get sent straight to

Figure 16-5

Acrobat Color
Management Preferences

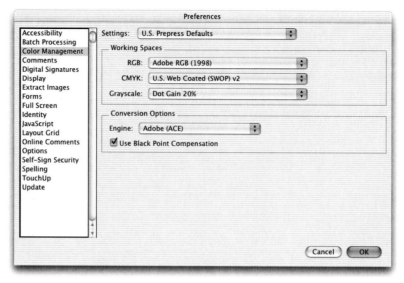

the display, so you're effectively getting no color management, but everything else gets color managed and there isn't anything you can do about it.

The Conversion Options only affect conversions for Proof Colors (described later) and for printing.

Printing

Source profiles are either embedded in the PDF document, or assumed by Acrobat's Color Management Preferences, but you need to specify a destination profile. Yet for non-PostScript printers, Adobe has provided absolutely no mechanism for specifying a destination profile or a rendering intent. When you print to a non-PostScript printer, it converts from the source profiles to the display profile.

So when you print to raster printers from Acrobat, you're best off selecting ColorSync or ICM in the printer driver. We've confirmed that Acrobat hands off the display profile to the operating system as the source profile for the data stream at print time. From there, the destination profile is dictated by the printer driver.

When you print to a PostScript printer, the Adobe section of the driver contains an Advanced button that doesn't appear in non-PostScript printer drivers. Clicking it opens the Print Settings dialog, with no fewer than seven color-management-related options, not one of which is a rendering intent setting—see Figure 16-6!

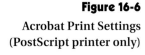

Figure 16-6

Acrobat Print Settings
(PostScript printer only)

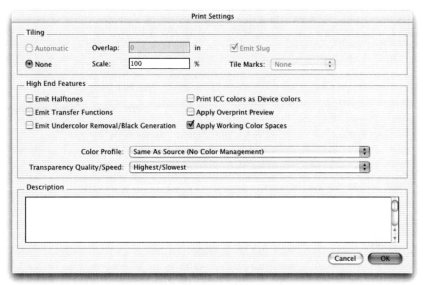

We generally ignore the first three checkboxes regarding halftones, transfer functions and UCR/GCR. If you need to use these features, you know it—if you aren't sure, only experiment when you have lots of spare time. The same goes for "Apply Overprint Preview" which is useful for forcing Acrobat to render the overprint function if your printer doesn't support it.

"Print ICC colors as Device colors" produces identical results whether checked or unchecked, so it seems to do nothing. (We're really unclear on what it would do if it *did* work—if you don't want conversions, just select Same As Source as you would in other Adobe applications, instead of a destination profile.)

"Apply Working Color Spaces," fortunately, does work, but we fail to understand why it's optional. When it's checked, Acrobat uses the Working Spaces in Color Management Preferences as source profiles for untagged objects in the conversion to print space. When it's unchecked, Acrobat uses a hardwired conversion that produces results charitably described as lurid and weird.

Last but not least is the Color Profile pop-up menu. This works like the Print Space pop-up menu in other Adobe applications, but it lacks rendering intent control—maybe someone from the Photoshop team should walk across the hall and have a chat with the color people on the PDF team to try to standardize user interface features and terminology.

InDesign 2 Export PDF

InDesign 2 can export PDFs directly, without the need for Distiller. We've heard some anecdotal reports in the chat rooms of problems with PDFs produced this way, but the sample size isn't large enough to let us draw any conclusions—we'll leave you to wrestle with this issue, we hope using better information sources.

When it comes to color management, InDesign's Export PDF capability is pretty good, with a couple of potential pitfalls. It produces fully color-managed PDFs, with or without embedded profiles for every object, or mixed-mode PDFs.

PDF Styles

The PDF Styles dialog, which you open by choosing PDF Styles from the File menu, lets you create and save presets for making PDFs, and is a real time-saver (see Figure 16-7).

Figure 16-7

InDesign 2 PDF Styles dialog box

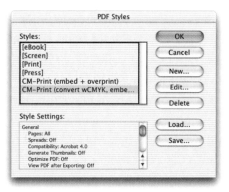

We suggest you familiarize yourself with the various PDF settings for two reasons—familiarity with them seems to make all the difference in the world between exporting problematic and problem-free PDFs, and we aren't going to talk about most of the settings since they don't pertain to color management.

Export PDF

The Export PDF dialog, which you open by choosing Export from the File menu, offers a Styles pop-up menu where you can select from the list of PDF Styles you created using the aforementioned PDF Styles feature. In the left column is an Advanced option, which is where you'll find the Color section (see Figure 16-8).

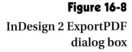

Figure 16-8

InDesign 2 ExportPDF
dialog box

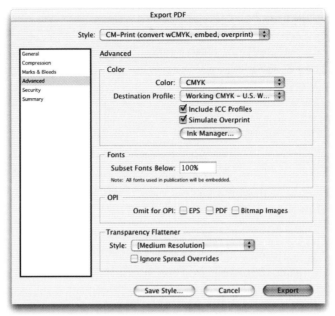

Color. Color offers three options. Leave Colors Unchanged does exactly that—if you create a document with mixed-mode images and elements, you'll create a mixed-mode PDF. Selecting either RGB or CMYK enables the Destination Profile pop-up menu, discussed next, and converts all the content in your document to the destination profile.

Destination Profile. Here you select a destination profile for output.

Include ICC Profiles. This option embeds ICC profiles into the PDF. If you selected Leave Colors Unchanged in the Color pop-up menu, each profile used in the document is embedded in the PDF. If you choose to convert the document to RGB or CMYK, only the destination profile is embedded, since all document content is converted to that destination.

Simulate Overprint. This option does two things. It makes InDesign do the overprint itself before producing the PDF, which is useful for making dual-purpose PDFs for screen and print because many consumer devices— and even some PostScript RIPs—have no idea what overprinting is. But it also converts spot colors to process, so it's not an option you want to use when preparing PDFs for press—use the Ink Manager instead.

Ink Manager. The Ink Manager can perform a variety of functions, which are described in the InDesign User Guide. If you make changes here, they affect the exported PDF, not your InDesign document. Be careful with these settings if you rely on InDesign to perform trapping, because some of them are used by InDesign's trapping engine.

If you select the option to convert all spot colors to process, they're converted using the CMYK equivalents supplied by Pantone in whichever Pantone library you used to specify the spots. They aren't converted using ICC-based color management, so your process Pantone colors probably won't look right unless you're really lucky.

EPS Objects

InDesign makes some peculiar assumptions about placed EPS files when exporting as opposed to printing. During printing, InDesign simply passes the values in the EPS to the printer, but during export, it color manages them instead. InDesign ignores profiles embedded in the EPS—so as far as it's concerned, EPSs with embedded profiles are untagged. But it honors embedded CSAs, and sees EPSs with embedded CSAs as tagged.

For the untagged variety, InDesign assumes the Document Profile (RGB or CMYK, as the case may be) as source, and converts them to the destination profile you select in the Export PDF>Advanced dialog, unless you selected Leave Colors Unchanged.

For the CSA tagged variety, InDesign uses the CSA as the source profile, and converts them to the destination profile, unless you selected Leave Colors Unchanged.

The resulting objects in the PDF have associated profiles like any other object, if you choose to embed profiles in the PDF.

The only ways to prevent EPSs from being converted during PDF export are:

▶ Select Leave Colors Unchanged.

▶ Choose the same profile for Document Profile (the assumed source for untagged EPSs) and for the destination profile you select in Export PDF.

Third-Party Stuff

There are a number of really good products on the market, but the one we've worked with the most, and hence can discuss with some authority, is Enfocus PitStop Pro 5.

Enfocus PitStop Pro

This plug-in for Acrobat lets you do all kinds of manipulation and editing on PDFs, but we'll only look at the ones that are color-management related. Consider it one of the necessary tools in the arsenal if you're a heavy PDF user. (Or for high-volume workflows, consider the industrial-strength PitStop Server—for more information, go to www.enfocus.com.)

PitStop Pro strengths. PitStop Pro offers the following useful capabilities for creating and massaging color-managed PDFs:

▶ It distinguishes between device-dependent (RGB, CMYK, Gray) and LAB and ICC-Based color spaces on a per-object basis.

▶ It lists the embedded profile associated with each object.

▶ It lets you untag objects, reassign profiles to objects, and embed profiles on saving the PDF.

▶ It lets you specify a destination profile to which any object can be converted. It supports RGB-to-CMYK, CMYK-to-RGB, and RGB- or CMYK-to-grayscale conversions using ICC profiles.

▶ It lets you do any of the above object-by-object, or globally.

▶ It preflights and produces certified PDF/X-1a documents with a preflight report, and tracks changes to the PDF as it moves through production.

▶ It offers downloadable "PDF Profiles" that extend its ability to preflight PDFs for other target viewers, such as the Internet.

PitStop Pro weaknesses. However, it isn't perfect, and has the following weaknesses:

- It offers no rendering intent control for conversions, which use the destination profile's default rendering intent.

- It doesn't directly support RGB-to-RGB or CMYK-to-CMYK conversions, though you can work around the limitation by first converting an object into LAB as an intermediary space.

- It doesn't support DeviceLink profiles.

Other Products

We haven't worked with these products as much as we have with PitStop Pro, but they come recommended by people whose judgement we trust:

- Apago PDF/X Checkup, www.apago.com

- Callas PDF/X Inspektor (free), and PDF Inspektor, www.callas.de/

- Dalim TWiST and SWiNG, http://www.dalim.com

- OneVision (various products), www.onevision.com

The Wave of the Future

If, as we suspect, print publishing will be forced by brute economics to make the transition from arcane craft to modern manufacturing process, it seems likely that PDF workflows, whether based on the current PDF/X standards or on ones that don't yet exist, will become prevalent. But while unambiguous communication of documents between creator and producer will ultimately benefit both sides, note that the shift from delivering application files, fonts, and linked graphics to delivering a print-ready PDF/X-1a involves a shift of responsibility back to the content creator.

In some ways, PDF/X is a 21st-century equivalent of the PostScript dumps Bruce used to send to service bureaus in the mid-1980s—when things went wrong, the blame was always his. PDF workflows hold huge promise, but they're still experimental, and you can always spot the pioneers by the arrows protruding from their backs—so if you're considering PDF workflows, take it one step at a time, test thoroughly, and don't attempt untried procedures when you're facing critical deadlines.

Automation and Scripting

The Smart Way To Be Lazy

Unfortunately, our desktop applications and our equipment—scanners, RIPs, and printers—don't always give us the exact color-management options we need. Fortunately, automation and scripting provide us not only with solutions to these limitations, but also bring a lot of power and flexibility to workflows that we may not otherwise have considered.

The purpose of this chapter isn't to cover every conceivable automation or scripting option, or even to serve as a primer. Instead, it's meant to give you a taste of the kinds of things automation and scripting can do, and teach you the right questions to ask when you look for products to solve your particular needs.

Why Automate?

We use automation for the following reasons:

▶ To free humans from repetitive, brainless grunt-work that doesn't require intelligent human decision-making or intervention

▶ To make efficient use of our available processing power

▶ To work around color-management limitations in our applications or equipment.

For example, we may have scanners or digital cameras that we've profiled, but the software that drives them doesn't embed profiles. We know which profile we need to assign to the images they produce, so rather than doing so manually in Photoshop, we can use automation (or scripting) to batch embed the appropriate profile in a single image, in multiple images, or even in folders of images. Since we don't need to open or display the images, the performance advantages can be significant, especially with RAM-gobbling high-resolution images, and we free ourselves from mind-numbing, repetitive button-pushing.

A good example of using automation to work around an application's limitations is using a color server to address desktop applications' near-universal lack of color-management support for vector EPS—many automation products can process EPS files, and sometimes even embedded EPSs or TIFFs within EPS files. On the device end, it's not uncommon for an imagesetter, platesetter RIP, or proofing device to have no idea what ICC profiles are. Color servers placed in front of such hardware can perform color management tasks before PostScript or PDF get to the RIP.

Color management offers one other very specialized type of automation—so specialized, in fact, that many people don't even recognize it as an automation feature. DeviceLink profiles offer an elegant way to store specific, hardwired device-to-device conversions—see the sidebar, "DeviceLink Profiles," later in this chapter.

Color Servers

Color servers are sometimes called batch processors, or generically, automation products. Color servers placed at the front-end of another device/RIP do their work by parsing PostScript or PDF files, changing only the numeric values—they don't damage the integrity of the PostScript or PDF files. When they process bitmap information (such as TIFF, JPEG, or bitmap EPS), they effectively open the file, perform the conversions, then rewrite the file.

Common color server features include:

▶ Processing multiple files or folders of files.

▶ Performing color conversions on TIFF and JPEG. Some also support EPS (both bitmap and vector).

▶ Supporting embedded profiles, with a mechanism for assuming profiles if no embedded profile is present.

▶ Using a LAB-based look-up table for converting Pantone (sometimes also Focoltone) colors to custom RGB or CMYK builds.

▶ Batch embedding profiles, or batch removing embedded profiles.

▶ Most support hot folders. Some support print queues that appear on the network as though they were PostScript printers.

Color Server Pros

Like any other technology, color servers have their pros and cons—we'll look at these in a general way before getting into specific examples.

▶ **Fast processing**—processing is much faster than doing an equivalent procedure in an application such as Photoshop, because the files don't need to be opened or displayed.

▶ **Configurability**—you can set up color servers to do tasks ranging from simply embedding profiles into images to simultaneously producing multiple converted files for scatter proofs and monitor soft-proof versions. You can set it to color manage TIFF, but not EPS. You can set it to color manage RGB images, but not CMYK.

▶ **Front end to almost any hardware**—sticking a color server into a workflow provides a single front end for color-managing a variety of devices. When you add a new proofer, you can simply add another queue to support that device without having to worry if it supports ICC profiles, and your future purchasing decisions don't depend on built-in color management support.

▶ **Hotfolders and print queues available over network**—you can set up hot folders to accommodate remote clients over a network and publish print queues on the network, too. Users don't have to deal with configuration issues or decide which profiles to use for source and destination—instead they simply place the files into the appropriate hot folder. Faster, and less prone to error.

▶ **Named color system support**—lets you deal effectively with named color systems like Pantone and Focoltone by generating custom CMYK equivalents for your specific devices. Equally important, it uses the *same* CMYK equivalents for all instances of a given Pantone or Focoltone color, effectively solving the seemingly unending problem of applications that use libraries containing different CMYK equivalents for the same solid colors.

Color servers are very well suited to repurposing already separated jobs (coated to uncoated, or between inksets) or to turning any device with a large enough gamut into a proofer, even if it doesn't have explicit color management support.

Color Server Cons

Lest the picture we've painted above sounds overly rosy, we feel bound to point out the following downsides to most server-based automation products:

▶ **Costly**—especially if you're used to the prices for desktop applications. Prices range from just under $1,000 to about $3,000.

▶ **Limited rendering intent control**—if you plan on using a server in late-binding workflows—such using all-RGB page layout, and printing RGB PostScript to a color server that converts to the appropriate CMYK space—you generally can't specify per-object rendering intent control. (We don't know of any page-layout applications that can generate a PostScript stream that contains rendering intents.) You can, however, specify rendering intents for classes of objects, such as "images" and "vector graphics," to use something else.

▶ **Limited source profile control**—when a page-layout application generates a PostScript stream, it doesn't embed ICC profiles for formats other than EPS, and it only does so for EPSs that already contain embedded profiles. If you use TIFF or JPEG file formats with a variety of source profiles, the color server can only assume source profiles. Again, you can specify source profiles for different classes of objects, but that's it.

Most of these cons have workarounds. The subtle differences between relative colorimetric and perceptual rendering may be within acceptable tolerances for many workflows, so the limited choice of rendering intent may only be a problem in workflows aimed at very high-quality output. And if you can standardize on a single source space in the page layout, the limited source profile control isn't a problem because the assumed profile is always correct.

Late-binding workflows that use color servers for final conversion simply don't provide per-image control over conversions—but even in high-end workflows that demand per-image control, servers can still do conversions to use devices that don't have explicit color-management support as proofers, and to assist with solid-color matching.

Examples

This is by no means an exhaustive review of every server-based automation product available. We've chosen the following examples both because we're familiar with them and because they provide good illustrations of the capabilities of server-based automation in general.

Praxisoft ICC Autoflow. ICC Autoflow, available for Macintosh and Windows, processes PostScript, EPS, and—on Windows only—PDF. A reduced-cost desktop version doesn't support hot folders—you point it manually to a folder, then the files it contains are processed according to the configured settings. Both versions let you create and save multiple configuration sets (see Figure 17-1). Note that this product doesn't process grayscale content—it simply passes through unchanged.

As discussed in Chapter 15, *Color Management in QuarkXPress*, VectorPro creates custom palettes which are also supported in ICC Autoflow.

Figure 17-1

Praxisoft ICC
Autoflow

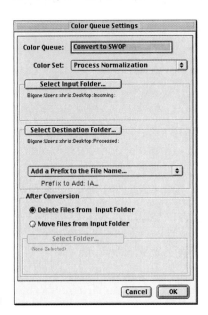

Main window

Color Queue Settings

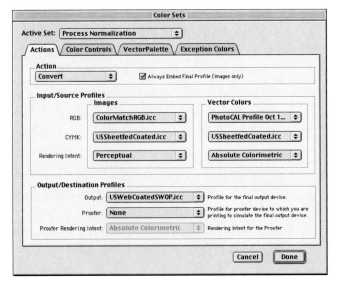

Color Sets

Gretag Macbeth iQueue. iQueue comes in several flavors: 110, 120 and 140. The primary differences are that 110 doesn't support PostScript (or EPS), while the other two do. In addition to 120's features, 140 adds PDF and print queue support instead of just hot folders. A few other features:

▶ Explicit support for PDF/X-1a and PDF/X-3 (140 version)

▶ DeviceLink and abstract profile support

▶ Additional file formats: BMP, Scitex CT, and PNG

▶ A built-in mini-Web server lets you obtain job status from any workstation.

Figure 17-2

Gretag Macbeth iQueue

Main window, Queue Setup window, and ICC Options

Color Server Questions

If you're contemplating a server-based automation product, here are three important questions you need to ask:

► **Which file formats are supported?** Most though not all workflows require PostScript (and hence EPS) support. Increasing numbers want PDF support.

► **What black-preservation options are offered? Does black-only text remain black-only when converted? What about black-only drop shadows?** Most products have some means of ensuring that black-only text is ignored, and thus remains device black instead of being converted to a rich black.

► **What is my intended use for the color server?** As we've previously discussed, color servers are well-suited to repurposing and proofing. They can also make separations in high-volume workflows in which the separation is subsequently checked by a skilled operator. The lack of per-image rendering intent or source profile control may be acceptable in some workflows and not in others.

Prepress Solutions

Prepress solutions are proprietary modules that fit into an existing prepress workflow, such as Creo Prinergy or the Rampage System made by Rampage, Inc. Their features vary widely—some only offer color-management capability as an extra-cost add-on; others have very limited color-management functionality. While they vary in their capabilities, these types of solutions generally share two common characteristics:

► The workflows into which they integrate are inherently late-binding. Conversions happen at the prepress stage, immediately prior to printing, rather than at the design or customer approval stages. You can't get much later than that.

► The solutions are proprietary. In contrast to color servers, which are designed to work with practically anything that has a profile, integrated prepress solutions work only in the specific prepress workflow system for which they were designed.

DeviceLink Profiles

DeviceLink profiles are one of the seven profile classes defined by the ICC specification. A DeviceLink doesn't describe a device—instead, it's a concatenation of two or more profiles that act as source and destination, and trigger a conversion. They're an automation feature, which is why we cover them in this chapter. Three things make them different from the device profiles we've discussed throughout this book:

▶ They're an apparent exception to the rule that you need at least two profiles to make a conversion happen. Well, you need at least two *device* profiles to make a conversion happen—devicelinks aren't device profiles (and they always contain at least two device profiles).

▶ There's no PCS in most devicelink profiles. The source and destination tables both contain device values, so the conversions are directly from RGB to CMYK, or CMYK to CMYK, depending on the profiles concatenated into the single devicelink. (The PCS is involved in the initial joining of the two profiles, but once the DeviceLink is built, the PCS has played its role.) Devicelinks are always unidirectional—conversions are only from the profile that was originally defined as the source to the profile that was originally

defined as the destination at the time the device link was created.

▶ You can't embed them into images. They don't describe a single color space, but a hardwired conversion from one set of device values to another, so there's no point in embedding them.

Why use devicelinks? Normal profile-to-profile conversions sometimes do things we don't want. For example, we usually want 100% black (C0 M0 Y0 K100) to stay 100% black, but CMYK conversions through the PCS always turn the four original channels into three before turning them back into four, so there's just no way they can preserve black-only text. It turns into a rich black, with the attendant registration headaches, instead. A devicelink lets you force the conversion to 100% black.

For generating devicelink profiles, our favorite tool is *Art Link-o-lator*, by Left Dakota Inc. (www.leftdakota.com), because it offers controls and options we haven't found anywhere else. Two features are particularly valuable:

▶ You can build in black point compensation, so you get a devicelink profile that simulates a profile-to-profile conversion using Adobe's proprietary black point compensation (see "Black

Point Compensation" in Chapter 12, *The Adobe Common Color Architecture*. For non-Adobe products, it's the *only* way to get conversions using black point compensation.

▶ You can specify black channel preservation *with scaling*. Most products offering black channel preservation do only that, preserving the black channel exactly so the pre-conversion and post-conversion black is identical.

This is rarely useful, because the source and destination devices often have different black dot gains. Black channel scaling preserves the black channel tone reproduction while compensating for the dot gain difference, so you still get a black-only drop shadow when you repurpose CMYK images, but the tonal characteristics of the black channel are preserved.

Finally, how do you use these darn things? None of the major color-managed applications discussed in this book support devicelink profiles. While long in the tooth, Apple's free ColorSync Plug-ins for Photoshop provide support for devicelinks on import and export, but most of the time devicelink profiles belong in RIPs, in color servers, and in prepress equipment that explicitly supports them.

Who Should Consider Prepress Solutions?

These products plug into complex and expensive prepress workflow systems that cost tens or even hundreds of thousands of dollars, and critiquing such systems is well beyond the scope of this book. If you're an individual or a small shop, and such workflow systems are something you neither want nor need, the only reason to read this section is to gain some insight into the kinds of things that happen to your job once you submit it.

This discussion deals solely with the pros and cons of the color-management aspects of the products, and its only purpose is to help you decide whether you'd be better served by a proprietary color-management module for your existing (or intended) workflow system or an open color-management solution. The trade-off is typically one between convenience and cost. A proprietary color-management module offers the convenience of seamless integration into your workflow system and one-stop shopping for service and support, but you can expect to pay a hefty price for something that more or less replicates the standard color-management features found in desktop applications. That said, prepress solutions can help in several situations.

Effective late-binding workflow solutions. For workflows where the intended output is unknown during the design process, products in this category offer per-object source profiles and per-object rendering intent control, so that you can prepare the content for separation without actually knowing the destination. Once the destination becomes known, everything is ready to create final separations. In lower volume workflows, you can color manage the content in QuarkXPress at print time, but that's less practical in high-volume workflows that rely on high-end prepress solutions.

Hard proofing. Some of the products in this category offer explicit inkjet printer support. Enabling color management can turn an inkjet with a sufficiently large gamut into a proofing device.

Postflight normalization. If preflight rejects a submitted job solely because contains a few RGB images, the workflow system can assign appropriate source and destination profiles, and convert those silly RGB images into CMYK. This is much more efficient than the traditional alternatives, which are either to reject the job, or to have someone open the images in Photoshop, convert them, update the placed images in the page-layout application, then output another PostScript file....

Solid color substitution. Prepress systems can often parse the PostScript to find instances of solid-to-process Pantone or Focoltone color conversions. When it finds them, it can substiture your custom hand-tuned CMYK equivalents, so you get the best possible simulation of solid colors, no matter which application originally specified them.

The Downsides

You need to judge the downsides to these solutions in the larger context of the entire workflow system, of which the color-management component may be a relatively tiny part.

Price. None of the vendors we've spoken to are willing to quote exact prices because "they vary" depending on the particular workflow bundle. That said, while pricing covers a fairly wide range, the approximate number we keep seeing "thrown out there" is $5,000, which sounds like a hefty chunk of change to replicate what boils down to the basic desktop color-management features.

With growing demand, we predict that color-management capabilities will become standard in future prepress solutions, but for now, they often cost extra. The best piece of advice we can offer you is to be a savvy consumer—ask lots of questions, and see demos (including ones with typical, and maybe a few atypical, jobs) to see just what they'll buy you.

Training. The challenge with closed proprietary systems is finding people who can train you how to use them and integrate them into your specific workflow. The few people who are really knowledgeable about integrating color management into proprietary workflow products tend to command top dollar.

Examples

The two products presented here typify the potential differences in this class of product and illustrate the need for careful research. Color-management support is available in Xinet, Rampage, and Apogee, among others. But the term "color-management support" means quite different things to different vendors. You need to dive in and find out what each one means.

Helios ImageServer and PDF Handshake. These are separate products, but are complementary in many workflows. ImageServer used to be called Helios EtherShare OPI, and is an image handler more than a prepress workflow solution. It combines OPI and color-management features, so it can change image size, resolution, and compression, in addition to doing color management. Unique features we like about this product include:

▶ **Print queue support.** In Helios ImageServer, configured print queues appear as virtual priinters, so the user simply prints to the appropriate print queue—such as "Coated Stock #2" or, for a proofing queue, "Eps10K Mgl CS#2" (to denote an Epson 1000 using a Mitsubishi glossy coated paper, simulating the press using coated stock #2). Naming systems are workflow-specific—the point is that you can name the queue as whatever makes sense for your workflow and your people.

▶ **Remote proofing.** You can upload PDFs to PDF Handshake, which rasterizes and color manages it, then soft-proof the result in a Web browser on a suitably calibrated and profiled display. Note, however, that PDF Handshake honors embedded profiles in all content, both bitmap and vector. For bitmaps, PDF Handshake lets you remove or reassign profiles in bitmaps when you don't want to use the embedded one, but for text and vector content, you'd need to use something like PitStop Pro or Server.

Creo Prinergy. Prinergy is a full-blown prepress workflow system that's similar to Scitex Brisque, except that it's PDF-based, so everything that goes into Prinergy is in PDF format. Prinergy offers two levels of color-management support:

▶ **Standard.** The standard level sees and uses the embedded profiles for each object in the PDF as source profiles, and converts them to one hardwired SWOP-based destination profile. If you're satisfied with a workflow that converts from the embedded source profiles to a SWOP destination, the standard level of color management is all you need.

▶ **Advanced.** The advanced color-management license lets you override or assign source profiles for each object in the PDF, and select a custom profile for the destination. It supports not only CMYK, but up to eight-channel ICC output device profiles, so you can use it to make Hi-Fi separations. It also supports DeviceLink profiles, black preservation, and proofing.

Prinergy can perform color-management tasks (embed, change embedded, or convert) when the job is first brought into the workflow, or at any time thereafter, but proofing conversions happen only when you generate the output stream to the proofer, so it doesn't create a separate proofing file. You select the job, the proofing device, and the proofing profile, then the job is converted so that the proofer simulates the selected destination (the press or a contract proofing system). If your proofing system does its own color management, and you prefer it, you can submit the job for proofing as final press CMYK without specifying a proofer profile, so that you don't end up with double color management.

Important Questions

If you're contemplating introducing such a product into your workflow, here are some of the questions we think are critical:

▶ **Does the product support black preservation?** It's almost always a problem when 100% black-only text and drop shadows get converted to rich black, or when your carefully crafted black channel vanishes because it gets converted to LAB, then reseparated. This always happens when you use color management for repurposing (CMYK-to-CMYK) conversions.

▶ **Does the product support black scaling?** A black channel for a low-quality uncoated stock won't give good results when the job is repurposed for a higher-quality coated stock if the black channel is simply preserved. What's really needed is to preserve the tone reproduction curve of the black channel, not the original numeric values. For this, you need a scaling function for the black channel to compensate for the differences in dot gain between the source and destination devices. If the product you're looking at doesn't have this feature, and you think you need it, see if it supports devicelink profiles instead (see the sidebar, "DeviceLink Profiles," earlier in this chapter).

▶ **Can automatic RGB-to-CMYK conversions give me the quality I need?** This is something you can test without buying or upgrading existing equipment. Profile conversions are made with no knowledge of the image content—they're one-size-fits-all, treating a picture of a black cat in a coal cellar exactly the same way as a picture of a polar bear in the snow. With good profiles, you may be able to create acceptable separations without any intelligent human intervention, but premium-quality work usually needs image optimization either before or after separation. You need to look at the work you do, and test the quality of your automatic profile-to-profile conversions, before you can answer this question.

In-RIP Color Management

In-RIP color management is most commonly used for proofing, because the total lack of control inherent in in-RIP separations usually doesn't work in other workflows. It occurs in three different ways:

▶ **Front-end.** The conversions are done before the PostScript is interpreted. This is like having an integrated color server in your RIP product, and is most common in proofing products such as the BestColor RIP. You can treat bitmap and vector objects separately, and automatically replace solid Pantone colors with process CMYK equivalents.

▶ **Back-end.** The PostScript is interpreted, creating a rasterized page image which is then color-managed and sent to the output device. Since there's only one raster object, there can be only one source and one destination. This approach is usually adequate for basic proofing needs—an example is the now-orphaned Adobe PressReady.

▶ **In-RIP.** This is literally in-RIP conversion—color management is performed by the PostScript interpreter as part of the PostScript interpretation process. The two flavors are PostScript color management and ICC-based in-RIP color management. In theory, any PostScript level 2 RIP at version 2017.xxx or higher supports PostScript color management, but in practice, workable PostScript color management is rarer than hen's teeth. Global Graphics' Harlequin RIP has an ICC option that literally builds an ICC-based color-management engine into the RIP, so it uses regular ICC profiles to perform the conversions.

The Good

We're generally not fond of solutions that rely on sending our jobs into a mysterious black box, but proofing is a simple enough and unambiguous enough conversion—from output CMYK to proofer CMYK or RGB via absolute colorimetric rendering—that it's an exception to our general rule. The main advantage it confers is simplicity—you simply send the final output files to the proofer, and the RIP takes care of the necessary conversion.

The Bad (and The Ugly)

In-RIP separations *do* involve sending your data into a mysterious black box, and hoping that the mysterious black box does the right thing. In-RIP separations tend to rely on assumed source profiles and rendering intents—there's no consistent or reliable mechanism for specifying custom, per-object source profiles and rendering intents.

InDesign 2 does provide a consistent mechanism for creating Post-Script source profiles for each object (Color Space Arrays, also called CSAs), and PostScript destination profiles with the proper rendering intent for each object (Color Rendering Dictionaries, also called CRDs). But you need a RIP that consistently uses them. Some RIPs ignore CSAs and CRDs entirely, others honor RGB CSAs and ignore CMYK CSAs, and some use CSAs but ignore downloaded CRDs and use only the RIP's built-in CRD. If you're tenacious enough or lucky enough to sort through the mess and create a functioning system for anything more complex than basic proofing conversions, we take our hats off to you—and as we mentioned elsewhere, maybe you should write a book!

Scripting

We sometimes find it strange that smart people who use computers every day to carry out tasks of great complexity simply glaze over as soon as the word "scripting" is mentioned. If pressed, we'd have to confess that we often number ourselves among those smart people—we're far from being scripting mavens, but we often use simple scripts, and we've seen what the more complex ones can do.

Scripting can save enormous amounts of time and eliminate equally enormous amounts of mind-numbing drudgery. But making it do so demands a hefty initial investment of time and energy.

What is Scripting?

Scripting is the act of writing a script in a language like AppleScript, JavaScript, or Visual Basic, that makes the computer do useful things. As such, it's a bit like programming in the way parking a car is a bit like landing the Space Shuttle—both require attention to detail and skills that you have to learn, but one requires attention to a lot more details, and learning a lot more skills, than the other.

Writing scripts is a great deal simpler than writing code, but it *does* require you to learn a scripting language, and while scripting language resembles natural human language much more than programming languages do, it's not by any stretch of the imagination natural human language.

What Can Scripting Do?

Scripting can do almost anything you can imagine. It lets you leverage existing applications—for example, Photoshop 7 offers extensive JavaScript support, and almost anything you can do in Photoshop can be JavaScripted. You can also write scripts that automate the communication *between* applications—for example, an AppleScript could pass off images to Photoshop, have it run a JavaScript to resize, rotate, and color manage them, and then pass them onto QuarkXPress for automated layout. The possibilities are nearly endless.

Scripting Advantages

One of the biggest advantages that scripting has over other automation tools is that it's essentially free—the tools for scripting are already built into your operating system. (Of course, your time is probably worth something too.) But scripting offers other advantages—here are the ones we find most compelling.

Customizability. Perhaps the biggest benefit of scripting is that it can automate almost any custom task as long as you can break it down into manageable chunks. Some scripting languages and tools—such as AppleScript with AppleScript Studio, and VisualBasic—let you create actual standalone applications, including a user interface to prompt the user for information or to provide status report feedback.

Leveraging existing applications. With AppleScript, you can leverage the unique capabilities of existing applications as well as existing scripts. For example, you can create a script that launches Photoshop, asks it to open a folder full of images, embed a profile, then resave the image in a different format.

You can do many of the same kinds of automation using Photoshop's Actions, but Actions don't allow conditionals, while scripts do. If you simply use an Action to embed a profile in a folder full of images, it will fail if the folder contains images in different modes; with a script, you can make Photoshop run a different action to embed the appropriate profile in RGB and CMYK images.

Speed. By eliminating unnecessary human interaction, you can drastically reduce the total time from beginning to completion. We've seen advanced, moderately complex scripts cut task time from 30–45 minutes down to 1–2 minutes.

Scripting Disadvantages

The only real disadvantage to scripting is that you have to learn to do it, and complex scripting seems to require a certain mindset that some people have and others simply have not. You can't buy scripts off-the-shelf the way you can other automation products, though the Macintosh platform supplies some handy scripts that automate simple color-management tasks. On Mac OS 9, they're in the Apple Extras:ColorSync Extras:AppleScripts folder; on Mac OS X, they're in the /Library/ColorSync /Scripts folder.

Learning the scripting language is only one part of the challenge. While you can eventually save time using custom scripts to automate common tasks, the development, testing, and debugging time is often quite lengthy.

Scripting Examples

The three scripting methods that we've selected—Photoshop Actions, JavaScript, and AppleScript—certainly aren't the only ones, but they're the most widely supported, and probably the most widely used. Photoshop Actions are mostly cross-platform, JavaScripts are almost completely cross-platform, while AppleScript is only available on Mac OS.

Our example scripts show what it takes to make all three scripting methods assign a profile to an image (ColorMatch RGB), convert it to U.S. Sheetfed Coated v2, and then save it with U.S. Sheetfed Coated v2 embedded. These scripts were provided courtesy of Nathan Wade, who can be reached at nwade@nwade.org (in case you'd like to hire him instead of learning scripting yourself).

Photoshop Actions are by far the easiest of the three—if you can do it with your mouse in Photoshop, you can probably record it as an Action. Then you can either run it manually, make it into a droplet, or use it with the Automate:Batch command. Photoshop Actions are largely cross-platform—the main problem area is file and folder navigation, which uses somewhat different syntax on each platform (see Figure 17-3).

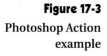

Figure 17-3

Photoshop Action example

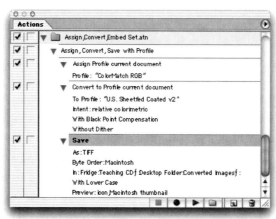

Photoshop also supports JavaScript, which has more cross-platform capability than Actions, but demands that you know something about JavaScript. If you can do it with the mouse, you can do it with JavaScript, and even you can't do it with the mouse, you might *still* be able to do it with JavaScript. See Figure 17-4 for the JavaScript version of our scripting example—it does the same thing as the Photoshop Action.

Figure 17-4

JavaScript example

```
if ( documents.length > 0 )
{
        try
        {
            var docRef = activeDocument;
        var cmykProfileName = "U.S. Sheetfed Coated v2";
            docRef.colorProfileName = "ColorMatch RGB";
docRef.convertProfile( cmykProfileName,
Intent.RELATIVECOLORIMETRIC,
true, false );
        alert( "Your document has been converted
from ColorMatch RGB to U.S.Sheetfed Coated v2,
using Relative Colorimetric Intent, Black Point
Compensation, and No Dither. — The file will now
be saved with embedded profile." )
            docRef.save();
        }
        catch( e )
        {
            // An error occurred.
            throw e;
        }
        // Everything went Ok.
}
else
{
        alert( "You must have a document open to
add the filename!" );
}
```

Last, but not least, is AppleScript. AppleScript is unique in that it can not only access ColorSync directly and do transformations on supported image types, but it can also drive scriptable applications. A single AppleScript can ask Photoshop to do a series of tasks—even ask it to run a pre-written JavaScript—and then forward the processed files to QuarkXPress or InDesign for automatic formatting and layout.

AppleScript Studio, new in Mac OS X, is an AppleScript development application that lets suitably motivated individuals create full-blown applications with an actual user interface. AppleScripts in Mac OS X can also access UNIX command-line scripts, and make XML-RPC calls and SOAP requests for remote procedures over the Internet. Very cool stuff for those that understand it.

In the AppleScript example we've included, you'll first notice it's a lot longer, because AppleScript assumes nothing. You have to teach it pretty much everything, including the fact you want to open an image. While you need to be a lot more specific and detailed when using AppleScript, it lets you do things that would otherwise only be possible if you became a programmer (see Figure 17-5).

Figure 17-5

AppleScript example

```
on run
        display dialog "Assign the default RGB
        Profile to an image, Convert to the default CMYK
        Profile, and Save with Profile Embedded. Modify
        the script to embed another profile instead."
        set somefile to choose file with prompt "Choose an
image"
        open somefile
end run
on open draggeditems
        tell application "ColorSyncScripting" to launch
        display dialog "Assign the default RGB
        Profile, Convert to default CMYK Profile, and
        Save with Embedded Profile?"

        set sourcefiles to
        filelistFromSelection(draggeditems)
        repeat with thisFile in sourcefiles
           tell application "Finder" to reveal item
           thisFile
           set thisFile to thisFile as alias
           tell application "ColorSyncScripting"
                   set sourceProf to default RGB profile
                   set matchProf to default CMYK profile
                   try
                           match thisFile from source
                           sourceProf to destination
                           matchProf matching with relative
                           colorimetric intent using quality
                           best
```

Figure 17-5

AppleScript example,
continued

```
                                   on error errmsg
                                      activate
                                      display dialog errmsg
                               end try
                       end tell
               end repeat


               tell application "ColorSyncScripting" to set quit
               delay to 5
       end open
       —returns dragged files OR files at first level of one dragged
       folder
       on filelistFromSelection(theselection)
               set hasfolder to false
               tell application "Finder"
                   repeat with thisItem in (theselection as list)
                           if (class of item thisItem is folder) or
                           (class of item thisItem is disk) then
                                   set hasfolder to true
                           end if
                   end repeat
               end tell
               if ((count item of (theselection as list)) > 1)
       and hasfolder then
                       display dialog "Drag multiple files or a single
                       folder." buttons {"OK"} default button 1
                   return ""
               end if
               tell application "Finder"
                   if hasfolder then
                           set filelist to (every item of folder
                           (item 1 of (theselection as list))) as
                           alias list
                   else
                           set filelist to (theselection as list)
                   end if
               end tell
               return filelist
       end filelistFromSelection
```

The Automation Trade-Off

The trade-off inherent in automation is that you gain efficiency at the expense of control over individual elements. It's up to you to decide where that trade-off needs to lie in your workflow, but a good rule of thumb is that if you find yourself doing exactly the same task over and over again, it's a good candidate for automation. The kind of automation you choose will depend on your workflow, your budget, and your skills, but it's always a good idea to keep your eyes open for aspects of your work that cry out for automation. When you think about it, you probably have more computing power on your desktop than NASA had in its entire organization when it launched the Voyager program. If that power can free you from repetitive drudgery, why not let it?

18

Building Color-Managed Workflows

Bringing It All Together

And so we come to the end of our color management odyssey. You've learned all about the many and varied ways our eyes interact with photons to produce the sensation we call color; how we use colorants such as inks, filters, and phosphors to make our color-reproduction devices emit or reflect photons that we interpret as color; and how we use profiles and CMMs to control these colorants so that we have a better chance of seeing the color we want. We've also told you repeatedly that color management does only two things—if you can't remember what they are, you aren't ready for this chapter!

More importantly, we hope you now realize that color management is part of a bigger picture. It's more than just making or using ICC profiles—it requires calibration, process control, collecting good measurement data, understanding application and driver settings, and above all, bringing all these together into a coherent workflow.

We've tried to give you the insights and the vocabulary you need to think critically about color management, to understand the hidden meaning behind the often-abstruse menu commands and dialog boxes that you encounter in your applications and device drivers, and to break down the color-management operations those menu commands and dialog boxes control into their component parts.

Why? Because in this chapter, we'll show you how to bring all this knowledge together to build a color-management workflow that suits your unique requirements.

We can't possibly spell out every possible color-management workflow, because there are probably as many workflows as there are practitioners. We don't want to simply tell you which buttons to push—because for one thing, you won't really learn anything except for a rote set of steps, and for another, as soon as you've learned the steps, one or another vendor will rename, move, or change the functionality of the buttons, leaving you back at square one.

Instead, we'll show you how to break a workflow down into its essential components, step you through the questions you need to ask, and show you the possible strategies to use in building your workflow. We will, of course, include some examples, but you should take them as illustrations of the possibilities rather than hard-and-fast rules.

The Four Stages of Color Management

All color-management workflows can be broken down into four basic steps, and understanding these steps is the key to analyzing, and then meeting, your needs. The basic steps are:

▶ Defining color meaning—specifying just what colors your RGB and CMYK numbers represent, or collecting LAB measurements of colors that you'll eventually translate into RGB or CMYK.

▶ Normalizing color—bringing all your color elements into a common color space. This step is optional, but most workflows benefit from the simplicity it brings.

▶ Converting for output—producing the set of numbers that will make your final output device(s) produce the desired color appearance.

▶ Proofing—making sure that your final output will, in fact, have the desired color appearance.

Let's examine these steps in detail.

Defining Color Meaning

You can't match a color until you know what that color is, so the first step in a color-management workflow is always to attach a specific color meaning to the document or object. Just how you accomplish that, and which color meaning you attach, depends on the nature of the document and its source.

Profiled captures. Profiled captures are pretty straightforward. If the capture device driver can embed the capture profile, allow it to do so. If it can't, you must assign the profile manually, either in an editing application (such as Photoshop) or using automation (such as AppleScript).

Unprofiled captures. Unprofiled captures are trickier. You have to decide on a color appearance, perhaps arbitrarily. Typically, you'll either assign a profile that produces something close to the desired appearance, or just assign an editing space. In the first case, you should convert to an intermediate editing space, and in either case, you'll probably color-correct the document—see "Workflow Into and Out of a Color-Managed Environment" in Chapter 10, *Color-Management Workflow*.

Unprofiled legacy images. Unprofiled legacy images present similar challenges to unprofiled captures. With RGB images, there's a good chance that a monitor-based profile such as Colormatch RGB (gamma 1.8) or sRGB (gamma 2.2) will produce close to the desired appearance, since they're almost certainly based on monitor appearance (see "When Color Management Starts" in Chapter 10, *Color-Management Workflow*).

With CMYK images, our philosophy is that when the CMYK destination is known, you should simply assign that CMYK profile and edit as necessary—if the CMYK destination is unknown, you have no business working in CMYK in the first place. In desperate situations, though, we may try assigning different CMYK profiles, then convert to *our* CMYK space.

Vector art. Some vector art applications insist that all the content in a document must be either RGB or CMYK, though you can force them to accept imported graphics in the other mode. In the case of legacy vector art files, you have two options:

▶ If you know the new destination, make it the source profile, and rework the file.

▶ If you know the original destination, make it the source profile, then repurpose the file (either by converting at print time in a desktop application, or using automation).

In the case of new vector art files, you have three options:

▶ Work in RGB using the same space you use in your other applications, but realize many of the colors in this space won't exist in the final output space. Take advantage of soft-proofing to a generic CMYK space (such as SWOP) to get a general idea of such limitations.

▶ Work in the widest-gamut device space in which the artwork could possibly be used, and the one with which you're most familiar.

▶ If the destination is known, assign that profile, and work in that space.

Spot colors. Spot colors probably cause more trouble than any other type of color element. First, unless the color will actually be printed as a spot color, it makes little or no sense to choose a spot color from one of the many Pantone or Focoltone libraries, because many of these colors simply aren't reproducible by CMYK printing—yet a depressingly large number of people continue to do so, with accompanying disappointment when the job hits production. Second, the published CMYK values in the various solid-to-process color guides are only valid for the printing process that was used to print the guides—if you use these values in *your* job, the resulting color may bear little resemblance to the intended one.

Currently, only the non-process Pantone libraries in Photoshop 7 use LAB—they automatically produce custom RGB and CMYK values based on the active document's profile. All other applications use libraries containing RGB values for on-screen display, and CMYK ones for print (see Chapter 15, *Color Management in QuarkXPress*, and Chapter 17, *Automation & Scripting* for suggestions on how to deal with solid-to-process).

Normalizing Color

Once you've defined all your color, you may well find that you have a raft of profiles—several different capture devices, a default RGB and a default CMYK profile in each application, and possibly some legacy CMYK profiles. It's conceptually possible, and even, with some difficulty, practically possible to carry these profiles through the workflow to final output—but your life will be made a great deal easier if you *normalize* all your color by converting it to a single space, or, more practically, to a single RGB and a single CMYK space.

Normalizing your color simplifies your life in two ways:

▶ It frees you from having to deal with profile mismatch warnings in all stages of production except the initial ones.

▶ It lets you rely on assumed profiles. Even if you prefer to embed profiles, most vector applications don't embed profiles in EPS files, so they force you to rely on assumptions. Normalizing your color makes it much more likely that the default assumed profiles will be the correct ones.

In addition, most RGB capture spaces don't work particularly well as editing spaces since they're typically neither perceptually uniform nor gray-balanced. So for all these reasons, we recommend that you normalize your color as soon as is practical.

Standardize defaults. All color-managed applications let you set default profiles for RGB and CMYK. Your sanity will be much less endangered if you make sure that all *your* color-managed applications use the *same* default profile for RGB and CMYK. Even if you're fanatical about embedding profiles, the occasional untagged file may slip through, and as noted above, vector EPS files often don't contain embedded profiles. If you normalize all your color by converting to a single RGB and a single CMYK, and then set your defaults to these same profiles, your workflow will be much more robust than if you fail to do either.

When to normalize. In the vast majority of cases, we recommend normalizing RGB color as soon as your applications will allow you to do so. Ad and marketing agencies can normalize stock photography to the desired RGB intermediate space early in the design process, and ask photographers to supply files in the same space.

Prepress and printing shops already have dedicated preflighting, and can include normalization as a part of it. Typically, prepress shops will normalize everything to CMYK, converting RGB content to CMYK and repurposing CMYK content when the source is different from the intended destination. Converting RGB content to CMYK before the CMYK destination is known isn't normalizing—it's premature binding (see the sidebar, "Premature Binding," in Chapter 10, *Color-Management Workflow*)—and is an idiocy we'd like to see stamped out!

The one exception is black-only text. For example, both InDesign and QuarkXPress don't exclude black-only text from color management—in InDesign, it's in Document CMYK, and in QuarkXPress it uses the CMYK Default Source Profile for Solid Colors. If these sources aren't identical to the destination profile used on output, you'll get rich black text, and registration headaches on press. We'd like to see vendors treat black text by default as device-dependent, and untouchable by color management.

Converting for Output

At some point, you need to convert your color to the final output space. The question is, when? Obviously, you can't convert to the output space until you know what that output space is. Once you know, two issues bear on the decision of when to convert.

One output or many? If you're going to a single output process, the question of when to convert essentially boils down to the trade-off between seeing and editing your color in final output space, and working with smaller, more agile RGB files. If you find that automated conversions in a color server, or even in the RIP itself, give you acceptable results, you can achieve significant productivity gains by working entirely in RGB and adopting a late-binding workflow. The downside is that you don't see the separations until they're on press.

If you have multiple output destinations, the question then becomes, do you prepare separate files for each output scenario, or do you rely on late-binding separations? The issues are confidence and quality. If you're confident that you can obtain usable results from automatic separations, a late-binding workflow where final separations happen in a color server or RIP may make sense.

Editing in output space. Our experience has taught us that for the ultimate in quality, you need to make final edits in the output space. Automated conversions can get you in the ballpark, but they only know about color spaces, not about the colors in the actual document. Hence they treat all content identically, ignoring the kinds of perceptual issues we raised all the way back in Chapter 1 (see "Where the Models Fail" in Chapter 1, *What Is Color?*), and so they sometimes produce results that fall short of ideal. If you need to edit color in the final output space, you need to make separate files for each output scenario.

You can, however, edit in an RGB working space while looking at a simulation of the final output, which in many cases is almost as good as editing in final output space (see "Soft-proofing," below). But if you need to make different edits for different outputs, you'll need to make separate files for each output.

Proofing

You can't, obviously, proof your color until you know the final destination. But you can proof your color before converting it to the final output space.

Soft-proofing. Most color-managed applications let you view a simulation of final output while you're working on files in some other space—for example, previewing CMYK output while working in RGB (see the sidebar, "Soft-Proofing Basics," in Chapter 10, *Color-Management Workflow*). While some types of edits, such as tweaks to the black plate, can only be made in CMYK, you can easily make many other kinds of optimization for tone and color on an RGB file prior to conversion, using an accurate display simulation as a guide.

Hard proofing. The majority of color-managed applications let you print a simulation of your final output to a composite printer, even if you haven't yet converted to final output. We don't recommend using prints made in this fashion as contract proofs, even if you can get the other party to agree to them, but they can be helpful in cutting the number of contract proofs you eventually need down to a single set. In a multiple-output scenario, this feature is particularly useful, because you can proof the different outputs before converting to final output from the same master file by simply changing the final output profile.

More-sophisticated proofing systems let you send the final output data to the proofer, and either perform an internal conversion in the RIP or color server, or configure the hardware to emulate the final output. In either case, you can make your color-managed application perform the conversion to final output space as part of the print process—so again, when dealing with multiple output scenarios, you can proof each one from the same master file by simply changing the final output profile.

Step-by-Step Color Management

The breakdown of color management that we've presented above should help you conceptualize the necessary steps in the workflow, from color capture or specification, through editing, to proofing and final output. The next stage in building a workflow is figuring out just what you need it to do.

Determining Your Needs

At the beginning of this chapter, we pointed out that there are probably as many color-management workflows as there are practitioners. We can't possibly spell out all possible workflows in detail. Instead, we'll step you through the questions you need to answer to determine your specific workflow needs.

Software, File Formats, and Devices

The first set of questions deal with the software and hardware you use to do your work. Ask yourself the following:

▶ Which applications will I use?

▶ What file formats will I need to support?

▶ What devices will I use to capture and reproduce color?

Applications. Your workflow options depend on the capabilities of the applications you use. Some applications let you attach a different profile to each element in a job, some are limited to a single RGB and a single CMYK profile, and some force you to normalize all your color into a single profile's space.

If you're working with a single application, the choices are relatively straightforward, but if you're working with multiple applications, you need to make sure that your workflow accommodates them all—and that almost invariably means making sure that the workflow can handle the most limited application of the set.

File formats. TIFF, JPEG, and PDF have robust support for embedded profiles, though you need to be vigilant for applications that either fail to detect embedded profiles or use them incorrectly. EPS and DCS EPS, however, are much less reliable in terms of profile embedding.

You need to figure out which parts of your workflow can rely on embedded profiles, and which parts must rely on assumed profiles. Then you need to make sure that you have appropriate safeguards in place to make sure that the *correct* profiles are assumed.

Devices. Capture devices vary widely in their ability to handle and embed profiles. Can your input devices, or their drivers, embed profiles correctly, or do you need to assign them manually? Can they convert the captures into an intermediate space and produce normalized captures, or do you need to handle normalization elsewhere?

Proofing devices also vary in their capabilities. In theory, you can use any device whose gamut wholly contains the gamut of the final output as a proofer. The question is whether you can configure the proofer to accept final output data (as you can with a proofing RIP or color server), or whether you need to rely on application-level color management to send a simulation of final output to the proofer.

What Outputs Do I Need?

Your output needs may vary from a single output that's known before you start the job, to multiple outputs that may be unknown until the last minute, or may even be unknown until after you've submitted the job. The issue is when to convert to final output space. You can't do that until you know what the final output is.

Known output. If you know the output right from the start, and you're dealing with a single output process, an early-binding workflow, where everything is converted to output space early in the process, makes a great deal of sense, particularly if you have to interact with outside providers who aren't color-management savvy.

If you have to deal with multiple known outputs, things become a little more complex. Early binding keeps things simple, but increases the workload because you have to prepare separate documents for each output process.

One possible solution is to keep images and critical vector color in RGB until it's time to generate final output, while defining black text and noncritical native color elements in CMYK, then assign the final output profile when you generate final output. You may have to tweak some CMYK color builds, but your black-only elements such as text stay black-only, and your imported RGB elements get separated to final CMYK when you create the final output file.

Unknown output. If you have to prepare files for unknown outputs, you'll almost certainly find that the political issues outweigh the technical ones. From a technical standpoint, the best solution is to submit the job in a device-independent form such as profiled RGB color, or even LAB. In the real world, though, the chances of such a job getting processed correctly after it's left your hands are uncertain at best. If you can obtain a signed contract stating unambiguously that the downstream operation will accept files in a specified, named RGB space (or in LAB), and will take full responsibility for the color from then on, by all means submit profiled RGB or LAB. Absent such a contract, you're almost certainly inviting trouble.

Often, you'll be forced into a premature-binding workflow instead (see the sidebar, "Premature Binding," in Chapter 10, *Color-Management Workflow*). From a color-management standpoint, such workflows make no sense, but we do have to live in the real world, which of course doesn't always make sense. If you're stuck in a situation like this, we offer the following suggestions:

▶ Specify a contract proofing system, such as Kodak Approval or Fuji ColorArt, by name, then separate for the proofing system and submit proofer CMYK along with the hard-copy proofs created from the CMYK data.

▶ Obtain as much information as possible about the output—type of press, coated or uncoated stock, anticipated dot gain—and choose a generic profile that approximates those conditions. The press profiles that accompany Adobe Photoshop, Illustrator, and InDesign, for example, are fairly "safe," but the more you know about the printing process, the better your chances of picking an appropriate profile.

▶ Absent any better information, use Adobe's SWOP Coated v2 profile (or, if you know that the job will be printed on uncoated stock, the SWOP Uncoated v2 profile). The results may not be ideal, but they should be usable.

If you have to deal with multiple unknown outputs, the first and last of the three suggestions above are equally applicable. The unknown is the unknown, whether it's one or many—the best you can do is to provide a file that's approximately suitable for printing, preferably accompanied by hard-copy proofs that indicate your intentions clearly.

Automation and Quality

Automation can save a great deal of time and effort. But automated processes are dumber than the dumbest person you've ever had to deal with—we hold firm to the view that the acronym "AI" stands for Applied Ignorance rather than Artificial Intelligence!

Automated color management knows nothing about images, nothing about color context, nothing about memory colors. It simply performs one-size-fits-all operations, one pixel at a time, and it has no means of evaluating its own results. Automation does the same thing every time.

What you can automate. Good candidates for automation include things like normalizing profiled RGB captures to a single RGB editing space. For example, if all your image sources embed profiles, you can safely set Photoshop's Color Management Policy for RGB color to "Convert to Working RGB." Then, whenever Photoshop encounters an image whose embedded profile is different from the working RGB space, it converts it from the embedded profile space to working RGB.

The downside, of course, is that Photoshop has no way of knowing whether or not the embedded profile is the correct one—it just blithely goes ahead and makes the conversion. So if you also receive imagery from sources that don't embed profiles correctly, the automation may produce a bad result, creating work instead of eliminating it.

Automated output conversions can often work well, but again, they treat all color identically. So you'll get good quality, but not as good as you'd get with a skilled operator optimizing each image. You can, however, create optimized solid-to-process conversions for solid colors, then apply them automatically using a color server or Praxisoft's VectorPro.

What you can't automate. You can't really automate anything requiring intelligent human intervention—optimizing images, choosing different outcomes on a case-by-case basis. That said, it's often worthwhile, albeit humbling, to compare totally automated results with those produced by your careful handwork. The questions you need to ask in making such a comparison are:

▶ Is there a discernible quality difference between the two?

▶ Can you make a business case for preserving that quality difference?

Once you've defined your needs, the last step in building your workflow is to look at the workflow tools that your applications and device drivers offer, and decide how best to employ them in the four stages of color management.

Workflow Tools

You understand the stages of color management, and you've determined what you need to produce. The last step is to look at the various tools your software and hardware offer, and decide how to apply them.

Embedded or Assumed Profiles

Color management workflows really only offer two ways to define color meaning, which is always accomplished by associating a profile with the document or object:

▶ Embedding a profile

▶ Assuming a profile.

Each approach has its pros and cons. Our very basic rule of thumb is that we generally embed profiles in RGB, and we generally assume profiles for CMYK. We always try to use CMYK as a final destination—CMYK-to-CMYK conversions do work, but they rarely give as good results as going back to the original RGB and reseparating—so we seldom need to deal with more than one flavor of CMYK at a time. That makes CMYK an ideal candidate for an assumed profile, since we know we have only one flavor of CMYK.

CMYK. We often make families of profiles for a given CMYK process, with different black generation characteristics. For example, we used three different profiles to create the CMYK in this book, with different black shapes, but we only used the different profiles to convert from RGB to CMYK. Once the content is converted to CMYK, the black generation used in the profile is no longer relevant.

In this kind of workflow, all the assumed CMYK profile does is attach a color meaning to the CMYK values by acting as a source profile. Any of the three profiles we created can do that equally well—its sole purpose is to provide a source profile for display simulations and hard-copy proofing.

CMYK profiles are also quite large—the ones we used for this book are 2.4 MB each—so embedding would mean we'd have to sling a lot more data around, and since all our CMYK is the same CMYK, much of that data would be redundant.

RGB. RGB matrix profiles, on the other hand, are tiny. We normalize our RGB color into an editing space as soon after capture as is practical, and editing space profiles are tiny, so we always embed them.

One key difference between embedded-profile workflows and assumed-profile workflows are that in the former, the color meaning is automatically attached to each element, while in the latter, the color meaning is applied manually by you, the user.

The other key difference is that, in an embedded-profile workflow, each element can have a different profile embedded, while in an assumed-profile workflow, you can generally have only one RGB and one CMYK profile. Therefore, the trick to making assumed profiles work is normalization—making sure that *all* your content is converted to just *one* flavor of RGB and just *one* flavor of CMYK before it enters the assumed-profile part of your workflow. Do that, and you can safely rely on assumed profiles. Fail to do so, and all bets are off!

Normalization and Editing Spaces

The case for normalizing CMYK in an individual job should be obvious—ultimately, it's all going to print using the same four CMYK inks on the same paper. The case for normalizing RGB is a little less so. Here are the main reasons we tend to do so:

▶ We prefer not to edit images in capture spaces because they're usually far from gray-balanced or perceptually uniform, so we convert to an intermediate editing space. That being the case, it usually makes sense to settle on a single intermediate editing space.

▶ Applications vary in their ability to handle embedded profiles correctly, QuarkXPress being an example of one that often does not. If we know that all our RGB is, for example, Adobe RGB (1998), we can set it as the default RGB. Then, even if an application fails to honor the embedded profile, we know that it will use the correct interpretation of RGB because it's the only interpretation available.

▶ It simplifies the workflow.

Some very quality-conscious workflows may need multiple RGB spaces: all editing spaces represent a series of trade-offs, and no single one can produce ideal results for all image sources and destinations—see "One Pixel's Journey …," later in this chapter, for an example. In most cases, though, the incremental gain from using multiple RGB spaces is outweighed by the increase in complexity that doing so brings.

Choosing an RGB space. Our main criterion when choosing an RGB space is that its gamut provides a reasonable match to the gamut of our intended output without wasting a lot of bits on color definitions that don't correspond to anything we can capture, reproduce, or possibly even see. This is always a trade-off.

Spaces defined by RGB primaries, white point, and tone curve all have a distinctive 3-D shape. An RGB space that completely encompasses the gamut of most CMYK outputs has to be very large indeed—so large that a lot of the color definitions it contains don't correspond to real colors. For example, in ProPhoto RGB (which is certainly large enough to encompass any output process we've experienced), R 0, G 0, B 255 corresponds in LAB to a blue that's fully saturated but has a luminance (L*) of zero! That doesn't correspond to anything we can see—all colors with a luminance of zero look the same to us, and they're black.

We use a variety of specialized editing spaces for different purposes, but our general recommendation is to start out with a single mainstream editing space such as Adobe RGB (1998) or Colormatch RGB, and stick with it unless and until you run into a specific limitation that another space can better address.

Some workflows avoid RGB altogether, and use LAB as the normalized space. Hardly anyone in the United States seems to use such a workflow, but they're quite popular in Europe, where Heidelberg has evangelized them for years (see the sidebar, "LAB—The Great Normalizer").

The Cop at the Door—Warnings

Some applications, notably the Big Three from Adobe—Photoshop, InDesign, and Illustrator—can be configured to warn you when they encounter color that hasn't been normalized—that is, it contains an embedded profile different from the one specified as the default, or in Adobe terminology, the "Working Space." You set this option by turning on the "Profile Mismatch: Ask When Opening" checkbox in the respective applications' Color Settings (see "Warnings—Manual Overrides" in Chapter 12, *The Adobe Common Color Architecture*). Unfortunately, no applications warn you when you *save* a file in a space other than the default.

Most other applications lack such features, so you have to develop your own procedures for checking and enforcing normalization, perhaps using scripting (see "Scripting" in Chapter 17, *Automation and Scripting*).

LAB—The Great Normalizer

LAB-based workflows may seem like a great idea—LAB is relatively unambiguous (you do need to specify white point and standard observer, but unless otherwise indicated, it's safe to assume D50 2-degree LAB), and by definition, it contains all colors. So why not simply use LAB until it's time to convert to output?

Well, if the output is known, and you deal with all your image optimization issues before you convert to LAB, a LAB workflow is just fine. Likewise, if you're willing to accept the gamut mappings you get from automated conversions, a LAB workflow is equally fine. But if you plan to optimize your color for different outputs, a

LAB workflow has the following disadvantages:

▶ Eight-bit-per-channel LAB files are fairly fragile things. Since LAB encoding has to cover the entire range of vision, the data points in LAB channels are stretched pretty far apart. So it's hard to make subtle edits on eight-bit-per-channel LAB files.

▶ Since LAB encoding has to contain all the colors we can see, it's also forced to contain many values that don't correspond to colors we can see. The estimates we've heard indicate that somewhere between five and seven million of the 16.8

million possible eight-bit-per-channel LAB values actually correspond to real colors, so encoded LAB contains a lot of values for which there are no real colors.

▶ LAB isn't the most intuitive space for editing or specifying colors.

▶ Many key applications and some key file formats don't support LAB.

If you understand the limitations and the requirements of LAB-based workflows, you can make them work, but they're quite specialized.

Black Preservation and Device-Dependent Data

One of our biggest reasons for avoiding CMYK-to-CMYK conversions is that K-only elements such as black text or black-only drop shadows almost always wind up being converted to a rich black that contains other inks besides black. This is almost never a desirable outcome since it introduces all kinds of registration problems on press.

The simplest solution for page-layout applications is to define all native elements in RGB so they can be repurposed, and to define black-only text and anything else for which you want specific CMYK values preserved in CMYK. Then ensure that their CMYK source profile is the same as the destination profile to prevent conversion.

Early-binding workflows don't usually have this problem, but late-binding workflows often do. There's no single ideal solution. For QuarkXPress users, Praxisoft's Compass Pro XT XTension lets you exempt 100% black-only objects from color conversions (see "Compass Pro XT" in Chapter 15, *Color Management in QuarkXPress*). For other users, server-based conversion products or devicelink profiles, both of which we discuss in Chapter 17, *Automation and Scripting*, provide possible solutions. Otherwise, you simply have to watch out, and assign the output profile manually to prevent any undesired conversion.

Named-Color Systems

Named-color systems such as Pantone and Focoltone present some special color-management problems. Some are technical—Pantone is noted for revising its libraries, so that different applications often wind up with different definitions of the same color. Some are human—users specify spot colors for process jobs, or specify the CMYK values from a spot-to-process swatchbook, failing to realize that the CMYK values provided may be totally inappropriate for the job at hand. Both cause trouble.

Libraries. Wherever possible, standardize your named-color libraries so that all your applications use the same definitions. Sometimes this isn't possible—applications tend to use proprietary formats for their color libraries—but it's always a good idea to check for updates, then apply those updates in a controlled fashion so that all your applications match.

The solid-to-process values for Pantone colors changed around May 2000 as a result of a change in the press behavior Pantone selected. The applications containing the post-May 2000 guide values are Photoshop 7,

InDesign 2, Illustrator 10, and QuarkXPress 5. FreeHand 10 and CorelDRAW 10 both use pre-May 2000 equivalents. Also, Illustrator 10 contains a series of Pantone colors with equivalents that would look wrong to the Three Blind Mice—the Illustrator 10.03 update fixes this problem on Windows, but Mac OS requires a separately downloadable Pantone update. All are available from Adobe's Web site.

However, we've found that we can almost always improve on profile-driven solid-color simulations by creating our own hand-tuned color builds. If accurate simulations of spot colors are very important in your workflow, consider one of the automated solutions for substituting hand-tuned color values for spot colors that we discussed in Chapter 17, *Automation and Scripting.*

Applications. Applications exchange named color through EPS or DCS. When you create artwork in an application, the CMYK equivalents defined in the libraries are included in the EPS file so that it can print on composite four-color devices. So artwork prepared with Illustrator 10 and Freehand 10 produce EPSs that contain different CMYK equivalents for the same Pantone color, and those are the values that get honored. Neither QuarkXPress nor InDesign modifies the CMYK equivalents for Pantone colors in EPS files.

However, if you open a QuarkXPress 4 document into QuarkXPress 5, or vice versa, native colors get updated—the CMYK equivalents used at print time for native Pantone elements are determined by the libraries belonging to the application from which you print.

People. It's not easy, and it's sometimes impossible, but we always try to train our users to refrain from specifying spot colors for process jobs. Many spot colors in the commonly used systems are outside the gamut of CMYK printing, and specifying one of them for a CMYK job inevitably leads to disappointment (or worse) later in the production process.

Simulations and Soft Proofs

Most color-managed applications let you force the monitor to simulate the final output. We find this vital in image-editing applications such as Photoshop, but we also find it surprisingly useful in page-layout applications. Our eyes always force us to judge color in context, and elements that look great in isolation sometimes look quite different when they're placed in the final layout. When we're working on a job with a single known output, we always view the simulation. If we're working on a job with multiple known outputs, we look at the worst one!

Even when the final output is unknown, we often use a CMYK simulation (assuming the job will eventually wind up being printed with some kind of four-color-process printing). Doing so helps us anticipate the excesses of over-optimistic designers who make use of the full RGB palette. If you *are* one of these over-optimistic designers, try setting your monitor simulation to Adobe's U.S. Sheetfed Coated v 2 profile—CMYK may get a *little* better than that on very high-quality jobs, but if you're designing for print, it will give you a reasonable estimate of the color palette you can use for the job.

Hard Proofs

We don't typically bother with hard-copy proofs before we know the output process—they basically won't tell us anything that our monitor can't do less expensively—but we often make use of our applications' capability to produce a hard-copy simulation of final output before we actually convert to final CMYK.

Printing hard-copy simulations of your final output can alert you to potential problems with the final conversion, so that you can take any necessary remedial action before the potential problem turns into an actual one. It's also a good idea to print hard-copy proofs after you've converted to final output—you may find very slight differences between the proof of the simulation and the proof of the final converted result.

It's unrealistic at this stage in the acceptance of color management to try to use cross-rendered proofs as contract proofs (though many periodicals do so, having achieved a confidence level through repetition). But they are useful for guidance. Of course, they don't show problems with screening or defects on the film or plates, but neither do most other digital proofing systems short of a Kodak Approval or Creo Spectrum. That said, inkjet printers are beginning to approach the resolution needed to produce actual dot-based proofs—we expect to see a lot of action in this area in the next few years.

One of the consequences of the adoption of direct-to-plate printing seems to be that nobody knows how to proof anymore. We've had the experience where a printer provided film-based proofs—Matchprints, in fact—for a job being printed direct-to-plate. More disturbingly, the Matchprints were all around 20 percent heavy on the cyan: a call to the printer provided us with the assurance that "the red always heavies up on press"—which left us wondering why they'd gone to the time and expense of running film in the first place!

In the end, the profiles we'd built for the press proved accurate, and at the press check, the press matched our Epson inkjet guidance prints closely as soon as it was brought up to density. The moral of this little tale is that contract proofing is as much about responsibility and confidence as it is about accurate color matching.

Output Conversions

Converting all your color accurately to the final output is the ultimate goal of color management. The keys to achieving that goal are first to make sure that you've selected the correct profile for output—that's the trivial part—and second, to make sure that each element in the job has the correct source profile—that's the nontrivial part.

Early binding. In an early-binding workflow, each element is either created in final output space or is converted to final output space early in the process, so early-binding workflows are relatively straightforward. It's always a good idea to preflight the job, either using the built-in tools offered by the applications or a dedicated preflighting tool, to make sure that no stray RGB images have slipped through—but in general, early-binding workflows usually mean that someone, somewhere in the production process has seen and checked the final color.

Late binding. In a late-binding workflow, things are a lot trickier—in extreme cases, the final color may not exist until you burn plates. So you need to be very sure that every element in the job is handled correctly.

Normalization is a good safeguard for late-binding workflows, because it reduces the final output conversion to one conversion from a single source to final output—you still need to make sure that each element has the correct rendering intent applied, but you don't have to worry about multiple source profiles.

Final Analysis

If you've planned your workflow carefully, you should know exactly what's going to happen to every element in the job, including the tricky ones like black-only text, and spot colors destined for conversion to process. Remember the stages of color management, and ask yourself the following questions:

▶ Has each element's color been correctly defined?

▶ Has each element been normalized as needed to either default RGB or output CMYK?

▶ Does each element have the correct rendering intent applied?

▶ Have special cases such as black-only text, black-only drop shadows, and spot-to-process conversions been adequately addressed?

▶ Are all the color-reproduction devices in the chain properly calibrated to ensure that they behave the way the profiles predict they will?

When you can answer each question with a yes, you can be pretty certain that you have a relatively bulletproof color-management workflow.

One Pixel's Journey ...

To illustrate at least part of the workflow we used to create this book, we thought it might prove instructive to trace the journey of just one of the many pixels that went into its making. This particular pixel started life one atypically sunny San Francisco afternoon in August 2001, as photons reflected from one of the many fine specimens in the Dahlia Garden in Golden Gate Park.

Capture a Pixel

Bruce captured these photons in his Kodak DCS 460 digital camera, took them home, and found, upon opening the image in the Kodak DCS Acquire plug-in, that they produced an RGB value of R 248, G 13, B 0 (see Figure 18-1). He then acquired the image into Adobe Photoshop.

Figure 18-1

The capture

Define the Color

Like many Photoshop Import plug-ins, the Kodak DCS Acquire plug-in doesn't embed profiles. In fact, it has no facility for using profiles at all. In the ProPhoto RGB working space that Bruce usually uses for Kodak digital captures, the pixel's values translated to a screaming fluorescent orange with LAB values of L* 60, a* 128, b* 103, quite different from the dahlia red that first attracted Bruce's attention.

So the first step on the pixel's color-management journey was to obtain the right color meaning by assigning a profile that correctly described its appearance—in this case, a custom profile he built for the camera using MonacoPROFILER 4.0. Assigning this profile in Photoshop changed the translation from RGB to much more reasonable LAB values of L* 50, a* 90, b* 72 (see Figure 18-2). Thus we gave the pixel (along with all its siblings that made up the rest of the image) not only a specific color meaning, but the desired color meaning.

Figure 18-2

Defining the color

Normalize the Color

Unfortunately, L* 50, a* 90, b* 72 simply isn't a color that our four-color press can reproduce, so we knew that the image would need significant editing to preserve the spirit, if not the literal color values, of the original when rendered in print. The DCS 460 profile space doesn't provide a good editing environment—it's neither gray-balanced nor perceptually uniform—so we decided to convert the image to the ProPhoto RGB working space for editing, using Photoshop's Convert to Profile command (see Figure 18-3).

Converting to ProPhoto RGB with relative colorimetric rendering preserved the LAB L* 50, a* 90, b* 72 values, while changing the RGB values to R 174, G 53, B 19. (We used ProPhoto RGB because converting the same pixel to Adobe RGB produced R 215, G 0, B 0—clipping both the green and blue channels—and LAB L* 53, a* 80, b* 69. It's not that Adobe RGB is a bad space, it just doesn't work well in the extreme reds with this particular camera and profile.)

Simulate the Output

In this workflow, our final output was known from the start—we'd printed other books on this press, and we'd already profiled it—so we went for relatively early binding. Before converting to CMYK, though, we

Figure 18-3

Normalizing the color

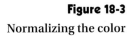

opted to view a simulation of the CMYK conversion using Photoshop's Proof Setup feature (see "Simulations and Soft-Proofing" in Chapter 12, *The Adobe Common Color Architecture*).

Optimize for Output

The soft proof immediately confirmed our fears—the predicted CMYK values of C 0, M 88, Y 89, K 0 produced corresponding LAB values of L* 52, a* 68, b* 48. We edited the image, still in RGB mode, while viewing the CMYK simulation, and by increasing saturation and reducing lightness we were able to change the predicted CMYK to C 0, M 91, Y 93, K 1, which we felt was as far as we could go in RGB mode. We decided to defer further editing until we'd converted to output CMYK.

Convert for Output

We converted the image to our output CMYK, using the settings that we'd determined worked best by looking at the soft proof—our heavy GCR press profile gave us the best saturation while still holding detail. One more edit produced a final output value of C 0, M 93, Y 95, K 2, LAB L* 50, a* 69, b* 48—a far cry from the original, but the best we could do in the circumstances (see Figure 18-4).

Figure 18-4

Converting for output

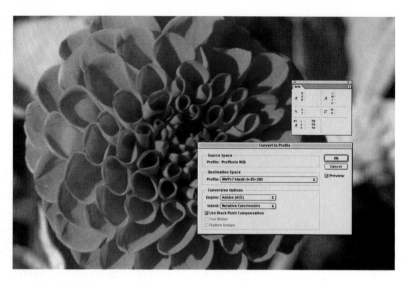

Proof the Output

Thus far, we've described the journey of our sample pixel from capture to output. But it also took some side-jaunts in the various proofing scenarios. Photoshop always does a conversion on the data sent to the display: to make the monitor reproduce our ProPhoto R 174, G 53, B 19, it had to send R 221, G 0, B 0 to the monitor. (You can't get this information directly because the conversion happens under the hood, and it isn't anything that normal people need to track anyway—we just mention it to illustrate that the pixel's journey isn't quite as straightforward as might seem at first glance.)

And it's also mildly interesting that when we proofed the image on our Epson 2200 using Premium Luster paper, Photoshop sent R 245, G 41, B 102 to the printer to make it produce the same color as press C 0, M 93, Y 95, K 2.

Hand Off the Color

We saved the converted image as a CMYK TIFF with no profile embedded, and placed it in PageMaker, where the default CMYK source profile and the Separations profile were both set to our final output press profile. This ensured that our pixel had the final output profile assumed as its source, so no conversion would take place on output, but we could still enjoy accurate display and accurate inkjet proofing. The final image is shown in Figure 18-5—our pixel is in one of the petals on the left edge of the dahlia.

Figure 18-5

The final image

The Devil Is in the Details

Throughout this book, we've pointed out that color management is in essence quite simple, since it does only two things: define a color meaning and preserve that color meaning. But in a complex production workflow, you'll encounter a host of details, each one of which must be addressed.

In Part I, we laid out the foundations for color management—the way we see color, the ways we make our devices produce color, the models we use to relate what we tell our devices to do with the results we see, and the basic operation of color management systems. We also pointed out the limitations of color management, and showed a few of the perceptual effects that the models simply don't take into account.

In Part II, we told you not only how to build and tune profiles for your various devices, but also the things you must do before and after profiling to make sure that your devices behave—and continue to behave—the way their profiles predict. No color management system can compensate for uncontrolled device variation. We also pointed out the importance of the environment in which you make your color judgements—correct lighting is critical.

In Part III, we laid out the ground rules for parsing color-management workflows. We examined the color-management features of some key applications, and walked you through their uses and their potential pitfalls, but if we've done our jobs correctly, we also gave you the vocabulary and insights necessary to analyze new applications, and to build a color-management workflow that suits your unique needs.

The rest is up to you!

PART IV

Appendices

Appendix A

Profile Anatomy

The ICC specification prescribes a format for various classes of what are generically referred to as ICC profiles. The intent of the format is to be both platform-independent and application-independent. Before the work of the ICC, profiles were either platform-specific or application-specific.

This appendix provides color geeks with more technical information about what various ICC profiles contain. Naturally it's not a substitute for the ICC spec itself, which is available at www.color.org, the Web site of the International Color Consortium.

Profile Structure

All ICC profiles have the following three segments: a profile header, a tag table, and tagged element data (see Figure A-1).

Figure A-1

ICC Profile cross-section

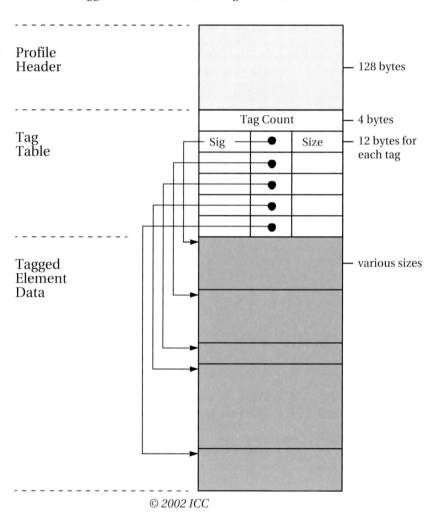

© 2002 ICC

Profile Header

The profile header contains information that allows searching and sorting ICC profiles—the header is always exactly 128 bytes. The profile header contains the following encoded parameters, in order:

Profile size. The total profile size in bytes.

CMM Type signature. This specifies the preferred CMM—effectively the default CMM. It's possible to define no preferred CMM. Signatures must be registered to avoid conflicts.

Profile version. The version of the ICC specification to which the profile conforms. There are place holders for major revisions (defined as newly added/changed required tags, necessitating an updated CMM to use the profile); minor revisions (defined as newly added/changed optional tags that don't require an updated CMM to use the profile); and bug fix revisions.

Profile Class. This defines the class of profile.

Device Class:	Signature:
Display	mntr
Input	scnr
Output	prtr

Additional profile classes are:

Profile Class:	Signature:
DeviceLink	link
ColorSpace Conversion	spac
Abstract	abst
Named Color	nmcl

Color space signature. There are 25 possible signatures for both device and non-device color spaces. This includes XYZ, CIELAB, CIELUV, YCbCr, CIEYxy, RGB, gray, HSV, HLS, CMYK and CMY explicitly, and any custom color space containing between 2 and 15 channels.

Profile Connection Space signature. There are only two options for the PCS: CIEXYZ or CIELAB.

Primary platform signature. Defines the platform on which the profile was created. The six possibilities are: Apple Computer, Inc.; Microsoft Corporation; Silicon Graphics, Inc.; Sun Microsystems, Inc.; Taligent, Inc.; and no primary platform.

Profile flags. There are two flags. One specifies whether the profile is currently a standalone profile (not embedded) or is embedded in a document. The other specifies whether or not the profile, when embedded, can be extracted from the document in which it's embedded, and made into a standalone profile.

Device manufacturer and model signatures. Signatures for devices must be registered with the ICC. Too many devices are registered to list here.

Device attributes. This describes the media associated with the device the profile applies to. Options are: reflective or transparency; glossy or matte; positive or negative; color or black and white. This frequently contains incorrect data, which doesn't affect the performance of the profile (like all of the data in this segment), but forces us to differentiate profiles using the profile name rather than the device attributes signature.

Rendering intent. This specifies the default rendering intent table in the profile. Options are perceptual, media-relative colorimetric, saturation, and ICC-absolute colorimetric. See Figure A-2 for the "mother" cross-reference of rendering intent tags.

Profile Creator signature. This identifies the creating manufacturer of the profile from the device manufacturer signatures list (mentioned previously).

Profile ID. This is generated with the MD5 fingerprinting method—a value of zero indicates the ID hasn't been calculated. This signature is currently optional.

Figure A-2

Profile class to rendering intent cross-reference

Profile Class	AToB0 Tag	AToB1 Tag	AToB2 Tag	TRC/ Matrix	BToA0 Tag	BToA1 Tag	BToA2 Tag
Input	Device to PCS: perceptual	Device to PCS: colorimetric	Device to PCS: saturation	colorimetric	PCS to Device: perceptual	PCS to Device: colorimetric	PCS to Device: saturation
Display	Device to PCS: perceptual	Device to PCS: colorimetric	Device to PCS: saturation	colorimetric	PCS to Device: perceptual	PCS to Device: colorimetric	PCS to Device: saturation
Output	Device to PCS: perceptual	Device to PCS: colorimetric	Device to PCS: saturation	Undefined	PCS to Device: perceptual	PCS to Device: colorimetric	PCS to Device: saturation
Color Space	Color Space to PCS: perceptual	Color Space to PCS: colorimetric	Color Space to PCS: saturation	Undefined	PCS to Color Space: perceptual	PCS to Color Space: colorimetric	PCS to Color Space: saturation
Abstract	PCS to PCS	Undefined	Undefined	Undefined	Undefined	Undefined	Undefined
DeviceLink	Device1 to Device2: rendering intent defined according to Table 9	Undefined	Undefined	Undefined	Undefined	Undefined	Undefined
Named Color	Undefined	Undefined	Undefined	Undefined	Undefined	Undefined	Undefined

© 2002 ICC

Tag Table

The tag table is the second and smallest segment of a profile, but is as vital to a profile as the index file is to a database, or the table of contents is to a book. It contains a tag count listing the total number of tags in the profile, followed by a sequential list of each tag contained in the profile. The list refers to each tag using a 4-byte tag signature registered with the ICC, a 4-byte offset to denote where the data for that tag starts, and a 4-byte size value to denote how long that tag is.

Tagged Element Data

This third segment of a profile contains the meat and potatoes—white point information, the profile description that appears in pop-up menus, rendering intent tables, tone response curves, etc.

One way to envision this is that the tag table is like the card catalog in a library, while the tag element data portion of the profile is the books—the analogy works better if you imagine books with no covers, just page after page with no obvious beginning or end to each book. The tag table tells the CMS what each tag is, and where it's located in the profile. It's important because the tags can come in any order, and some tags can be any length.

Required Tags

The ICC profile specification includes both required and optional tags. The following required tags must be in every ICC profile.

profileDescriptionTag

This contains the profile name that appears on menus. The file name and profile name are two different things. The profileDescriptionTag is the real profile name. This is required by the additional profile classes as well.

mediaWhitePointTag

This is the measurement of media white, in CIEXYZ, which is used in the calculation of the absolute colorimetric rendering intent. Absolute colorimetric rendering is computed from the AtoB1Tag and BtoA1Tag in conjunction with a mediaWhitePointTag.

chromaticAdaptationTag

If the actual illumination source is not D50, this tag is required, and is used to convert the actual illumination source to the PCS illuminant (which is D50).

copyrightTag

The profile copyright is stored as a 7-bit ASCII string, also required by the additional profile classes.

Input Profiles

Input profiles support grayscale, RGB, and CMYK input devices. In theory, they could describe multichannel input devices as well, although we don't know of a package that makes CMYK input profiles, let alone multichannel ones. (We aren't aware of a package that makes monochrome input profiles either.) So the options are, RGB matrix, RGB table-based, and RGB matrix-and-table-based input profiles.

Matrix-Based Profiles

For RGB matrix-based input profiles, only two additional tag types are required, for a total of 10 tags. The data contained in these two tags is very small which is why RGB matrix profiles are typically only a few kilobytes in size. The additional required tags are:

MatrixColumnTag. The three required MatrixColumn tags are redMatrixColumnTag, greenMatrixColumnTag, and blueMatrixColumnTag. They contain the XYZ tristimulus value of the primary (red, green, or blue, respectively). CIELAB is not supported in matrix profiles.

TRCTag. There are also three Tone Reproduction Curve (TRC) tags: greenTRCTag, redTRCTag, and blueTRCTag.

Table-Based Profiles

For RGB table-based input profiles, there is only one additional tag required, but it can contain a substantial amount of information when compared to matrix-based profiles.

AtoB0Tag. This table contains device-to-PCS data for the perceptual rendering intent. Only the perceptual rendering intent is required for table-based input profiles, although other rendering intents are supported as well. Both 8-bit and 16-bit precision are supported. The PCS data may be represented as either CIEXYZ or CIELAB.

Hybrid Profiles

The ICC specification, version 4.0, supports input profiles that are both matrix- and table-based.

Display Profiles

Monochrome display profiles are supported by the ICC spec with just a single grayTRCTag, but the much more common color display profiles are, like input profiles, RGB matrix-based, RGB table-based, and RGB matrix-and-table-based profiles.

The required tags for RGB matrix-based display profiles are identical to those for RGB matrix-based input profiles. Table-based and hybrid display profiles require one additional tag:

BtoA0Tag

This contains the PCS-to-device perceptual table. This tag is required to ensure that display profiles are reversible. Though the perceptual table is required, this does not mean that perceptual rendering is used: this tag almost always contains colorimetric data, so renderings are always colorimetric—either relative or absolute.

Output Profiles

The ICC specification allows for TRC-only monochrome output profiles, although we're again hard-pressed to think of a package that makes them. For all practical purposes, you'll find that output profiles are generally RGB, CMYK, and (much more rarely) grayscale table-based profiles. The ICC spec currently supports up to 15-channel profiles (in version 4.0.0), but the common CMMs support only up to 8-channel output profiles. Here are the required tags.

AtoBTag and BtoATag

There are six possible tags representing both the rendering intent and the direction (to the PCS or from the PCS). It's easy to get them confused—one way to remember is to think "A to P" and "P to A" instead of "A to B" and "B to A," where "P" is the PCS and "A" is the device.

- ▶ The AtoB0Tag is device-to-PCS perceptual rendering

- ▶ The AtoB1Tag is device-to-PCS colorimetric rendering

- ▶ The AtoB2Tag is device-to-PCS saturation rendering

- ▶ The BtoA0Tag is PCS to device perceptual rendering

- ▶ The BtoA1Tag is PCS to device colorimetric rendering

- ▶ The BtoA2Tag is PCS to device saturation rendering

Notice that there's only a single colorimetric table. See "mediaWhitePointTag" for more information. For a description of how rendering intents are actually applied in conversions, see the sidebar "Rendering Intents and Conversions."

gamutTag

This table contains PCS values on the input side, and on the output side a single value, either 1 or 0. A value of one means the PCS value is out-of-gamut, and a value of zero means the PCS color is in-gamut.

Rendering Intents and Conversions

When we perform conversions, most applications only let us choose a single rendering intent, yet both source and destination profiles contain rendering intents that can apply to the conversion. Here's how it works.

If both source and destination profiles contain the rendering intent you specified, it's used for both the source-to-PCS and PCS-to-destination conversions.

However, matrix-based profiles only contain a single rendering intent, usually (as we noted earlier in this Appendix) relative colorimetric, even if it's often labeled as perceptual. Conversion between matrix profiles and the PCS can

only use the rendering intent in the matrix profile, so if either source or destination profile is a matrix, the conversion between it and the PCS uses the matrix rendering intent. If the other profile contains the specified rendering intent, that intent is used in the conversion between the PCS and that profile.

If no rendering intent is specified, either because the user interface doesn't allow it or because you chose "Automatic," the destination profile's default rendering intent is used for both source-to-PCS and PCS-to-destination, *if* the source profile supports that rendering intent.

For example, if you request a conversion from a matrix-based editing space profile such as Adobe RGB (1998) to a CMYK output profile using Perceptual rendering, the source-to-PCS conversion will use relative colorimetric rendering because that's the only intent Adobe RGB (1998) contains, and the PCS-to-destination conversion will use perceptual rendering.

This is why rendering intents sometimes appear to have no effect—if you convert from one matrix profile to another, the conversion can only use the rendering intents contained in the profiles.

Additional Profile Classes

Besides device profiles (including "virtual device" profiles such as Adobe RGB (1998), Colormatch RGB and sRGB), the ICC specification allows for four additional classes of profile. The additional profile classes are: devicelink, color space conversion, abstract, and named color.

DeviceLink

DeviceLink profiles allow for direct device-to-device conversions—they're essentially profiles that contain a conversion from one profile to another. While they typically contain only a single source and destination profile, any number of device and non-device spaces in series can be combined in a devicelink profile, though the first and last profiles in the chain must represent device spaces. Four tags are required for devicelink profiles: profileDescriptionTag, AtoB0Tag, profileSequenceDescTag, and copyrightTag.

DeviceLinks may appear to break the rule that you always need two profiles to make a conversion, but under the hood, a devicelink contains at least two profiles even though it's a single file.

ProfileSequenceDescTag. This describes the sequence of the profiles contained in the link.

ColorSpace Conversion

ColorSpace conversion profiles are used by CMMs to convert between different device-independent color spaces, such as between CIELAB and CIELUV. These profiles can be embedded in images—if you have a LAB image that isn't based on D50, you need a suitable ColorSpace Conversion profile embedded in it.

Abstract

Abstract profiles are intended to perform image editing by transforming color data within the PCS. In practice they are rarely, if ever, used. We know of only two packages that create them: Kodak ColorFlow Profile Tools (a.k.a. Profile Editor), and ITEC ColorBlind Edit.

Named Color

Named color profiles (often referred to as NCPs) are used to support named color systems such as Pantone, Focoltone, or vendor-specific custom colors. The requirement is for the named colors to be associated with a device-independent (typically LAB) value. The optional, but most practical aspect of NCPs is to reference each named color to device values, thereby ensuring the best possible reproduction of a named color on a specific device.

Appendix B

Workflow Templates

Some time after the topic of workflow templates came up, Chris stumbled upon a Mac OS X-only application called OmniGraffle. Developed by the OmniGroup (www.omnigroup.com), OmniGraffle is used primarily for diagramming and charting (see Figure B-1). It's an amazingly deep application with too many features to list here, but—in addition to supporting layers, transparency, and tons of other stuff—the one that really rings our chimes is its unique auto-layout feature.

The more complex the workflow, the more useful this auto-layout feature can be. It uses the established relationships between your workflow components to alter the layout, using settings in Layout Info. The auto-layout results may not be the prettiest thing you've seen, but they let you see your workflow in new and often surprising ways.

One of Chris' more endearing qualities is his boundless energy and enthusiasm, and he immediately hatched grandiose schemes for exquisitely diagramming all kinds of color-management workflows. When Bruce pointed out that fully diagramming even the relatively simple workflow we used to produce this book would demand an eight-page foldout, Chris finally relented, realizing just what a rabbit hole it could turn into. So what we're providing in this appendix is simply a taste that diagrams some specific workflow situations.

The more complex your workflow, the more important it is to plan, and to figure out the interactions between departments and customers, whether or not they are using color management. We find OmniGraffle incredibly useful in assisting the diagramming of color-managed workflows, and recommend it to anyone who needs to sit down and figure out complex production scenarios.

Figure B-1
OmniGraffle

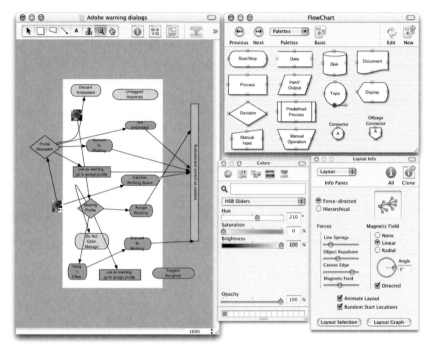

A screen capture of an early attempt at diagramming Adobe's Missing Profile and Profile Mismatch warnings.

We've used the same conventions in all the templates contained in this appendix—they're shown in Figure B-2—to distinguish between user actions, user decisions, and application options.

Figure B-2
Legend

action
user
needs to
take

decision
user must
make

dialog box option

Figure B-3
The four stages of
color management

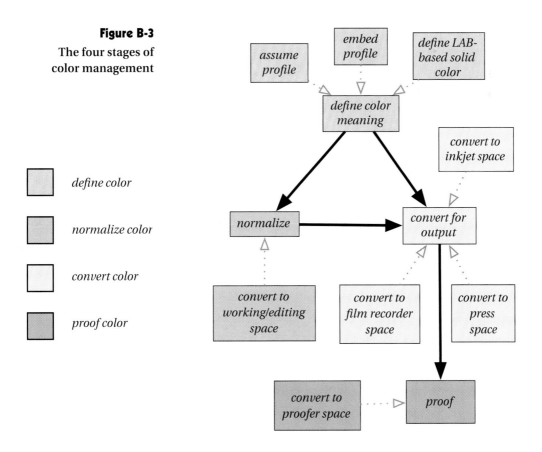

define color

normalize color

convert color

proof color

assume
profile

embed
profile

define LAB-
based solid
color

define color
meaning

convert to
inkjet space

normalize

convert for
output

convert to
working/editing
space

convert to
film recorder
space

convert to
press
space

convert to
proofer space

proof

Figure B-4

A rational workflow for
content creators

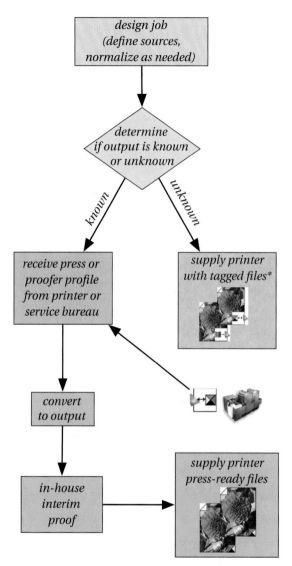

design job
(define sources,
normalize as needed)

determine
if output is known
or unknown

known

unknown

receive press or
proofer profile
from printer or
service bureau

supply printer
with tagged files*

convert
to output

in-house
interim
proof

supply printer
press-ready files

**and an explicit notation of the profiles to be
assumed for files that don't support
embedded profiles*

Figure B-5

A sadly typical workflow
for content creators

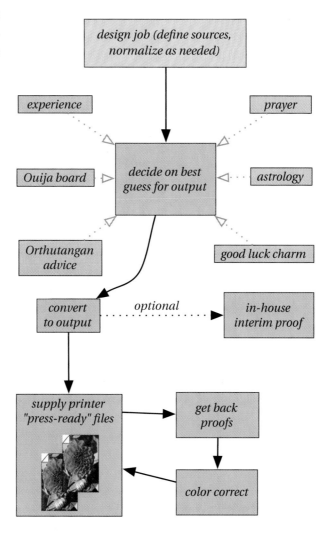

The iterative proof-then-color-correct cycle ends when:
1. The proofing budget dries up,
2. You get fed up (or someone gets injured or killed),
3. The proofs come back looking the way you want.

Figure B-6

Traditional and ideal
workflows for print
providers

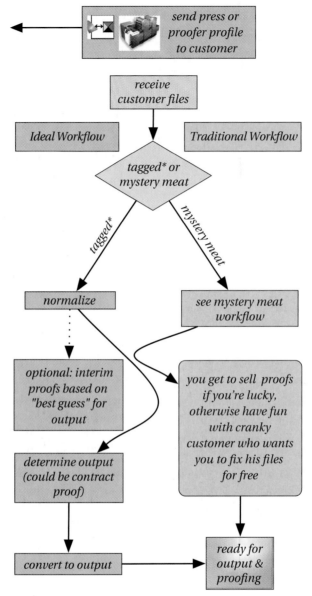

send press or
proofer profile
to customer

receive
customer files

Ideal Workflow

Traditional Workflow

tagged* or
mystery meat

tagged*

mystery meat

normalize

see mystery meat
workflow

optional: interim
proofs based on
"best guess" for
output

you get to sell proofs
if you're lucky,
otherwise have fun
with cranky
customer who wants
you to fix his files
for free

determine output
(could be contract
proof)

convert to output

ready for
output &
proofing

*embedded or assumed profile
well documented

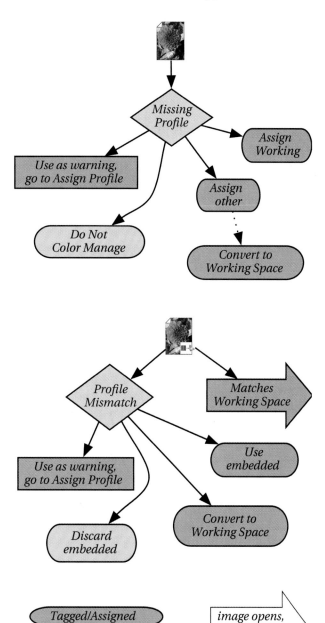

Figure B-8   Dealing with CMYK Mystery Meat

The image is effectively color managed because you're evaluating it in a calibrated environment. The numbers may not produce the desired color appearance, but they produce a known, rather than a random, color appearance.

The image is "officially" color managed because it's tagged with a profile.

The gray areas represent bad options. You have no idea what this image is, so you aren't in a position to assign a profile without looking at the image. (And if you want tradition, well, we can't help you.)

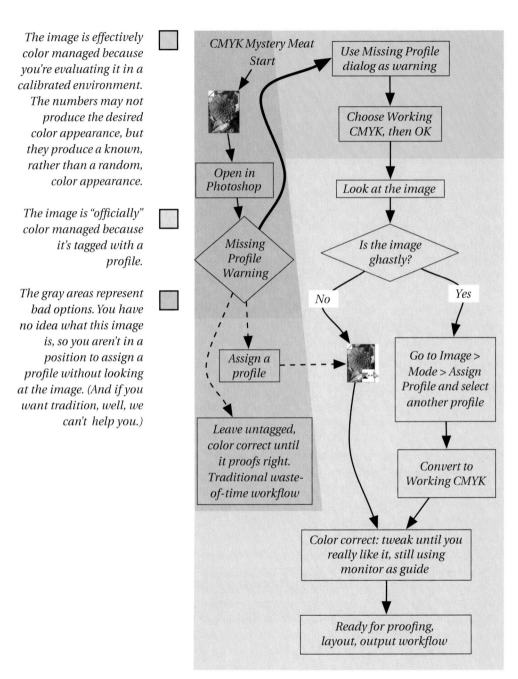

Figure B-9 Dealing with RGB Mystery Meat

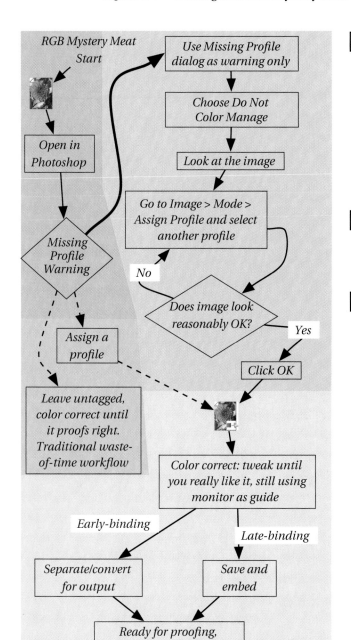

The image is effectively color managed because you're evaluating it in a calibrated environment. The numbers may not produce the desired color appearance, but they produce a known, rather than a random, color appearance.

The image is "officially" color managed because it's tagged with a profile.

The gray areas represent bad options. You have no idea what this image is, so you aren't in a position to assign a profile without looking at the image. (And if you want tradition, well, we can't help you.)

Glossary

ΔE (Pronounced "delta-E.") Generically, the computed degree to which two colors appear to match. Usually calculated in *CIELAB*, but other color-differencing systems exist.

absolute colorimetric See *colorimetric intent*.

achromatic The attribute of light from a surface or light source related to the amount of light—specifically, its *brightness*. Contrast with *chromatic*.

additive primaries Three light sources chosen so that they can reproduce other colors by addition of *wavelengths*. One primary contributes long wavelengths (red), another the medium wavelengths (green), and the other the short wavelengths (blue). See also *subtractive primaries*.

AM screening Also known as a *halftone*. In printing, a method of doing *screening* where the frequency of the dots (the *screen frequency*, or the number of dots per inch) does not vary throughout the screen. Instead, the effect of tones is created by varying the size of the dots (hence "amplitude modulation"). Contrast with *FM screening*.

anisotropy The phenomenon whereby a printer produces slightly different color depending on the orientation of the paper movement through the printer.

aperture   A small opening. Color-matching experiments usually involve the test subject viewing colors through a small aperture, and measurement instruments also view samples through a small aperture.

artifact   Something added artificially. In general, any undesirable effect that is visible in a displayed or printed image, but was artificially introduced by the equipment or software. Examples are *banding*, compression artifacts, moiré patterns, etc.

assigning a profile   The term used in Adobe applications for the act of *tagging a document* with a profile. See the sidebar on page 270.

assumed profile   The *profile* that acts as the *source profile* for untagged documents (or ones that the active application sees as untagged). See the sidebar on page 270.

banding   An *artifact* where there are noticeable jumps from one tone level to the next.

black generation   In four-color printing, the method used to generate the black, or K, channel from the color channels. The two main kinds of black generation are *UCR* and *GCR*.

black level   On a monitor, the setting that controls the base black of the display. On a *CRT*, this is just the brightness (or offset) control on the monitor.

black point   The *density*, and occasionally the color, of the darkest black reproducible by a device. For a printer, this is the density and neutral color balance of the darkest black achievable using the printing inks; for a monitor this is the density of the monitor when displaying black, and can be adjusted by setting the *black level*.

black point compensation   A setting in Adobe Photoshop that makes sure that the *black point* in the *source profile* is mapped to the black point of the *destination profile*, and the rest of the tonal range is scaled accordingly.

blackbody radiator A light source whose *photons* are entirely due to heat energy given off by the source. According to the laws of physics, there's a very predictable correlation between the temperature of the blackbody and the color of the light—lower temperatures are red, higher temperatures are white, and the highest temperatures are blue.

brightness The perceived response to light intensity. This response (in a human observer) is *non-linear*.

calibration Modifying or adjusting the behavior of a device (such as a color reproduction device or a measurement instrument) to a desired state (often a factory specification, or some state that helps simulate some other device).

camera metamerism The type of *metamerism* where two color samples match to a human observer, but not to a certain camera, or vice versa (the human does not see a match, but the camera does).

candela The unit of *luminous intensity*.

cathode ray tube See *CRT*.

CCD Charge-Coupled Device. A light-sensitive microchip, used in scanners and digital cameras as the basis for capturing a digital image.

characterization See *profiling*.

chroma Technical word for *saturation*.

chromatic The attributes of light from a surface or light source related to the *wavelength* composition of the light—specifically, its *hue* and *saturation*. Contrast with *achromatic*. The chromatic attributes describe the properties of the *photons* in the light, while the achromatic component describes the quantity of photons in the light.

chromatic adaptation See *color constancy*.

CIE Commission Internationale d'Éclairage. (International Commission on Illumination). An international association of color scientists that has assembled many of the standards used as the basis for *colorimetry*.

CIE LAB (Also known as L*a*b*.) One of the two main *color spaces* proposed by the *CIE* to attempt a *perceptually uniform* color space. L* is the lightness value, a* is the red-green *opponency*, and b* is the blue-yellow opponency. CIE LAB is one of the two color spaces used as a *PCS* in *ICC*-based color management.

CIE LUV (Also known as L*u*v*.) One of the two main *color spaces* proposed by the *CIE* to attempt a *perceptually uniform* color space.

CIE xy diagram (Also known as the CIE xy chromaticity chart.) The horseshoe-shaped diagram representing the relationships of the colors in the CIE system.

CIE XYZ Shorthand for the CIE XYZ *color space*. This defines colors in terms of three theoretical *primaries*, X, Y, and Z, that are based on the *CIE* research into human color response (the CIE *Standard Observer*). XYZ is not *perceptually uniform* and therefore can't be used for computing color distance. XYZ is one of the two color spaces used as a possible *PCS* in *ICC*-based color management.

click-balancing *Gray-balancing* an image by clicking on an area in the image that you know should be neutral.

CMM Color Management Module. Some people know it as an abbreviation for Color Matching Method, or Color Manipulation Model. In any case, a CMM is a drop-in component that provides the "engine" for profile-to-profile conversions. It defines how colors are computed using the sample points in the *profiles* as guidelines.

CMS Color Management System. Software dedicated to handling device-to-device conversion of colors. The *ICC*-based model for a CMS consists of four components: a *PCS*, *device profiles*, a *CMM*, and a set of *rendering intents*.

colorant Something, such as a *dye* or *pigment*, or *phosphors* on a monitor, that produces color on some other medium.

color bar A strip of color patches, usually printed in the margin of a printed page, and used for process control. A color bar is by definition *device-dependent* and should be created in the *color model* of the printing device. Color bars contain at least the maximum (100%) of each primary and *complementary color*. Many also contain 50% coverage areas of *primaries* and their overprints, as well as neutrals.

color constancy The tendency of the visual system to consider the color of an object to be constant despite changing viewing conditions. If all the colors in a scene change in the same way, the eye tends to attribute this to a change in *illuminant*, and discounts the change.

color gamut See *gamut*.

color management system See *CMS*.

color-mixing function In a visual system or color-measurement device (such as a scanner, camera, or *colorimeter*), the unique mixture of red, green, blue responses to different color samples. Visual systems and measurement devices don't really have a *gamut*; they have a color-mixing function.

color model A general system for assigning numbers to colors. An example would be the RGB color model, where each color is defined in terms of three numbers; the first the amount of some (as yet undefined) red primary, the second a green primary, and the third a blue primary. Contrast with *color space*.

color space An instance of a *color model* in which every color is represented by a specific point in space, and thus has a specific set of three or more numbers that describe it. An example would be the RGB space of a particular monitor, where a certain color has a specific set of three numbers representing the amounts of the red, green, and blue *phosphors* needed to produce that color. Note that there can be many color spaces that use the same color model (for example, every monitor essentially has its own specific color space, but all use the RGB color model).

color temperature   A description of the color of light in terms of the temperature of the light source, in *kelvins*. Lower temperatures are redder, higher temperatures are white, and the highest temperatures are bluer. Technically we should only refer to the exact color temperature of a *blackbody radiator*. If the light source is not a true blackbody radiator, then it's more correct to speak of the *correlated color temperature* of the light source.

colorant   Something used to produce color, such as the *dyes* in inks or toner, or the *phosphors* in a monitor.

colorimeter   A device for computing *colorimetry* (color matches) from measurements of a surface.

colorimetric intent   The two *rendering intents* that try to preserve *colorimetry* of colors— colors are mapped to an exact match wherever possible, and where not possible (because the color is out of the target *gamut*), the color is mapped to its nearest equivalent. In most cases, this conversion should include a remapping of the *white point* so that this colorimetric match is relative to the target white point—this is known as *relative colorimetric*. In some cases (in certain stages of proofing), the colorimetric match should be absolute—the colors should be converted as if the match were being done relative to the source device's white point—this is known as *absolute colorimetric*.

colorimetry   The science of predicting color matches based on ever-growing research into typical human color vision. Much colorimetry is based on the work of the *CIE*.

ColorSync   Apple's implementation of *ICC*-based color management. On Macintosh computers, the components in the Mac OS that handle such things as making *profiles* and *CMMs* available to programs that need to convert colors.

complementary colors   Two colors that make gray (or white) when combined. For example, red and cyan are complementary colors.

cones   See *photoreceptors*.

continuous tone   A device that can represent many tonal values for each unit pixel. A laser printer is not continuous tone as it can only lay down a printer dot or leave it blank—to produce tones, it needs to use the trick of *screening*. A monitor is continuous tone as every displayed pixel can represent tone levels by varying the intensities of the red, green, and blue light.

contone   Shorthand for *continuous tone*.

contrast   The difference between the lightest and darkest areas of an image.

correlated color temperature   See *color temperature*.

CRD   Color Rendering Dictionary. In PostScript color management, the CRD is the equivalent of the *destination profile*, and either resides in the *RIP* or is sent to it at print time.

CRI   Color Rendering Index. A measure of how well colors are rendered by different lighting conditions as compared to a standard light source. CRI values range from 1 to 100, whereby 100 means that all colors that match under the standard would also match under the measured lighting conditions.

CRT   Cathode Ray Tube. The most common type of computer monitor, consisting of tube with a source of electrons (a cathode) at one end, and a flattened end coated with *phosphors* that glow when excited by the electrons. (See also *LCD*.)

CSA   Color Space Array. In PostScript color management, the CSA is the equivalent of an ICC *source profile* that is downloaded to a PostScript *RIP* together with the documents it describes.

curing time   Time needed after printing by some *colorants*—for example, the inks in inkjet printers—for the printed image to arrive at a stable appearance.

D50   One of the CIE standard *illuminants*. D50 is a specification of daylight with a *correlated color temperature* of 5000 K.

D65   One of the CIE standard *illuminants*. D65 is a specification of daylight with a *correlated color temperature* of 6504 K. This is the standard *white point* that we recommend for monitor *calibration*.

delta-e   See ΔE.

densitometer   A device for computing *density* from measurements of a surface.

density   The degree to which a surface absorbs light. Density is a *logarithmic* value—a density of 3.0D is ten times darker than a density of 2.0D, and a hundred times darker than a density of 1.0D.

destination profile   In a color conversion, the *profile* that defines how to convert colors from the profile connection space (*PCS*) to the target *color space*. See also *source profile*.

device profile   See *profile*.

device-dependent   The property of a *color model* whereby the exact meaning of a set of numbers depends on the specific device. For example, RGB is a device-dependent color model because a specific set of RGB numbers (say, 10, 20, 30) will "mean" a different thing—i.e. it will produce a different color—depending on what RGB device you are using. See also *device-independent*.

device-independent   The property of a *color model* where the exact meaning of a set of numbers is unambiguous and does not depend on any specific device.   For example, *LAB* is device-independent because a specific set of LAB numbers "means" the same thing—i.e. it represents the same color—regardless of any device. See also *device-dependent*.

display profile   Also known as a *monitor profile*. A profile for a display device such as a computer monitor.

dithering   (1) *screening*;

(2) Any technique that simulates colors or tones by intentionally printing or displaying dots of various primary colors in various patterns to give the illusion of a larger set of colors. A halftone is a type of dither (called an *ordered dither*) where the dot pattern is uniform and uses the primary ink colors together with paper white to give the illusion of many colors. Another example of dithering can be seen when viewing a full color image on a monitor in 256-color mode—the illusion of additional colors is created by displaying the limited palette of 256 primary colors in various dot patterns.

dot gain   The growth of *halftone* dots during print reproduction. The main cause of dot gain is the spreading of ink as it hits paper, but slight dot gain can also be introduced during imaging to film.

dpi   Dots Per Inch. Usually, but not always, used when referring to the resolution of printers. Often incorrectly used as synonymous with *ppi,* or sometimes *spi.*

dye   A soluble *colorant.* Dye-based inks exhibit color drift over time, especially when exposed to light and other elements. Often used in inkjet printers. Contrast with *pigment.*

dynamic range   A range from brightest white to darkest dark as measured in *density.* The dynamic range of measurement devices (such as scanners, cameras, or *densitometers*) describes the distance between the darkest black the device can measure before it is unable to detect differences in brightness, and the brightest white it can measure without overloading. Also applied to media (for example, prints or. transparencies), and images, to describe the range from the darkest black to the brightest white.

early-binding   A workflow strategy that converts all colors to the final output space as soon as possible; for example, converting all scans immediately to printer CMYK.

editing space   A *color space* intended specifically for editing of color values. An RGB editing space should ideally (1) be *gray-balanced*; (2) be *perceptually uniform*; and (3) have a *gamut* large enough to contain the values being edited.

electrophotostatic   The class of printing devices that use a laser to set a static charge on a point-by-point basis, to control where toner particles stick.

embedding a profile   Saving a *profile* in a document file. The profile defines the *source profile* used when converting the color values in the file to any other *color space.* The embedded profile effectively provides the meanings of the color numbers in the file. See the sidebar on page 270.

emissive Having the property of emitting (giving off) light. A light bulb and a computer monitor are emissive.

encoding (1) In a *color space*, a specific set of numerical values that can represent a specific color. For example, in a monitor's RGB space, each encoding is a specific triplet of eight-bit numerical values, and approximately 16.7 million encodings are available;

(2) The act of assigning specific numerical values to colors.

error diffusion A form of *FM screening*.

fluorescence The absorption of light energy at one *wavelength* and re-emission at a different wavelength.

FM screening In printing, a method of *screening* in which the dots are all the same size, but the effect of tones is created by varying the frequency of the dots in a given area (hence "frequency modulation"). Contrast with *AM screening*.

fovea The area at the center of the *retina* that is populated predominantly by *cones*. This is where color vision occurs and where visual acuity (sharpness) is highest.

foveal vision The viewing condition where the image is focused on the *fovea* of the viewer, and thus produces the best acuity and color vision.

gamma (1) The degree to which a device or *color space* is *non-linear* in tonal behavior, represented as the exponent of a power function.

(2) In *CRT* display systems, the relationship between input voltage and output *luminance*.

(3) In *color spaces*, the mapping of tonal values to perceived *brightness*. A gamma value of around 2.2 is generally considered *perceptually uniform*.

gamma curve A simple example of a *tone reproduction curve* typical of most devices. This is a simple *non-linear* curve.

gamut The range of colors and *density* values reproducible on some output device such as a printer or monitor. This is sometimes split into the *color gamut*—the range of colors limited by the *primaries* used—and the *dynamic range*—the range of *brightness* levels from the darkest black to the brightest white of the device.

gamut compression The remapping of color and tone values from a large *gamut* to a smaller one.

gamut mapping The remapping of color and tone values from one *color space* to another. If the destination color space has a smaller *gamut*, this remapping will require *gamut compression*.

GCR Gray Component Replacement. A method of *black generation* that replaces a certain percentage of CMY with the equivalent amount of K.

GDI Graphics Device Interface. Microsoft's name for the display engine in Windows.

geometry See *measurement geometry*.

gray-balanced A *color space* in which any neutral pixel has equal R, G, and B values is said to be *gray-balanced*.

gray-balancing (1) Correcting RGB values in an image so that neutral grays have balanced R, G, and B values;

(2) Adjusting the behavior of a device to achieve good reproduction of neutrals.

halftone In printing, the most commonly used method for *screening*. The effect of tones is created by dividing the image into equally spaced halftone cells, each of which is filled with a dot of a known size—larger dots create darker tones; smaller dots create lighter tones.

high-bit A general term for anything higher than the minimum 8 bits per channel (256 tone levels). A high-bit file is a 16-bit file. A high-bit scanner may be a 10-, 12-, 14-, or 16-bit scanner.

HLS An adaptation of the RGB *color model*, stands for *hue, lightness, saturation*. When lightness is at maximum, the color is white.

HSB An adaptation of the RGB *color model*, stands for *hue, saturation, brightness*. Common in many color-managed applications. Similar to *HLS* except that when brightness is at maximum, the color is at its brightest.

HSV An adaptation of the RGB *color model*, stands for *hue, saturation, value*, and is synonymous with *HSB*.

hubris   Overbearing pride or presumption, arrogance. A condition that leads those afflicted to attempt to write books on color management.

hue   The property of the light from a surface or light source by which we perceive its dominant *wavelength*.

ICC   International Color Consortium. A consortium of color-related companies that have cooperated to standardize *profile* formats and procedures so that programs and operating systems can work together.

ICM   Image Color Management. The implementation of the *ICC* profile specification in Microsoft Windows.

illuminant   A light source defined spectrally—in other words, by the relative amount of energy at each point in the *visible spectrum.*

infrared   (*IR*) The non-visible region of the electromagnetic *spectrum* just below the low-energy, or red end, of the *visible spectrum.*

input profile   A *profile* for an input device such as a camera or digital camera. Not to be confused with a *source profile.*

intensity   The sheer amount of light from a surface or light source, without regard to how the observer perceives it; the number of *photons* in the light. Compare to *brightness*, which is the perception of the light's intensity.

interpolation   The computation of unknown values that fall between known (usually measured or sampled) values.

IR   See *infrared.*

ISO   The International Organization for Standardization. An organization that coordinates networks of standards bodies around the world. (ISO is not an acronym, but rather derived from the Greek "isos," meaning "equal.")

IT8   One of a family of targets used for *calibration* and profiling of scanners and printers.

kelvins   (K) The unit physicists use to describe temperature, with the scale starting at absolute zero—the temperature at which all atomic activity stops.

LAB   See *CIE LAB*.

late-binding   A workflow strategy that delays conversions to final output as long as possible, perhaps even doing this conversion in the *RIP*.

LCD   Liquid Crystal Display. The second most common type of computer monitor, consisting of two layers of polarized plexiglass between which are liquid crystals that change shape in response to electrical currents. (See also *CRT*.)

lightness   Relative *brightness*. The brightness of a surface or light source relative to some absolute white reference.

linear   A simple relationship between stimulus and response, whereby (for example) doubling the stimulus produces double the response. The human sensory system is predominantly *non-linear*.

linearization   (1) *calibration*;

(2) The act of making a device *linear* (which is a specific form of calibration).

liquid crystal display   See *LCD*.

logarithmic   A method of arranging numbers on a scale that compresses as the numbers get larger. This is convenient when the same scale has to represent both very small and very large numbers. (See the sidebar on page 33.)

lookup table   (*LUT*) A table that allows input values to be looked up and replaced by corresponding output values. For example, an RGB-to-XYZ lookup table would let you (or a color management system) look up an RGB triplet and find the equivalent *XYZ* triplet.

lpi   Lines Per Inch. This always refers to the resolution, or *screen frequency*, of a *halftone*. Not to be confused with *dpi*, which refers to the resolution of the microdots used by a digital printer, not the resolution of halftone dots.

luminance   The amount of light energy given off by a light source, independent of the response characteristics of the viewer. More precisely, luminance is the *luminous intensity* per unit area of the light-emitting surface. (For a more detailed description of luminance, *luminous flux*, and *illuminance*, see sidebar on page 211.)

luminous intensity — The amount of light energy given off over time from a point light source. This is measured in *candelas*. (See also *luminance*, and sidebar on page 211.)

LUT — (Pronounced "luht.") See *lookup table*.

LUV — See *CIE LUV*.

matrix — An ordered set of numbers listed as a rectangular grid. A 3x3 (or "3-by-3") matrix can be used to convert from one 3-channel color space to another—for example, it can convert any triplet of numbers representing the RGB values of a color, to another triplet of numbers representing the *CIE XYZ* values for the color. All *profiles* use either a 3x3 matrix, or a *lookup table* (*LUT*), to convert values.

measurement geometry — The physical geometry of a measurement device that defines the relative angles of the light source, measured surface, and detector. These are important when dealing with such effects as glare and surface texture on the measurements.

memory color — A color—such as a skin tone, grass green, or sky blue—that has a special association for the viewer, and is therefore more important to get right than other colors for which the viewer has no memory reference.

metameric ink/dye — A slight, but common misuse of the term *metamerism*. When someone says that a printer has "metameric inks," he generally mean that the inks are vulnerable to wide shifts in apparent color depending on lighting conditions.

metamerism — The condition where two color samples, with different spectral properties, produce the same color sensation under certain viewing conditions, and a different color sensation under different conditions.

metamers — Two color samples that exhibit *metamerism*. In other words, they match under some, but not all, viewing conditions.

monitor profile — Also known as a *display profile*. A *profile* for a computer monitor.

monochromatic light — Light consisting of *photons* all of the same energy level or *wavelength*. An example would be a laser.

nanometer (*nm*) One billionth of a meter.

non-linear A complex relationship between stimulus and response, where (for example) increasing the stimulus produces less and less response. The human sensory system is predominantly non-linear.

null transform When the *source profile* and *destination profile* are the same, *CMM*s ensure no conversion occurs.

observer metamerism The type of *metamerism* where two color samples match to one observer, but not to another observer. Examples of this are *scanner metamerism* and *camera metamerism*.

opponency The theory of color vision (now well verified by experiments) that we experience color in terms of various opponent pairs: red-green, blue-red, and light-dark. This has now been reconciled with *trichromacy* with research that shows that one layer of the *retina* has the three *photoreceptors*, and the next layer seems to sort this information into the opponent pairs.

ordered dither A *halftone*.

output profile A *profile* for an output device such as a printer or proofing device. Not to be confused with a *destination profile*.

PCS Profile Connection Space. The *color space* used as the intermediate form for conversions from one profile to another. In the *ICC* specification, the PCS is either *CIE XYZ* or *LAB*.

perceptual intent The *rendering intent* that tries to preserve the perceptual relationships in an image, even if this means remapping all colors both in-*gamut* and out-of-gamut. This is usually, but not always, the preferred *rendering intent* for images that contain many out-of-gamut colors, but if all colors are in-gamut for the target *color space*, *relative colorimetric* may be preferred.

perceptually uniform The property of a *color space* whereby distances between points in the space correspond well to perceived distances between the colors they represent. Close colors are represented by close points; different colors are represented by distant points.

phosphor   A substance that absorbs energy and gives off *photons*, usually of a very specific *wavelength*. The photons are not the result of heat energy (in other words, this is not *blackbody radiation*), but rather of specific properties of the atoms in the substance. Prime examples are the red, green, and blue phosphors in a *CRT* monitor.

photon   A fundamental packet of electromagnetic energy traveling through space. In some ways photons behave like particles and in other ways photons behave like waves.

photoreceptors   Light-sensitive nerve cells in the *retina*. (Sometimes called simply receptors.) The two main types of photoreceptors are *rods* and *cones*, so called because of their shape. Rods are responsible for low-light vision, and cones for daytime vision. There are three types of cones, each sensitive to a different part of the *visible spectrum*.

pigment   An insoluble *colorant*. Pigment-based inks greater stability over time, even when exposed to light (including *UV*) and other elements, than dye-based inks. Used in press inks, toners, and outdoor printing. Contrast with *dye*.

polarization   filtering light in such a way that only light waves of a particular orientation pass. Polarization is a key part of how *LCD* monitors work. Many measurement instruments also incorporate polarizing filters to reduce glare issues with glossy targets.

posterization   See *banding*.

ppi   Pixels Per Inch. This is usually used when referring to the resolution of a digital image. Contrast with *dpi*.

primaries   Shorthand for color primaries. A set of colors that, used together in controlled amounts, can reproduce all other colors. See also *additive primaries* and *subtractive primaries*.

process color   The combination of three or more *primaries*, in various amounts, to simulate the reproduction of full color. In printing, often used as a shorthand for four-color process—printing using cyan, magenta, yellow, and black (CMYK) inks.

profile　A file that contains enough information to let a *CMS* convert colors into or out of a specific *color space*. This may be a device's color space—in which we would call it a *device profile*, with subcategories *input profile*, *output profile*, and *display profile* (for input, output, and display devices respectively); or an abstract color space such as a *working space* like Adobe RGB (1998).

profile mismatch　The condition that arises when you open a file that contains an *embedded profile* other than the opening application's *assumed profile* or *working space*.

profiling　The act of creating a *profile* by measuring the current state of the device. Sometimes also known as *characterization*.

Quartz　Apple's name for the display engine in Mac OS X.

QuickDraw　Apple's name for the display engine in Mac OS 9 and earlier. See also *Quartz*.

reflectance　(*R*) The ratio of light shone onto a surface to the light reflected back to a detector. This is the measurement used by a reflection *densitometer* to compute *density*.

reflective　Having the property of reflecting light off a surface. A sheet of paper and ink have reflective components. See also *transmissive*.

relative colorimetric　See *colorimetric intent*.

rendering intent　The setting that tells the color management system how to handle the issue of converting color between color spaces when going from a larger *gamut* to a smaller one. The *ICC* specifies four rendering intents: *perceptual*, *saturation*, and two types of *colorimetric intents*.

retina　The layer of nerve cells lining the back of the eye and receptive to light.

RIP　Raster Image Processor. The RIP is either part of a digital printer or a separate computer attached to the printer. The job of the RIP is to convert the page image from vector form (usually expressed in PostScript) to the raster form needed by the marking engine of the printer. Some color-management processing and conversions can also happen in the RIP.

rods   See *photoreceptors*.

saturation The property of the light from a surface or light source by which we perceive the purity of the light—how much does the light contain photons of only a certain *wavelength* (highly saturated) or a mixture of many wavelengths (less saturated).

saturation intent The *rendering intent* that tries to preserve the saturation properties of colors as much as possible, even at the expense of *hue* accuracy or perceptual relationships. This is usually, but not always, the preferred rendering intent for information graphics such as graphs or maps, where it's desirable to maintain saturated vivid colors, or where the saturation of different regions is designed to convey information.

scanner metamerism The type of *metamerism* where two color samples match to a human observer, but not to a certain scanner, or vice versa (the human does not see a match, but the scanner does).

screen angle In a *halftone*, the angle of the lines that form the halftone screen, relative to horizontal.

screen frequency In a *halftone*, the number of halftone cells, or "lines" per inch or centimeter.

screening In printing, the method used to simulate different tones and tints of ink by breaking the ink into dots of controlled size and frequency.

simultaneous contrast The effect where the perception of a color is affected by other colors seen simultaneously in the same field of view. (Compare to *successive contrast*.)

smart monitor A monitor with a direct connection to the host computer (rather than just an analog connection via the video card), that lets the computer control the monitor's analog controls directly .

soft-proofing Using your monitor as a proofing device—displaying a simulation of how a document will appear when printed.

source profile In a color conversion, the *profile* that defines how to convert colors from the first *color space* to the profile connection space (*PCS*). See also *destination profile*.

space (1) The final frontier;

(2) In color and color management, shorthand for a *color space*. We often refer to the "RGB space" of a monitor, or the "CMYK space" of a printer, when referring to the specific definitions of the colors reproducible on that device in terms of its *primaries*.

spectral data A sampling of *spectral power distribution*, limited to the number of bands supported by the measurement device. *Colorimetric* and *density* data can be derived from spectral data.

spectral power distribution The amount of each *wavelength* contained in a sample of emitted or reflected light.

spectrophotometer A device for measuring the spectral properties of a surface—teh degree to which the surface reflects light in different regions across the *spectrum*.

spectrum The full range of possible energy levels (*wavelengths*) of *photons*. The *visible spectrum* refers to the range of energy levels (wavelengths) visible to the eye.

spi Samples Per Inch. This is usually used when referring to the resolution of a digital camera, scanner, or a scan. See also *dpi*.

spot color A non-process color, usually based on a named color system, printed on a separate plate on a press.

sRGB A "standard default" RGB *color space* intended for images on the Internet.

Standard Illuminant One of the standardized list of *illuminants* defined by the *CIE* as representative of typical light sources. The best known of these are the A illuminant (incandescent bulb), and the *D50* and *D65* daylight illuminants.

Standard Observer The definition formalized by the *CIE* of the visual response of a typical human observer.

stochastic screening A form of *FM screening*.

strip reader   An instrument designed to read a row or several rows of color patches at a time. You feed the target, in strips, into the instrument.

subtractive primaries   Three *pigments* chosen that can reproduce other colors by the subtraction of *wavelengths* from white. One primary (cyan) subtracts long wavelengths, another (magenta) subtracts the medium wavelengths, and the other (yellow) subtracts the short wavelengths. See also *additive primaries*.

successive contrast   The effect whereby the perception of a color is affected by other colors seen immediately before. (Compare to *simultaneous contrast*.)

tagging a document   The act of associating a *source profile* with an object. You can tag an object either by *assigning* a profile inside an application, or *embedding* a profile in the object as you save it to a file. (See the sidebar on page 270.)

target descriptor file   (*TDF*) A file, used for scanner and digital camera profiling, that contains the premeasured values for the color patches on a profiling target.

TDF   See *target descriptor file*.

tonal compression   The remapping of tonal values from a wide *dynamic range* to a narrower one. Often part of *gamut compression*.

tone reproduction curve   (TRC) The graphed curve that describes the tone reproduction properties of a device. The graph shows the relationship between input values to the device and the resulting tone.

total ink limit   The limit on the maximum amount of ink allowed at a time during four-color printing. If you allowed 100% of all four inks to get printed at a time, this would be a 400% coverage. As paper cannot hold this much ink, the limit is usually set well below 400%.

transmissive   Having the property of transmitting light through a surface. Backlit media and the RGB color filter layer of an *LCD* display are transmissive. See also *reflective*.

transmittance   (*T*) The ratio of light shone onto a surface to the light transmitted through to a detector. This is the measurement used by a transmission *densitometer* to compute *density*.

trichromacy The theory of color vision (now well verified by neurophysiology) that we have three types of *photoreceptors*, each responsive to different regions of the *visible spectrum*.

tristimulus Consisting of three stimuli. Used to describe measurements and experiments that ask a test subject to match a target stimulus by adjusting the intensities of three pre-chosen stimuli.

UCR Under Color Removal. A method of *black generation* that uses black only in the neutral and gray areas.

ultraviolet (*UV*) The non-visible region of the electromagnetic *spectrum* just above the high-energy, or violet, end of the *visible spectrum*.

UV See *ultraviolet*.

UV brighteners Additives used in papers, inks, and even detergents, to make whites look brighter by absorbing non-visible *ultraviolet* light and re-emitting visible light.

videoLUT The *lookup table* (*LUT*) located in the memory of a video card. The videoLUT is accessible by software on the computer, which can use it to convert all RGB values as they are sent to the monitor. This provides an easy way for software to control the overall *gamma* and *white point* characteristics of the video system.

visual calibrator Software used for monitor *calibration* that requires you to make visual judgments based on targets displayed on the screen, rather than exact measurements using a device.

visible spectrum That part of the *spectrum* containing the range of *wavelengths* visible to the eye, approximately 380–720 *nanometers*.

wavelength In a periodic wave, such as a light wave propagating through space, the distance from one wave crest to the next. Light wavelengths are measured in *nanometers* (billionths of a meter). The wavelength of a *photon* is related to its energy—the higher the energy, the shorter the wavelength.

white luminance The *luminance* of the *white point* of a monitor.

white point (1) The color (often described in terms of *color temperature*) and intensity (often measured as either *luminance* or *density*) of the brightest white reproducible by a device. For a printer, this is the color and brightness of the paper. For a monitor this is the color temperature and luminance of the monitor when displaying white, and can be modified.

(2) The color (usually described in terms of color temperature) of a light source.

white point adaptation The ability of the eye to adapt to a change in *white point*. This is related to the perceptual task of *color constancy*.

working space The *color space* chosen as the default space for documents of a certain mode. For example, in Adobe Photoshop an RGB working space is used as the default color space for new RGB documents, and a CMYK working space is used as the default for new CMYK documents. In most cases the best choice of working space is an *editing space*, but any bidirectional space can be used.

xy chromaticity chart See *CIE xy diagram*.

XY plotter A rig used with a measurement instrument for measuring a page full of color patches. The instrument is mounted in the XY plotter, which can move the instrument precisely in horizontal or vertical position on the page. See also *strip reader*.

XYZ See *CIE XYZ*.

Index

GATF RHEM Light Indicator

One of the most frequent sources of color-management problems is an incorrect viewing condition. The GATF RHEM Light Indicator, attached to the inside back cover of this book, provides a quick, easy way to check your viewing light. It's printed with two inks that produce a metameric match under D50 lighting, and a mismatch—where you can see obvious stripes—under non-D50 lighting.

Place it on the print that you're evaluating and check its appearance. If you can see obvious stripes rather than a solid color, your lighting is unsuitable for making critical color judgements such as the ones you need to make for profile editing or proofing. Two caveats:

▶ This target is designed to invalidate bad lighting conditions, not to validate good ones.

▶ Different D50-simulators have different spectra, and some may cause *slight* striping—this isn't normally a cause for concern. But if you see obvious stripes, as in the illustration below, your lighting isn't suitable for critical color work.

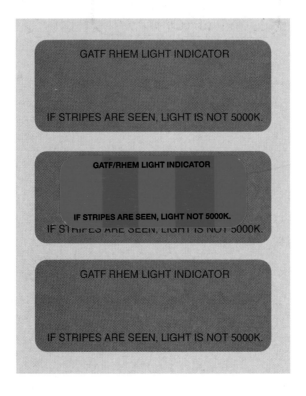